THE UNIVERSE, GOD, AND GOD-REALIZATION

Works by Swami Satprakashananda

METHODS OF KNOWLEDGE: ACCORDING TO ADVAITA VEDANTA

HINDUISM AND CHRISTIANITY

SRI RAMAKRISHNA'S LIFE AND MESSAGE IN THE PRESENT AGE: WITH THE AUTHOR'S REMINISCENCES OF HOLY MOTHER AND SOME DIRECT DISCIPLES

MEDITATION: ITS PROCESS, PRACTICE, AND CULMINATION

THE GOAL AND THE WAY: THE VEDANTIC APPROACH TO LIFE'S PROBLEMS

THE UNIVERSE, GOD, AND GOD-REALIZATION

and other Vedantic treatises

THE UNIVERSE, GOD, AND GOD-REALIZATION

From the Viewpoint of Vedanta

By

Swami Satprakashananda

THE VEDANTA SOCIETY OF ST. LOUIS

ISBN 0-916356-57-4
LC 77-79829

205 South Skinker Boulevard
St. Louis, Missouri 63105

Printed in the United States of America

CONTENTS

SYNOPSES OF CHAPTERS 7

PREFACE 15

NOTE ON THE PRONUNCIATION OF TRANSLITERATED SANSKRIT ALPHABET 17

ABBREVIATIONS 19

INTRODUCTION 21

Part One THE UNIVERSAL SIGNIFICANCE OF VEDANTA

I. What is Vedanta? 33

II. The Fundamental Teachings of Vedanta; Its Specialities 40

III. The Applicability of Vedanta to Ancient and Modern Life 57

Part Two THE UNIVERSE: ITS ORIGIN AND NATURE

IV. The Efficient and the Material Cause of the World Order and Its Empirical Reality 71

V. Īśvara and His Māyā 87

VI. The Process of Creation 110

VII. The Creation from the Word 132

Part Three THE QUEST FOR GOD, REALITY OF REALITIES

VIII. The Search for the One in the Many 150

IX. What is Reality? The Objective and the Subjective Approach 165

X. The Direct and the Indirect Knowledge of the Supreme Being 176

XI. Reality as Affirmed by the Scriptures and Experienced by the Seers 188

Part Four REALIZATION OF GOD, THE ALL-PERFECT SUPREME BEING, THE IDEAL ONE, IS THE ULTIMATE GOAL

XII. Brahman, All-transcendent and Immanent 200

XIII. Karma-yōga — The Stepping Stone to the Spiritual Path 221

XIV. The Interrelation of the Four Yōgas 231

XV. Bhakti-yōga, the Way to the Realization of Saguṇa Brahman 243

XVI. Jñāna-Yōga, the Way to the Realization of Nirguṇa Brahman 254

Appendix I The First and the Last Message of Śrī Kṛṣṇa, the Pioneer Teacher of the Practical Phase of Vedanta (Smṛti-prasthāna) 263

Appendix II The Abundant Life 276

Appendix III Life Here and Hereafter 284

Appendix IV Available Editions of Extant Vedic Texts 292

BIBLIOGRAPHY I English Works quoted from in this book 295

BIBLIOGRAPHY II Sanskrit Works quoted from in this book 297

INDEX 303

SYNOPSES OF CHAPTERS

PART ONE

THE UNIVERSAL SIGNIFICANCE OF VEDANTA

I. What Is Vedanta?

1. The relation of Vedanta to the Vedas. The two main sections of the Vedas. 33
2. The triple basis of Vedanta. 36
3. The two main divisions of the Hindu scriptures. Their interrelation. 37
4. The extant Vedic texts. 38

II. The Fundamental Teachings of Vedanta: Its Specialities.

1. One undifferentiated Reality — Pure Being-Consciousness-Bliss — underlies all diversities. 40
2. The same Supreme Being, immanent and transcendent—Saguṇa and Nirguṇa Brahman. Two main schools of Vedanta — monotheistic and monistic (nondualistic). 41
3. The Supreme Being is the inmost self in every living being. The basic difference between the living and the nonliving. 43
4. The inner self of man is luminous, free, pure, and immortal. 44
5. Man's twofold ajñāna (ignorance). The real and the apparent man. 45
6. The four Vedic mahāvākyas (the cardinal sayings). Their significance. 46
7. Each of the four cardinal sayings points to two main approaches to the Supreme Being: Bhakti-yōga (the path of devotion) and Jñāna-yōga (the path of knowledge). 48
8. To realize Brahman, Saguṇa or Nirguṇa, is the supreme goal of life. 50
9. How can the human mind turn to the Eternal, while its general tendency is to seek the temporal? The importance of virtue. 51
10. The necessity for the practice of Karma-yōga; its basic principle. It is preparatory to Bhakti-yōga and Jñāna-yōga. 53
11. The fundamental teachings of Vedanta summed up. 54
12. The same All-pervading Self (Paramātmā) dwells within every individual as the inmost self and is apparently limited or individualized. As such this is called *jīvātmā*. 54
13. Two specialities of Vedanta. 55

III. The Applicability of Vedanta to Ancient and Modern Life

1. The appeal of Vedanta to the human mind from ancient times has been due to (1) its universality, (2) its rationality, and (3) its practicality. 57

2. The universal Truths upheld by Vedanta. Everywhere human life must conform to them. Their recognition is conducive to world-unity urgently needed in the present age. 58
3. The Vedantic view of religion. The necessity for harmony of religions. 60
4. The rationality of Vedanta. The efficacy and limitations of human reason. 61
5. The need of mystical experience. Its relation to reason. 62
6. The practicality of Vedanta. Application of the highest spiritual principles to man's everyday life. 64
7. The place of Karma-yōga in spiritual life. The narrow and wide view of it. Its wide application by Swami Vivekananda. 64
8. Further application of Vedanta in practical life by Swami Vivekananda: (1) Arousing man's faith in himself, and (2) urging him to serve God through men. 66
9. Swami Vivekananda's method is an extensive application of the ancient teachings. 67
10. By looking upon all things and beings as manifestations of Divine Forms one can contemplate on God with the eyes open. Gradual stages of this practice. 68

PART TWO

THE UNIVERSE: ITS ORIGIN AND NATURE

IV. The Efficient and the Material Cause of the World-order and Its Empirical Reality

1. The universe a standing mystery to the human mind. Man's inquiries about its origin. 71
2. The root of the universe is the Reality underlying it. 72
3. Brahman is the material as well as the efficient cause of the universe comprising the living and the nonliving. 73
4. Brahman has not changed into the diversified world but appears as such through māyā. 75
5. What is māyā? Brahman associated with māyā is the cause of the manifold. 76
6. The role of reason in determining the cause of the universe. 78
7. The empirical reality of the world-appearance. The distinction between good and evil is valid in the relative order. 80
8. Vedanta views the perceiver, the object perceived and perception as the triple manifestation of the one fundamental Reality. It repudiates both realism and idealism. 82
9. Further refutation of the Buddhist Idealists' views. 84
10. The distinction between the external objects and the internal ideas is to be recognized until Brahman is realized. 86

V. Īśvara and His Māyā

1. The jīva, jagat, and Īśvara constitute the triple relative order. 87
2. No beginning of the three. 89
3. How are the jīva and jagat related to Īśvara? 90
4. The solution of the problem is the nondualistic conception of māyā. 91
5. The appearance of the world of phenomena is due to māyā or ajñāna (antiknowledge) that disguises Reality. 93
6. Māyā has different names. It is indefinable either as real or as unreal. Nor is it both real and unreal. 94
7. Māyā is evident as contraries that mark the universe 95
8. By associating the dissociated, māyā causes individualization. 97
9. The cosmic and the individual aspect of māyā. Īśvara and the jīva. 98
10. Īśvara, the Lord of māyā, is the All-pervading and All-transcendent Being. 99
11. The tripartite relative order vanishes when the Absolute (the unconditioned Brahman) is realized. 101
12. Īśvara is the highest manifestation of the Absolute. The Unconditioned and Conditioned Brahman. 101
13. Any difference is irreconcilable with absolute unity. Māyā solves the metaphysical crux. Its inscrutability is its special characteristic. 103
14. Māyā produces the jīva and jagat through two different kinds of adhyāsa (apparent superimposition). 104
15. Māyā is beginningless, but comes to an end. 106
16. The question why Īśvara creates the world is untenable. He is all-free. The significance of līlā. 107

VI. The Process of Creation

1. The Advaita theory of creation called *vivarta-vāda.* 110
2. The beginning of the creation. The causal state of the animate and the inanimate world. 111
3. The Advaita theory of the preexistence of the effect in the cause. 113
4. How Īśvara starts the creation 114
5. The position of Īśvara as the Creator and Ruler of the universe. 115
6. The aim of Vedanta in delineating the process of creation is to maintain the unity underlying the diversity. 117
7. How the living and the nonliving arise. Hiraṇyagarbha, the first created being. 118
8. The origination and nature of the five subtle elements constituting the jīva's subtle body and of the five gross elements constituting his physical body and the physical cosmos. 119
9. The psychophysical constitution of the jīva. 122
10. The continuity of the evolutionary process from the lowest to the highest order of life without the transformation of one species into another. Evolution presupposes involution. 124

11. The jīva's spiritual self does not evolve but has greater and greater manifestation with the evolution of the psychophysical organism. 126
12. The role of Hiraṇyagarbha (the cosmic soul) in the cosmic process. 128
13. The Supreme Being, the Prime Mover of the universe, ever shines in His transcendent glory. He is the Adorable Lord. 131

VII. The Creation from the Word

1. This is an ancient view prevalent in varying forms among the Indo-Aryans, the Greeks, the Hebrews, and the Christians. 132
2. The significance of *Vāk* (the Word) in the Vedic texts quoted above. 134
3. *Vāk* (the Word) as the origin of the universe. 137
4. The monosyllabic word *Ōm* as the symbol of Vāk. Its significance. 139
5. The manifestation of the Vedas and the role of the Vedic words in creation. 141
6. The instrumentality of Vāk in creation. 143
7. The Vedantic conception of the Word compared with that of Philo and of St. John. 145
8. The Christian and the Vedantic view of the Divine Incarnation. 147

PART THREE

THE QUEST FOR GOD, REALITY OF REALITIES

VIII. The Search for the One in the Many

1. Its is man's innate tendency to seek the ideal in the real. 150
2. That the Ideal Reality can be attained is evidenced by great spiritual leaders' experiences, words, and deeds. 151
3. Vedanta declares the Ideal Reality to be the Goal attainable by all. 153
4. The Vedantic view of the manifold is not illusionism or pantheism. 156
5. The world of experience keeps man in bondage, whereas the knowledge of the Reality beyond the relative leads him to Freedom. 158
6. The quest of the many is the way of ignorance, the quest of the One is the way of knowledge. 160
7. The Vedantic view of the Ultimate One. Its consistence with empirical knowledge. 161

IX. What is Reality? The Objective and the Subjective Approach

1. Reality defined. Pure existence underlies all changing forms. It is invariable and undeniable. 165
2. The order of becoming cannot be real in itself. 168
3. What is objectively known as pure Being is subjectively found to be Pure Consciousness. So by realizing the inmost self one can realize That. 170

4. The inmost self of man is uncontradicted Being-Consciousness-Bliss. 172
5. The three orders of existence. 174

X. The Direct and the Indirect Knowledge of the Supreme Being

1. The close relation between the two. 176
2. The gulf of difference between the two types of knowledge—the direct and the indirect. 178
3. The imperative need of internal discipline for the realization of Brahman. 180
4. To realize Brahman is the supreme purpose of human life. 181
5. Nothing less than the direct knowledge of Brahman can make man sorrowless. 182
6. Inner purity is an essential prerequisite for the direct knowledge of Brahman. 185
7. The ways of the illumined ones. 186

XI. Reality as Affirmed by the Scriptures and Experienced by the Seers

1. The ultimate One is a fact of experience. 188
2. The realization of Nondual Brahman as Pure Consciousness. 190
3. Pure Being is Pure Consciousness and Pure Bliss. 192
4. The meaning of "The One only without a second." 194
5. The ultimate One beyond the range of thought and speech is betokened by negatives. 195
6. Similarity between the Vedantic and the Neo-Platonic view with regard to the Ultimate Reality. 197
7. The Real is the Ideal. 198

PART FOUR

REALIZATION OF GOD, THE ALL-PERFECT SUPREME BEING, THE IDEAL ONE, IS THE ULTIMATE GOAL

XII. Brahman, All-transcendent and Immanent

1. Defining the Indefinable. 200
2. Nondual Brahman can be comprehended and expounded as well in relation to the apparent manifold as its substratum. Extrinsic and intrinsic marks of Reality. 202
3. Brahman as immanent in the universe. 204
4. Though immanent, Brahman is All-transcendent. 206
5. Intrinsically undifferentiated Brahman is apparently differentiated. 207
6. A true knower of Brahman sees Brahman in both the aspects. 208

7. The distinction of the Ultimate One as transcendent and immanent is also recognized by other mystical religions. 212
8. The two ways of viewing the all-pervading Supreme Being. 215
9. The unique position of Īśvara (the Lord of the Universe) in Nondualistic Vedanta. 215
10. He is the Adorable One. 217

XIII. Karma-Yōga — The Stepping Stone to the Spiritual Path

1. Karma which binds a man to the continuous rounds of birth and rebirth, leads him to full freedom and infinite joy when done in the spirit of yōga or perfect equanimity. 221
2. Karma-yōga is not mere unselfish work or ethical deeds. 222
3. Preparation for Karma-yōga. 223
4. The practice of Karma-yōga — the common basis of all the other yōgas. 225
5. Karma-yōga paves the way to the practice of other yōgas through the purification of the mind. 228

XIV. The Interrelation of the Four Yōgas

1. That Karma-yōga is preparatory to the practice of Jñāna-yōga as well as Bhakti-yōga is expressly stated by Śrī Kṛṣṇa in the *Bhāgavatam*. 231
2. Through Karma-yōga, an aspirant of Dhyāna-yōga acquires the two prerequisites of the meditative life: nonattachment and calmness of mind. 232
3. Śaṅkara's view of jñāna and karma are not self-contradictory. 233
4. No actual contradiction between Śaṅkara and Swami Vivekananda. 236
5. Thus, the contradiction between Śaṅkara and Swami Vivekananda can be said to be mostly verbal. 237
6. The difference of viewpoints with regard to jñāna and karma naturally find different expressions in Śaṅkara and Swami Vivekananda. 238
7. In one respect Swami Vivekananda has made a distinct contribution to the conception of Karma-yōga. 240
8. Swami Vivekananda's message is the logical conclusion of the teachings of the Upaniṣads and the *Gītā*. 242

XV. Bhakti-Yōga, the Way to the Realization of Saguṇa Brahman

1. The threefold distinction of Reality, according to Advaita Vedanta. The goal of Bhakti-yōga and the goal of Jñāna-yōga. 243
2. Bhakti-yōga as related to Karma-yōga and Jñāna-yōga. 244
3. Two distinct stages of devotion: (1) Preparatory, and (2) Spontaneous. 245
4. Marks of spontaneous devotion: closer and closer relationship with God. 246
5. Whole-hearted devotion is the greatest treasure of human life. The development of spiritual insight. 248

6. Of all the means for the development of devotion, association with holy men is most efficacious. Divine grace descends through them. The devotee should continue his efforts without relaxation. 249

7. The worship of God is the universal duty of all human beings. 250

8. Even by practicing meditation on God through an image the devotee can realize Him as an Omnipresent Being. 251

9. God's grace descends upon the devotee with his self-surrender. Śrī Kṛṣṇa also mentions how one realizes God through His grace. 251

10. The devotee who realizes God within himself also sees Him in all beings. 252

XVI. Jñāna-yōga, the Way to the Realization of Nirguṇa Brahman

1. The goal of Jñāna-yōga is the realization of the identity of the individual self with the Supreme Self. 254

2. The importance of Self-knowledge. The triple method of its attainment. 255

3. The fourfold requisite for Self-knowledge with which the pupil should approach a competent teacher. 257

4. The identity of the individual self and the Supreme Self is the quintessence of the Vedic knowledge. 258

5. How Brahman is realized through meditation as the Self within. 260

PREFACE

This is a supplementary volume to my previous book — *The Goal and the Way,* which presents the Vedantic view of a human individual and his goal.

In this volume I have tried to dwell on the Vedantic view of the cosmos in relation to man and God under the title *The Universe, God, and God-Realization.*

After the General Introduction dwelling on the importance of religion in the modern world, a preliminary section: "The Universal Significance of Vedanta," serves as the opening theme. The book contains altogether four major parts:

1. The Universal Significance of Vedanta
2. The Universe: Its Origin and Nature
3. The Quest for God, Reality of Realities
4. Realization of God, the All-Perfect Supreme Being, the Ideal One, Is the Ultimate Goal

Each part consists of several chapters. Each chapter is divided under appropriate subheadings.

The book is attended with cogent Appendices followed by Bibliographies of English and Sanskrit works quoted from, and closed with a regular Index.

I deeply appreciate the devoted service of my Vedanta students in going through the manuscript and suggesting emendations, in preparing the final typescript and seeing it through the press.

SATPRAKASHANANDA

The Vedanta Society
St. Louis, Missouri
June 8, 1977

NOTE ON THE PRONUNCIATION OF TRANSLITERATED SANSKRIT ALPHABET

a	as in all
ā	as in far
i	as in tin
ī	as ee in deep
u	as in full
ū	as oo in loop
ō	as in note
ṛ	as ri in prick
ṁ	as ng in Hongkong
ḥ	as in oh!
g	hard as in good
ṅ	as ng in king
c	as ch in church
ch	as chh in thatch-hut
jh	as geh in hedge-hog
ñ	n (palatal)
ṭ	as in tool
ṭh	as th in boat-house
ḍ	as in dog
ḍh	as in Godhood
ṇ	n (cerebral)
th	as in thin
d	as th in then
dh	as in Buddha
n	(dental) as in noun
ph	as in loophole
bh	as in abhor
v	as w
ś	as in short (palatal sibilant)
ṣ	(cerebral sibilant)

ABBREVIATIONS

AB	*Ātma-bōdha*
Ai.Br.	*Aitareya Brāhmaṇa*
Ai.U.	*Aitareya Upaniṣad*
BG	*Bhagavad-gītā*
BP	*Bhāṣā-pariccheda*
Br.U.	*Bṛhadāraṇyaka Upaniṣad*
BS	*Brahma-sūtras*
Ch.U.	*Chāndōgya Upaniṣad*
com.	commentary
CW	*The Complete Works of Swami Vivekananda*
GSR	*The Gospel of Sri Ramakrishna*
Is.U.	*Īśa Upaniṣad*
Jab.U.	*Jābāla Upaniṣad*
Ka.U.	*Kaṭha Upaniṣad*
Kai.U.	*Kaivalya Upaniṣad*
Kau.Br.	*Kauṣītakī Brāhmaṇa*
Kau.U.	*Kauṣītakī Upaniṣad*
Ken.U.	*Kena Upaniṣad*
Ma.U.	*Māṇḍūkya Upaniṣad*
Mbh.	*Mahābhārata*
MK	*Māṇḍūkya Upaniṣad Kārikā*
MS	*Manu-Smṛti*
Mu.U.	*Muṇḍaka Upaniṣad*
NPT.U.	*Nṛsiṁha-pūrvatāpanīya Upaniṣad*
NS	*Naiṣkarmya-siddhi*
NUT.U.	*Nṛsiṁha-uttaratāpanīya Upaniṣad*
Pd.	*Pañcadaśī*
PMS	*Pūrva-mīmāṁsā-sūtras*
Pr.U.	*Praśna Upaniṣad*
Rg V.	*Ṛg-Veda*
Sat.Br.	*Śatapatha Brāhmaṇa*
SB	*Śrīmad-bhāgavatam*
S.com.	Śaṅkara's commentary
SD	*Sāṁkhya-darśanam*
SK	*Sāṁkhya-kārikā*
SLS	*Siddhānta-leśa-saṁgraha*
Sv.U.	*Śvetāśvatara Upaniṣad*
Tai.Ar.	*Taittirīya Āraṇyaka*
Tai.Br.	*Taittirīya Brāhmaṇa*
Tai.U.	*Taittirīya Upaniṣad*
VC	*Viveka-cūḍāmaṇi*
VP	*Vedānta-paribhāṣā*
VS	*Vedānta-sāra*
VV	*Vākya-vṛtti*
YS	*Yōga-sūtras of Patañjali*

INTRODUCTION

THE IMPORTANCE OF RELIGION IN THE MODERN WORLD — THE SPECIAL NEED OF THE RELIGION AND PHILOSOPHY OF VEDANTA

In these days so many forces other than religion — cultural, social, scientific, economic, political, and military — are at work to make a better world, man's secular interests are so pressing, varied, and captivating, that one may wonder if religion is essential in modern life, if religion is going to be outworn or outmoded. But a careful analysis of the situation assures one that religion has to play a vital, a unique role in the complex life of today and that it can effectively contribute to man's happiness and security in this progressive age.

1. Modern Problems and Their Root Cause

Many are the problems of the modern man. How can religion solve them? One of the outstanding problems is how to avert the nuclear war that threatens mankind with extinction. Warlike men are prone to think that the very fear of total destruction can serve as a deterrent to war. But this is not a safe course to follow. It is most hazardous and inhuman. If civilization has to live by such diabolic means, then it is not worth the name. In the very process of saving civilization, you are killing it. The safe and sane measure is, of course, to cultivate mutual understanding, trust, and fellow-feeling among individuals and nations. This is what religion urges. By frightening one another, nations can never be united. The leaders of mighty nations, however, feel the necessity of solving the problem of war by negotiation. But, unfortunately, they rely too much on military might and diplomatic tactics, while their success depends on their moral integrity, their adherence to truth, justice, and humanitarianism. As long as they think more intensely of war than of peace, how can they find the way to peace? Let them explore all of the avenues of peace as zealously as they are trying to develop the means of destruction. Then they will find peace by a peaceful approach.

Usually, the socio-political leaders aim at solving life's problems by an adjustment of the external conditions. Many are the courses they follow. With the aid of science and technology, they try to alleviate the miseries of men and promote their well-being. They develop arts and industries and establish technical institutes and research centers. They carry on an extensive program of social work and establish hospitals and clinics. They introduce new political, economic, and social systems, enact laws, national and international, and make pacts and treaties among countries. Even then they cannot cope with the situation. The point is that all these measures for the welfare of mankind, for the peace and progress of the world, varied and extensive though these be, are by nature inadequate for the purpose, because they do not go to the root of human problems.

To solve life's problems effectively we have to remove their root cause. If we trace their origin, we find that they arise, in most cases, not exactly from man's external conditions, but from his inner weaknesses. His social, economic, and political problems are more often than not grounded in his moral nature. Usually, it is lack of self-control and right understanding that either creates or aggravates man's difficulties. Human problems are primarily psychological and secondarily biological. As long as a person carries within him any of the dark forces, such as greed, pride, hatred, anger, jealousy, fear, and suspicion, he will have trouble wherever he may be. He can make a hell of heaven.

There is no question that the lack of moral integrity in individuals and nations makes the world problems all the more complicated and difficult to solve. Their solution depends, in the last analysis, on man's inner goodness. None of these can be solved satisfactorily if man's inner life is not sound. The world is confronted basically with moral problems. If human nature deteriorates, if man deliberately subordinates ethical ideals to material interests, and if expediency be the golden rule, no law, no system, no pact, and no social gospel, however well-advised, can save the world.

Here religion comes to our aid. It pays particular attention to man's inner life. To unfold the inner man is its special function. By developing the spiritual outlook on life, it stabilizes man's moral nature, which is essential to his material well-being. We shall explain how.

2. The Message of Religion is for One and All

Despite the divergences of doctrines, beliefs, and practices, three fundamental truths form the common background of all religions worth the name.

Firstly, there is, in the view of all religions, an ideal Reality, which answers to man's conception of perfection. This is declared to be the Supreme Being that sustains and manifests the universe. This is also conceived as "spiritual" reality, self-existent and self-aware, distinct from the psychophysical realm of phenomena.

Secondly, all religions acknowledge, directly or indirectly, an inherent relation between man and the Supreme Being. Man is essentially a spiritual being. His real self is neither the physical body nor the body-mind complex, but the immortal Spirit, akin to the Highest. The spiritual relation between man and the Supreme Being is the keynote of religious life.

Thirdly, according to all religions, man's self-fulfillment is the realization of his essential relation with the Supreme Being. This is the highest goal of human life. In the view of most theistic faiths the relation culminates in union with God; in the view of nondualistic Vedanta, in identity with the God-head.

Spirituality is the core of religion. He who recognizes the above three spiritual principles and tries to live in conformity with them is regarded as a spiritual aspirant. He is said to have developed a spiritual outlook on life. This serves two important purposes. In the first place, it makes life meaningful. Secondly, it makes life sound and secure.

With the development of the spiritual outlook on life, a person clearly apprehends the true purpose of life. The world we live in, howsoever real it may appear to be, is far from an ideal existence. It gives us no assurance even for the fulfillment of our legitimate hopes and desires. Notwithstanding all human endeavors to ameliorate the conditions of life, notwithstanding all dreams of "inevitable progress" and "ever-increasing perfection," the world persists in being a battleground of good and evil forces, a welter of such opposites as pleasure and pain, growth and decay, order and disorder, light and darkness. There is no prospect of unmixed blessing here. Yet man cherishes in his heart the highest ideals of beauty, goodness, joy, and freedom. There is within him an innate longing for the Best, the Perfect.

So the questions arise: Is there no way to its fulfillment? Is this noblest urge for the supreme Good bound to die out? Should man ignore or suppress it? The spiritual leaders answer: No. There is an ideal Reality transcending all dualities, which man can reach, beyond which there is nothing more to seek. This is the culmination of all knowledge; this is the fulfillment of all desires; this is what he has to live for. To seek security in the insecure is not his destiny. Death is not his final end. He can attain the imperishable through the perishable; the infinite through the finite; the Perfect through the imperfect. With this end in view, he should regulate all the affairs of life, harmonize all his movements, and coordinate all his thoughts, words, and deeds.

This is the message of religion. And it is for one and all. Anyone, at whatever level of life, can turn to the Highest, because the kinship between an individual and the Supreme Being holds good, whether the person is young or old, pure or impure, wise or unwise, rich or poor, whole or maimed. Thus religion holds before all the promise of complete freedom from all miseries and the attainment of supreme peace and blessedness. In case you deny the spiritual ideal, in case you hold to earthly prosperity, power, and pleasure as the main objectives of life, what message can you have for the aged in their declining years, or for the young whose future prospects are blighted by mishap?

3. Material Values and Moral Virtues

We have seen how religion unveils the meaning of life. Now, we shall see how it promotes order and security. Material progress, unsupported by moral ideals, is insecure and deceptive. Wealth proves to be a curse when the owner does not know its right use. Power misdirected is a positive evil. Scientific knowledge abused proves to be a menace to humanity. Freedom — political or economic — without a regulative principle, does more harm than good. The edifice of world prosperity and power has to be built on a sound moral foundation. What weakens man's moral nature is the tendency to attach more importance to material values than to the moral. It is delusive. Religion turns man's attention to the inner life and impresses on him the value of moral ideals. He learns that while moral virtues insure inner strength, joy, and freedom, material power and possessions, however glaring, do not. One may gain prosperity by unfair means, but not peace of mind. Wealth does not necessarily make a man purer, stronger, happier, or wiser. It is true that external resources are necessary to life, yet a person should not barter away inner goodness for them. Whatever wealth he may acquire, whatever pleasures he may seek, he should always keep firm on the path of virtue.

He who strives for the spiritual ideal knows that material power and possessions cannot help him as much as moral virtues. While inner purity is indispensable to spiritual growth, worldly prosperity is not. None can see the light of Truth unless the mind is tranquil and transparent. It is incumbent on a spiritual aspirant to adhere to moral principles.

Further, religion points out that man's real interest is not in self-seeking, but in self-denial. Unselfishness is the basic moral quality. It fosters other virtues. It is a blessing in itself. It leads to self-expansion. Selfishness is detrimental to man's best interests. It is the root of all vices. It causes self-contraction. As a result, whatever power, love, joy, and freedom a selfish person may have becomes more and more restricted. On the other hand, an unselfish person develops all these qualities with self-expansion. Self-fulfillment lies in self-expansion. The more you feel your unity with others in spirit, the closer you come to the Supreme Being, who enfolds and unites all individual selves as the Soul of all souls. The more you feel your kinship with the Supreme Being, the deeper is your relationship with your fellow-creatures. You look upon them not only as brothers and sisters, but as the varied images of yourself. Then you can follow the precept: "Love thy neighbor as thyself." Thus, the spiritual outlook transforms man's inner life, remodels his dealings with others, and is therefore conducive to world order, security, and peace.

The imperative need of moral and spiritual values for the stability of material progress cannot be ignored. The politico-social leaders may develop machinery, fully industrialize a country, and raise the living conditions of the people very high, yet their economic problem will not be solved, if proper care is not taken for the moral advancement of the people.

As long as greed dominates the minds of the people, as long as inordinate sense-desires provoke them, wants will multiply, competition will become keener, and the conflict between the employer and the employed will grow increasingly severe. Similarly, clinics and hospitals cannot solve the problems of disease, unless the people learn to live with moderation.

Peace treaties cannot solve the problem of war as long as nations seek self-interest at the cost of truth, justice, and humanitarianism. At the present time, juvenile delinquency is alarmingly high in the U.S.A. Can we say police forces and criminal laws can solve the problem, while the minds of the youth receive no moral and spiritual inspiration?

4. This-Worldly Attitude and Its Consequences

The twentieth-century man in general is not opposed to religion. He is rather indifferent to it. He is not an atheist, nor an agnostic, nor a sceptic of the nineteenth-century type. This change of attitude towards religion may be due partly to the advancement of scientific thought in the present age. Physical science no longer holds to the old materialistic and mechanistic outlook on life and the world, but has a deeper view of the phenomenal existence and the underlying reality. Its conception of the universe does not contradict the existence of God as Supreme Being beyond the range of sense-perception. The modern man does not usually deny God, but has a tendency to ignore Him. He thinks that he can take care of the world without the help of God, that he can make this life self-sufficient without taking into account what is beyond. Equipped with scientific knowledge and technology, he is set on making this earth a happy, prosperous, and secure place in which to live. He has a this-worldly attitude, which is very often applauded as life-affirmation. But, unfortunately, it does not produce the desired effect. One can very well see through its speciousness. It is considerably responsible for the present predicament of the world.

The point is this. If we do not include in our scheme of life any higher existence beyond, our minds naturally become focused on the world perceivable by the senses. As a result, the sensuous outlook on life prevails. To enjoy earthly existence in all the variety and richness of sense-experience becomes the ideal of life. Knowledge is cultivated for practical ends. Science, philosophy, arts, and ethics become increasingly subservient to the interests of the sense-life. Consequently, they degenerate; they lose their uplifting force. Material achievement is acclaimed as the measure of man's happiness, intellectual ability, and even moral advancement. As a matter of fact, such a false idea of human progress has prevailed in the western world for over three hundred years. Sense-appetites are insatiable by nature. If not well regulated, they debase the mind. It has already been pointed out that when man's inner nature deteriorates, material power and prosperity become insecure and perilous. In fact, cold and hot wars, on a large or small scale, ensue. This is what has happened in modern times.

Even the spread of education, which is usually considered to be the panacea of evil, can be of little help, when the sensuous outlook is predominant. The educational policy of a nation is determined by its basic attitude towards life. There cannot be a sound system of education without a sound philosophy of life. If material advancement is the main objective of a nation, economic values will invariably be given priority in its educational scheme. The general trend of its system of education will be such as to impress upon the minds of the youths the necessity of wealth, rather than the necessity of virtue. They will learn the secret of making money without caring to learn the secret of right living. They will be much more eager to be prosperous and powerful than to be virtuous and spiritual.

5. Spiritual Idealism Is Necessary Even for Temporal Interests

We have seen that, while the spiritual outlook on life tends to strengthen man's moral nature, the sensuous outlook tends to weaken it. Spiritual idealism is as necessary for temporal interests as for the eternal values. Intellectual culture does not promote human solidarity as much as the cultivation of virtues does. Mutual understanding and appreciation cannot be as strong a bond of unity among men as fellow-feeling and compassion. Moreover, intellect of a high order does not develop without moral goodness. Virtue brightens intellect and turns it into insight. Reason does not properly function unless the mind is free from emotional involvement. Man's rational nature depends more on his moral well-being than does his moral well-being on his rational nature. Mere intelligence without inner purity often turns a man into a clever animal capable of exploiting the world.

It is true that man can develop an ethical sense through intellect, independent of religion. As a rational being, he can see that his weal and woe are interconnected with the weal and woe of his fellow-beings. None can grow in isolation. For social harmony, individual interests are to be interwoven into collective interests. If each person clamors for his own interest, regardless of the interests of others, then there will be chaos and the interest of all will suffer as a consequence. So it is to his advantage that a person makes his self-interest conformable to the common interest.

To all appearance, man can live by this ethical standard of enlightened self-interest and attain prosperity and peace in the world. But actually this cannot go very far. Enlightened self-interest is too flimsy an ethical ideal to provide a stable basis for the well-being of mankind. It is not as good as unselfishness. It does not regard selflessness as a virtue or a value in itself. Our moral life cannot be sound or mature until we practice selflessness for the sake of selflessness, until we know that our self-fulfillment is in the effacement of the egoistic self, in loving and serving our fellow-beings as an end in itself and not for any selfish motive.

This is possible only when we feel a spiritual oneness with all. No human relationship based on common secular interests can make us unselfish in the true sense. It is the recognition of the Supreme Being as the indwelling spirit in all that makes us aware of our spiritual kinship with others. Some may, however, feel this kinship vaguely without actual knowledge of the spiritual Reality. A few in whom this feeling becomes strong turn altruists without being avowedly spiritual. The egoist can find reason only for enlightened self-interest. His ethical life cannot go beyond this limit. But for an all-embracing spiritual relationship, disinterested love would have no meaning in human life.

6. Religion Offers Solutions to Modern Problems

Let us see what the specific problems of modern life are and how religion solves them. Modern man wants peace with progress. He does not care for the peace of renunciation or seclusion, which is usually associated with religious life. He is acquisitive. He wants order and security in prosperity. He desires the continuity of the material progress achieved through scientific discoveries and inventions, which characterize the present age.

Religion is not opposed to man's search for power, possession, or pleasure. It does not look down on the marvelous accomplishments of physical science, but wants us to remember that material values, howsoever glaring, should not be rated higher than moral values. None should seek prosperity at the cost of his moral life. It defeats its own purpose. One can gain wealth by unfair means, but not inner peace, freedom, or joy. Man's moral nature is the very basis of life's development. His physical, intellectual, aesthetic, and spiritual well-being rests on this. Let man acquire wealth in abundance, in any form whatsoever; let him enjoy life in diverse ways; but let him not deviate from righteousness: this is the behest of religion. Assuredly, one can gain prosperity by honest ways, if one has the patience to try them.

Religion, however, does not want man to be tied down to the temporals even at their best. Its object is to lead him gradually from the search of the transitory to the search of the eternal. It recognizes the fact that man is born with inveterate sense-desires, and he has to outgrow them in a well-regulated life of experience, before he can have any longing for the suprasensible ideal Reality.

Another problem pressing on the modern man is how he can be intensely active and yet have inner poise and peace. Shortly after his arrival in the United States, the author gave a series of lectures on Vedanta in Washington, D.C. One evening, after the meeting, a lady greeted him and said, "Swami, what we need in America is not more of religion, but the secret of inner poise and peace. If you can teach us this, you will do us a great service. We have to be relieved of nervous tension."

Evidently, the American lady did not realize how very necessary the religious spirit is for maintaining inner peace and self-possession. It did not, perhaps, occur to her that the basic cause of mental unrest and nervous disorders, common in western life, is the sensuous outlook. Emotional disturbance is inevitable when the mind is in the grip of sense-desires. Greed, pride, anger, hatred, jealousy, lust, fear, etc., must prevail in him who is inordinately attached to mundane things. To hold to the hedonist ideal and, at the same time, remain free from emotional involvement, is self-contradictory. To have poise and peace of mind, one has to be interested in higher values and detached from the lower. He who holds to moral values can maintain self-possession.

Religion goes further and tells us that what is pleasant is not necessarily good. The highest Good is beyond the duality of pleasure and pain. It is the ideal Reality. When we seek that as the ultimate goal and view this life as a means to that supreme end, then we become free from worldly attachment. Consequently, we live with a dispassionate attitude and do our duties without being swayed by success and failure, praise and blame, pleasure and pain. We remain unperturbed under the varying conditions of life. We can see things objectively, because we do not count on transitory pleasures and possessions, because material values do not mean as much to us as the inner development through the passing phases of the earthly life.

A third problem besetting modern life is how man's ever-widening contact with others can be free from all discordance, all tension. A modern man has various connections with the world—social, cultural, political, economic, and so forth. He is in communication with numerous personalities. He travels fast, far and wide. From day to day he encounters men and women of different nationalities, races, and cultural ideals. For the well-being of mankind, it is essential that his association with persons of various temperaments, tastes, ideologies, customs, and manners should be harmonious and cordial. Mere tolerance, goodwill, and cooperation, without a deeper understanding of one another's position, cannot accomplish this.

Not only that, there should be a genuine feeling for others, regardless of common interests. What else besides religion can help us adequately on this point? Religion teaches us that he who is considered an alien is but a brother in disguise, nay, our very self in another form. So in helping others we help ourselves; in hurting others we hurt ourselves. The one Supreme Being is the Soul of all souls. When we recognize this truth, we establish a spiritual relationship with all. This is the way to disinterested and universal love.

Spiritual unity is all-embracing. It underlies all differences; it is the unity of all unities. So spiritual vision gives us the most comprehensive view of things. We learn to look upon multiplicity as the manifestation of one transcendent Reality. To live harmoniously with various cultural groups, we have to develop not only an international, but a universal outlook. Religion tells us that there is but one source of all power, all knowledge, all beauty, all love, and of all goodness and greatness. There is no essential difference between one expression of power and another. The difference is in the mode of manifestation. When we become aware of the essential unity underlying the diversity of forms, no manifestation, howsoever low it may appear to be, can create any adverse feeling within us. We approach all with sympathetic understanding.

7. The "One World" Ideal

The problem of problems of the modern man is how to make "one world," how to integrate the world politically, economically, socially, and culturally, so there will be no conflict of interests anywhere, so that the nationals of various countries will feel themselves to be world-citizens, and mankind will be like one family. The demand for human solidarity has been all the more insistent because of the physical unification of the world, by such advanced methods of transportation and communication as intercontinental airways, radio, telephone, cable, and so forth. As a matter of fact, though the distant parts of the world have been closely knit together, human hearts have not come correspondingly nearer. However, there is a growing desire in man for a better relationship with his fellow-beings.

The formation of the United Nations, a world organization for peace and security, is a symbol of men's willingness to live harmoniously. Persistent efforts of the U.N. to remove the causes of friction in the international field have lessened the chance of war. It can succeed in localizing war, even though it may not be able to prevent it. By international laws, agreements, and coordinated actions, it may be able to bring about a complete political and economic adjustment throughout the world. By promoting mutual understanding and appreciation of various cultural groups, it can establish a close relationship among them. But it is to be noted that the successful operation of the U.N. and its organs depends, in the last resort, not on the political sagacity or the practical efficiency of the member nations, but on their sincerity and fellow-feeling.

According to some men of light and leading, cultural relationship is the sound basis of world unity. The meeting of the eastern and the western races can be very well effected by mutual understanding and appreciation of their cultural patterns. As far as we can see, cultural affinity must be deeper than political or economic accord; yet it cannot be a universal meeting ground for humanity. The nations of the world at any time must be more or less advanced culturally. All cannot be at the same level of development. Even now, in this age of progress, there are many backward and primitive races. So the relationship is likely to be confined within groups of nations of the same cultural status. Spiritual unity, which transcends all worldly distinction, cultural or otherwise, is the sole universal ground of human relationship. In their deepest spiritual nature, there is no difference between man and man, far apart as they may appear to be in every other way, physically, intellectually, culturally, socially, and so forth.

8. The Eternal Role of Religion

To sum up. Religion has a twofold function: to transform human personalities and to transform human relationships. This can be regarded as its eternal role. Its operation varies, of course, under the changing conditions of human history. Religion is more concerned with man's inner nature than with his external affairs. It adheres to the simple truth that there cannot be a better world without better men and women. It makes man aware of his real self, ever pure, free, immortal, and divine. This arouses in him self-faith, which is the key to inner unfoldment. The animal-man turns into god-man. Man's growing consciousness of his inner potentialities in the present age makes him particularly receptive to this teaching. Being aware of the spiritual self as the ruler of the psychophysical system, an individual finds himself in a position to control his body and mind and to integrate his personality.

This self-awakening leads to the recognition of the spiritual self in others. So the aspirant's attitude towards his fellow-creatures changes. He finds that the mortal man is essentially immortal. Pure or impure, strong or weak, wise or unwise, though he may appear to be, the same divine principle shines within man as his innermost self. Consequently, the aspirant's heart is filled with due regard for all. He deals with each and every individual with proper esteem. He even tries to see God as the indwelling spirit in all and to worship Him by serving man. Thus, by teaching man to see God in himself and to see God in others, religion transforms human personality, improves interpersonal relationships, and paves the way to universal love. "Let us be divine and help others to be divine. 'Be and make,' let this be your motto," says Swami Vivekananda.

These teachings bring us close to the religion and philosophy of Vedanta. The special need of Vedanta in the present age is due to its universality, rationality, and practicality as explained in the main text — see Chapter III.

PART ONE

THE UNIVERSAL SIGNIFICANCE OF VEDANTA

CHAPTER I

WHAT IS VEDANTA?

1. *The relation of Vedanta to the Vedas. The two main sections of the Vedas.*

The term *Vedanta* (Veda + anta) literally means "the *anta* (culmination) of *veda*," that is to say, knowledge, primarily suprasensuous knowledge. Secondarily, *Vedanta* means the culmination of the Vedas, the basic scriptures of the Indo-Aryans, which dwell on that knowledge. The original Vedic texts collected and classified under four distinct heads constitute the four Vedas, from which derives the religio-philosophical system known as Hinduism. So the primary name of Hinduism is *Vaidika-dharma* (the Vedic Religion). It is also called *Sanātana-dharma* (the Eternal Religion), because it upholds the fundamental truths, which are eternal and universal.[1]

The four Vedas are the *Ṛg*, the *Yajuḥ*, the *Sāma*, and the *Atharva*. Each Veda consists of two main divisions: the Saṁhitā and the Brāhmaṇa. The Saṁhitā is the collection of the *mantras* — hymns,

[1]It is to be noted that "Hindu" and "Hinduism" are foreign designations. So are "India" and "Indians." The former two came from the Persians and the subsequent two from the Greeks. Towards the close of the sixth century B.C. the Persians under Darius I, whose empire extended from the eastern border of Greece to the western border of India, occupied a territory close to the river *Sindhu,* the Sanskrit name of the Indus. The Persians mispronounced *Sindhu* as "Hindu" and gradually the inhabitants of the regions adjoining the river Sindhu became known as "Hindus." In course of time the term was extended to the entire population of the country and their religion came to be called "Hinduism."

The Greeks had similar difficulty in pronouncing the Sanskrit name *Sindhu.* They called the river "Indus." Through them the country became known as "India" and the people as "The Indians." The original name of the country is *Bhāratavarṣa* and that of the people *Bhāratavāsī.* Both are often shortly called *Bhārata.*

prayers, and formulae meant to be used for the invocation of deities and the pouring of oblations in fire in sacrificial rites.[2] The Brāhmaṇa section is basically an explanatory treatise on the application of the mantras and is written mostly in prose. To the Brāhmaṇa proper are added the Āraṇyakas and the Upaniṣads. Consequently, in a wide sense, the Brāhmaṇa section includes both of these.

The Āraṇyakas (lit. Forest-treatises) were so named because they were usually taught and studied in the forest by the anchorites (the Vānaprasthīs), who, in the advanced stage of life, retired from the world and lived in forest retreats for contemplation on deeper truths.

The term *Upaniṣad* signifies the knowledge of Brahman, the Supreme Being, the ultimate Reality, which being duly received by a deserving pupil from a qualified teacher, eradicates his *ajñāna* — inapprehension and misapprehension of Truth — the root-cause of all his bondages and sufferings, and reinstates him in his intrinsic freedom and blissfulness. As explained by Śaṅkara:

> This knowledge of Brahman is called "upaniṣad" inasmuch as it entirely does away with the transmigratory life together with its root-cause for those who betake themselves to its cultivation, for the root *sad* prefixed by *upa* and *ni* means that. Books are called "Upaniṣads" because they have this end in view.[3]

They are meant to be studied especially by the seekers of Liberation (mōkṣa).

There are many Upaniṣads. Only one of them, the *Īśa,* belongs to the Saṁhitā part of the Veda; the rest belong either to the Brāhmaṇa proper or its Āraṇyaka section. Each Upaniṣad invariably forms the concluding chapters of the Saṁhitā, the Brāhmaṇa, or the Āraṇyaka, to which it belongs. This is one of the reasons why the Upaniṣads are

[2]The Sāṁhita is the primary part of the Vedas. This is the collection of the mantras, which are hymns and formulae recited at the sacrificial rites. Some mantras were like hymns chanted for the invocation of the deity. These are called "Ṛk Mantras." Some mantras were recited while pouring oblations into the sacrificial fire. These are in prose and are called "Yajuḥ Mantras." At the same time some other mantras were sung like odes in praise of the deity. These are known as "Sāma Mantras." In each of the four Vedas there are these three types of mantras — Ṛk, Yajuḥ, and Sāma. In the *Ṛg-Veda* there is the preponderance of Ṛk Mantras, in the *Yajur Veda* there is the preponderance of Yajuḥ Mantras. In the *Sāma-Veda,* there is the preponderance of Sāma Mantras. In the *Atharva-Veda,* there are those mantras and other mantras as well. In all the four Vedas there are these three types of mantras — Ṛk, Yajuḥ, and Sāma. For this reason the four Vedas are collectively known as *Trayī* (the triad).

[3]Br.U. I:1, intro.

known singly and jointly as the Vedanta (the end of the Veda). The other reason is that the Upaniṣads form the crown of the Vedas, the culmination of the Vedic knowledge, inasmuch as they teach the highest truths regarding the individual, the universe, and the Supreme Being. This is why they are called the *Śruti-śira* (lit. the head of the Sruti, that is, the crown of the Veda). The term *Śruti* literally means that which is heard. It applies to the Vedic texts as the embodiment of suprasensuous knowledge orally transmitted by the seers from the beginning. In the orthodox view the Śruti is Divine Revelation without beginning.

From the standpoint of the subject matter the Vedic texts are divided into two main parts: the Work-section (karma-kāṇḍa) and the Knowledge-section (jñāna-kāṇḍa). The Upaniṣads comprise the knowledge-section and the remainder of the Vedas the work-section. By "knowledge" is meant the direct knowledge of Brahman, beyond which there is nothing more to know. This is called *parāvidyā*, the supreme knowledge. As stated in the *Muṇḍaka Upaniṣad,* "But the *Para* is that by which the Imperishable One is known."[4] This is the central theme of the Upaniṣads.

The knowledge of the sacrificial rites and ceremonies, of the duties of life and their results, and of all arts and sciences is termed *aparāvidyā* (the subsidiary knowledge). This is the theme of the work-section of the Vedas. It prescribes rites and duties and moral rules for the seekers of the temporal good, so that they can attain by their observance not only well-being in this life but also utmost felicities in the celestial abode or paradise (svargalōka) hereafter, until they can be convinced of their limitations. The knowledge-section teaches that the Supreme Being alone is eternal, ever-free, pure and perfect. He is the Light of lights. He alone is self-manifest. He is to be realized by the removal of ignorance (ajñāna). There is a unity of purpose between the two sections, for both aim to lead man from the search for the transitory to the search for the Eternal One. The work-section is preparatory to the knowledge-section.

The term Vedanta is, however, used in a wide sense to cover all the sacred texts that have the Upaniṣads as their basis and elucidate their teachings. As defined by the *Vedānta-sāra*:

> Vedanta means the Upaniṣads, the source of right knowledge, the *Śārīraka-sūtras* [widely known as the *Brahma-sūtras*], and other

[4]Mu.U. I:1.5.

treatises which elucidate them [e.g., the *Bhagavad-gītā* and the commentaries on the Upaniṣads, the *Brahma-sūtras*, and the *Bhagavad-gītā*].[5]

2. *The triple basis of Vedanta.*

The three standard works on Vedanta are the Upaniṣads, the *Brahma-sūtras* and the *Bhagavad-gītā*. They form its triple basis, and are collectively called *prasthāna-traya* (the threefold norm).

The Upaniṣads consist of the suprasensuous truths revealed to the mystic vision of the seers, who declare what they see. They do not, as a rule, argue or reason. Speculation is not their way. In course of time there arose the necessity of systematizing the Upaniṣadic statements in order to resolve their apparent contradictions and to convey their import in terms of reason. The transcendental truths, although beyond the reach of reason, admit of rational interpretation. Otherwise, they cannot be universally accepted. Several attempts were made from the earliest days to present the Upaniṣadic truths in terms of reason, but none of these treatises is available in the present age except Bādarāyaṇa Vyāsa's *Brahma-sūtras* mentioned above. This forms the basis of Vedanta as a rational philosophy and is highly esteemed as authoritative by all schools of Vedanta — the monistic (nondualistic) and the monotheistic.

The *Bhagavad-gītā* dwells on the problem of the application of the Upaniṣadic truths to active life.[6] It forms the third stage of Vedanta — that of applied truths, while the Upaniṣads constitute the mystical and the *Brahma-sūtras* the rational basis of Vedanta. These three — the Upaniṣads, the *Brahma-sūtras* and the *Bhagavad-gītā* — are respectively known as the *Śruti-prasthāna,* the *Nyāya-prasthāna,* and the *Smṛti-prasthāna* Vedanta, inasmuch as they follow the way of revelation, of reason, and of regulation of life, indicated by the terms *Śruti, Nyāya,* and *Smṛti,* respectively. All the schools of Vedanta are grounded on this triple foundation. Thus we find that in the system of Vedanta mysticism is harmonized with rationality, and the philosophy of life is allied with the way of life.

Usually the Upaniṣads, like the Brāhmaṇas and the Āraṇyakas, have been separated from the rest of the Vedas and used as independent treatises, with the result that it is not possible in many cases to ascertain to which of the Vedas, or to which recension or part of it a particular Upaniṣad belongs. The difficulty is especially due to

[5] *The Vedānta-sāra* of Sadānanda, sec. 3.

[6] See Appendix I, "The First and the Last Message of Śrī Kṛṣṇa."

the fact that many Brāhmaṇas, Āraṇyakas, and their recensions have long been extinct.

Of the extant Upaniṣads, numbering about three hundred, only one hundred and eight enumerated in the *Muktika Upaniṣad* (I:30-40) are regarded as genuine. Among them twelve are counted primary, viz., *Īśa, Kena, Kaṭha, Praśna, Muṇḍaka, Māṇḍūkya, Aitareya, Taittirīya, Chāndōgya, Bṛhadāraṇyaka, Śvetāśvatara,* and *Kauṣītakī.* Śaṅkara has written commentaries on the first ten of the group. He has also written commentaries on the *Brahma-sūtras* and the *Bhagavad-gītā.* In his commentary on the *Brahma-sūtras* he has referred to the *Jābāla, Paiṅgala* and *Mahānārāyaṇa* Upaniṣads, in addition to the above-mentioned twelve. Other than these fifteen, several minor Upaniṣads — such as *Kaivalya, Maitreyī, Ātmabindu, Tejōbindu, Ātmōpaniṣad* — have been current among the spiritual aspirants. (See Appendix IV— "Available Editions of Extant Vedic Texts.")

3. *The two main divisions of the Hindu scriptures. Their interrelation.*

Before the Vedas were committed to writing they were transmitted orally through an unbroken line of teachers and pupils. Consequently they are called the *Śruti,* literally, hearing or what is heard. The term signifies direct knowledge or the truths revealed to the suprasensuous perception of the seers. It is used to distinguish the Vedic texts from later Hindu scriptures designated the *Smṛti,* lit. remembering or what is remembered. It signifies indirect knowledge. While the Vedas are esteemed by orthodox schools as Divine revelations, the *Smṛtis* are regarded as human compositions and considered authentic as far as they are in conformity with the Vedas.

In a restricted sense the term *Smṛti* is applied to "Dharma-śāstras," that is to say, the scriptures dealing with social and moral observances, religious rites, and spiritual disciplines. These include — (1) The Institutes of Law (social and moral codes) by Manu, Yājñavalkya, Parasara, Āpastamba, and other sages. (2) The two Epics — the *Rāmāyaṇa* and the *Mahābhārata.* (3) The Sāṁkhya and the Yōga systems of philosophy. (4) The Tantras (the treatises on the ritualistic worship) of the Śaivas, the Vaiṣṇavas and the Śāktas.

As defined by Manu: "By *Śruti* is meant the Veda, and by *Smṛti,* the Dharma-śāstra."[7]

[7]MS II:10.

In a wide sense the term *Smṛti* includes, other than the Dharmaśāstras, the four systems of philosophy, i.e., Pūrva Mīmāṁsā, Uttara Mīmāṁsā, Nyāya, Vaiśeṣika, and eighteen Purāṇas, e.g., *Viṣṇu Purāṇa, Agni Purāṇa, Śrīmad-bhāgavatam,* and so on.

4. *The extant Vedic texts.*

We cite below a classified list of the extant Vedic texts, viz., the Saṁhitās, the Brāhmaṇas, the Āraṇyakas, and the Upaniṣads, showing their mutual relation. The following five Saṁhitās, eighteen Brāhmaṇas, four Āraṇyakas, and sixteen Upaniṣads are considered most authentic among the available Vedic treatises. It is to be noted that *Yajur-Veda* has two main divisions — Black (kṛṣṇa) and White (śukla).

I. *Ṛg-Veda*

Ṛk Saṁhitā	*Brāhmaṇa*	*Āraṇyaka*	*Upaniṣad*
	1. *Aitareya*	1. *Aitareya*	1. *Aitareya*
	2. *Kauṣītakī (or Sāṁkhyāṇa)*	2. *Kauṣītakī*	2. *Kauṣītakī*
	3. *Paiṅgi*		

IIA. *Kṛṣṇa (Black) Yajur-Veda*

Kṛṣṇa Yajuḥ Saṁhitā	*Brāhmaṇa*	*Āraṇyaka*	*Upaniṣad*
	1. *Taittirīya*	1. *Taittirīya*	1. *Taittirīya*
	2. *Ballavī*		2. *Kaṭha*
	3. *Śāṭyāyanī*		3. *Śvetāśvatara*
	4. *Maitrāyanī*		4. *Mahānārāyaṇa*
	5. *Kaṭha*		5. *Maitrāyaṇīya*

IIB. *Śukla (White) Yajur-Veda*

Śukla Yajuḥ Saṁhitā (or Vājasaneyī Saṁhitā)	*Brāhmaṇa*	*Āraṇyaka*	*Upaniṣad*
	1. *Śatapatha*	1. *Śatapatha*	1. *Īśa*
			2. *Bṛhadāraṇyaka*
			3. *Jābāla*
			4. *Paiṅgala*

III. *Sāma-Veda*

Sāma-Saṁhitā	*Brāhmaṇa*	*Āraṇyaka*	*Upaniṣad*
	1. *Tāṇḍya-Mahābrāhmaṇa (or Pañcaviṁśa with the supplement Ṣaḍviṁśa)*		1. *Chāndōgya*
	2. *Talavakāra*		2. *Kena*
	3. *Ārṣeya*		
	4. *Vaṁśa*		
	5. *Daivatādhyāya*		
	6. *Mantra*		
	7. *Sāma-vidhāna*		
	8. *Saṁhitōpaniṣad Brāhmaṇa*		

IV. *Atharva-Veda*

Atharva-Saṁhitā	*Brāhmaṇa*	*Āraṇyaka*	*Upaniṣad*
	1. *Gōpatha*		1. *Muṇḍaka*
			2. *Māṇḍūkya*
			3. *Praśna*

(For available editions of extant Vedic texts, see Appendix IV.)

CHAPTER II

THE FUNDAMENTAL TEACHINGS OF VEDANTA; ITS SPECIALITIES

1. *One undifferentiated Reality — Pure Being-Consciousness-Bliss — underlies all diversities.*

From the earliest days the Vedas have declared One Reality underlying the universe of endless variety and ceaseless change. Throughout the *Ṛg-Veda Saṁhitā*[1] we find such statements as:

"Reality is One; the sages call It by various names: Agni (the god of fire), Yama (the god of death), Mātariśvan (the god of wind)."[2]

"The Infinite One is the Lord of the moving and the unmoving, of all that walk and all that fly, of the multiform creation."[3]

"He who, though One, assumes the names of many gods."[4]

"The One Existence is conceived as many."[5]

The One undifferentiated Being is the sole support and substance of the manifold. Just as a clay pot has no existence apart from clay, similarly, multiple things and beings have no existence apart from Pure Being. The undiversified One appears diversified by diverse names and forms. It is names and forms that undergo changes constantly, while the underlying Reality ever remains the same, unaffected, unstained by the diversities and mutations of the phenomenal order. We invariably deal with forms and misapprehend them as things in themselves. There is no difference between one piece of wooden furniture and another, so far as their substance, wood, is concerned; it is but the difference of names and forms that creates differences in their practical efficacy. Immanent in the order of phenomena, Pure Being is all-transcendent, "partless, actionless, tranquil, flawless, stainless."[6]

[1] *Ṛg-Veda Saṁhitā* (Text with exhaustive Index), edited by Sreepada Sarma Satavalekara, Svadhyaya-Mandala, Paradi, Surat, India.

[2] *Ibid.* I:164.46. (i.e., Maṇḍala I, Sūkta 164, Mantra 46).

[3] *Ibid.* III:54.8.

[4] *Ibid.* X:82.3.

[5] *Ibid.* X:114.5.

[6] Sv.U. VI:19.

Pure Being is not an inert material entity lacking self-awareness. It is identical with Pure Consciousness, and is All-Bliss. So It is said to be Sat-Cit-Ānandam Brahman. As stated in the *Bṛhadāraṇyaka Upaniṣad:* "Brahman that is Consciousness and Bliss is the supreme Goal of the giver of wealth as well as of him who realizes Brahman and lives in That."[7] Being of the nature of Pure Consciousness, Brahman, the Supreme Being, is All-Awareness. Self-manifest, He manifests all else including the resplendent sun. The *Kaṭha Upaniṣad* graphically presents this truth:

> There the sun shines not, nor does the moon, nor do the stars; nor are these lightning flashes there, what to speak of this fire. He shining everything shines after Him. By His radiance all these are manifested.[8]

Thus, according to Vedanta, the whole universe comprising the animate and the inanimate, arises from Pure Consciousness, is sustained by It and manifested by It. Consequently, it rejects the view that the physical cosmos has emerged from dull blind matter and that life and consciousness have evolved from the same source — a view that has been held by not a few philosophers, psychologists, physical scientists, and biologists in the modern time and in preceding ages.

Pure Consciousness is All-Bliss, being the very perfection of existence. So it is said in the *Taittirīya Upaniṣad:* "He (the pupil) came to know that Bliss is Brahman; from Bliss indeed all these things originate; having originated, they are sustained by Bliss; they move towards and enter into Bliss."[9] Further, "The illumined one who realizes the Bliss of Brahman has nothing to fear."[10] According to the *Chāndōgya Upaniṣad:* "The Infinite alone is Bliss. There is no Bliss in what is finite. Only the Infinite is Bliss. One must desire to know the Infinite."[11]

2. *The same Supreme Being, immanent and transcendent — Saguṇa and Nirguṇa Brahman. Two main schools of Vedanta — monotheistic and monistic (nondualistic). (See also Chap. XII)*[12]

That the fundamental Reality is One without a second and is

[7]Br.U. III:9.28.7.
[8]Ka.U. II:2.15.
[9]Tai.U. III:6.
[10]*Ibid.* II:9.
[11]Ch.U. VII:23.1.
[12]For further treatment of Saguṇa and Nirguṇa Brahman, see the author's book *Meditation, Its Process, Practice, and Culmination,* Chap. VII, pp. 173-76.

Being-Consciousness-Bliss (Sat-Cit-Ānanda) is recognized by all schools of Vedanta — monistic and monotheistic. This is the very perfection of existence, man's Highest Ideal, the ultimate Goal. Not only is there One Supreme Being, one God; He is the sole Reality. Nothing exists apart from Him or independently of Him. Each and everything, living or nonliving, minute or vast, has its being in Him. As immanent in the manifold the One Supreme Being has different aspects in relation to it: He is the Omniscient, Omnipotent Internal Ruler of the universe; its origination, preservation, and dissolution are due to Him; He is its One All-pervading Self; He dwells within every individual as the inmost self; He is the All-gracious Adorable One worshipped by the seekers of Liberation. Such is Brahman in relation to the universe constituted of the three guṇas.[13] This is Saguṇa Brahman, who is possessed of all blessed qualities. All schools of Vedanta, nondualistic and monotheistic, accept Saguṇa Brahman.

But Nondualistic Vedanta, of which Śaṅkara is the greatest exponent, does not consider Saguṇa Brahman to be ultimate. According to this school Brahman is absolutely nondual, free from all distinctions and differences; even the distinction of substance and attribute does not hold there. All multiplicity is mere appearance, which we perceive in the state of ignorance, and consider as real. The human mind invariably conceives of God in relation to the universe. Though immanent in the universe God is all-transcendent, unaffected by multiplicity. Though Saguṇa He is Nirguṇa as well.

We can hardly think of God without reference to the creative order. But God exists even when there is no creation at all. Such is Brahman — beyond all characterization. Words are inadequate to express *That*. Beyond the range of speech and thought is *That* (avāṅgmanasōgōcaram). Such expressions as "Nirguṇa Brahman,"

[13]Before the manifestation of the universe, the guṇas remain in a state of equilibrium; they balance one another. Then prakṛti or māyā is in its causal state. It is indiscrete and undifferentiated. As the guṇas lose their equilibrium the process of evolvement starts. From the grossest to the finest, everything in nature (physical and psychical) is composed of the three guṇas, which invariably coexist and are inseparable. But everywhere one or another of the triad predominates the other two. It is the preponderance of one or another of the triad in varying degrees that makes all differences in things.

The guṇas are not the attributes of prakṛti, but its constituents like the three strands of a rope. They may be conceived as substantive energies. Sattva is the principle of poise conducive to purity, knowledge, joy. Rajas is the principle of motivity leading to activity, desire, restlessness, or disquietude. Tamas is the principle of inertia resulting in inaction, dullness, and delusion. Sattva is light, tamas heavy, rajas medium. Sattva is represented as white, rajas as red, tamas as dark.

"Satcitānandam Brahman" only point to *That* by implication.

According to the monotheistic schools of Vedanta, Saguṇa Brahman — God with attributes, generally known as the Personal God — is the Ultimate One. The direct approach to Him is the path of devotion, Bhakti-yōga, characterized by a form of relationship between the worshipper and the Adorable One. The strong adherents of the path of devotion are the five principal monotheistic schools of Vaiṣṇavism, which are well grounded on the triple basis of Vedanta. They are the worshippers of Viṣṇu, the all-pervading Preserver. Other than the schools of Vaiṣṇavism, there are the monotheistic schools of the Śaivas and the Śāktas, who all acknowledge the authority of the Vedantic texts, and worship Saguṇa Brahman as Śiva and Śakti. Śiva represents the static and Śakti the dynamic aspect of Saguṇa Brahman. Śakti (lit. power, specifically, the Divine Power) is conceived as the Mother of the universe and worshipped as such.

The Nondualistic school esteems the worship of Saguṇa Brahman as an indirect way to the realization of Nirguṇa Brahman. The direct approach to Nirguṇa Brahman is the path of knowledge, Jñāna-yōga; Bhakti-yōga is proximate to Jñāna-yōga as preparatory to it.

3. *The Supreme Being is the inmost self in every living being. The basic difference between the living and the nonliving.*

All-pervading Supreme Consciousness underlying every form of existence, animate and inanimate, is manifest within every living being as the inmost self (sarvabhūtāntarātmā).[14] It is said in the *Śvetāśvatara Upaniṣad:* "One Self-effulgent Being, hidden in all beings, all-pervading, is the inner self of all animate beings."[15]

Because of the luminous self man is ever aware of his own existence and of all else within his scope. His existence is self-evident. Each and every human being knows that he exists: he requires no proof for that. This shows what man really is. No material object, not even the resplendent sun, the ruler of the solar universe, is ever aware of its own existence or of anything else, vast or minute, bright or dark. But man is of contrary nature. He is self-effulgent pure spirit. The fundamental difference between matter and spirit is that matter is devoid of self-awareness, while spirit is awareness itself.

The inner self is the central principle of consciousness in a living being that integrates the heterogeneous constituents of the organism

[14]Usually termed *Pratyagātmā, Sākṣī, Kūṭastha.* [15]Sv.U. VI:11.

and their functions. It is living beings and not inanimate objects that give evidence of inner consciousness. The reason is this — in a living being there is the mind, more or less developed, which has the capacity to transmit or reflect consciousness according to its development. This is how all-pervading Consciousness is apparently particularized or individualized by each finite mind. To give an illustration: wide-spread sunlight being reflected in a mirror or transmitted through a glass-pane inside a room, assumes a distinctive character according to the condition of the mirror or the glass.

4. *The inner self of man is luminous, free, pure, and immortal.*

In a human being the mind is more highly developed than in other living beings. It is not just the difference of physical form that demarcates the human from the subhuman order, but the distinctive character of the mind. Of all the living beings man alone is capable of thinking. The senses present their respective objects as agreeable and disagreeable. Birds and beasts respond to them instinctively. But human beings judge, evaluate, and deal with these objects according to their mental capacities.

Because of the distinctive character of the mind, consciousness is manifest in a human individual as distinct self-awareness. Not only is he aware of his own existence spontaneously, he also recognizes himself as an individual distinct from all external objects as their cognizer. Further, he cognizes the conditions of the body, the organs, and the mind. As a cognizer he must be distinct from all that are cognized. But while man recognizes himself as distinct from the external objects, he does not readily recognize himself as distinct from the body, the organs, and the mind, even though he is aware of their changing conditions. On the contrary, he is identified with the psychophysical garb because of his ignorance (ajñāna) of the true nature of the self.

Nevertheless, the cognizer and the cognized cannot be identical. While the cognized vary, the cognizer remains constant as the witness of the changing conditions, external and internal. The one and the same cognizer experiences waking, dream, and deep sleep states from day to day, and also childhood, youth, and maturity as years roll on. Being constant the cognizer maintains an individual's identity despite all variations of external events and of the psychophysical constitution as well. Further, there is an essential difference between the cognizer and the cognized. Consciousness is intrinsic in the cognizer, while the object cognized is devoid of it. The knower is ever the knower. It cannot be objectified. There is no subject-object relation in man's self-awareness. The self is self-manifest.

While the objects cognized, external and internal, undergo changes, the cognizer remains constant, invariable in the midst of the variable. So the inmost self of man is changeless, and therefore beyond birth, growth, decay and death; beyond hunger and thirst; beyond weal and woe. And it is ever shining, being of the nature of consciousness. It is ever pure, free, immortal.

5. *Man's two fold ajñāna (ignorance). The real and the apparent man. (See also Chap. V, sec. 8.)*

Although man is vaguely aware of the nature of the self, he does not realize what he really is, due to ignorance as we have already noted. The presence of ignorance is evident from the fact that a man can use such expressions as "I do not know myself," "I am ignorant of myself" in consequence of a certain measure of introspection. It is absurd that the knower should be ignorant of his own nature. Yet, it is a fact. The knower testifies to his ignorance with regard to his true nature, as its witness. But he cannot repudiate his own existence.

This ignorance is twofold. Not only does man fail to apprehend the nature of the self, he even misapprehends it. Being associated with the psychophysical garb, he is more or less identified with it and ascribes to himself the conditions of the body, the organs, and the mind, although he is ever distinct from them as their cognizer. This is evident from such expressions as, "I am dark," "I am fair," "I am tall," "I am short," "I am deaf," "I am blind," "I am lame," "I am happy," "I am unhappy," "I am honest," "I am ignorant," and so forth.

The veil of ignorance (ajñāna), which shrouds the nature of the luminous self, underlies the psychophysical garb. It is the immutable self, ever united with the all-pervading Self as the wave with the ocean, that supports ajñāna as its basis. As such the self is called "Kūṭastha (the rock-steady)." It is unaffected by the veil of ajñāna of which it stays as the witness (sākṣī). Ajñāna can be counted as the primary constituent of the psychophysical garb. Next to ajñāna is the individual mind. The immutable self in association with ajñāna, being reflected in the cognitive aspect of the mind (buddhi), becomes identified with the mental mode characterized by "I-ness" and invariably appears as the ego, the individualized self. This is the apparent self, the Self identified with the not-self. It is the ego that imposes upon itself not only the varying states and functions of the mind, the organs, and the body, but also the external conditions. This is how the limitless self appears limited, the changeless as changeful, the luminous as nonluminous. So the ego, the apparent self, with all its transformations, is no other than the real self appearing different from what it is. For instance, the sun, rising or setting, bright or dim, large or small, is but the same immense, radiant, stationary sun unaffected by its varying appearances.

6. *The four Vedic mahāvākyas (the cardinal sayings). Their significance.*

The fact that the individual self manifest as the ego is essentially identical with the all-pervading Supreme Self is the central theme of Vedanta. In each of the four Vedas there is a terse sentence declaring this truth. This is called *mahāvākya* (lit. the great saying). The four mahāvākyas are:

(1) "Consciousness [manifest as the individual self] is Brahman" as declared by the *Aitareya Upaniṣad* of the *Ṛg-Veda.*[16]

(2) "I am Brahman" as declared by the *Bṛhadāraṇyaka Upaniṣad* of the *Yajur-Veda.*[17]

(3) "Thou art That" as declared by the *Chāndōgya Upaniṣad* of the *Sāma Veda.*[18]

(4) "This ātman [the self within] is Brahman" as declared by the *Māṇḍūkya Upaniṣad* of the *Atharva Veda.*[19]

It is to be noted that these highly significant Vedic sayings point to the identity of the individual self and the Supreme Self, in their essential nature as Pure Consciousness beyond all distinctions. The individual self represents finite consciousness, and the Supreme Self all-pervading Consciousness. As Consciousness pure and simple divested of their respective adjuncts the two are identical. But as long as the individual self under the spell of ajñāna holds to the psychophysical adjunct it is virtually limited in every respect. Then there is an immense gulf of difference between the individual self and the Supreme Self. The Supreme Self is the Omniscient, Omnipotent Internal Ruler of the universe, whereas the individual self can barely control the psychophysical adjunct. To give an illustration, the wave limited by its apparent form is but an insignificant part of the ocean.

[16]Ai.U. III:1.3. [17]Br.U. I:4.10. [18]Ch.U. VI:8.7, *passim.* [19]Ma.U. II.

As such the wave belongs to the ocean, and not the ocean to the wave. But as pure and simple water, the wave is identical with the ocean; there is no essential difference between the two. The implication of each of these mahāvākyas is the sole reality of Nondual Consciousness. Each points to this as the ultimate Reality (akhaṇḍārtha-bōdhaka).

Over and above, the great Vedic dictum imparts a twofold knowledge not attainable by perception or speculative reason. On the one hand, by declaring the oneness of the individual self with the Supreme Self it removes man's deep-seated misconception of himself, viz., that he is bound, insignificant, impure, and mortal — and points to his real self as ever shining, ever free, ever pure; as beyond decay and death, beyond weal and woe. On the other hand, by declaring the Supreme Self as the inmost self of every individual, it removes man's equally inveterate misconception of the Supreme Being — that He is far away, inaccessible, and hidden — and presents Him as the nearest of all, ever manifest, immediate and direct. What is imagined to be unattainable is already attained. The seeker has only to discover Him, to open his inner eye and see. By knowing the inner self he can reach God. The direct way to the Supreme Being is an inner approach. This is the burden of the Upaniṣadic teachings. It will be evident from the following passages:

> Smaller than the small, greater than the great is the Self hidden in the heart of every living being. He who is free from desires realizes the greatness of the Self through the tranquility of the senses and the mind, and goes beyond sorrow.[20]
>
> He is not grasped by the eyes, or the organ of speech, or by any other organ. Nor is He attained through austerity or good work. Being pure-minded through the clarity of understanding, a person sees Him, the Indivisible One, through meditation.[21]
>
> That which is not revealed by speech, but by which speech is revealed, know that alone to be Brahman and not what people worship outside.
>
> That which is not comprehended by the mind, but by which the mind is said to be comprehended, know that alone to be Brahman and not what people worship as outside.[22]
>
> The Self alone is to be meditated upon, for all these [multiple objects] are unified in It [being nondifferent from It]. Of all these, this Self alone should be realized, for one knows all these through It, just as one finds an animal by its footmark. [The reason is that the Self is the foothold of the entire manifold.][23]

[20]Ka.U. I:2.20. [21]Mu.U. III:1.8. [22]Ken.U. I:5,6, et seq. [23]Br.U. I:4.7.

7. *Each of the four cardinal sayings points to two main approaches to the supreme Being: Bhakti-yōga (the path of devotion) and Jñāna-yōga (the path of knowledge). (For elaborate treatment of the Four Yōgas, see Chaps. XII-XVI.)*

Further, each of the four great Vedic sayings, being resolved into two distinct factors, signify two distinct courses, the one for the realization of Nirguṇa Brahman, and the other for the realization of Saguṇa Brahman. For instance, the dictum "I am Brahman" can be resolved into the two factors "I am He" and "I am His." "I am He" implies the identity of the individual self with the Supreme Self. It betokens the direct approach to Nirguṇa Brahman, which is called Jñāna-yōga, the path of knowledge. Consciousness of the identity of the individual self with the Supreme Self is typical of the seekers of Nirguṇa Brahman, the followers of the path of knowledge, Jñāna-yōga.

The other factor, "I am His," implies the relationship between the individual self and the Supreme Being. It betokens the direct approach to Saguṇa Brahman, which is called *Bhakti-yōga,* the path of devotion. A deep feeling of relationship with the Adorable One is the characteristic mark of the seekers of Saguṇa Brahman, the followers of the path of devotion, Bhakti-yōga.

It is worthy of note that Jñāna-yōga, the path of knowledge, is not wholly an intellectual approach, nor is Bhakti-yōga, the path of devotion, just an emotional approach. Without the intense longing of the heart for the realization of Nirguṇa Brahman, the follower of the path of knowledge cannot reach the Goal merely by the exercise of intellect — in the manner of a speculative philosopher or a research student. Because of the predominance of reason in this approach, it is technically called Jñāna-yōga, the path of knowledge. Similarly, without the exercise of reason, the seeker of Saguṇa Brahman, the follower of the path of devotion, cannot have a clear understanding of the Goal and the approach. Consequently, his mind cannot be free from doubts, prejudices, narrowness, bigotry, fanatacism, and other obstacles on the way.

After being fully convinced of the truth through intense meditation in the depth of the heart on the identity of the individual self with the Supreme Self as Pure Consciousness, the follower of the path of knowledge, Jñāna-yōga, realizes Nirguṇa Brahman beyond all distinction in nirvikalpa samādhi, the culmination of mystical experience.

As regards the path of devotion, the Vedantic teachers have recommended different forms of relationship with the Adorable One according to the adorer's inner attitude. After worshipping Him devotedly as the Supreme Ruler, or as the Supreme Master, or as the Eternal Father, or as the Eternal Mother, or as the sole Dependable Friend, or as the Dearest Child, or as the Supreme Beloved, the worshipper realizes with the intensification of his devotion and the deepening of his spiritual insight, that the Supreme Being is all in all, that He is the Soul of all souls, that He dwells within every individual as the inmost self. The devotee becomes convinced that his inner self belongs to Him completely as the wave belongs to the ocean. Through intense meditation on the unity of the individual self with the Supreme Self in the depth of the heart, as his mind becomes completely absorbed in Him, the worshipper realizes the unification of the two in savikalpa samādhi, the mystical experience in which the distinction between the two is not obliterated. This is the culmination of the path of devotion, Bhakti-yōga.

The efficacy of both Bhakti-yōga and Jñāna-yōga has been clearly demonstrated in the present age in the life of Sri Ramakrishna. During the last twenty years of his life not a day passed when he did not experience either savikalpa or nirvikalpa samādhi, or both. His experiences have been recorded in his own words as far as possible by his direct disciples.

> "Ah, what a state of mind I passed through! My mind would lose itself in the Indivisible Absolute. How many days I spent that way! I renounced bhakti and bhakta, devotion and devotee. I became inert. I could not feel the form of my own head. I was about to die. I thought of keeping Ramlal's aunt [referring to Sri Sarada Devi, the Holy Mother] near me.
>
> "I ordered the removal of all pictures and portraits from my room. When I regained outer consciousness, when the mind climbed down to the ordinary level, I felt as if I were being suffocated like a drowning person. At last I said to myself, 'If I can't bear people, then how shall I live?' Then my mind was again directed to bhakti and bhakta. 'What has happened to me?' I kept asking people. Bholanath [a clerk of the Dakshineswar temple garden] said to me, 'This state of mind has been described in the *Mahābhārata*.' How can a man live, on coming down from the plane of samādhi? Surely he requires devotion to God and the company of devotees. Otherwise, how will he keep his mind occupied?"[24]

[24] *The Gospel of Sri Ramakrishna according to "M"* (a lay disciple), Eng. tr. by Swami Nikhilananda, New York, Ramakrishna-Vivekananda Center, 1942, p.767.

> The Master himself said to us on many occasions, "The natural tendency of this mind is upwards towards the Nirvikalpa plane. Once in samādhi, it does not feel inclined to come down. It has forcibly to be brought down for your sake. This force is also not sufficient for coming down, so I catch hold of some trifling desires of the lower plane, as 'I will smoke tobacco,' 'I will drink water,' 'I will take sukta,' 'I will see so-and-so,' 'I will talk'; these also have to be retained in the mind by effective repetition. It is only then that the mind gradually comes down to the state of body-consciousness. Again, when coming down, it flies off in that (upward) direction. It has to be brought down again by means of such desires."[25]

The access to Nirguṇa Brahman by Jñāna-yōga is a direct but very steep course. This suits only highly qualified spiritual aspirants. So says Śrī Kṛṣṇa: "Greater is the difficulty of those whose minds are set on the unmanifested (Nirguṇa Brahman), for the Goal of the Unmanifested is very hard to attain for those who are in the grip of the body-idea."[26] The mediocre seekers of Nirguṇa Brahman are therefore instructed to first realize Saguṇa Brahman in savikalpa samādhi by Bhakti-yōga and later realize Nirguṇa Brahman in nirvikalpa samādhi by the practice of Jñāna-yōga. This is a less arduous venture.

8. *To realize Brahman, Saguṇa or Nirguṇa, is the supreme goal of life.*

Whoever succeeds in realizing Brahman, Saguṇa or Nirguṇa, becomes free from all bondages and sufferings and attains everlasting light and bliss. That the realization of Brahman is the Supreme Goal of life has been affirmed by the Vedantic seers and sages from time immemorial and reiterated from age to age.

We quote below a few relevant Upaniṣadic passages:

> I have realized that Supreme Being who is effulgent like the sun and beyond darkness. It is by knowing Him and Him alone that one goes beyond death. There is no other way out.[27]
>
> While in this very body, we have been able to know That [Brahman]. Otherwise, we would have been ignorant. Then there would have been a great calamity. Those who know That [Brahman] become immortal, while others undergo misery alone.[28]

[25]*Sri Ramakrishna, The Great Master,* by Swami Saradananda, Eng.tr. by Swami Jagadananda, Madras, India, Sri Ramakrishna Math, 1952, p. 364.

[26]BG XII:5. [27]Sv.U. III:8. [28]Br.U. IV:4.14.

> This great birthless Self is undecaying, immortal, unconditioned, without fear, and infinite, Brahman [the Infinite One] is indeed fearless. He who knows the Self as such becomes the fearless Brahman.[29]

> When He who is both high and low [existing as the Cause and the effect] is realized, then the fetters of the heart are broken, all doubts are dispelled, and the deposit of karma is eliminated.[30]

> If a person knows the Self then he attains the true goal of life. If he cannot know That here, great misery awaits him. Having realized the Self in every being, the wise withdraw from the world [give up "I-ness" and "my-ness"] and become immortal.[31]

This is the keynote of Vedanta. In the modern age Sri Ramakrishna and his disciples have emphasized the same Vedantic ideal of God-realization by precept and by example as well. To see God is the supreme purpose of human life. He can be seen by more ways than one, and every religion worth the name represents one or more of them. It is worthy of note that the two characteristic marks of each way are the purification of the heart and the development of longing for God. This is the burden of Sri Ramakrishna's message.

9. *How can the human mind turn to the Eternal, while its general tendency is to seek the temporal? The importance of virtue.*

Now one may argue thus: How can man be interested in the spiritual venture leading to the ultimate Goal? How can his mind turn away from transitory pleasures and possessions within his reach to the search for eternal treasures, which are far away, dubious, and inaccessible to all appearance? Obviously, human beings in general are engrossed with temporal values in one form or another. They are attached to the sense-world and strive after sense-enjoyment by all possible means. Even those who believe in the hereafter aim at sense fulfillment in the celestial realm. Among the believers in God not a few worship Him for the transitory rather than for eternal life.

Far from condemning the aspirants seeking temporal values here and hereafter, the Vedic seers have recommended courses for their attainment until the seekers can realize their shortcomings by actual experience and turn to the eternal. Indeed, this is the main purpose of the work-section of the Vedas. Besides the right performance of domestic and social duties essential to an individual's well-being in

[29] *Ibid.* IV:4.25. [30] Mu.U. II:2.8. [31] Ken.U. II:5.

this life, the Vedas have prescribed rites and ceremonies by which the seekers of celestial joys and glories can attain them. There is no inherent contradiction in the Vedic view between the search for the temporal and the search for the eternal, because, being rightly directed, the one leads to the other. But the absolute condition for the success of either is adherence to the moral course. He who deviates from the path of virtue (dharma) is not qualified for the performance of the Vedic rites, because it is detrimental to his own interests, secular and spiritual.

"That is dharma (virtue) by which human beings can attain affluence and the Supreme Good as well," says Kaṇāda, the founder of one of the six Vedic systems of philosophy, called "the Vaiśeṣika."[32] We shall see how the practice of virtue promotes both.

The cultivation of virtues is attended with the overcoming of vices. These two constitute the moral course. Such qualities as kindness, sincerity, truthfulness, humility, forgiveness, contentment, are regarded as virtues. These indicate man's fellow-feeling towards his fellow-beings. They are conducive to internal peace and poise. As a result, the inner vision of a virtuous man becomes clear and his judgment ripens. These are essential to the right use of one's inner and outer resources and their development.

On the contrary, vice is associated with man's ill-feeling towards his fellow-beings. It proceeds from selfishness. Whoever succumbs to any of the vices, such as hatred, anger, pride, jealousy, cruelty, hypocrisy, greed, cannot maintain the balance of mind. He loses his power of understanding. His judgment is vitiated. Consequently whoever succumbs to vice runs the risk of abusing his inner and outer resources and of losing them as well.

According to the Vedic teachers the one universal duty of all human individuals, irrespective of their religious views, social rank, pecuniary situation, cultural standing, political status, and physical condition, is the observance of virtue. It is their strong behest that under no circumstances should one deviate from the path of virtue. "Virtue protects him who protects her," says the *Mahābhārata.* Further, "From virtue arises happiness." "Virtue is the only friend that accompanies man beyond death."

Virtue harmonizes individual and social interests. It is the stable basis of every aspect of the individual and the collective life. A man's physical, intellectual, aesthetic, as well as spiritual well-being, rests on this. Unsupported by the inner goodness of individuals, social

[32] *Vaiśeṣika Sūtras* I:1.2.

institutions, political organizations, economic systems, judiciary administration, scientific research, technological advancement, defense measures, howsoever well devised, cannot establish peace, harmony, and welfare among men.

A seeker of secular good in whatever form who keeps firm on the path of virtue gets the utmost for his capacities and situation in life. By actual experience of power, position, learning, fame, health, wealth, beauty, pleasure, and so forth, he realizes their inherent shortcomings. He becomes convinced that there is no assurance of security in the temporal order, there is no prospect of unmixed blessing in the relative universe characterized by dualities. Yet in the depth of his heart there is a cry for life beyond death, for light beyond darkness, for joy beyond sorrow. Where else but in God can he find them? He understands that there is One Supreme Being, who alone is eternal, who alone is free, who alone is perfect, while all else is short-lived, bound, and imperfect. Unless disillusioned of all charms and glories of life none can accept God as the sole Goal, as the sole Refuge.

10. *The necessity for the practice of Karma-yōga; its basic principle. It is preparatory to Bhakti-yōga and Jñāna-yōga. (See also sec. 7 of this chapter.)*

So we see that it is not the experience of the bitterness of adversity, but the comprehension of the emptiness of affluence gained by virtue that turns the human mind Godward in the true sense. This is the beginning of spiritual life. But ardent devotion to God does not develop at the same time. Nor does intense longing for Liberation. The one prerequisite for following the path of devotion, the direct approach to Saguṇa Brahman, is ardent devotion to Him. Similarly, the one precondition for following the path of knowledge, the direct approach to Nirguṇa Brahman, is intense longing for Liberation. For the development of either of these prerequisites the seeker has to practice Karma-yōga. We shall dwell on this in detail in due course. Here we shall indicate its basic principle.(See also Chap.XIII, sec. 2.)

When a person accepts God as the Supreme Goal and lives with that Ideal in view, he does not look upon any temporal value, howsoever high, as an end in itself, but as a means to the highest end. Naturally he deals with all that concerns him with composure, but not with indifference. Being free from all attachment to the temporal he is unshaken by the changing conditions of life. He performs his duties, domestic and social, with equanimity, being unperturbed by success and failure, pleasure and pain, praise and blame. This is the basic principle of Karma-yōga. "Equanimity is said to be yōga,"[33] says Śrī Kṛṣṇa with reference to Karma-yōga. With the further development of the aspirant's inner nature Karma-yōga is practiced with different mental attitudes. Along with this Vedanta recommends the formal worship of God by physical, verbal, and mental methods for the cultivation of devotion to the Supreme Being. This is the preparatory stage of devotion.

11. *The fundamental teachings of Vedanta summed up.*

Nondual, pure Being-Consciousness-Bliss is the sole Reality. It is the very basis and being of the apparent manifold. As such It is immanent and all-transcendent. Beyond the distinction of substance and attribute, the all-transcendent One is designated Nirguṇa (attributeless) Brahman.

As immanent in the manifold the same Reality has different aspects and attributes in relation to it and is called Saguṇa Brahman. This has different names:

(1) As the One All-pervading Self of the universe this is called Paramātmā.
(2) As the All-knowing, All-powerful Ruler of the universe this is called Parameśvara (the Supreme Lord).
(3) As the All-gracious Giver of Liberation this is called Bhagavān.

12. *The same All-pervading Self (Paramātmā) dwells within every individual as the inmost self and is apparently limited or individualized. As such this is called* jīvātmā.

The real self of man is luminous, pure, free, and immortal. To realize its essential *unity* or *identity* with the Supreme Self is the Goal of life.

Thus there are two main ways to attain this: the one is called Bhakti-yōga, the path of devotion, which culminates in the realization of the unity. The other is called Jñāna-yōga, the path of knowledge, which culminates in the realization of the identity of the individual self with the Supreme Self.

[33]BG II:48.

(1) The one is the approach to Saguṇa Brahman. This is the path of devotion, Bhakti-yōga, characterized by the consciousness of relationship between the individual self and the Supreme Self. Relationship implies distinction between the related.

(2) The other is the approach to Nirguṇa Brahman. This is the path of knowledge, Jñāna-yōga, characterized by the consciousness of the essential identity of the individual self and the Supreme Self.

(3) As we have indicated above, it is the practice of Karma-yōga that paves the way to either approach. But none can practice Karma-yōga until he can accept the Supreme Being as the Goal of life and make a determined effort to be free from attachment to the temporal.

In order to turn away from the search of the temporal to the search of the Eternal, the seeker must be disillusioned of dualities by experiencing adequacy consequent on righteous living. A person of righteous living who follows the path of virtue, has no anti-feelings toward his fellow beings. Being free from emotional disturbances, such as jealousy, hatred, pride — his understanding, his judgment, function rightly. Consequently, he can utilize his outer and inner resources as well as possible. As a result he gets the most out of this life. After enjoying wealth, beauty, power, position and so forth he recognizes their shortcomings. In this world of pairs of opposites, growth and decay, life and death, prosperity and adversity, hope and despair, enjoyment and suffering, ascent and descent, are correlated. We cannot have just the one to the exclusion of the other. This is how a righteous person becomes disillusioned of the inevitable dualities of life. Until then one cannot turn to the Eternal One, the Changeless One, beyond this world of dualities.

An unrighteous person can also acquire wealth, beauty, power, position, and so forth and experience them. But he cannot escape the inevitable failure and frustrations. Such a person may be disgusted with the life of dualities, but he cannot turn to the Eternal One. He is not disillusioned of the pairs of opposites, unavoidable as they are.

13. *Two specialities of Vedanta.*

One speciality of Vedanta is that it prescribes varied and graded courses according to the inner development of man and his situation in life, so that by pursuing those that are best suited to him he can reach the ultimate Goal in due course, proceeding from where he is. Even from the lowest level a person can reach the mountain-top by rightly guiding his steps.

It is said in a Hymn on The Greatness of Śiva (Śiva-mahimnah stōtram) by Puṣpadanta, st. 7:

> The triple Veda (Trayī),[34] Sāṁkhya and Yōga systems, Pāśupata (Śaiva) and Vaiṣṇava doctrines prescribe diverse courses. This is the best, that is wholesome, they say.
>
> As the different streams having their sources in different places all mingle their water in the sea, so, O Lord, the different paths which men take through different tendencies, various though they appear, crooked or straight, all lead to Thee.

Another notable speciality of Vedanta is its comprehensiveness. It sees life as a whole — it takes into consideration all the aspects of life such as physical, intellectual, aesthetic, moral and spiritual. Of these the moral is the basis and the spiritual is the ideal, as explained above. In Vedantic thought and culture, mystical experience, philosophic reason, faith, religious rites and ceremonies, domestic and social duties, humanitarian deeds, renunciation, meditation, devotional rapture, ethics, aesthetics, have their due places. There is no inherent contradiction in the Vedantic view between worldly duties and spiritual disciplines; between Divine Law and Divine Grace; between science and religion; between poetry and philosophy; between the individual and the society — all have their appropriate places in human existence.

According to Vedanta, humanity must move as one body in an orderly procession in which every individual, every nation, will have a distinctive role to play. Unity in variety, and not uniformity, is the pattern of world culture. Physical, intellectual, aesthetic, moral and spiritual development must continue hand in hand. Science and religion, arts and ethics, philosophy and mysticism will have their appropriate places in human life. One expression of life does not contradict another as long as each contribute to the highest good that man has to achieve. For instance, various types of building materials, and of manual and skilled labor can be used in conformity with an architect's plan to construct a masterpiece of architecture. Similarly, all facets of life can be utilized in building a "masterpiece" of social organization, if each facet is accorded its rightful place in the scheme of life. The goal of civilization cannot be different from the goal of religion. (See Appendix II — "The Abundant Life.")

[34]See footnote on the Vedas, p. 34.

CHAPTER III

THE APPLICABILITY OF VEDANTA TO ANCIENT AND MODERN LIFE

1. *The appeal of Vedanta to the human mind from ancient times has been due to (1) its universality, (2) its rationality, and (3) its practicality.*

We shall dwell on these points successively.

From ancient times spiritual and cultural ideas have flowed from India to the outside world, Eastern and Western. For centuries Alexandria was the meeting place of Oriental and Western culture and thought. It is there that Plotinus, the Roman Neo-platonic philosopher, who was born in Egypt, imbibed Eastern views. According to some historians it was through Neo-platonism that India's spiritual ideas influenced the medieval mystics of Christianity.

In his book *Mysticism and Catholicism* H. Stutfield remarks:

> Evidently there seems to be a growing probability that, from the historical standpoint at any rate, India was the birthplace of the fundamental imaginings, the cradle of contemplative religion, and the nobler philosophy.[1]

Further,

> The mind of Plato was heavily charged with Orphic mysticism mainly derived from Asiatic sources. India, always the home of mystical devotion, probably contributed the larger share.[2]

According to many Western Orientalists, such as Horace H. Wilson (1786-1860), Sir Monier-Williams (1819-1899), Frederick Max Müller (1823-1900), Paul Duessen (1845-1915), Indian literature had been continuously influencing European scholars in

[1]Hugh E.M. Stutfield, *Mysticism and Catholicism,* London, Fisher Unwin, 1925, p. 31.

[2]*Ibid.,* p. 74.

Germany, France, and England from before the close of the 18th century.

Previous to the Vedanta movement initiated by Swami Vivekananda, Indian spiritual ideas influenced the scholars of the Concord group in Massachusetts, particularly Henry David Thoreau (1817-1862) and Ralph Waldo Emerson (1803-1882). In his lecture on "Plato; or, the Philosopher" in *Representative Men* Emerson observes:

> In all nations there are minds which incline to dwell in the conception of the fundamental Unity. The raptures of prayer and ecstasy of devotion lose all being in One Being. This tendency finds its highest expression in the religious writings of the East, and chiefly in the Indian scriptures, in the Vedas, the Bhagavat Geeta, and the Vishnu Purana.[3]

2. *The universal Truths upheld by Vedanta. Everywhere human life must conform to them. Their recognition is conducive to world-unity urgently needed in the present age.*

In the Vedantic view the One Immutable Ultimate Reality underlies all diversities. It is the very perfection of existence, to realize which is the goal of human life. Here is the culmination of human knowledge. Human knowledge cannot go beyond the ultimate unity of existence. To find unity in diversity is the objective of every branch of knowledge. While every branch of physical science seeks unity in its limited sphere, philosophy seeks the unity of unities. Religion aims to experience the Ultimate One.

The Ultimate One is Pure Being-Consciousness-Bliss. The Supreme Being is Supreme Consciousness and Supreme Bliss. This is the very perfection of existence, the Ideal Reality.

Swami Vivekananda says:

> If you go below the surface you find that Unity between man and man, between races and races, high and low, rich and poor, gods and men, and men and animals. If you go deep enough, all will be seen as only variations of the One, and he who has attained to this conception of Oneness has no more delusion. What can delude him? He knows the reality of everything, the secret of everything. Where is there anymore misery for him? What does he desire? He has traced the reality of

[3]Ralph Waldo Emerson, *Representative Men,* in *The Complete Works of Ralph Waldo Emerson,* Vol. IV, Boston, Houghton Mifflin, 1903, p. 49.

everything to the Lord, the Centre, the Unity of everything, and that is Eternal Existence, Eternal Knowledge, Eternal Bliss.[4]

Further, the All-transcendent One is the All-pervading Self of the universe. This shines within every individual as the inmost self. What is innermost in the universe is innermost in man. As declared by the Upaniṣad:

> The Nondual Self-effulgent Being is hidden in all that is created. He is all-pervading. He is the inmost self of all beings.[5]

So the real self of man is the central principle of consciousness, self-evident, ever-shining, pure, free, immortal. This is ever united with the Supreme Self, although man is not aware of it due to a peculiar ignorance (ajñāna; see Chap. V, sec. 8).

To realize the oneness of the individual self with the Supreme Self is the goal of human life. There is the end of all delusion, all misery. The Upaniṣad says:

> When to the man of realization all beings [animate and inanimate] become the Self, then what delusion and what sorrow can there be for that seer of oneness.[6]

The basic urge in man is the urge for the Highest and Best, the urge for the Infinite. This is at the back of all his undertakings, even though he is not aware of it. Knowingly or unknowingly, rightly or wrongly, man is constantly struggling to reach That. This is why he can never be satisfied with anything limited or imperfect. He who understands this cannot but be sympathetic to all. Free from hatred or malice, he will try to help the wrongdoer as far as he can. Abiding peace dwells within him who knows the Supreme Goal of life and judiciously endeavors for that one end.

A great desideration of the present age is the unity of humanity despite all diversities. Because of the unprecedented facilities of transportation and communication consequent on the advancement of scientific knowledge and technology, human beings of diverse races, religious beliefs, cultural standards, economic conditions, have been brought close together. In this situation, the only way to mutual regard, love, and harmony among men, on which rest peace and progress in life, is to find a common ground of human relationship

[4]CW II, pp. 153-54. [5]Sv.U. VI:11. [6]Is.U. 7.

that transcends all distinctions of color, creed, nationality, rank, merit, and so forth. The recognition of the unity of the individual self with the Supreme Self provides such a ground. This is the way to universal love. This is the rationale of ethics and spirituality.

"Love thy neighbor as thyself,"[7] says The Holy Bible. Why? Because your self is nondifferent from the neighbor's self, due to the essential oneness of both with the Supreme Self.

Explicit or implicit, four basic truths underlie all religions despite the differences of doctrines and practices. These can be summed up as follows:

1) Supreme Consciousness — Ideal Reality — is the All-pervading Self of the universe.
2) This is the indwelling self in every individual. "The Kingdom of God is within you," says Jesus Christ.[8]
3) The real self of man is luminous, pure, free, immortal.
4) To realize the unity of the individual self with the Supreme Self is the Goal of human life.

3. *The Vedantic view of religion. The necessity for harmony of religions.*

In all religions there have been great saints and seers who have realized God in the depth of the heart. Their words of wisdom and whole-souled devotion to God testify to the validity of their inner experience.

Vedanta looks upon every religion worth the name as a way to God-realization. It stands for harmony of religions. In the present age it was the genius of Sri Ramakrishna to exemplify how different religious courses, including those of Islam and Christianity, lead to the same goal, the realization of God. From his own experience he declared: "To realize God is the Goal of human life."[9] "Each religion is a pathway to God."[10]

Two essential requisites for realizing the unity of the individual self with the Supreme Self are the purification of the heart and the cultivation of devotion to the Supreme Being. Religious practices and spiritual disciplines vary according to the capabilities of the aspirants in conformity with these two basic requirements.

[7]Leviticus 19:18; Matthew 19:19, 22:39; Mark 12:31.
[8]Luke 17:21. [9]GSR, p. 453. [10]*Ibid.*, p. 265.

In the Vedantic view different religions are varied expressions of the one eternal religion, which is man's search for God and the realization of God. The avowed objective of different religions is the establishment of peace and harmony among men. How is it possible as long as bigotry, fanaticism, and feuds prevail among them? By mutual understanding, regard, and recognition of truths common to all, the followers of different religions should at first reconcile all contradictions among themselves before they can set the stage for world peace. They must learn to look upon themselves as pilgrims to the same shrine of Truth.

It is to be noted that one deficiency of the modern mind is its lack of knowledge of the fundamental truths, despite its knowledge of many details of the psychophysical realm.

4. *The rationality of Vedanta. The efficacy and limitations of human reason.*

Modern man is inclined to reason. Unless rationally convinced he will not accept anything to be true. Vedanta is also in favor of reason. It does not recognize irrational authority. Faith, according to Vedanta, is reliance on the trustworthy. It is not unreasonable to rely on the reliable. The words of such persons as are free from delusion, error, deceit, and deficiency of the senses and the mind, are to be accepted as authentic. As a matter of fact, a major part of our knowledge is built on verbal testimony — oral and written words. We hardly verify the authentic sources from which we derive the bulk of our knowledge. Just as there are specialists in secular subjects, so are there also specialists in spiritual themes.

But reason has its limitations as well. It leads to inferential knowledge, which is indirect and not definite. When we infer the existence of fire from the sight of smoke from a distance, we cannot be sure as to the nature of the fire or to its exact location. Reason does not unveil the object of knowledge to us. If it be true with regard to the sensible objects, far more it must be true with regard to the suprasensible truths. We cannot deny the existence of the suprasensible, because the explanation of the sensible world is in the suprasensible. The universe as perceived by us is not self-explanatory. We need the knowledge of the unseen in order to understand the seen.

The truths declared by the Vedas — such as the ultimate unity of existence, the immortal self of man, the attainment of Liberation — are suprasensuous and suprarational. They are beyond the ken of the senses and the reach of reason. Speculative philosophy cannot determine them indubitably and far less unveil them. But although suprarational, they are not irrational. They admit of rational explanation. Being the basic facts of existence they explain the different aspects of life — physical, mental, vital, aesthetic, moral, social and spiritual. They evaluate and illumine the relative truths.

As regards the incompetence of reason to unveil suprasensuous truths Swami Vivekananda remarks:

> The field of reason, or of the conscious workings of the mind, is narrow and limited. There is a little circle within which human reason must move. It cannot go beyond. Every attempt to go beyond is impossible, yet it is beyond this circle of reason that there lies all that humanity holds most dear. All these questions, whether there is an immortal soul, whether there is a God, whether there is any supreme intelligence guiding this universe or not, are beyond the field of reason. Reason can never answer these questions. What does reason say? It says, "I am agnostic, I do not know either yea or nay." Yet these questions are so important to us. Without a proper answer to them, human life will be purposeless. All our ethical theories, all our moral attitudes, all that is good and great in human nature, have been moulded upon answers that have come from beyond the circle. It is very important therefore that we should have answers to these questions.[11]

5. *The need of mystical experience. Its relation to reason.*

One may ask, "How does man know the truths that are beyond the range of the senses and out of the reach of reason?" According to most religions great saints and seers intuit these truths in a supraconscious state above reason. As declared by Patañjali:

> In that state [of samādhi] knowledge can be said to be "filled with truth."
>
> The knowledge that is gained from testimony and inference is about common objects. The knowledge gained from samādhi is of a much higher order, being able to penetrate where inference and testimony cannot go.[12]

Many Eastern and Western philosophers concur on this point that the human mind can develop a suprasensuous and suprarational faculty of "intuition," which is far superior to intellect and can penetrate facts that are otherwise inaccessible.

[11]CW I, p. 181. [12]YS I:48, 49.

On the necessity of mystic intuition for the perception of Truths beyond reason Dr. Radhakrishnan observes:

> We have to pass beyond thought, beyond the clash of oppositions, beyond the antinomies that confront us when we work with the limited categories of abstract thinking, if we are to reach the real where man's existence and divine being coincide. It is when thought becomes perfected in intuition that we catch the vision of the real. The mystics the world over have emphasized this fact . . .
>
> According to the Upaniṣads there is a higher power which enables us to grasp this central spiritual reality. Spiritual things require to be spiritually discerned. The yōga method is a practical discipline pointing out the road to this realization. Man has the faculty of divine insight or mystic intuition, by which he transcends the distinctions of intellect and solves the riddles of reason. The chosen spirits scale the highest peak of thought and intuit the reality.[13]

But without undergoing the necessary spiritual disciplines none can develop the mystical intuition for the perception of suprasensuous truths. This is true for the seeker of Saguṇa Brahman and for the seeker of Nirguṇa Brahman as well. When, as a result of following the preparatory courses including the study of the Vedic scriptures, the seeker of Nirguṇa Brahman develops intense longing for Liberation, he should approach a qualified teacher, a man of realization who is well-versed in the scriptural knowledge as well. After hearing from him the Vedic *mahāvākya* he must grasp its import through reasoning. Then through further reasoning he has to be convinced of the truth of the statement. Next he should meditate on the truth — the identity of the individual self with the Supreme Self. Through intense meditation he succeeds in realizing the truth. Hearing the scriptural truth, reflecting on it, and meditating intensely on it, are said to be the threefold means of Self-realization. The scriptural text, reason, and the pupil's experience must be in conformity.

The seers' experiences corroborate the Vedic truths. They restate from their own experiences what the Vedas declare. Their lives of unsullied purity, their whole-souled devotion to the Divine Being, their selfless service to their fellow-beings, their words of enlightenment testify to the genuineness of their experiences and pronouncements.

[13]S. Radhakrishnan, *Indian Philosophy, Vol. 1,* London, Allen & Unwin, 1931, p. 176.

6. *The practicality of Vedanta. Application of the highest spiritual principles to man's everyday life.*

The appeal of Vedanta to modern man is due not only to its universality and rationality but also to its practicality. The Vedantic teachers have shown how the highest truths can be applied to active life; how a person can live in the world according to fundamental spiritual principles. The *Bhagavad-gītā* dwells particularly on the application of spiritual truths to man's everyday life. It teaches how a man can live in the world free from worldliness. Śrī Kṛṣṇa has pointed out how intense activity and serenity of mind can go together, how a person can walk on the spiritual path in any field of life, be it a marketplace or a battleground, a laboratory or a workshop, how from the lowest level of life a man can reach the highest by rightly guiding his steps.

Vedanta holds before man the one Supreme Goal, but prescribes a gradation of ethical and spiritual discipline suited to the inner capacities and external conditions of individuals, so that a person in any level of life can proceed towards the highest from where he is by following the appropriate courses. This is the application of "The doctrine of differentiation of the capabilities of the aspirants." Says Swami Vivekananda:

> Take man where he stands and from there give him a lift.[14]
>
> Our duty is to encourage everyone in his struggle to live up to his own highest ideal, and strive at the same time to make the ideal as near as possible to the truth.[15]
>
> All the men and the women in any society are not of the same mind, capacity, or of the same power to do things; they must have different ideals, and we have no right to sneer at any ideal.[16]

7. *The place of Karma-yōga in spiritual life. The narrow and wide view of it. Its wide application by Swami Vivekananda. (See also Chaps. XIII, XIV.)*

In the Vedantic view, as we have noted, there is no inherent contradiction between the search for the temporal and the search for the eternal. Being rightly directed the one leads to the other. We have seen how a seeker of temporal values who keeps firm on the path of virtue becomes disillusioned of dualities in due course, turns to the

[14]CW II, p. 382. [15]CW I, p. 41. [16]CW I, p. 39.

Eternal and accepts God as the Supreme Goal. But although he tries to get rid of desires, they cling to his mind persistently. It is through the practice of Karma-yōga — the right performance of domestic and social duties with self-dedication to the Supreme Being — that one gains the competence for the path of devotion (Bhakti-yōga) or the path of knowledge (Jñāna-yōga), according to one's inner attitude. Usually it is through the development of ardent devotion to God that a Karma-yōgī becomes qualified for the practice of Bhakti-yōga, the direct approach to Saguṇa Brahman, and it is through the development of intense longing for Liberation that he becomes qualified for the practice of Jñāna-yōga, the direct approach to Nirguṇa Brahman.

He who is qualified for the practice of Bhakti-yōga or the practice of Jñāna-yōga can devote himself wholly to spiritual deeds. The performance of secular duties is not indispensable to his inner development as in the case of a Karma-yōgī. But he can still continue to perform his secular duties as before if his situation in life requires this. In that case his karma is usually regarded as a form of devotion or a form of knowledge, and he is not counted a Karma-yōgī anymore. But taking an objective view, some prefer to call him a Karma-yōgī. So in their view Karma-yōga associated with Bhakti-yōga or Jñāna-yōga can lead an aspirant to the realization of Brahman, Saguṇa or Nirguṇa.

Śrī Kṛṣṇa says in the *Śrīmad-bhāgavatam* to his disciple Uddhava:

> He who worships me constantly and exclusively, through the performance of his duties, knowing my presence in all beings, soon attains to steadfast devotion to Me. O Uddhava, through his undying devotion he comes to Me, the great Lord of all beings, the originator and reabsorber of all, their cause, the Brahman. Having his mind thus purified by the performance of his duties, and knowing My Divinity, he becomes endowed with knowledge and realization and soon attains to Me. All his duties, consisting of specific rites, of those belonging to the castes and orders of life, if attended with devotion to Me become supreme and conducive to liberation.[17]

Considering the need of the age Swami Vivekananda has taken a similar far-reaching view of karma. In the present active, busy, complex life of intellectual triumph and material achievements — a life which cannot be readily turned into primitive simplicity or

[17]SB XI:18.44-47.

meditative quietude — there is dire necessity for some spiritualizing principles of karma which can serve as a pivot for this maddening course of activity. It is more possible for the modern man to practice renunciation *in* work rather than renunciation *of* work.

8. *Further application of Vedanta in practical life by Swami Vivekananda: (1) Arousing man's faith in himself, and (2) urging him to serve God through men.*

Besides taking an extensive view of Karma-yōga, Swami Vivekananda has emphasized a twofold application of Vedanta in practical life.

(1) Arousing man's faith in himself by making him aware of the true nature of the self, which is pure, free, immortal and luminous. According to him, the man who has no faith in himself cannot have faith in God. With what intense feeling he says:

> Aye, let every man and woman and child, without respect of caste or birth, weakness or strength, hear and learn, that behind the strong and the weak, behind the high and the low, behind everyone, there is that Infinite Soul, ensuring the infinite possibility and the infinite capacity of all to become great and good. Let us proclaim to every soul — "Arise, awake and stop not till the goal is reached." . . . Teach yourselves, teach everyone his real nature, call upon the sleeping soul and see how it awakes. Power will come, glory will come, goodness will come, purity will come, and everything that is excellent will come when this sleeping soul is roused to self-conscious activity.[18]

Further,

> Manifest the divinity within you, and everything will be harmoniously arranged around it.[19]

The knowledge of this divinity is the secret of man's development both in individual and collective life, secular as well as spiritual. It finds expression in two distinct ways: "I am divine" and "Thou art divine." As a man becomes aware of his own divinity, he becomes aware at the same time of the divinity of his fellow-beings. Along with the development of his faith in himself his regard for others develops. His potentialities grow as his self-faith is intensified. His capacity for serving his fellow-creatures necessarily increases.

(2) In addition to arousing man's faith in himself by making him

[18]CW III, p. 193.

[19]CW IV, p. 351.

aware of his divine nature, Swami Vivekananda has emphasized a second method of carrying Vedantic truth into practice. It is serving man in the spirit of serving God. Says he:

> Look upon every man, woman, and everyone as God. You cannot help anyone; you can only serve; serve the children of the Lord, serve the Lord Himself, if you have the privilege.[20]
>
> You may invent an image through which to worship God, but a better image already exists, the living man. You may build a temple in which to worship God, and that may be good, but a better one, a much higher one, already exists, the human body.[21]

9. *Swami Vivekananda's method is an extensive application of the ancient teachings.*

In Swami Vivekananda's view all domestic and social duties and humanitarian deeds as well can be performed in the spirit of worshipping God in man. His message is the logical conclusion of the teachings of the Upaniṣads and the *Bhagavad-gītā*. Truly speaking, it is not altogether a new message. But its practical application in every sphere of life has not been tried before. In the *Śrīmad-bhāgavatam* Śrī Kṛṣṇa urges Uddhava to see God in all beings and deal with them as such:

> With a pure mind one should observe in all beings as well as in oneself only Me, the Ātman, who am both inside and out, and all-pervading like space.
>
> This looking upon all beings as Myself in thought, word, and deed, is to My Mind, the best of all methods of worship.[22]

This mode of seeing and worshipping God in all beings is natural with the seers and the lovers of God who attain illumination. It is the spontaneous expression of their inner experience. Rare individuals highly advanced in spiritual life have also carried this ideal into actual practice. But its application in the lives of the spiritual aspirants in general has not been tried before. Such a course has been recommended by Sri Ramakrishna in the present age. He says:

> It is God Himself who plays about as human beings. If God can be worshipped through a clay image, then why not through a man?[23]

[20]CW III, p. 246. [21]CW II, p. 311. [22]SB XI:29.12,19. [23]GSR, p. 407.

Further, as recorded by Swami Saradananda:

> Some time in 1884 A.D. a friend of ours came to Dakshineswar and found the Master sitting in his room surrounded by the devotees. Sri Narendra also was present there . . . There arose the topic of the Vaishnava religion in the course of the conversation and, explaining briefly the essence of that doctrine to all, the Master said, "That doctrine teaches that one should always be careful to observe three things, namely, a taste for God's name, kindness to all beings and the worship of Vaishnavas. . . ." No sooner had he uttered the words, "kindness to all beings," than he suddenly went into samādhi. Regaining partial external consciousness in a short time, he continued, "Talk of compassion for beings? . . . No, no; not compassion to Jīvas but service to them as Śiva."
>
> All went on listening to those words of the Master in Bhāvasamādhi; but none could detect and understand their hidden import at that time. It was Narendranath alone who, coming out of the room at the end of the Master's samādhi, said, "Ah! what a wonderful light have I got today from the Master's words! In synthesizing the Vedantic knowledge, which was generally regarded as dry, austere and even cruel, with sweet devotion to the Lord, what a new mellowed means of experiencing the Truth has he revealed today!" . . .
>
> "If the divine Lord ever grants me an opportunity, I'll proclaim everywhere in the world this wonderful truth I have heard today. I will preach this truth to the learned and the ignorant, to the rich and the poor, to the Brāhmaṇas and the Caṇḍālas."[24]

It was the genius of Swami Vivekananda to find new light in this precept of the Master, and seek its practical application in the modern age for the amelioration of man's condition in every sphere of life.

10. *By looking upon all things and beings as manifestations of Divine Forms one can contemplate on God with the eyes open. Gradual stages of this practice.*

The seer who realizes his oneness with the Supreme Self in the state of samādhi does not lose sight of Him anymore. In the state of normal experience he sees everything in God and God in everything. All things and beings appear to him as varied manifestations of the One Supreme Being. This vision is natural to him.

However, a seeker of God, although he does not see Him, is asked to think of His presence everywhere, to look upon all things and

[24]Swami Saradananda, *Sri Ramakrishna, the Great Master,* pp. 821-22.

beings, vast and small, high and low, as the manifestation of the Divinity. But most spiritual aspirants find this difficult to practice in the beginning. So they are advised to proceed by stages. They are told at first to look upon the objects of special beauty, sublimity, goodness, and greatness as manifestations of God's glory. As they recognize God as the one source of all beauty, all power, all greatness, all goodness, gradually they become accustomed to thinking of every expression of beauty as His beauty, every expression of power as His power, every expression of greatness as His greatness, every expression of goodness as His goodness. Eventually they succeed in contemplating on God as the one origin of all things and beings, as the One Being underlying them all.

Such gradual stages of meditation on Divine manifestations in the world around us have been indicated by Śrī Kṛṣṇa in the tenth chapter of the *Bhagavad-gītā*. Just as a spiritual aspirant is expected to meditate on God in the depth of his heart with the eyes closed, so he is also expected to contemplate on Him in the world outside with the eyes open. Before delineating to Arjuna His various manifestations in the universe around us, Śrī Kṛṣṇa speaks of Himself as the One Self existing in the hearts of all:

> I am, O Guḍākeśa [an epithet of Arjuna, meaning conqueror of sleep], the Self dwelling in the hearts of all creatures. I am the beginning, the middle, and the end of all beings.[25]

Then He relates to Arjuna His special manifestation as the highest and best in every class of objects. To cite a few instances:

> Of the bodies of water, I am the Ocean. Of the mountains I am the Himālayas. Of the rivers I am the Ganges. Of the seasons I am the spring. I am the goodness of the good. I am the knowledge of the wise.[26]

And so on. In conclusion he says:

> And further, whatsoever is the seed of all beings that am I, O Arjuna. There is no being moving or unmoving that can exist without Me.
>
> There is no end of My divine manifestations, O Queller of Foes. This is but a brief statement of my endless glories.

[25] BG X:20.
[26] BG X:21-38.

> Whatsoever being there is possessed of greatness, beauty, splendour, know that to be a product of a fragment of my glory.
>
> Or, what avails thee to know all these details; I exist pervading this entire universe by a portion of Myself.[27]

The ideal is to see God in everything. The *Īśa Upaniṣad* opens with this instruction:

> All this — whatsoever moves [changes] in this moving [changing] universe should be covered by the Lord.

Each and every individual can proceed towards the Highest from where he is by following courses suited to his stage of inner development.

[27]BG X:39-42.

PART TWO

THE UNIVERSE: ITS ORIGIN AND NATURE

CHAPTER IV

THE EFFICIENT AND THE MATERIAL CAUSE OF THE WORLD-ORDER AND ITS EMPIRICAL REALITY

1. *The universe a standing mystery to the human mind. Man's inquiries about its origin.*

The world has puzzled the human mind from the day it had the power of inquiry. To ancient and modern man alike, the panorama of the universe, vast and varied, without beginning or end, marked as much by complexity and horridness as by order and beauty, has proved to be the greatest riddle awaiting solution. The boundless azure sky with clouds of many hues and forms, the countless luminaries shining overhead, the sun running its daily round, the earth with its variegated features, the astounding phenomena of nature, and above all the tragi-comedy of life — have stirred man's imagination and made him wonder as to the cause and the character of the sensible world. He inquires: "Where does it come from? How has it come? How does it exist? Where does it go?" Religion, philosophy, science, and mythology have come to his aid, and man's investigations into the problems have led to various conclusions.

Long, long ago similar inquiries were made by the students of Vedic India. One of the Upaniṣads opens with the report of such an inquiry:

> The seekers of Brahman inquired: What is the cause of the universe? Is it Brahman? Whence are we born? Why do we live? Where is our ultimate goal? At whose command, O the Knowers of Brahman, are we bound by the law of happiness and suffering? Time, the inherent nature of things, destiny, chance, the elements, primal energy, the ego

— none, nor any combination of these, can be considered the cause of the universe, for they depend on the existence of the knowing self.[1] The empirical self, too, cannot be the cause, for being subject to the law of happiness and suffering it is not free.

> Following the process of meditation, they perceived within themselves the self-luminous Supreme Being with His power hidden by the manifestations of Its own guṇas. It is He who presides over all the causes beginning with time and ending with the individual self.[2]

2. *The root of the universe is the Reality underlying it.*

What the Vedic thinkers recognized as the Ultimate Cause is neither the object nor the subject, but the Supreme Self (Ātman) underlying both. One infinite Being interweaves the two. In their view no unintelligent principle belonging to the object-world can be the ultimate cause, be it time, or nature, or necessity, or accident, or energy, or vital force, or blind will. Not being self-aware or self-operative, these cannot bring about the cosmic order singly or jointly. Moreover, they all presuppose a cognizing subject. The object implies the subject as its precondition. It has been observed by Śaṅkara, "To say that there is an object but that it is not known is absurd. It is like saying that something is seen but there is no eye."[3] The existence of the universe points to an all-knowing, all-controlling eternal Being to whom it is related as an object. Transcending the innumerable apprehending subjects and the phases of the universe apprehended by them, there is One Self-effulgent Reality, One Ātman, which holds, penetrates, observes, and regulates them all. This is the warp and woof of the whole fabric of relative existence. This is the origin, the abode, and the goal of everything. So the Upaniṣads declare:

> All this is Brahman. In That all this originates, rests, and merges.[4]
>
> All these are guided by Pure Consciousness and exist in Pure Consciousness.[5]
>
> It is from Bliss that all beings arise, by Bliss all that are born are sustained, and into Bliss they return and re-enter.[6]

[1]The knowing self is beyond the ego. In deep sleep when the ego ceases to function, the self, the basis of the ego, endures as the passive witness of unspecified ignorance. So after waking an individual can say: "I did not know anything, I had no knowledge even of myself. I did not know myself as a man or a woman or as anything else."

[2]Sv.U.I:3.

[3]Pr.U. VI:2, S. com.

[4]Ch.U. III:14.1.

[5]Ai.U. III:3.

[6]Tai.U. III:6.

3. *Brahman is the material as well as the efficient cause of the universe comprising the living and the nonliving.*

The implication is that Brahman is both the efficient and the material cause of the universe. He is not only the Creator but also the created. In the words of the Upaniṣad, "In the beginning this [the sensible world] was undiversified Brahman. That by Itself diversified Itself. Therefore That is called the Self-created."[7] The idea is clarified by these illustrations:

> As the spider brings forth and withdraws its thread,[8] as plants grow on the earth, as hair grows on a living person, so does everything in the universe arise from the Immutable Being.[9]
>
> As from a blazing fire thousands of sparks, identical with it in nature, come forth, so, my good friend, from the Immutable Being various creatures arise and unto That they return.[10]

In the Vedantic view there cannot be creation out of nothing, for existence cannot come out of nonexistence. The effect is the cause in another form — the one cannot be quite contrary to the other. Something cannot turn into nothing, nor can nothing turn into something. In fact, there is no creation in the absolute sense. Origination means only transformation of the potential into the actual. It is the transition from the unmanifest into the manifest state. The principle *nihil ex nihilo fit* (nothing comes into being out of what is nonexistent), which was recognized by such Greek philosophers as Anaximander, Parmenides, Aristotle,[11] and others, was maintained by the Vedic teachers as an axiomatic truth. Āruṇi says to his son Śvetaketu:

> In the beginning it was Existence only, the One without a second. Some say in the beginning there was nonexistence only and from nonexistence the universe arose. But how could that be? How could

[7]*Ibid.* II:7.

[8]That a spider can withdraw its web is a popular belief, but not a scientific truth. This does not, however, invalidate the illustration. Common knowledge and not scientific accuracy is involved here. We often use the illustration of the sun moving round the earth, although it is not an astronomical truth.

[9]Mu.U. I:1.7.

[10]*Ibid.* II:1.1.

[11]See Aristotle's *Physics* I, 4, 187a: "the dogma common to all the physicists that 'nothing can come out of what does not exist.' " Trans. by the Rev. P. Wicksteed and F.M. Cornford, Vol. I, 1929; Metaphysics, IV,5,1009a, trans. by H. Tredennick, Vol. I, 1958. The Loeb Classical Library, London, William Heinemann.

existence be born of nonexistence? No, my child, in the beginning there was Existence only, One without a second. . . . Of all these created things and beings, my child, Pure Existence is the origin, Pure Existence is the support, Pure Existence is the end. . . . In that subtle essence all this has its being.[12]

Being is all-in-all according to the Upaniṣads; there is no possibility of void or nonexistence.

Vedanta also rejects the view that God creates the universe out of preexisting material by His power eternally working on it: that He is only the efficient cause of the world as is the potter of the pot. There cannot be anything outside God, the Supreme Being, the One without a second. Pure Existence is the immutable essence of all finite objects. This is why none of them can ever be annihilated. Their forms change, but the essence remains the same throughout. Underlying the apparent forms there is one and the same Reality. God is in everything and everything is in Him. He is the one Self of all. Man should meditate on Him as his innermost Self. So it is said:

That which cannot be expressed by speech, but by which speech is expressed — That alone know as Brahman, and not that which people worship as apart from themselves. That which cannot be apprehended by the mind, but by which, they say, the mind is apprehended — That alone know as Brahman, and not that which people worship as apart from themselves.[13]

According to the Upaniṣads an extra-cosmic God is a naive conception of the Supreme Being. It does not satisfy man's inquiry about the efficient and the material cause of the universe. As long as there is opposition between matter and spirit, they must limit each other. Neither can be supreme. The questions — Where does the universe come from? How does it exist? remain unanswered. As observed by Swami Vivekananda:

"A ruler of the universe does not explain the universe and much less an external ruler, one outside of it; He may be a moral guide, the greatest power in the universe, but that is no explanation of the universe."[14] Further, ". . . the explanation of a thing must come from inside and not from outside."[15]

Nor does Vedanta uphold the idea that the universe emanates from God. In that case God cannot be immutable. Fixed in Brahman

[12]Ch.U. VI:2.1,2, et seq.
[13]Ken.U. I:5,6.
[14]CW I, p. 349.
[15]*Ibid.*, p. 369.

the universe is conceived of as a huge tree with the root above and the branches below: "This is that eternal Aśvattha Tree with its root above and branches below. That root, indeed, is the Shining One; That is Brahman, and That alone is called the Immortal. In That all worlds are contained and none can go beyond."[16] While giving a detailed account of the creative process Vedantic cosmology aims to bring out the great truth that Reality is One; that Brahman is the sole ground and explanation of the manifold; that It is both the efficient and the material cause of the universe.

4. *Brahman has not changed into the diversified world but appears as such through māyā.*

One may pertinently ask, "How can Brahman, the One without a second, change into the world? How can the Unmoving move, the Unchanging change, and the Perfect become imperfect?" The answer is that Brahman does not move but appears to move. It does not change but appears to change. It does not become manifold but appears as such. This appearance is māyā. So says Gauḍapāda:

> This unborn Brahman appears to undergo modification only through māyā and not otherwise. For, if this modification were real, the Immortal One would become mortal. . . . The immortal cannot become mortal, nor can the mortal become immortal. For it is never possible for a thing to change its nature.[17]

The manifold universe is real from the viewpoint of the finite self under the spell of māyā. What the unillumined experience as the ever changing world of plurality, the illumined realize as Nondual Brahman. Diseased eyes may see things as yellow even though there is no yellowness in the things seen. In the same way, the world-appearance is real from the human end, but altogether absent in Brahman. Just as the apparent movements and changes of the sun cannot be traced to the sun, on which they are only superimposed, so the multiplicity of names and forms cannot be traced to Brahman, being a mere superimposition. The point is, no causal relation exists between appearance and Reality. The Absolute is beyond all relations. "Between the real and the apparent there is no positive relation definable by words," remarks Śaṅkara.[18]

Brahman is the ground of multiplicity from the viewpoint of

[16]Ka.U. II:3.1. [17]MK III:19,21. [18]Ma.U. VII, S. com.

appearance, just as the sun is the locus of apparent movements and changes noticeable from the earth. So the question of the origin of the universe is tenable only from the empirical standpoint. From the standpoint of the absolute it has no meaning. The sun appears to rise and set and looks large or small, bright or dim, to those who inhabit the earth. These are facts from the earthly position, but from the position of the resplendent and stationary sun, pure myths.[19]

5. *What is māyā? Brahman associated with māyā is the cause of the manifold.*

The term māyā applies to world-appearance in all its stages of development. It includes all diversities. The entire relative existence is the domain of māyā. Broadly speaking, the world has two distinct stages, latent and manifest. The origin of the universe can be traced at best to Brahman associated with māyā in its potential state. Beyond māyā is the absolute Nondual Brahman without time, space, and causation. Māyā in its potential state is the beginning of the manifest universe, just as the seed is the beginning of the tree. It is the causal state in which all diversities remain latent. We cannot go beyond that. Absolute beginning of anything is illogical. Like the rotation of seed and sprout the universe revolves from the latent to the manifest state and from the manifest to the latent state. So māyā is beginningless (anādi).[20] But though without beginning, it is not without end (ananta). It ends with the realization of the absolute Brahman, just as the snake disappears when the rope mistaken for it is found. Māyā has no existence apart from Brahman, just as the illusory snake has no existence apart from the rope, its basis.

Brahman associated with māyā is the origin, the support, and the goal of the universe. This is called Saguṇa Brahman, who is immanent in the universe as the Supreme Self and acts as Īśvara, the Supreme Ruler, the dynamic God. He controls the universe from within. Māyā in its potential form contains the seed-force or potency (śakti) that leads to all its later developments. As such it is the creative power of Īśvara. It belongs to Him and is wholly dependent on Him. It is not a separate entity like prakṛti of Sāṁkhya philosophy. It forms an adjunct of Īśvara, the Great First Cause, and is the origin of the whole range of causes and effects. It is not inherent in His being as Brahman.

Īśvara with māyā as His power causes the projection, the

[19]See Tai.U. II:8, S. com.

[20]See BS II:1.36.

preservation, and the dissolution of the universe. In the development of the universe all transformations are in māyā, the source of all appearance; there is no change in Brahman, in Reality Itself. "He moves and He does not move."[21] "Undivided, He exists, as it were, divided in beings."[22] Any transition from the potential to the actual is a transformation (pariṇāma) of māyā and an apparent modification (vivarta) of Brahman.[23] But māyā in itself has no essence of being. So Brahman associated with māyā, the principle of appearance, is the material as well as the efficient cause of the universe. As the wielder of māyā, Saguṇa Brahman or Īśvara is the efficient cause of the universe and as the ground of māyā its material cause. "Know Nature (prakṛti) to be māyā and the Supreme Lord to be the holder of māyā," says the Upaniṣad.[24] "By Me presiding, māyā produces all things moving and unmoving," says Śrī Kṛṣṇa.[25] Being the Supreme Lord incarnate in human form, Śrī Kṛṣṇa refers to himself as such.

Saguṇa Brahman, because of His association with the phenomenal world, is conditioned, so to speak. He is Self-aware. He knows Himself as the Master of māyā. He is not Pure Consciousness, the same at every point of existence, like Nirguṇa (attributeless) Brahman. There is no distinction of substance and attribute in Nirguṇa Brahman, but Saguṇa Brahman is possessed of attributes (guṇas). As Īśvara He is the Personal God. The term *Personal* is used to indicate that He has attributes. It does not mean that He has a form like a human being. He possesses all excellences in the highest degree. He is the repository of all greatness and goodness. He is All-knowing, All-powerful, All-embracing.

Nirguṇa Brahman is designated as the Higher (Para) Brahman and Saguṇa Brahman as the lower (Apara) Brahman. However Saguṇa Brahman, apart from māyā, His limiting adjunct, is no other than Nirguṇa Brahman. As pointed out by Swami Vivekananda, "The very idea of causation exists only in the phenomenal world, and God as the cause of this universe must naturally be thought of as limited, and yet He is the same Impersonal God."[26] So Īśvara is described in the Upaniṣad both as personal and impersonal.

> Just as the sun shines lighting up all space above, below, and across, even so does that one adorable Being, the repository of all blessed qualities, preside over everything that can be characterized as a cause.

[21]Is.U. 5.
[22]BG XIII:16.
[23]See SLS I; VP VI.
[24]Sv.U. IV:10.
[25]BG IX:10.
[26]CW II, p. 336.

> He is the one Source of the world. He causes Nature to evolve. He transforms all created things. He engages all the guṇas in their functions. Thus He controls the whole universe.
>
> One effulgent Being is hidden in all that has come into being. He is all-pervading and is the inmost Self of all creatures. He presides over the law of Karma. All beings reside in Him. He is the Witness and He is Pure Consciousness free from the guṇas and transcendent.
>
> He is the one destroyer of ignorance in the phenomenal world. He alone is the fire stationed in water. Realizing Him alone one overcomes death. There is no other way of Liberation.[27]

The three guṇas — sattva, rajas, and tamas — are the primal constituents of māyā.[28] They balance one another in its potential state. This is a state of equilibrium. Māyā becomes operative with the disturbance of this equilibrium, which releases the latent force that is behind all its manifestations. This seed-force or potency (śakti) is the subtlest aspect of māyā. The term māyā is often restricted to this aspect. Viewed as the source of the phenomenal world it is called prakṛti (the primary cause). It is hidden by the manifestations of its own guṇas, for it is the causal phase of the universe of mind and matter and not easy to comprehend. We have seen how some students of Vedic India in their search for the cause of the universe followed the method of meditation and found within themselves the self-luminous Supreme Being with His power "hidden by the manifestations of its own guṇas." (See sec. 1.) Etymologically, the term *prakṛti* means perpetual action, that is, the principle of becoming, distinct from the Immutable Being. Māyā, the principle of appearance, is prakṛti, the principle of becoming. It is the world of names and forms that undergoes change, whereas the bedrock of Reality is ever the same. We shall dwell on "Īśvara and His Māyā" at length in the next chapter.

6. *The role of reason in determining the cause of the universe.*

It is evident that the Vedic thinkers found speculative reason inadequate for determining the exact nature of the origin of the universe; so they resorted to intuitive perception through the practice of meditation. The knowledge gained by reason is indefinite and indecisive. Being mediate, it lacks the assurance that immediate perception conveys. Inferential knowledge cannot, therefore, remove

[27]Sv.U. V:4,5; VI:11,15.
[28]See footnote 13 on the three guṇas, p. 42.

the seeker's doubts and misconceptions as to the object of knowledge. This is true of all sensible things that we may know by inference. In the case of suprasensuous reality there is still more difficulty. In order to infer the presence of one thing from the perception of another we must be sure from direct experience of their invariable concomitance, or causal relation.

We can infer the presence of fire within a house on seeing smoke coming out of its chimney, because we have found by direct experience the causal relation between the two, e.g., it is fire that causes smoke. In the case of God and the world we have had no chance of observing any causal relation subsisting between the two, because while the world is an object of sense-perception, God is not. Therefore, from the perception of the world we cannot logically deduce the existence of God as its Creator. We can only say that the world, being of the nature of effect or a series of causes and effects, must have some ultimate cause. We can also form an idea of the cause by supposition. But we cannot come to a definite conclusion about the nature of the final cause by the reasoning process.

Argument, howsoever cogent, can at most make the existence of God possible but not actual. Only suprasensuous experience or intuitive perception can make God real to us. According to Kapila, the founder of the Sāṁkhya system of philosophy, there is no logical proof to establish the reality of God.[29] It has also been pointed out by Kant that all the three kinds of arguments, cosmological, teleological, and ontological, are insufficient to prove the existence of God.[30]

Śaṅkara holds that though reason cannot establish the existence of God, yet it is an invaluable aid in gaining the direct knowledge of Him.[31] After knowing about God from authentic sources, such as the revealed texts and illumined teachers, the aspirant can have

[29]See SD I:92.

[30]Immanuel Kant, *Critique of Pure Reason,* trans. by J.M.D. Meiklejohn, New York, Willy, 1781; revised 1787, p. 331. "There are only three modes of proving the existence of a Deity, on the grounds of speculative reason.

"All the paths conducting to this end, begin either from determinate experience and the peculiar constitution of the world of sense, and rise, according to the laws of causality, from it to the highest cause existing apart from the world — or from a purely indeterminate experience, that is, some empirical existence — or abstraction is made of all experience, and the existence of a supreme cause is concluded from *a priori* conceptions alone. The first is the *physico-theological* argument, the second the *cosmological,* the third the *ontological.* More there are not, and more there cannot be.

"I shall show it is as unsuccessful on the one path — the empirical, as on the other — the transcendental, and that it stretches its wings in vain, to soar beyond the world of sense by the mere might of speculative thought."

[31]See BS I:1.2, S. com.

intellectual conviction of the truth of God through reasoning. Then it becomes possible for him to attain immediate knowledge of God by the practice of meditation on His true nature. So it is said: "One should hear [about the Self] from the words of the *Śrutis*. Then one should reflect on It through reasoning. After reflection one should constantly meditate on It. These are the means of the realization [of the Self]."[32] The *Śrutis* are the only reliable source of the knowledge of God; we have to accept their testimony. Though God is beyond the reach of reason, His existence is not irrational, but admits of rational exposition. In fact, we cannot explain the universe without acknowledging the reality of God. The existence of God is a necessary postulate, not a logical conclusion.

7. *The empirical reality of the world-appearance. The distinction between good and evil is valid in the relative order.*

It is true that, according to Vedanta, Brahman alone is real and the world is unreal. But the unreality of the world does not mean, as is often inferred, that the world is a mere shadow without substance, a pure illusion, or a void. The point is that the world as it appears to us is unreal, because this appearance has no absolute existence. In its essential nature as Brahman the world is ever real, because it is Brahman that is mistaken for the world. Śaṅkara observes:

> As Brahman, the Cause, does not lack existence at any of the three periods of time, so does the world, the effect. Since there is only one Existence pure and simple, the effect is non-different from the cause.[33]
>
> All effects with different names and forms are real only as Pure Existence but unreal in themselves.[34]

Just as a clay pot has no existence apart from clay so the manifold has no existence apart from Brahman, its ground. In itself it is a conglomeration of names and forms. It should not be regarded as a subsistent entity. As identical in essence with Brahman it is real.

While Vedanta denies the absolute reality of the world of experience, it recognizes its empirical reality. It acknowledges from the viewpoint of appearance all diversities and distinctions that prevail in the phenomenal world. It maintains a distinction between

[32]*Smṛti* text quoted by Rāmatīrtha in his commentary on *Vedānta-Sāra,* sec. 4. See also Br.U. II:4.5.

[33]BS II:1.16, S. com.

[34]Ch.U. VI:2.1.

existence (sattvam) and reality (satyam). Something can exist without being real. Anything that is contradicted is not real in the true sense. The dream world is contradicted by the matter-of-fact world of experience, which again is falsified by the full awareness of Nondual Brahman. From the viewpoint of the world of appearance there are three orders of existence according to Vedanta: (1) absolute existence (pāramārthika sattvam), (2) empirical existence (vyavahārika sattvam), and (3) illusory existence (prātibhāsika sattvam).[35]

Neither the empirical nor the illusory is nonexistent as is a barren woman's son, which is entirely false (tuccha, alīka), imperceptible even in illusion. Then again the empirical is not unreal in the same way as the illusory. As stated by Śaṅkara, "Relative to the illusory objects, such as a mirage, actual water and the like are real."[36] While the illusory appears and disappears, the empirical existence of cause and effect persists until the direct knowledge of Brahman is attained, which is a rare prospect for bound jīvas.

As long as a person cannot realize Brahman all differences of kind, quality, and quantity in the relative plane are facts for him. He cannot ignore the distinction between virtue and vice, happiness and misery, knowledge and ignorance, the saint and the sinner, the living and the nonliving, the action and the result, the fine and the gross, the great and the small, the high and the low. It is through the observance of these distinctions that he can go beyond them and reach the Nondual Brahman. Dream objects are quite real to the dreamer until he wakes up. Day and night exist for him who sees the sun rise and set, even though they are nonexistent from the viewpoint of the sun.[37] True, all are in essence Brahman, yet there is difference in their manifestations in the relative plane. A sentient being is a higher manifestation of Brahman than an inanimate thing. Good is a higher manifestation of Brahman than evil. So one must rise from the lower to the higher and higher in order to attain Brahman, which transcends all relativity.

Both good and evil are positive existences according to Vedanta. It is not true that one is the negation of the other, as some philosophers, Eastern and Western, have maintained. Had pleasure been just the absence of pain, as the Sāṁkhya system holds, then a passive state of mind, such as composure, could not be experienced. Hatred is not mere lack of love. Cruelty is not mere absence of kindness. Between the two there is the attitude of dispassion. One can be neutral or indifferent. Virtue is contrary to vice. It is more than

[35]VP II. [36]Tai.U. II:6, S. com. [37]MK III:36, Ānandagiri.

innocence. Similarly, disease is not just the negation of health; grief is not just the negation of happiness; wickedness is not just the negation of goodness; poverty is not just the negation of prosperity. Vedanta is neither optimistic nor pessimistic in the ordinary sense. It sees life as a whole, in all its aspects, and also what is beyond. Brahman, which is all-Bliss (ānanda-rūpam), underlies and transcends the duality of good and evil. Being the higher manifestation of Brahman, good is nearer the Truth than evil. So one has to reach the Goal through good and not through evil. A supreme note of optimism pervades the Vedantic view and way of life in an extraordinary sense.

Therefore the truth is that the phenomenal world is existent from the relative standpoint, but nonexistent from the viewpoint of the absolute. On this twofold world-view Śaṅkara observes:

> This phenomenal world, caused by diversification and unreal, is a fact for those who hold that things are different from Brahman and also for those who do not. The adherents of the supreme truth, however, while investigating, in accord with the Śruti, the true nature of things, whether they really exist or not, arrive at the conclusion that Brahman alone is, the One without a second, beyond all relativity. So there is no contradiction between the two views. We do not maintain the existence of anything but Brahman in the state in which the supreme truth is attained, as the Śrutis say, "One only without a second" and "Without interior or exterior." Nor do we deny in the relative plane of name and form the validity for the ignorant of the empirical facts comprising action, its agent, its instrument, its result, and so forth. Therefore, the scriptural and the empirical outlooks rest on knowledge and ignorance. So there is no fear of contradiction between them. No school can deny that the existence and the nonexistence of the phenomenal world depend on the relative and the absolute standpoint.[38]

8. *Vedanta views the perceiver, the object perceived and perception as the triple manifestation of one fundamental Reality. It repudiates both realism and idealism.*

Moreover, Vedanta holds that the difference between the subjective and the objective is quite valid in the relative plane. One cannot be reduced to the other. Vedanta recognizes (1) the coexistence of the knowing selves, (2) the internal ideas, and (3) the external objects. These three orders of existence are distinct from one another as facts of experience and are interrelated. They form a triple

[38]Br.U. III:5.1, S. com.

existence. To deny any one of the three, or to identify one with another, is not right. None of them, as such, is ultimately real. From the absolute standpoint all the three are nonexistent, nondual Brahman or Pure Consciousness being the sole reality.

Vedanta may be characterized as metaphysical or absolute idealism, inasmuch as it maintains the ultimate reality of one undifferentiated Supreme Consciousness and views everything as identical with It in essence. But the point is that its world-view differs fundamentally from subjective idealism on the one hand and objective realism on the other. It has been aptly remarked by Prof. Radhakrishnan, "The essential correlativity of subject and object, which is the central truth of all idealism, is accepted by Śaṅkara, who sets aside both mentalism and realism as inadequate to the facts of experience."[39] The mental idea and the physical object both are appearances with reference to the fundamental Reality. But so far as the phenomenal existence is concerned, they endure as distinct entities.

The external world can be said to be unreal in two different senses: either it is altogether nonexistent, or it is a mere form of inner consciousness appearing as something outside as in dream. Subjective idealism (Vijñānavāda) maintains the second position. But Vedanta holds neither of these two views. Had the external things been nonexistent like the horns of a hare, they could not be perceived by the senses. Since they are objects of perception, their existence cannot be denied. Nor can they be reduced to mere forms of internal cognition, as subjectivism assumes. In the perception of an object we are conscious not only of the act of cognition but also of the object as distinct from and external to it. No one perceives the object as identical with cognition itself. The object and its cognition are two distinct facts of experience. The one is external and the other internal. Since the object is perceived as external to and distinct from the act of cognition its separate existence should be acknowledged. Thus argues Śaṅkara[40] while refuting the subjective idealism of the Yōgācāra School.[41]

[39]S. Radhakrishnan, *Indian Philosophy,* 2nd edn., London, George Allen & Unwin Ltd., 1931, II:498.

[40]BS II:2.28, S. com.

[41]The Yōgācāra is one of the four principal speculative systems of Buddhism. Two of them, the Vaibhāṣika and the Sautrāntika schools, are realists. While the former upholds direct realism, the latter supports indirect realism. They belong to the Hīnayāna branch of Buddhism. The two other schools, the Yōgācāras and the Mādhyamikas, belong to the Mahāyāna branch. The Yōgācāras are idealists. The Mādhyamikas are known as nihilists — they deny the reality of all but the absolute.

The Yōgācāra contends that he does not deny the perception of an object, but he denies that in perceiving an object one perceives anything but a mode of inner consciousness, for it is the very cognition that one wrongly perceives as something external, and so the object is identical with cognition. Śaṅkara replies: "Nobody perceives cognition itself as a pillar, as a wall, and so forth, but everybody perceives them as objects of cognition."

Like the Yōgācāra, George Berkeley admits the perceptibility of things and identifies them with perceptions; they exist only in being perceived. Says he:

> That the things I see with my eyes and touch with my hands do exist, really exist, I make not the least question. The only thing whose existence we deny is that which *philosophers* call Matter or corporeal substance.
>
> . . . we eat and drink and are clad with the immediate objects of sense, which cannot exist unperceived or without the mind . . .
>
> Ideas imprinted on the senses are real things, or do really exist, this we do not deny, but we deny they can subsist without the minds which perceive them, or that they are resemblances of any archetypes existing without the mind, since the very being of a sensation or idea consists in being perceived, and an idea can be like nothing but an idea.[42]

Jadunath Sinha rightly observes: "Berkeley argues that the existence of a sensible object consists in being perceived — esse est percipi — and therefore it is an idea of the mind. Śaṅkara, on the other hand, argues that an object is perceived because it actually *exists* external to the mind; an object is distinctly perceived as existing independent of the act of perception. No one can argue a fact of experience out of existence."[43]

9. *Further refutation of the Buddhist Idealists' views.*

Vedanta also distinguishes between the states of waking and dream and repudiates the Buddhist Idealists' view that waking and dream cognitions are similar in nature. The Yōgācāra holds that the distinction of subject and object is within consciousness itself in waking experience as in dream; it is inner consciousness that appears in a dream as apprehending cognition and also as objects

[42]George Berkeley, *The Principles of Human Knowledge,* Chicago, Open Court, 1920, sec. 35,38,90.

[43]Jadunath Sinha, *Indian Realism,* London, Kegan Paul Trench, 1938, p. 231.

apprehended, while there are no external things corresponding to them; similarly, all that we perceive as external objects in the waking state are only modes of consciousness. Śaṅkara points out that the analogy is wrong, because waking and dream cognitions are not of the same nature; there is a vital difference between them. The dream experiences are falsified by the waking experiences, but the latter are not falsified by either dream or hallucination. In fact, our experience of the world in waking life endures and is not contradicted by any other empirical experience. It is sublated, that is, contradicted only by the knowledge of Brahman. Besides, the dream state is of the nature of recollection, which is due to the impressions acquired by previous experience of objects. But the waking state is of the nature of perception. It is the direct experience of the objects present. Therefore, the waking experience cannot be likened to the dream experience.[44] However, dream imagery, too, has a reality of its own. No experience, be it imagination, illusion, or hallucination, is unreal according to Vedanta, Prior to awakening to the Reality of Self each is real in its own sphere.[45] None can be regarded as false as a rabbit-horn or a barren woman's son.

Then again, Śaṅkara urges, how can the Idealists account for the variety of cognitions in the absence of external objects? The Yōgācāra argues that the variety of cognitions, such as pot, cloth, etc., depends not on the variety of external objects but on the variety of subconscious impressions. Diverse perceptions arise from previous impressions, as in dream, and leave new impressions on the mind. Thus, the Yōgācāra postulates an infinite series of mental impressions and perceptions related to each other as causes and effects. Śaṅkara points out that there can be no internal impressions, because, according to the Yōgācāra, there is no experience of external objects.[46] Mental impressions originate from perception, and not perception from mental impressions. So the assumption of a beginningless series of mental impressions as causes and effects is groundless. It cannot account for the variety of perceptions. If perceptions arise from internal impressions they cannot be of a different nature. Novel experiences are not possible in that case.

Further, Śaṅkara points out, mental impressions cannot subsist if the perceiving self be momentary.[47] No recollection or recognition of past experience is possible unless the experiencer endures. In the Yōgācāra's view everything is momentary; it admits no abiding self,

[44]See BS II:2.29, S. com.
[45]Ch.U. VIII:5.4, S. com.
[46]BS II:2.30, S. com.
[47]BS II:2.31, S. com.

but only a series of momentary subject-cognitions or forms of ego-consciousness (ālaya-vijñāna) in addition to a series of object-cognitions. If the Yōgācāra school concedes the ego-consciousness (ālaya-vijñāna) permanence, then it contradicts its doctrine of momentariness.

10. *The distinction between the external objects and the internal ideas is to be recognized until Brahman is realized.*

Thus Vedanta rejects the idealist's view of the world. While it denies the absolute reality of the world order, it acknowledges its empirical reality. As long as Brahman is not realized and as long as the perception of the manifold endures both the external and the internal worlds are to be accepted as relatively existent. The Realists accept the external world as real independently of the perceiver's mind. The Idealists deny the reality of the external world independently of the mind. In their view external objects are but mental ideas. Vedanta denies absolute reality to both — external objects and mental ideas — but accepts both as facts in the relative existence; they are not incompatible. Says Swami Vivekananda:

> Without the "I" there can be no "you" outside. From this some philosophers came to the conclusion that the external world did not exist save in the subject; that the "you" existed only in the "I." Others have argued that the "I" can only be known through the "you" and with equal logic. These two views are partial truths, each wrong in part and each right in part. Thought is as much material and as much in nature as body is. Both matter and mind exist in a third, a unity which divides itself into the two. This unity is the Ātman, the real Self.[48]

So we see that Vedanta in no way ignores but accepts the world before denying it. A twofold purpose is served by this acceptance. Firstly, to disprove the world one has to acknowledge it. Secondly, without accepting the various conditions of life as facts one cannot get beyond them. The truth behind appearance has to be attained methodically by each individual through such progressive measures as are suited to his psychophysical status.

[48]CW VII, p. 99.

CHAPTER V

ĪŚVARA AND HIS MĀYĀ

1. *The jīva, jagat, and Īśvara constitute the triple relative order.*

The individual experiencer (jīva)[1], the world of experience (jagat), and their Supreme Ruler (Īśvara) are the three main categories of the relative existence. These are acknowledged by most religious and philosophical systems. The central fact, however, is the individual, the embodied soul. It is from his position that all inquiries begin. He is the investigator. He judges reality and unreality. He cannot deny his own existence, which is self-evident. Every other existence has, as a matter of course, a reference, direct or indirect, to the individual. In the Vedantic view of the relative order the individual is in no case out of the picture. It is his experience of the universe that ascertains its reality. The existence of the individual (jīva) and the universe (jagat) presupposes the existence of the Supreme Lord (Īśvara), because neither of them is self-existent or self-sustaining. Their origination and sustenance must be due to an omnipotent, omniscient, and omnipresent Being. Indeed, the existence of Īśvara is the necessary condition for the existence of the jīva and jagat. There cannot be the jīva and jagat without Īśvara.

Again, it is man's ignorance regarding the true nature of himself and the universe that sets him in quest of the Ultimate Reality, and it is his Self-realization as the undivided, limitless consciousness beyond all diversity and relativity, including the duality of the subject and the object, which proves the illusoriness of all that are finite and the absolute reality of Brahman, the One only without a second. Nothing can convey to him the truth about Brahman more directly than Its reference to his own self in such terse expressions as "This

[1]The word *jīva* literally means a living being. Every living creature, be it a plant, a worm, an insect, a bird, a beast, a man, or a deity, is, according to the Hindu view, an embodied soul. The jīvas have varying degrees of consciousness. Even the plants are sentient. Of all the jīvas man alone is capable of Self-knowledge. The jīva, jagat, and Īśvara are also termed respectively *bhōktā* (experiencer), *bhōgya* (the experienced), and *preritā* (the Mover, the Internal Ruler), who interrelates the two (see Sv.U. I:12).

Ātman is Brahman";[2] "Thou art That";[3] "I am Brahman";[4] "Consciousness is Brahman."[5] Essentially, man is Brahman, but as an individual being he is bound to be in the triple existence of the jīva, jagat, and Īśvara. With the jīva there must be jagat and Īśvara. It is to be noted that while monistic (nondualistic) Vedanta maintains the identity of the individual self with the Supreme Being, monotheistic Vedanta maintains the relationship between the two. While the monist says, "I am He," the monotheist says, "I am His."

One may assume that in Nondualistic Vedanta Īśvara is a projection of the jīva's ajñāna (antiknowledge). Such a view, though upheld by some of its later interpreters, is not its true intent. On the contrary, the trend of the Vedantic texts, if we can see aright, is to maintain that the jīva's ajñāna (antiknowledge),[6] the limiting adjunct of the finite self, is a product of the cosmic māyā of Īśvara. As long as the jīva is subject to ajñāna he sees Reality as it appears to him through māyā. Meditation on Īśvara can make him free from ajñāna and remove the veil of māyā completely.[7] The vast difference between the jīva and Īśvara is recognized throughout the Vedantic texts.[8] At the same time their essential identity with Nondual Brahman is maintained. The cardinal Upaniṣadic dictum (mahāvākyam), "Thou art That," which is the keynote of Vedanta, is based on this distinction. Īśvara is all-free, all-powerful, all-knowing, while the jīva's freedom, power, and knowledge are ever limited. The released soul that attains Brahmalōka[9] gains all lordly powers except the powers of creation, etc., which belong to Īśvara alone.[10] While Īśvara is one, the jīvas are many. Īśvara is the controller of the jīvas and the dispenser of the fruits of their actions.[11] He manifests the jīvas and jagat, and is ever associated with them as their eternal ruler.[12] The three are coexistent, but not of the same grade.

[2]Ma.U. II; Br.U. II:5.19; IV:4.5.
[3]Ch.U. VI:14.3.
[4]Br.U. I:4.10.
[5]Ai.U. III:1.3.
[6]See sec. 8 and 9 of this chapter and Chap. VIII, sec. 3; also footnote 13 in sec.4.
[7]Sv.U. I:11.
[8]See BS II:1.22, "But on account of the statement [in the Śrutis] of difference [between the individual soul and Brahman as Creator] [He is] something more [than the individual soul]."
[9]The region or the abode of Brahmā, Īśvara the Creator. The devout who reach its uppermost sphere are not reborn. It is parallel to heaven or the kingdom of God where the redeemed souls go.
[10]*Ibid.* IV:4.17.
[11]VV 36.
[12]Cf. Sv.U. VI:17, "Who rules over this universe eternally."

2. *No beginning of the three.*

In fact, the jīva, jagat, and Īśvara are interrelated. We cannot account for any of the three without reference to two others. All the attributes of Īśvara imply His relation to the jīva and jagat. Any expression with regard to Him, such as "God the Father," "the Almighty Creator," "the Adorable Lord," "the Supreme Ruler," "the Benign Providence," "the Omnipresent Being," "the Divine Master," has a reference to either of them.

Like Īśvara the jīva as well as jagat have no beginning in time. All of the three are said to be unborn (aja).[13] As pointed out by Śaṅkara, their beginning is untenable.[14] The universe with the living and the nonliving must have existed in the causal state before its manifestation; because nothing cannot turn into something, just as something cannot turn into nothing. Moreover, had the living beings arisen accidentally without their previous existence in potential forms, then their weal and woe would have been unmerited and the difference in their sufferings and enjoyments unaccounted for. Nor would it have been proper to hold God responsible for such a situation. How could He be regarded all-wise and impartial since He allowed some to suffer and others to enjoy without cause? The same problems would have to be faced, even if the living creatures originated from undiversified, homogeneous Nature. Therefore, prior to their manifestation the living and the nonliving constituting the universe must have existed in the causal state in primordial Nature. The world ever *is*, whether manifest or unmanifest, and its sole ruler is Īśvara. "There is no one else able to rule it."[15]

The Sanskrit word corresponding to *creation* is *sṛṣṭi*, which literally means "throwing," that is to say, "projection from the latent to the manifest form." In the Vedantic view the creation of the jīva and jagat does not imply their absolute beginning but their development from the potential to the manifest state. Just as every individual thing in this world has three distinct states of existence — origination, continuation, and destruction (which is but reversion to the cause) — so has the universe as a whole. The projection, the preservation, and the dissolution of the universe comprising the living and the nonliving form a complete cycle (kalpa) rotating continuously under the rulership of Īśvara. It is an eternal process. Rare individuals who attain Liberation by realizing Supreme

[13] Sv.U. I:9.
[14] BS II:1.36, S. com.
[15] Sv.U. VI:17.

Brahman go beyond it; while countless others continue to be in the cosmic order controlled by Īśvara.

The beginning of the universe actually means the beginning of a cycle. The dissolution of the universe with the animate and the inanimate does not mean its annihilation but its reabsorption in the causal state, from which it emerges again in the beginning of a new cycle. It is said in the *Ṛg-Veda,* "The Lord planned the sun and the moon as before."[16] As Creator, Protector, and Destroyer of the universe, Īśvara is designated respectively as Brahmā, Viṣṇu, and Śiva. The one and the same Lord has three different aspects or forms (trimūrti).

3. *How are the jīva and jagat related to Īśvara?*

How does Īśvara hold and control the jīva and jagat? The relation between God and the world has been a baffling problem in rational theology. We cannot explain the world without God nor can we easily harmonize the two. The crucial point is: How can this indubitable, imperfect world be reconciled with the existence of the Perfect Being? To conceive the jīva and jagat as different from or outside Īśvara implies a limitation of His infinitude. In the Vedantic view they have no existence apart from, or independent of, Īśvara. He is the Reality that supports and controls both. They depend on Him, and not He on them. He alone is eternal, while all else is non-eternal. He is the sole independent entity. He is the central principle that pervades everything, and is external to none. In the *Bhagavad-gītā* the Lord calls the jīva and jagat His higher and lower natures.[17] They are the manifestations of His being. There is no "other" in His Consciousness. He is not an individual. He is the cosmic whole including the jīva and jagat. The three form a unity in difference.

Truly speaking, Īśvara is the Supreme Self (Paramātmā) that manifests and sustains all finite existences, conscious and unconscious, the animate and the inanimate. As stated by Śaṅkara, "To the contemplative nothing other than the Supreme Lord exists. He is manifest in the eightfold form of the unmoving and the moving, such as earth, water, fire, air, ether, the sun, the moon, and the individual soul."[18]

[16] Rg.V. X:190.3.

[17] BG VII:4,5.

[18] *Dakṣiṇāmūrti Stōtram* (Hymn to the Benign Lord in the form of the guru), The Works of Śaṅkara, Vol. XI, Vanvilas Press, Srirangam.

According to all schools of Vedanta, monotheistic[19] as well as monistic (strictly speaking Nondualistic, Advaita), Īśvara is the sole self-existent Reality inclusive of the jīva and jagat. The unity of existence is the keynote of Vedanta. Absolute pluralism or dualism has no place in it. Says Śrī Kṛṣṇa, "Beyond Me there is naught else. All this is strung on Me as a row of gems on a thread."[20] Īśvara in Vedanta is called "the Internal Controller (antaryāmī)," who directs and guides the cosmic process from within. "He who inhabits all beings and is within all beings, whom none of the beings knows, whose body is all beings, and who controls all beings from within, is the Internal Ruler, He is your immortal Self."[21]

It is He who shines as the conscious self in every living creature. The one undivided luminous Self appears as myriad souls. "All faces are His faces; all heads His heads; all necks His necks; He dwells in the hearts of all beings. He is the Divine Lord pervading everything. Therefore, He is all-embracing and benign. The Self, indeed, is the mighty Lord who directs the intellect to the attainment of complete clarity of vision. He is the imperishable Light that controls everything."[22]

One may pertinently ask, how does the Imperishable include the perishable, the All-pure the impure, the All-good the evil? How can the Self-intelligent consist of the unintelligent? The explanation that the individual souls and Nature (prakṛti) form the outer aspect of Īśvara, as given by some monotheistic philosophers, does not prove to be a convincing answer. According to Rāmānuja, the jīva and prakṛti are accessory to Īśvara, being related to Him as attributes to substance or as body to the soul. Even so, it is difficult to conceive of Īśvara as an immutable, all-free, or perfect Being. As long as the jīva and prakṛti are inseparably associated with the being of Īśvara and form an integral part of Him, His nature cannot be altogether free from their imperfections and impurities.

4. *The solution of the problem is the nondualistic conception of māyā.*

Let us see how nondualistic Vedanta solves the problem. Both nondualistic and monotheistic schools of Vedanta hold that the

[19]The five monotheistic schools of Vedanta are: (1) Viśiṣṭādvaita of Rāmānuja, (2) Dvaitādvaita of Nimbārka, (3) Śuddhādvaita of Vallabha, (4) Dvaita of Madhva, (5) Acintya-bhedābheda of Baladeva.

[20]BG VII:7. [21]Br.U. III:7.15. [22]Sv.U. III:11,12.

universe is the manifestation of Īśvara's power (śakti), called māyā. There are, however, marked differences in their conceptions of māyā despite several points of agreement. All agree that māyā is the causal potency of primordial Nature or prakṛti, the origin of the universe, which is not a separate entity as the Sāṁkhya system maintains, but is subordinate to Īśvara and belongs to Him as His power (śakti). So the Upaniṣad says, "Know that prakṛti is māyā and that the Supreme Lord is the wielder of māyā. The whole universe is filled with what are but the parts of His being."[23] "Prakṛti is Īśvara's power of māyā," says Śaṅkara.[24] It is through His power of māyā that Īśvara is the all-knowing and all-powerful Creator, Preserver, and Destroyer of the cosmic manifold.

According to most monotheistic schools, the creative energy of God is inherent in Him. In the view of Śākta Tantra, which is closest to nondualism, the power of God is not different from the being of God, the power-holder. Śakti in her potential state is identical with Śiva. Now, if māyā, the creative energy, inheres in God, if it be inseparably connected with His being, then any change in it means change in God Himself and the seed of imperfection must be within Him. So the problem remains unsolved.

According to the Nondualistic school, the creative energy or prakṛti recognized as Īśvara's power of māyā is not an ultimate principle inherent in Him. It does not pertain to His essential nature as Nirguṇa Brahman. It adheres to Him as an adjunct (upādhi), so to speak, but in no way affects Him. Māyā is true so far as the world-appearance is concerned. It serves as the power of Īśvara in the realm of appearance, beyond which it has no existence. Māyā is something positive, but unique. It is not nonbeing, because it is instrumental to the appearance of multiplicity on the unity of Reality. Nor is it being, since it has no existence apart from Nondual Brahman. Īśvara, who knows māyā as such, holds and controls it. As the master of māyā He is the Projector, Preserver, and Destroyer of the manifold universe, of which He is the sole support. Nirguṇa is Saguṇa without undergoing any change. Being under the spell of māyā the jīvas regard the phenomenal world of plurality as real in itself and become bound to the wheel of mortal life. Māyā and its manifestations have no influence over Īśvara. To Him the unity of Reality is fully manifest despite the apparent multiplicity. Māyā is related to Him in the same way as an illusory object is related to its ground. Conjoined with

[23]*Ibid.* IV:10.
[24]BS II:1.14, S. com.

māyā by apparent superimposition Brahman is Īśvara. The term *māyā* is applicable to Īśvara's creation as well as to His creative power. It signifies both the causal and the manifest state of the universe.

Brahman as controlling māyā is Īśvara. Brahman as controlled by māyā is jīva. From the position of the jīva, this mysterious principle, māyā, is designated as ajñāna or avidyā, which is usually translated as ignorance or nescience. But ajñāna or avidyā does not mean the absence or the negation, but the reverse, of knowledge. It is antiknowledge, which terminates with the knowledge of Reality.[25] It has two distinct functions — it veils the Supreme Being and it projects the manifold. It is because of this that the jīva fails to perceive Nondual Brahman as his self and experiences multiple things and beings as real in themselves. Thus avidyā is the cause of both inapprehension and misapprehension. There *can* be inapprehension of the Real without its misapprehension, as in deep sleep, but there *cannot* be misapprehension without inapprehension. Any perception of duality is due to avidyā. Any relative knowledge as well as ignorance is in its domain.

5. *The appearance of the world of phenomena is due to māyā or ajñāna (antiknowledge) that disguises Reality.*

There are reasons for recognizing primal energy of the nature of ajñāna or avidyā as the creative power of Īśvara. In the first place, without power the creativity of the Immutable and Immovable Brahman is not possible. Then again, prakṛti, the primordial Nature, must not be apart from, or independent of, Nondual Being. There can be only one Absolute Being. This phenomenal world of change and interdependence cannot be a self-sustaining entity. Yet it appears to be self-existent and covers That on which its existence depends. Indeed, everything that we perceive seems to be real in itself, while in fact it is a mere form covering the real. Try as we may, we cannot know the real nature of anything. The forms, changing constantly,

[25]The jīva's ajñāna is eradicated by direct experience of Brahman (aparōkṣānubhūti). This is intuitive knowledge. With reference to this, ajnāna is said to be antiknowledge, that which is *contradictory* to knowledge. Brahman is the locus of ajñāna or māyā from the viewpoint of the world-appearance. In this sense ajñāna is *contrary* to Pure Consciousness that Brahman is. What are contradictory cannot exist together, like truth and untruth. What are contrary can exist together like two opponents. Light and darkness are contradictory; but light and a veil of mist are contrary. See sec. 9.

appear to be real because of Reality underlying them. We only deal with the forms and mistake them to be real in themselves, while the underlying Reality never comes into view. What but avidyā can create such a situation? As the cause is, so is the effect. The effect points to a corresponding cause.

Further, had the world of duality and dependence been absolutely real, had there been no ideal existence transcending it, then liberation from its bondage would not have been possible. But since it is rooted in false knowledge due to avidyā, liberation is attainable by its eradication through the knowledge of Reality beyond all limitation. It is said by Śaṅkara, "Truly, the seed force (potential energy), which has to be designated as avyakta (the indefinable), is of the nature of avidyā and is dependent on Īśvara. It is a monstrous sleep made up of māyā, in which lie the migratory souls lacking in Self-knowledge."[26]

6. *Māyā has different names. It is indefinable either as real or as unreal. Nor is it both real and unreal.*

The same primal energy, supported and directed by Īśvara, has different names. As undiversified or undifferentiated in its potential aspect it is called *avyākṛta.* Of course, all diversity is latent in it. As the origin of the universe it is called *prakṛti.* As it veils Reality and is counteracted by the direct experience or immediate knowledge of Reality, it is called *ajnāna* or *avidyā.* As instrumental to the projection of the world-appearance it is called *māyā.* Since its nature cannot be determined either as being (sat) or as nonbeing (asat) it is called *avyakta* (the indefinable).[27] Indeed, it is inexplicable in itself. Just as the world is not self-explanatory neither is its origin. The terms *prakṛti, avidyā, ajñāna, māyā,* and *avyakta* are often synonymously used.

The word *māyā* literally means "that which measures (the Immeasurable)." It is this inscrutable measuring or limiting principle that makes the Unlimited apparently limited, the Undifferentiated apparently differentiated, the Unrelated apparently related, the Unconditioned apparently conditioned by time, space, and causation. So māyā has been called *aghatita-ghatanā-patīyasī,*[28] she who is expert in making the nonexistent appear as existent. It is māyā that

[26]BS I:4.3, S. com.

[27]*Ibid.*

[28]See Śaṅkara's *Māyā-pañcakam* (Five Stanzas on Māyā) at the end of this chapter, p. 109.

makes Reality appear as different from what It is. Manifesting itself as the manifold of names and forms grounded on Nondual Reality, māyā is neither real nor unreal. It is not real (sat) because it has no existence apart from Brahman and is eradicated by true knowledge. That alone is real (sat), according to Vedanta, which is self-existent, which is not conditioned by time, space, and causation; in other words, which is in no way contradicted.

Nor is the phenomenal world of multiplicity unreal (asat), because it is a fact of universal experience and persists until the knowledge of Reality is attained. That is unreal (asat) which has no existence at all. The world of phenomena is not nonexistent as is a barren woman's son or a hare's horn. Though it has no self-identity, yet it is undeniable. It is also different from dream-experience, illusion, or hallucination, which is more or less private, has no practical efficiency, and endures for the time being.

Māyā cannot be regarded even as a participant in both existence and nonexistence, which are contradictory. Since the world of becoming is indescribable (anirvacanīya) either as real (sat) or as unreal (asat), it is characterized in Vedantic terminology as *mithyā,* which does not mean, as is often misconceived, "unreal" but "other than real and unreal" (sadasad-vilakṣṇa). The manifold has an apparent existence grounded on the Supreme Being like the illusory appearance of a serpent on a rope.

Māyā is thus defined by Śaṅkara:

> Māyā or avidyā, also called *avyakta* (unmanifested) is the power (śakti) of the Supreme Lord. She is composed of the three guṇas (sattva, rajas, and tamas), has no beginning and is imperceptible [in her potential state]. It is from the effects she produces that her existence can be inferred only by the wise. It is she who begets the entire universe. She is neither real nor unreal, nor both. She is neither different nor nondifferent [from Reality], nor both. She is neither a compound nor an integral whole, nor both. She is most peculiar. Her nature is inexpressible.[29]

7. *Māyā is evident as contraries that mark the universe.*

We cannot see māyā in its potential state. We see only the effects it produces; and it is from the effects that we can know the nature of the cause. Truly speaking, māyā is not a theory, but a fact of experience. The entire relative existence is the domain of māyā. Anything relative

[29]VC 108-9.

is neither real nor unreal. It has a conditional existence but no absolute reality. It is and it is not. The whole realm of cause and effect is such. The entire world of phenomena, physical and psychical, is conditioned by time, space, and causation. It exists because of the Absolute. It is not real in itself, and has only an apparent existence. It is based on the Absolute, yet not identical with It. The world as it appears to us is neither real nor unreal. It is mithyā. As an appearance it is neither different nor nondifferent from Brahman. But, essentially, it is nondifferent from Brahman, its basis and being.[30] In fact, the world of experience is an appearance screening Reality which exists in and through it. It is said by Gauḍapāda: "This manifold does not exist as identical with the Self nor does it stand by itself independent of the Self. The two are neither different nor identical; this is what the seers see."[31]

The following remarks of Swami Vivekananda are illuminating:

> Māyā is not illusion as it is popularly interpreted. Māyā is real, yet it is not real. It is real in that the Real is behind it and gives it its appearance of reality. That which is real in Māyā is the Reality in and through Māyā. Yet the Reality is not seen, and hence that which is seen is unreal and it has no real independent existence of itself, but is dependent upon the Real for its existence. Māyā then is a paradox — real, yet not real; an illusion, yet not an illusion. He who knows the Real sees in Māyā not illusion but Reality. He who knows not the Real sees in Māyā illusion and thinks it real.[32]

This coupling of the Real and the unreal is the act of māyā. It is the mysterious principle that associates the dissociated. It prevails everywhere as the meeting of the contraries. It is māyā that brings about the relativity of the subject and the object, the knower and the known. The two are dissimilar yet inseparable. One does not exist without the other. The universe is a conglomeration of pairs of opposites, such as life and death, light and darkness, joy and sorrow, knowledge and ignorance, plenty and want, beauty and ugliness, kindness and misery, love and hatred, good and evil, in which the antitheses are correlated; yet either factor appears to be an independent element and in vain we try our utmost to have the one of the pair to the exclusion of the other. This is the effect of māyā. There is no elevation without depression, no construction without destruction, no addition without subtraction. In each case the contraries form a single process. They are inseparable; yet they

[30]See BS II:1.4. [31]MK II:34. [32]CW VI, p.58.

appear disparate. This is the effect of māyā. Each organism lives by constant building up and breaking down. The seed disintegrates as it sprouts. The birth of the plant is the death of the seed-form. They go together. This is how māyā operates.

8. *By associating the dissociated, māyā causes individualization. (See Chap.II, sec. 5 — Man's twofold ajñāna.)*

The glaring instance of māyā is man's ego-idea. His very individuality is based on ignorance (ajñāna). He is not essentially a psychophysical being. He can know by self-introspection that he is the unchanging observer of physical and mental events and, therefore, ever distinct from the body-mind complex. Yet he fails to recognize the true nature of the self and mistakes the not-self for the self. The knower of the body and the mind gets identified with the known! This is absurd. Yet it is the commonest fact of life. All confusions and sufferings of man arise from this wrong identification, the outcome of ignorance. Here is the origin of the ego-idea that finds expression as "I-ness" and "my-ness." As we have noted, the ego is the self identified with the not-self.

The subject and the object are as contrary in character as light and darkness. The subject is self-luminous, for consciousness is its very nature. The object is stark blind, absolutely devoid of consciousness. The one is pure spirit; the other is dark matter. There is no reason why one should be confused with the other. Yet they become identified with each other and the attributes of one are ascribed to the other. But neither of them changes its nature in this process of superimposition, just as the stump of a tree suffers no change when mistaken for a policeman, or a thief, or a ghost.

This mistaking of one thing for another or the ascription of the attribute of one thing to another is called in Vedantic terminology *adhyāsa.* It is apparent association of the dissociated. What accomplishes this strange feat is māyā, expert in making the nonexistent appear as existent (aghatita-ghatanā patīyasī). It is evident in all human behavior and experience marked with "I-consciousness," such as "I am here," "I am writing," "I think," "I see," "I am hungry," "I am growing old," "I dreamt," "I am deaf," "I am virtuous," "I am wealthy," "I am happy," "I am a father," "My body feels tired," "My hands can grasp," "My mind can visualize," "I shall die," and so forth. Thus, unaware of the true nature of the Self, which is ever pure and free, man identifies himself not only with the body, the senses, and the mind, but also with external things and beings, and grieves helplessly in delusion.

That ajñāna is ever attendant on the individualized self is evident from such abiding feeling of man as "I do not know myself." Although he is aware of his own existence, being of the nature of consciousness, which is self-evident, he is not aware of his true nature. It is very strange that the knower whose essence is consciousness should be in ignorance with regard to his real nature. Yet it is a fact. Not only that. Each individual feels surrounded by a wall of ignorance which he struggles to break down throughout life. Ajñāna underlies the ego-idea and all its varied expressions. The volitional actions of an individual, his thoughts, feelings, memories, and imaginations proceed from the ego-idea. Even in dream it endures in different forms. In dreamless sleep all modes of the mind, including the ego-idea, merge in unspecified unawareness. While asleep, a teacher does not know that he is a teacher, a mother does not know that she is a mother, a robber does not know that he is a robber. From this causal ajnāna, unspecified unawareness, arises again the ego-idea and the consequent mental operations as one wakes up. The individual ajñāna, the limiting adjunct of the finite self, is a phase of the cosmic ajnāna or māyā held and controlled by Īśvara.

9. *The cosmic and the individual aspect of māyā. Īśvara and the jīva.*

Māyā can be viewed in the cosmic and also in the individual aspect. The cosmic māyā or the māyā associated with Īśvara is pure because of the full predominance of sattva over rajas and tamas. It does not obscure His consciousness in the least, but serves as His manifold power (śakti) of the projection, the preservation and the dissolution of the cosmos. Īśvara manifests and governs the whole universe by His very presence without any effort. His knowledge and rulership are natural and unconstrained. So the Upaniṣad says, "He has neither body nor organs. No one is known to be His equal or superior. His sovereign power is declared [by the Vedas] to be manifold and His creativity through knowledge and might is spontaneous."[33] He is the maintainer of dharma, the destroyer of sin, and the master of all blessed qualities.

Māyā that is associated with the individual soul is often distinguished from the cosmic māyā by the term ajñāna or avidyā in a restricted sense. Because of the preponderance of tamas over sattva

[33]Sv.U. VI:8.

and rajas, the individual māyā or ajñāna is impure. It obstructs the jīva's self-knowledge and creates the seeming ego-idea. It is the cause of his bondage. Consequently, his power is insignificant and his knowledge limited or obscure. The creation of the universe, physical and mental, is due to cosmic māyā. The individual ajñāna or avidyā is particularly responsible for the association of the self with the not-self, a fragment of the psychophysical universe. The finite self (jīvātmā) is related to the body-mind complex through ajnāna, its limiting adjunct. Īśvara (the Supreme Self) associated with māyā is the all-powerful and all-knowing Creator and Ruler. The finite self, the jīvātmā, associated with ajñāna functions as an experiencer and doer. In either case, the nature of the relation between caitanya and jaḍa (spirit and matter) is the same. It is a case of apparent superimposition.

As long as the jīva clings to the ego-idea he remains in bondage in the domain of māyā. But when he foregoes it and surrenders the ego to the Supreme Self, the Lord of māyā, he attains Liberation in union with Him. So says Śrī Kṛṣṇa, "Verily, this divine māyā of Mine, constituted of the guṇas, is hard to cross. But those who take refuge in Me solely go across it."[34] The Lord of māyā is the liberator from its bondage. Bondage and Liberation both are in the domain of māyā. Neither has any meaning in Nirguṇa Brahman, which is absolutely free. Māyā or ajñāna with tamas or rajas preponderant keeps man in bondage; with sattva preponderant the same leads him to freedom. These are like dark and bright aspects of māyā, and are sometimes distinguished as *avidyā* (in a restricted sense, of course) and *vidyā*. It is said, "Avidyā leads to mortality and vidyā to immortality. Brahman who [as Īśvara] controls vidyā and avidyā is above both."[35] Says Śrī Kṛṣṇa to Uddhava, "Know vidyā and avidyā to be My powers, which are respectively the cause of Liberation and bondage of the embodied souls. The two are the initial products of My māyā."[36]

10. *Īśvara, the Lord of māyā, is the All-pervading and All-transcendent Being.*

It has already been noted that Īśvara, though holding māyā with all its ramifications, is in no way affected by it. Such is His mastery over it. As illustrated by Śaṅkara, "Just as a magician is not himself

[34]BG VII:14.
[35]Sv.U.V:1.
[36]SB XI:11.3.

affected by the enchantment created by his magic since he knows it to be unreal, even so is the Supreme Lord unaffected by the world-appearance."[37] The purpose of the analogy is, of course, not to present Īśvara as a master-magician, but to convey the sense of His absolute purity and immutability even as the Creator, Preserver, and Destroyer of the variegated universe. Another apt illustration is given by Sri Ramakrishna: "The snake is not affected by the poison in its mouth, while those who are bitten by it are affected. Similarly, Īśvara is not affected by His māyā, though the finite selves are under its spell."[38]

The point is that Creatorship is not inherent in Īśvara. It is but His extrinsic characteristic (taṭastha lakṣaṇa). Intrinsically, He is immutable, immovable, Nondual Brahman beyond all diversities and distinctions. It is only in relation to the world-appearance arising from the adjunct māyā that Nondual Brahman is the all-knowing and all-powerful Ruler of the manifold. The phenomenal world is real to the individual (jīva), but cannot be reckoned as his creation. The existence of māyā, its origin, is a fact from his position. With the individual ajñāna there must be the cosmic māyā. The one betokens the other as the fruit betokens the tree. This does not mean that the cosmic māyā exists because of the individual ajñāna. The individual ajñāna derives from the cosmic māyā and not the cosmic māyā from the individual ajnāna. From the viewpoint of the world-appearance Brahman is their locus. With the adjunct of māyā Brahman is Īśvara, with the adjunct of ajñāna or avidyā Brahman is the jīva. Thus Īśvarahood is invariably linked with jīvahood. Both are the apparent aspects of Brahman, the Ultimate One.

Īśvara is ever related to the jīva as Ruler to the ruled. They are coexistent and without beginning. As observed by Śaṅkara:

> And He [Īśvara] stands in the empirical realm in the relation of the Ruler to the cognizing souls called jīvas, which are really one with His own Self (just as portions of ether inside jars are one with the universal ether), but are limited by the combination of the body and the senses composed of names and forms brought forth by Avidyā. Therefore, the Lordship of Īśvara, His omniscience and omnipotence, are relative to the individualization due to limiting adjuncts derived from avidyā, while in reality such expressions as the ruler, the ruled, omniscience, and so forth, do not apply to the Self from whose being all adjuncts are wiped out by right knowledge.[39]

[37]BS II:1.9, S. com. [38]GSR, p.102. [39]BS II:1.14, S. com.

11. *The tripartite relative order vanishes when the Absolute (the unconditioned Brahman) is realized.*

The fact that Īśvara as the Supreme Lord is not the Ultimate Reality is proved by the crowning mystical experience of an illumined soul. Īśvarahood is ever related to the cosmic manifold, which is associated with the jīva's empirical self rooted in ajñāna. As the knowledge of the true nature of the Self dawns upon man, he realizes not only the falsity of his identity with the psychophysical garment, but also the falsity of the psychophysical garment itself, nay, of the entire world of experience.

As long as an individual knows himself to be a physical or a psychophysical being, he dwells in the realm of phenomena and cannot see the Reality underlying them. But when he becomes aware of his indwelling self, the experiencer and sustainer of the psychophysical system, he perceives his affinity with the Supreme Being who supports and manifests the phenomenal world. Gradually, he recognizes his transcendental self, the basis of ego-consciousness, as the unchanging witness of the ever-changing physical and mental events; then he realizes his unity with the all-pervading, all-knowing Supreme Self. Finally, this experience culminates in the identity or the complete oneness of the two as integral, undivided, limitless, absolute Consciousness, where all distinctions of the knower, the known, and the process of knowing are obliterated and wherein the individual souls, the objective universe, and even the Supreme Lord dissolve.

The following remark of Śaṅkara is pertinent:

> Moreover, when the consciousness of the identity [of the individual soul with the Supreme Being] is aroused by such instruction of their identity as "Thou art That," then the finiteness of the individual soul and the creatorship of Brahman vanish at once, because all experience of difference proceeding from wrong knowledge is annihilated by perfect knowledge.[40]

12. *Īśvara is the highest manifestation of the Absolute. The Unconditioned and Conditioned Brahman.*

One should not, however, come to the conclusion that Īśvara is no more real than the phenomenal world. Actually He is the impersonal, absolute Brahman beyond all trace of māyā and is ever aware of His

[40]BS II:1.14, S. com.

true being as such. Though associated with māyā and its modifications, He is not the least affected being totally detached. As the highest manifestation of the Absolute on the relative plane He is the most adorable One. "Free from attachment [the Self] is unattached," says the Upaniṣad.[41] Īśvara is extolled as one with the attributeless Brahman: "He is the formless, self-luminous Being, unborn, existing within and without, having no prāṇa or mind, pure, beyond the indestructible cause of causes [the undifferentiated prakṛti]."[42] Arjuna praises the Lord: "Thou art the Imperishable, the Ultimate One to be realized. Thou art the Supreme support of the universe. Thou art the undying guardian of the eternal dharma. Thou art the Primal Being, I believe."[43] So does Uddhava praise the Lord: "Thou art the Supreme Brahman, limitless like the sky, the transcendent Being beyond Prakṛti."[44]

The Lord thus speaks of His complete transcendence: "As the mighty air moving everywhere ever rests in ākāśa [etheric space], in the same manner, know thou, all things rest in Me [without affecting Me]."[45] "Never do these acts [of creation, preservation, and dissolution of the universe], O Arjuna, bind Me, because I remain unattached to them as one unconcerned."[46] "As I am beyond the destructible [the manifest universe] and transcend the indestructible [the undifferentiated prakṛti], so I am renowned in the world and in the Veda as the Supreme Being."[47]

Metaphysical investigation also points to the truth that the Ultimate Reality is nondual and nonrelational, and cannot be attained by intellectual knowledge. That which faces any "other" must be limited. It is said in the *Chāndōgya Upaniṣad,* "That is Infinite where one sees no other, hears no other, knows no other; that is finite where one sees any other, hears any other, and knows any other. It is the Infinite that is immortal; it is the finite that is mortal."[48] In intellectual knowledge the relativity of the subject and the object prevails; the object is known in relation to the subject and the subject in relation to the object. So it fails to reveal the true nature of either. Intellect cannot go beyond the range of relative knowledge. It cannot reach the Absolute that underlies and transcends the subject and the object relation.

The end of knowledge is to be attained in intuitional experience, in which the subject and the object merge into nonrelational

[41] Br.U. III:9.26.
[42] Mu.U. II:1.2.
[43] BG XI:18.
[44] SB XI:11.28.
[45] BG IX:6.
[46] *Ibid.* IX:9.
[47] *Ibid.* XV:18.
[48] Ch.U. VII:24.1.

undifferentiated consciousness revealing the Absolute. The Ultimate Reality is neither the subject nor the object, neither substance nor attribute, neither cause nor effect. It is beyond all conditions and relations. Relation signifies dependence in some form or other. It also implies something beyond the related. Īśvara, as the Supreme Lord, is relative to the world and cannot be the Ultimate Reality. As such He is *Apara Brahma* (conditioned Brahman) and not *Para Brahma* (unconditioned Brahman). But the conditioning is apparent, being due to māyā.

13. *Any difference is irreconcilable with absolute unity. Māyā solves the metaphysical crux. Its inscrutability is its special characteristic.*

Most philosophers concur in the Upaniṣadic view that the Fundamental Reality is the Limitless, Undivided One. Nevertheless, plurality is undeniable. It is all that we perceive, externally and internally. What is the exact relation between the manifold of experience and the Absolute One? How can unity and multiplicity, the Infinite and the finite, Being and becoming be reconciled? This has proved to be a puzzling metaphysical problem. Some eminent philosophers, both Eastern and Western, such as Bhartriprapañca, Rāmānuja, Nimbārka, Jīva Gōswāmī, Hegel, Bosanquet, and Bradley, have sought in different ways to harmonize the order of becoming with the Ultimate Being, to accommodate diversity in the fundamental unity. In their view the Absolute is not free from internal differences and relations. It is not pure identity of being.

But Nondualistic Vedanta finds no actual relation between the cosmic manifold and the absolute unity of existence. The relation of conjunction is unimaginable. No causal or any other relation of inherence can be logically determined. The Uncaused, Immutable One cannot be the cause of any "other." The Absolute cannot be both changeless and changeable, undivided and divided, conscious and unconscious. Any difference in the oneness of Being is untenable. If unity is real, the difference must be false, because they are mutually contradictory. To explain contradiction is the function of philosophic reason. It cannot accept as final truth what it aims to dissolve. So the manifold cannot inhere in the Absolute One as its part, or mode, or attribute, or feature, or function, or potency.

As far as the human intellect can apprehend, finite existences have no place in the unbroken fullness of the Infinite. The Absolute is free from all difference and relations, internal as well as external. Yet, as a fact of experience plurality is indubitable. So Vedanta explains it as a mere appearance due to the mysterious limiting principle, māyā. That the relation between the cosmic manifold and the Ultimate Reality can neither be established by reason nor denied is the implication of *māyā* in Advaita Vedanta. It is the strange association of appearance with Reality. Says Sureśvarācāryya: "The characteristic of avidyā is its very inscrutability, that it cannot bear proof. Otherwise, it would be a reality."[49] The illusion of a snake on a rope is a fact, which admits of no explanation. If it could be accounted for, it would be a reality. "This cosmic illusion is without cause," says the same author elsewhere, "It is contrary to all reason. It stands no scrutiny, just as darkness stands not the sun."[50] If you investigate this world of māyā it vanishes. So says Sri Ramakrishna, "If māyā is once recognized, it feels ashamed of itself and takes to flight."[51]

14. *Māyā produces the jīva and jagat through two different kinds of adhyāsa (apparent superimposition).*

This association of the apparent with the real is signified by the term *adhyāsa* (superimposition). Māyā is the mysterious principle that brings it about. Adhyāsa, as defined by Śaṅkara, is the projection or the erroneous ascription of something where it does not exist.[52] As we have already noted, there are two distinct types of adhyāsa:[53] (1) the mistaking of one thing for another, and (2) the ascription of the attribute of one thing to another. A classical example of the former is a rope mistaken for a snake and of the latter is a white conch appearing yellow when seen through a yellow glass. In the first instance, one thing appears as another; the rope appears as the snake. In the second, a thing appears different; the white conch appears yellow. In both cases there is apparent identification of the true and the false without any change in their character. The rope does not partake of the nature of the snake nor does the snake of the rope. The whiteness of the conch is not affected by its apparent yellowness; nor is yellowness by whiteness. The world of experience and the jīva are two distinct cases of adhyāsa in point. As the world of

[49] Br.U. *Bhāṣya-vārttika,* 181, as quoted in *Vidvanmanōrañjinī* on *Vedānta-sāra.* The second line of the verse is different in Ananda Ashrama edn.

[50] NS III:66.

[51] GSR, p. 336.

[52] BS, intro., S. com.

[53] We are considering *arthādhyāsa,* leaving out *jñānādhyāsa.*

experience is superimposed on Brahman, so is jīvahood. In neither case does Brahman undergo any change. The world as well as the jīva is essentially Brahman.

Māyā veils Reality and projects the world-appearance. The apparent manifold rests in Brahman like the reflection of a city in a mirror. The mirror in the illustration is all that exists, the reflected city is but an appearance. To give another example, the whole phenomenal world is superimposed on Brahman like the illusory snake on the rope. Just as the illusory snake has no existence apart from the rope, its basis, similarly the world of phenomena has no existence apart from Brahman, its substratum. As the appearance of a snake in a rope does not mean a dual existence, because the rope alone actually exists, so the world-appearance implies no duality of existence, because Brahman is all that exists. Just as the rope is not the least affected by the illusory snake, similarly Brahman is in no way affected by the world-appearance. As the snake disappears when the rope is discovered, so does the world-appearance vanish when Brahman is realized. But the world-appearance does not obscure Brahman completely. In and through the world of phenomena the "being" or "is-ness" of Brahman is evident. The phenomenal appear to be real because of Reality permeating them; the Real appears to be phenomenal because of fleeting names and forms superimposed.

Brahman is the very being, the substratum, of the world of appearance. Throughout the world of names and forms, the product of māyā, Brahman is ever manifest as existence. The world is not merely a transformation of māyā. It is Brahman, Pure-Consciousness-Bliss, immutable and free from duality, that appears through māyā as the variegated ever-changing world of phenomena. It is adhyāsa of the first type: mistaking of one thing for another.

The appearance of Brahman as the jīva is the second type of adhyāsa: the ascription of the attribute of one thing to another. The Infinite Consciousness appears as finite or individualized consciousness being associated with ajñāna, just as the sun reflected in a mirror is apparently limited. It is the sun that appears as its reflection in the mirror. There is no basic difference between the two. The finite self under the spell of ajñāna ascribes to itself the characteristics of its psychophysical adjunct, a part of the world of phenomena. Thus, the limitations of the finite self are attributed to the Supreme Self. So the Unlimited appears as limited, the Unchanging as changing, the Immortal as mortal, the Unborn as born, the Pure as impure, the Free as the bound. Despite the superimposed limitation, the real nature of the self asserts itself. The self exists, shines, and is ever dear, being blissful. Freed from ajñāna the jīva realizes his very self as Brahman, whereas the world of appearance dissolves into It.

15. *Māyā is beginningless, but comes to an end.*

Although Brahman is the sole reality in the absolute sense, yet from the position of the individual the Nondualistic teachers have taken into account the following six categories: (1) the jīva, (2) Īśvara, (3) the difference between the jīva and Īśvara, (4) māyā, (5) the association of māyā with its locus Brahman, and (6) Brahman. They are all considered beginningless (anādi).[54] The first five are the primal categories of the relative order. Their beginning is indeterminable within the domain of relativity. Beyond it is the Absolute, where they are nonexistent. So the question as to the origin of the jīva, Īśvara, or māyā does not arise. They are interrelated. All differences vanish when māyā is dispelled by the knowledge of Brahman, the Absolute. "When the individual soul sleeping under the spell of beginningless māyā is awakened, he then realizes the Nondual Self beginningless, dreamless, sleepless."[55]

Nevertheless, one may ask: "Where does māyā come from?" It is to be noted that our inquiry into the origin of the universe cannot go beyond māyā, the potential state of the manifold. To predicate a cause of māyā is to lead to infinite regress (anavasthā). Like the seed and the sprout the universe moves from the unmanifest to the manifest state and from the manifest to the unmanifest state. It continues eternally. Neither nothing nor something else can be the origin of māyā, which is unique and unaccountable. So māyā has no beginning.

Then again, it is absurd that the individual soul under the spell of ajñāna will ascertain the beginning of māyā, which is at the very root of the individualization of the Self. When Self-knowledge is attained, māyā disappears. There is no trace of the universe or its origin, māyā, in the Ultimate Reality, Supreme Brahman. "No duality is there," says Gauḍapāda.[56] Though the beginning of māyā cannot be determined, it proves to be mithyā when we investigate into its nature. "That is māyā which does not really exist (but is perceived)."[57]

It is not beginningless in the sense in which Brahman is. Otherwise, it would have been a reality and there would have been no

[54]See SLS Ch.I, Kṛṣṇānanda-tīrtha's com.
[55]MK I:16. [56]*Ibid.* IV:75. [57]*Ibid.* IV:58.

end of it. So says Gauḍapāda: "If the world has no beginning it cannot have an end (some may contend)."[58] The answer is as follows: As the nonexistence of an object (a chair for instance) previous to its creation is beginningless, so is māyā. Just as the prior nonexistence (prāgabhāva) of an object has no beginning but has an end at its creation, similarly, māyā, though without beginning, comes to an end when Self-knowledge is attained. Since māyā has no beginning, the question, Why does māyā exist? is pointless. All "why's" are in māyā, the domain of ajñāna. So none can be finally answered. The "why" of māyā cannot be answered within māyā and beyond māyā there is no room for the question.

The following remarks of Swami Vivekananda are pertinent:

> The question — what is the cause of māyā? — is contradictory. Our position is that the Absolute has become this relative only apparently, that the Unconditioned has become the conditioned only in māyā. By the very admission of the Unconditioned, we admit that the Absolute cannot be acted upon by anything else. It is uncaused, which means that nothing outside Itself can act upon It. First of all, if It is unconditioned, It cannot have been acted upon by anything else. In the Unconditioned there cannot be time, space, or causation. That granted, your question will be: "What caused that which cannot be caused by anything to be changed into this?" Your question is only possible in the conditioned. But you take it out of the conditioned, and want to ask it in the Unconditioned. Only when the Unconditioned becomes conditioned, and space, time, and causation come in, can the question be asked. We can only say ignorance makes the illusion. The question is impossible. Nothing can have worked on the Absolute.[59]

16. *The question why Īśvara creates the world is untenable. He is all-free. The significance of līlā.*

Similarly, it is useless to ask why Īśvara creates the world. He who is all-free is free to create as well as not to create. No cause can prevail on Him. So the Vedas say: "Who can know it truly and who in this world can truly say whence arises this diversity of existence and why?"[60] We must not forget that for the All-powerful creation is no work at all. Work implies effort and also necessity. Neither is true in

[58]MK IV:30.

[59]CW V, pp. 203-4.

[60]Rg.V. X:129.6; Tai.Ar. II:8.9. Cf. T.H. Green, *Prolegomena to Ethics,* Oxford, Clarendon, 1906, sec. 100: "The old question, why God made the world, has never been answered, nor will be. We know not why the world should be; we only know that there it is."

the case of Īśvara. He creates out of the fullness of freedom and joy, without any effort, spontaneously, as if it is His very nature. It affects Him in no way. Throughout the whole course of creation — projection, preservation, and dissolution of the universe — His purity, immutability, and blissfulness are not impaired in the least.

Īśvara is all-sufficient; He has nothing to gain by creation; He has no unfulfilled desire to fulfill; and yet He acts. Though He has no necessity, still He creates. So it is said, "His act of creation is in mere sport (līlā) as in the world."[61] As explained by Śaṅkara: Just as in the world a king, whose desires are satisfied, engages himself in pastimes sportively, without any object to achieve; just as a man breathes naturally, without motive; similarly, God conducts the course of creation naturally without any purpose whatsoever, as if it is a mere sport (līlā).[62] It is to be noted that He creates neither out of necessity nor automatically. According to Gauḍapāda the creation is neither for His enjoyment nor for His diversion. It is His very nature to create. Says he, "This [the act of creation] is the very nature of the Divine Being. What desire can He have whose desires are ever attained."[63]

Indeed, God creates in full freedom. The term *līlā,* by which Vedanta characterizes the creative activity of Īśvara, is very significant. It differentiates the Divine act of creation from what we call work, which involves effort, necessity, and compulsion. The production of the universe by Īśvara is free from all these elements. Līlā implies His complete transcendence along with His immanence. Unrelated He abides everywhere. Unmoved He moves everything. He acts, still He does not act, because there is no effort, nor necessity, nor compulsion in His work. He is all-free, all-perfect. The universe proceeds out of His joyousness, so to speak. From the viewpoint of the egoistic self, the world is a conglomeration of multiple things and beings, a welter of dualities and differences. From the viewpoint of the transcendent Supreme Self the whole universe is the manifestation of one Reality — Pure Being-Consciousness-Bliss. The world appears as līlā only when we can view it from God's position.

Though Īśvara has no objective in the act of creation, still it serves a twofold purpose of the jīva. The world provides him with experience and leads him to Liberation. The whole universe is a moral order working in that direction. The evolution of life is a movement towards the jīva's progressive Self-realization.

[61] BS II:1.33.
[62] *Ibid.* S. com.
[63] MK I:9.

We conclude with the citation of Śaṅkara's poem — "Five Stanzas on Māyā" (Māyā-pañcakam):

> Expert in making the nonexistent appear as existent, māyā creates the differences of Īśvara, jagat [the world], and the jīva, in Ātman, Pure Consciousness, free from all imaginings, undivided, unparalleled, without component parts, and eternal!
>
> Expert in making the nonexistent appear as existent, māyā instantly debases by a show of prosperity and the like, human beings that are no better than quadrupeds, alas! even though they have threshed out hundreds of Vedic and Vedantic texts!
>
> Expert in making the nonexistent appear as existent, māyā causes the Nondual Ātman, all-awareness, of the nature of Consciousness and Bliss, to enter into, and constantly wander in, the ocean of the world composed of the elements — namely ether, air, fire, and so forth!
>
> Expert in making the nonexistent appear as existent, māyā brings forth such ego-ideas and delusions—as "I am a Brāhmaṇa," "I am a Vaiśya," "my son," "my wife," "my home" — in Ātman, which is Blissful Consciousness and is devoid of all distinction of caste, color, and merit!
>
> Expert in making the nonexistent appear as existent, māyā creates such distinctions as Brahmā, Viṣṇu, Śiva, and the like, in Brahman, undivided as It is, and alas! utterly confuses even the learned with these notions of differences![64]

[64] *The Works of Śaṅkara,* Vol. XI, Vanivilas Press, Srirangam.

CHAPTER VI
THE PROCESS OF CREATION

1. *The Advaita theory of creation called vivarta-vāda.*

The creative order proceeds from Brahman associated with māyā in its potential state. It is Saguṇa Brahman who holds and directs māyā as its Witness in all its stages. Māyā, the causal potency of the world-appearance, serves as His power. It has no existence apart from Him. With the aid of māyā He is both the efficient and the material cause of the universe. He is Īśvara, the Supreme Ruler of the creative process as the one all-encompassing Self. His agency consists in His all-knowingness, His will to create, and His act of creation. But His thought, will, and act are effortless, because they proceed spontaneously from His Omniscience. It is said in the *Muṇḍaka Upaniṣad:*

> He who knows all things in their universal and particular aspects, whose effort consists in His knowledge, brings forth the cosmic soul (Hiraṇyagarbha), and names and forms and foods.[1]

Without undergoing any change whatsoever He manifests Himself in diverse ways through the modifications of māyā. All changes are in māyā, the principle of appearance, but none in Reality. Being the sole ground of the apparent manifold, Brahman is its material cause.

> By "material cause" is meant the substratum of the superimposition of the universe, or the substratum of māyā that becomes transformed into the universe.[2]

It is said in the *Ṛg-Veda:*

[1]Mu.U. I:1.9. The cosmic soul, Hiraṇyagarbha, is also called *Brahmā.* Īśvara as the Creator has the same epithet *Brahmā.* It is worthy of note that Brahmā, the cosmic soul, is other than Brahmā of the Trinity or Trimūrti — Brahmā, Viṣṇu, and Śiva (Īśvara as the Creator, Preserver and Destroyer of the universe).

[2]VP VII.

The Lord on account of the modes of māyā is perceived in many forms.[3]

The One appears as the manifold. The change is only apparent. Such apparent modification of the causal substance is called in Vedantic terminology *vivarta.* The actual modification is termed *pariṇāma.* In the rope-snake analogy, the apparent snake is vivarta of the rope. A cloth is pariṇāma of the woven yarns. The creation is due to pariṇāma of māyā and vivarta of Brahman. To give a specific example, an iron pan is pariṇāma of iron empirically; both are modes of māyā, being mere appearances, but vivarta of the underlying Reality, Brahman.

The Advaita theory of creation is called *vivarta-vāda* (the theory of apparent modification). The implication is that the universe is not the product of Brahman. The causal relation between Brahman and the cosmic order is only apparent. Causation has, however, significance within the domain of māyā. It holds between one mode of māyā and another, but not between Brahman and the phenomenal world. Brahman supports but transcends the entire range of causes and effects.

2. *The beginning of the creation. The causal state of the animate and the inanimate world.*

In the beginning māyā or prakṛti is undifferentiated (avyākṛta). Not a single thing, living or nonliving, gross or fine, great or small, appears there. No manifestation of form or feature is there. No all-pervading, original element prevails there. No sound or movement of any kind is there. Even space-time is out of existence. It is a state of cosmic sleep, so to speak, marked by complete stillness and darkness. As stated by Manu, "All this was absorbed in darkness, imperceptible, without distinctive mark, out of the reach of intellect, incomprehensible, and totally immersed in deep sleep, as it were."[4] This boundless, profound quiescence has found poetic expression in a well-known hymn of the *Ṛg-Veda* (Nāsadīya-Sukta):

> Then there was neither aught nor naught;[5] there was neither earth nor vault of heaven, nor any region beyond. What was the pervading element? Where? For whose sake did the dark, deep waters exist?

[3]Rg.V. VI:47.18; Br.U. II:5.19.
[4]MS I:5. [5]Because māyā is neither real nor unreal (Sāyaṇa's com.).

There was neither death nor deathlessness. There was no distinction of night and day. That [Brahman] breathed without air. That existed united with His māyā. Nothing else beside That was there.

Like gloom hidden by gloom all this lay, in the beginning, in the womb of māyā, undistinguished from the cause. What was latent therein became manifest by the influence of His thought.[6]

The undifferentiated prakṛti is not simple or homogeneous. It is constituted of the three guṇas — sattva, rajas, and tamas.[7] Though distinct, the guṇas are inseparable. They form a unity in trinity. Prakṛti is a complex whole, in which each of the three guṇas is struggling perpetually for predominance over the other two. It is because of this peculiarity that they are capable of giving rise to countless varieties. In the undifferentiated state of prakṛti they are in equilibrium, that is, they fully counterbalance one another. There is no absolute rest in prakṛti. It is the principle of becoming, responsible for imposing the world of names and forms on Pure Being. The creative process starts with the disturbance of the equipose of the guṇas. In this context the term *guṇa* means "strand" and not "attribute," which is the usual meaning of the word. The guṇas are the irreducible constituents of prakṛti. They form, as it were, the three strands of the rope of māyā. Each and every product of prakṛti partakes of these three factors. The difference between one object and another is mainly in the degree of preponderance of one or another of the guṇas over the other two.

At the cosmic dissolution the manifold universe, composed of series of causes and effects, merges in inverse order into the undifferentiated prakṛti. Like the tree in the seed, the variegated world remains there in potential state. This is the seed force, the causal potency, of the entire cosmos. As observed by Śaṅkara:

Even when the world is being dissolved, it is dissolved only so far that its potentiality still remains; and from this root of potentiality it arises; otherwise, we should have to acknowledge that its origination is accidental (that is, without a cause).[8]

The unliberated souls lie dormant with their causal bodies merged in prakṛti. It is the causal body that contains the rudiments of the subtle and the gross body. Even Hiraṇyagarbha (the cosmic soul) leaves the cosmic body, the universal mind, and attains final

[6]Rg.V. X:129.1-3.

[7]See footnote 13 on the three guṇas, p. 42. [8]BS I:3.30, S. com.

Liberation in the supreme state of oneness with Brahman. Only Īśvara, the Eternal Ruler of prakṛti, endures.[9] This is the basic dissolution of the cosmos, which is called *prākṛta pralaya.*[10] This is distinct from the absolute dissolution (ātyantika pralaya) and the intermediary dissolution (naimittika pralaya), which we shall dwell on later.

3. *The Advaita theory of the preexistence of the effect in the cause.*

From the potential state the universe arises in new forms in the beginning of the next cycle. It is not nonexistent before its production. Creation is the development of the latent into the actual. As pointed out by Śaṅkara, "A nonexistent effect is not produced, nor an existent effect lost."[11] In the Vedantic view of causal relation the effect exists in the material cause before its production and is nondifferent from the cause. This theory of causation is called *satkārya-vāda* (the theory of preexistent effect). The Sāṁkhya school also maintains this theory, but in a different sense. According to Vedanta, pariṇāma, the transformation of the cause into effect, means only a change of form and not of substance, because there is no essential difference between cause and effect. But according to Sāṁkhya, it is substantial change.

A contrary theory of causation is upheld by the Nyāya and Vaiśeṣika schools. They maintain that the effect does not exist in the cause before its production; a nonexistent effect comes out of an existent cause. This is called *asatkārya-vāda* (the theory of non-preexistent effect). It is also known as *ārambha-vāda* (the theory of origination). Vedanta refutes this theory by the following argument: We see that particular causes produce particular effects. Cloth can be made of threads and not of iron filings; cream can be secured from milk and not from water; and so forth. This shows that there is an invariable relation between an effect and its material cause. Otherwise, for a desired effect it would not be necessary to seek a particular causal substance; it could be produced by anything. To produce a specific effect a thing must be causally related to it. But a thing cannot be related to an effect before its production, unless it is present there in some form or other. Therefore, the effect must be preexistent in the cause.

It may be argued that the effect is not preexistent in the cause, but certain power or potency of the cause produces the effect. This only

[9]Sv.U. VI:17. [10]VP VII. [11]Br.U. I:4.7, S. com.

means that the power which produces a particular effect is preexistent in the cause and related to the effect; in other words, the effect is potentially contained in the cause. As observed by Śaṅkara:

> The power is identical in essence with the cause and the effect is identical in essence with the power.[12]

As a matter of fact, the effect is the causal substance in another form. Essentially it is identical with the material cause. As the cause exists in the effect, so does the effect exist in the cause before its manifestation. They are actually the same substance in two different forms. Moreover, to say that the effect is nonexistent in the cause before its production is to maintain that the nonexistent becomes existent, which is absurd. "A barren woman's son is born neither in reality nor in illusion."[13]

4. *How Íśvara starts the creation.*

How does the process of creation start? What disturbs the equilibrium of the guṇas? Does undifferentiated prakṛti awake of itself? No. Prakṛti is insentient. It cannot operate without the animation of Consciousness. For its functions as well as for its existence, it depends wholly on the luminous Self. Two distinct factors are involved in starting the process of creation. The one is the animating vision (īkṣaṇa) of Īśvara; the other is the readiness of jīvas' karma (latent impressions of past actions and experiences) to bear fruit. They synchronize.[14] It is Īśvara's īkṣaṇa (literally, seeing) that quickens prakṛti. It is said in the *Aitareya Upaniṣad:*

> Before creation all this was one with the only Self [being indistinguishable from the Self]. There was nothing else active. He viewed: 'Let me create the worlds.' He created the worlds [for the living beings to reap the fruit of their diverse karma].[15]

[12]BS II:1.18, S. com.

[13]MK III:28.

[14]Cf. VP I, "Just as owing to the contact of the sense organs with the objects and other such causes, different modes arise in the mind, the limiting adjunct of the jīva; similarly, owing to the prevalence of karma of the jīvas that are about to be created, there arise in māyā, the limiting adjunct of the Supreme Lord, such modes as, 'Now this is to be created,' 'Now this is to be maintained,' 'Now this is to be destroyed,' and so forth."

[15]Ai.U. I.1.1-2.

The fact of Īśvara's *īkṣaṇa* (viewing, reflection) is also mentioned in the *Chāndōgya Upaniṣad.* He viewed: "May I be many. May I be born variously."[16]

It is indicated that the Supreme Self becomes diversified as the manifold. As stated in the *Taittirīya Upaniṣad:*

> He willed "Let Me be many. Let Me be born variously." He contemplated. Having contemplated He created all this, whatsoever there is. Having created it, He verily entered it. Having entered it, He became the manifest and the unmanifest, the defined and the undefined, the supported and the unsupported, the sentient and the insentient, the real and the unreal. The Supreme Being became all this, whatsoever there is.[17]

Īśvara plans the creation in view of the jīvas' karma and the unfoldment of their inner nature. Says Śaṅkara:

> He reflected concerning the order and the arrangement of the world to be created. Having thus reflected He created the universe with time and space, names and forms, as required by the karma and other conditions of the living beings. This is the universe that is being experienced by all creatures in all states according to their perception.[18]

As stated in the *Vedānta-paribhāṣā:*

> At the beginning of the creation the Supreme Lord associated with māyā of unlimited and inscrutable power and aided by the jīvas' past actions and experiences, which are the causes of the variety of the universe to be created, first conceives in His mind the entire universe consisting of names and forms, and resolves, "I will do this."[19]

The new creation is the development of the physical order in conformity with the psychical. It is a readjustment of the natural and the moral order. So the present cosmos is not a mere replica of the past. It is a new arrangement on the basis of the preceding one.

5. *The position of Īśvara as the Creator and Ruler of the universe.*

The Lord declares Himself to be the prime mover of prakṛti:

[16]Ch.U. VI:2.3.
[17]Tai.U. II:6.1.
[18]*Ibid.* S. com.
[19]VP Chap. VII.

> Under my super-vision prakṛti brings forth the moving and the unmoving. Because of this, O Son of Kuntī, the world revolves.[20]

The emergence of all beings from prakṛti is due to its impregnation by Īśvara. The differences among living creatures are due to the differences in their past karma. For these Īśvara is not responsible. He creates or manifests the living beings according to their inner nature containing merit and demerit. Śaṅkara explains Īśvara's position as the Creator by an analogy:

> Just as Parjanya (the god of rain) is the common cause of the production of rice, barley, etc., while the differences among these species is due to diverse potentialities inherent in their respective seeds; so Īśvara is the common cause of the creation of god, man, etc., while the differences among these beings are due to their respective karma belonging to their inner nature. Therefore, Īśvara, who takes into account jīva's merit and demerit, cannot be blamed for partiality or cruelty.[21]

Obviously, the Vedantic view of creation is contrary to accidentalism as well as naturalism. It is also different from the dualism of the Sāṁkhya system. According to the Sāṁkhya system, insentient prakṛti and self-intelligent puruṣa (soul) are two distinct entities. Prakṛti is the material cause of the universe. It functions because of the proximity of puruṣa (soul). As the spectator of the evolutionary process of prakṛti, puruṣa is aloof from it. It is the successive transmutation (pariṇāma) of prakṛti in the proximity of puruṣa that gives rise to the whole universe, psychical and physical. So the Sāṁkhya theory of creation is called *pariṇāma-vāda* (the theory of actual modification) in contradistinction to *vivarta-vāda* (the theory of apparent modification) of Nondualistic Vedanta.

In the Nondualistic view the Supreme Being is immanent in the whole creation. Without undergoing any change whatsoever He appears as the manifold through names and forms (nāma-rūpa), the products of māyā. He is the sole entity. Māyā or prakṛti has no independent existence. It is wholly dependent on Īśvara as His power. He holds, controls, and directs it. Even as the immutable Witness of the cosmic process He is dynamic, because He sets prakṛti working by His watchful eye, so to speak. He is not a mere onlooker like puruṣa of the Sāṁkhya system. He is "the unmoved mover" of prakṛti. "He presides over past, present, and future."[22] Under His sovereign

[20]BG IX:10.

[21]BS II:1.34, S. com.

[22]Ka.U. II:1.12,13. See also Sv.U. IV:10, et seq.

control each and everything, animate or inanimate, great or small, functions according to the law of its being.[23] "Through fear of Him wind blows, the sun rises, the god of fire, the god of rain, and, the fifth, the god of death, rush."[24] Yet He is unattached, being unrelated.[25] Just as electricity that puts a machine in motion is not accountable for the specific functions of its various parts, so Īśvara is not directly responsible for the particular ways of different things and beings. Says Śrī Kṛṣṇa:

> Neither agency nor actions does the Lord create for the people. Nor does He connect actions with their respective fruits. It is prakṛti that brings about all these. The all-pervading Self takes on neither merit nor demerit of any. Knowledge [of the self] is veiled by ignorance; thereby the creatures are deluded.[26]

But the situation changes when the jīva becomes aware of the supremacy of Īśvara as the sole support and mover of prakṛti, that is, māyā, and no longer yields to it and holds to the ego, but takes refuge in Him, its Lord. Then māyā no more binds the jīva, but rather helps him to reach the Goal. He receives the divine guidance and protection. He finds in Īśvara "the Goal, the Protector, the Master, the Observer, the Abode, the Refuge and the Friend."[27] Śrī Kṛṣṇa says: "This inscrutable māyā of Mine, constituted of the guṇas, is difficult to overcome; but those who take refuge in Me alone get over this māyā."[28]

6. *The aim of Vedanta in delineating the process of creation is to maintain the unity underlying the diversity.*

The Upaniṣads give us varying accounts of the order of creation. In later Vedantic literature, however, we find a common cosmogony derived from them. In delineating the creative process, the main purpose of the Upaniṣads has been to maintain the unity of existence in multiplicity.[29] In order to convey the sole reality of Brahman they have presented Him by various illustrations and other methods both

[23] See Br.U. III:8.9.
[24] Tai.U. II:8.1.
[25] See Br.U. III:9.26.
[26] BG V:14,15.
[27] *Ibid.* IX:18.
[28] *Ibid.* VII:14.
[29] VP VII, "The passages dealing with the process of creation are intended not to maintain creation but to establish Brahman, the One only without a second."

as the efficient and the material cause of the manifold universe and then pointed out the falsity of plurality.[30]

The true interest of the Vedantic teachers has been not in the process of origination, but in the very origin, the ultimate ground, of the world of phenomena. In accounting for the variegated creation in all its stages they have kept in full view the omnipresent, ever-shining Self. "Just as the spider moves by means of the thread [it brings forth], just as from one fire tiny sparks proceed in all directions, so from this Self arise all organs, all worlds, all gods, and all beings."[31] From Ātman all this originates, in Ātman all this rests, and into Ātman all this is reabsorbed. "The luminous Self projects the Self by the Self through His māyā. It is He who cognizes the manifold. This is the conclusion of the Vedanta."[32] As observed by Śaṅkara, "The description of the origination, the continuity, and the dissolution of the universe in all Vedantic texts is to confirm the idea of the unity of existence free from all distinctions and not to convince one of the reality of creation."[33]

7. *How the living and the nonliving arise. Hiraṇyagarbha, the first created being.*

As the process of creation starts Hiraṇyagarbha (the cosmic soul) arises first. He is the first self-conscious being, the subject in opposition to the object, spirit in opposition to matter. So it is said: "Hiraṇyagarbha is the first embodied being to be born and is different from the Trinity (Brahmā, Viṣṇu, and Śiva). 'He indeed is the first embodied soul. He indeed is called a person [puruṣa].' "[34] It is said in the *Ṛg-Veda,* "Hiraṇyagarbha appeared first of all."[35] Īśvara (also called Parameśvara, the Supreme Lord) is extolled as the originator of Hiraṇyagarbha: "He who, in the beginning, brought forth Hiraṇyagarbha."[36] "He who saw Hiraṇyagarbha being born."[37]

It is Īśvara who endows him with the subtle and the gross body. His subtle body is the universal mind or cosmic intelligence (mahattattva). His gross body is the physical universe. As the presiding deity of the physical universe he is called Virāt. The manifestation of various orders of animate beings and inanimate nature is due to him. The word *Hiraṇyagarbha* literally means "the golden womb." Being impregnated by Īśvara through His glance or

[30]See MK III:15.
[31]Br.U. II:1.20.
[32]MK II:12.
[33]Br.U. II:1.20, S. com.
[34]VP VII.
[35]Rg.V. X:121.1.
[36]Sv.U. III:4.
[37]*Ibid.* IV:1.

reflection (īkṣaṇa), prakṛti conceives the first born jīva, the cosmic soul, whose body is cosmic intelligence and therefore radiant. As explained by Śaṅkara, "In that primordial nature I [Īśvara] deposit the germ of the birth of Hiraṇyagarbha, the seed from which all beings originate. . . . From this act of impregnation arise all beings through the birth of Hiraṇyagarbha."[38]

In due course minor jīvas, the individual souls, arise. It is jīvas' karma, the latent impressions of past actions and experiences inherent in their causal bodies, that determine the nature of their subtle and gross bodies and also the external conditions in which they are born. The diversity of the objective universe, psychical and physical, follows from the diversity of jīvas' inner nature. Regarding the order of creation, Gauḍapāda says, "At first the jīva is manifested and then the variety of internal and external objects."[39] The manifestation of the objective universe is intended for the experience of the living beings and their progressive movement towards liberation.[40]

At the inception the jīva has the causal body, with which he lies dormant in undifferentiated prakṛti. Ajñāna, the limiting adjunct of the individual soul, is the causal body (kāraṇa śarīra), because it contains the germ of the subtle and the gross body. In fact, the subtle body with the deposit of karma, the impressions of past actions and experiences, remains there in potential form. After the development of the subtle body, the jīva is endowed with the gross, that is, the physical body. His physical body is renewed each time he is born, but the subtle body endures throughout his births and rebirths until he attains liberation from the cycle.[41]

8. *The origination and nature of the five subtle elements constituting the jīva's subtle body and of the five gross elements constituting his physical body and the physical cosmos.*

The subtle body of every jīva is composed of the five subtle elements (sūkṣma bhūtas): akāśa (ether), vāyu (air), tejas (fire), ap (water), and pṛthivī (earth). The gross or physical body of every jīva is composed of five corresponding gross elements (sthūla bhūtas), which are the compounds of the five subtle elements. Unlike the

[38]BG XIV:3, S. com.
[39]MK II:16.
[40]Cf. SK 21 and *Tattva-kaumudī.*
[41]See the author's book, *The Goal and the Way,* Chap. "How Is a Man Reborn?"

gross, the subtle element is simple, that is, unmixed with any other subtle element. So, it is designated tanmātrā (lit. that alone). For example, subtle ākāśa is pure and simple ākāśa, but gross ākāśa is a compound of all the five subtle elements with the preponderance of ākāśa. Similarly, subtle vāyu is pure and simple vāyu, but gross vāyu is a compound of all the five subtle elements with the preponderance of vāyu; and so on. The subtle body (sūkṣma śarīra), of which mind is the principal component, is also called liṅga śarīra (index body), because it indicates the nature of the jīva, whereas the causal does not.

The five subtle elements with tamas predominant in each, being compounded by the process of the fivefold combination called *pañcīkaraṇa* (quintuplication), produce the five gross elements. It is as follows:

> Divide each subtle element into two halves and subdivide the first half of each element into four equal parts; then add to the other half of each element one subdivision of each of the remaining four; so that each compound element contains all the five.[42]

Thus, gross ākāśa contains half subtle ākāśa and one-eighth of each of the remaining four subtle elements; gross vāyu contains half subtle vāyu and one-eighth of each of the remaining four subtle elements; gross tejas contains half subtle tejas and one-eighth of each of the remaining four subtle elements; and so on.[43]

These five gross elements (sthūla bhūtas) are all the ingredients of the sensible world. From the viewpoint of sense-perception the whole physical world consists basically of five kinds of material substances: (1) audible, (2) tangible, (3) visible, (4) tastable, and (5) smellable. They have the following five forms: (1) etheric, (2) aerial, (3) fiery, (4) liquid, and (5) solid. They are signified respectively by the terms: ākāśa (ether), vāyu (air), tejas (fire or light), ap (water), and pṛthivī (earth). These are the five gross elements. Ākāśa is the finest of them.

The five subtle elements (sūkṣma bhūtas), of which the gross are compounded, are rudimentary and imperceptible. They are the original states of the five types of sensible matter. To quote Dr. Seal:

[42]Pd. I:27.

[43]The table of quintuplication:

Gross elements		*Subtle elements*					
Ākāśa (ether)	= 1/2 ākāśa	+ 1/8 (vāyu	+ tejas	+ ap	+ pṛthivī)		
Vāyu (air)	= 1/2 vāyu	+ 1/8 (ākāśa	+ tejas	+ ap	+ pṛthivī)		
Tejas (fire)	= 1/2 tejas	+ 1/8 (ākāśa	+ vāyu	+ ap	+ pṛthivī)		
Ap (water)	= 1/2 ap	+ 1/8 (ākāśa	+ vāyu	+ tejas	+ pṛthivī)		
Pṛthivī (earth)	= 1/2 pṛthivī	+ 1/8 (ākāśa	+ vāyu	+ tejas	+ ap)		

> The sūkṣma bhūtas (subtle elements) are forms of homogeneous and continuous matter without any atomicity of structure; the mahābhūtas (gross elements) are composite; but even these are regarded as continuous and without any atomic structure. Vedanta speaks of aṇu, paramāṇu [minute particle such as atom], not as an ultimate, indivisible, discrete constituent of matter, but as the smallest conceivable quantum or measure of matter.[44]

Gross ākāśa has one property: sound. It is all-pervasive, imponderable, and inert. Gross vāyu has two properties: sound and touch; its special property is touch. It is aeriform matter instinct with kinetic energy. Gross tejas has three properties: sound, touch, and color; its special property is color. It is radiant matter instinct with the energy of heat and light. Gross ap has four properties: sound, touch, color, and taste; its special property is taste. It is odorless liquid matter that stimulates particularly the organ of taste. Gross pṛthivī has five properties: sound, touch, color, taste, and smell; its special property is smell. It is solidified matter that stimulates particularly the organ of smell. Fundamentally, there are only five sense-objects: sound, touch, color, taste, and smell, which invariably belong to some concrete thing.

The Nyāya and Vaiśeṣika schools, however, conceive four of the elements, namely, earth, water, light, and air, as atomic in their ultimate form. Each of them is constituted of a particular type of atom (paramāṇus). These atoms are indivisible, indestructible, infinitesimal, and supersensible. Ākāśa is infinite and all-pervading. Thus, there are four original types of atoms according to Nyāya-Vaiśeṣika; while, according to Greek atomic theory, as stated by Democritus, there is no qualitative, but purely quantitative, difference in atoms.

How do the elements originate? It is to be noted that each and everything arises from Brahman associated with māyā, because He is the one source of all. As the Reality underlying the apparent manifold He is the sole material cause. Evidently, a clay pot originates from clay. But the fact is that Brahman associated with māyā, appearing as a lump of clay, reappears as a pot. There is no other substance but Brahman. "Of all created things Pure Existence is the origin, Pure Existence is the support, and Pure Existence is the goal," says the sage Uddālaka to his son Śvetaketu.[45] It is said in the *Muṇḍaka Upaniṣad,*

[44]Brajendranath Seal, *The Positive Sciences of the Ancient Hindus,* Harlow, Essex, Longmans Green, 1915, p.88.

[45]Ch.U. VI:8,4.

"From Him (Saguṇa Brahman) arise the life principle, mind, all the sense organs, ākāśa (ether), vāyu (air), tejas (fire), ap (water), and pṛthivī (earth) that supports all."[46] Of all these ākāśa is the first to appear. "From this Supreme Self ākāśa is born."[47] It has been noted above (see Chap. V, sec. 4) that māyā or avidyā has two distinct functions: (1) veiling the Supreme Being, and (2) projecting the phenomenal world. From Brahman associated with the projecting power of māyā, while tamas is predominant, originates ākāśa, from ākāśa vāyu, from vāyu tejas, from tejas ap, and from ap pṛthivī. These are the five subtle elements. Each of them is constituted of the three guṇas (sattva, rajas, and tamas) with a preponderance of tamas. But tamas is not equally preponderant in all the five elements. There is greater preponderance of tamas in them successively from ether down to solid earth.

9. *The psychophysical constitution of the jīva.*

It is the subtle elements which develop the subtle body. All the seventeen component factors of the subtle body grow out of them. These are the two modes of mind (antaḥkaraṇa) — deliberative (manas) and determinative (buddhi), the five vital forces, the five organs of perception, and the five organs of action.[48] The cognitive mind has four modes representing four different functions: manas, buddhi, ahaṁkāra, and citta. Manas is the function of cogitation; buddhi is the function of determination or decision; ahaṁkāra is the function of ego-consciousness expressing itself as "I-ness" and "my-ness"; citta is the function of recollection. In every act of cognition there are these four functions of mind. It is a fourfold process. Vedanta considers cognition the primary function of mind, because its other functions, such as feeling, willing, imagining, etc., rest on this. So the four functions — manas, buddhi, ahaṁkāra, and citta — stand for the whole mind. Among the constituents of the subtle body only the first two functions are mentioned to signify the entire mind; the other two functions — ahaṁkāra and citta — are included in manas and buddhi.[49] In Vedanta mind is termed *antaḥkaraṇa,* lit. the internal instrument, being distinct from the external organs — the instruments of perception and action — which deal directly with the physical objects.

The five vital forces are prāṇa, apāna, vyāna, udāna, and

[46]Mu.U. II:1.3. [47]Tai.U. II:1.1. [48]See AB XII. [49]See VS XIII.

samāna.[50] Prāṇa is the general name of the life principle, which has these five names according to its five specific functions.[51] Though operating on the physical body, the five prāṇas belong to the subtle body.

The five organs of perception or sense organs are the ears, the skin, the eyes, the tongue, and the nose. These are the instruments of cognition or knowledge. Accordingly there are five types of sensible objects: audible, tangible, visible, tastable, and smellable. The five organs of action or motor organs are the organ of speech, the hands, the feet, and the organs of evacuation and generation. Obviously, these ten organs are located in the physical body. But these physical instruments are not, according to Vedanta, the actual organs (indriyas). Strictly speaking, the real organs (indriyas) are the subtle counterparts of the physical organs, through which they operate. They are located in the subtle body. The specific powers of the ten bodily organs are derived from their subtle counterparts, the real organs (indriyas). The subtle sense organs are distinct from the nerve centers as well. They are capable of immediate expansion and contraction. They function through the corresponding bodily organs or end organs.

Now we shall see how the different components of the subtle body develop from the five subtle elements. In all these elements sattva and rajas are more or less operative, while tamas preponderates in varying degrees. These three constituents are inseparable like the three sides of a triangle. The five subtle elements, however, can operate, singly or jointly, in any of these aspects. The sattva aspect of the five subtle elements, being combined, develops mind. Because of the essence of sattva, mind has the capacity to manifest the light of consciousness. The sattva aspect of the five subtle elements severally produces the five organs of perception in succession. Thus, the sattva aspect of ākāśa (ether) produces the organ of hearing, of vāyu (air) the organ of

[50]See Br.U. I:5.3, S.com.; Ch.U. I:3-5; VS XIII.

[51]*Prāṇa,* specifically, is the life principle operative in the lungs and the heart and responsible for respiration. It functioning, other vital forces function. *Apāna* functions below the heart down to the navel and helps elimination. *Samāna* (lit., the equalizer) is located in the stomach; it digests and assimilates food and drink, and causes circulation of blood. *Vyāna* (lit. the pervading one) is so called because it pervades the body and operates on the nerves. It is responsible for utterance of speech and actions of great effort. It regulates prāṇa and apāna as their nexus. *Udāna* maintains bodily heat and promotes growth. It also helps the soul in passing out of the body at death. As it leaves, the body loses all heat.

Prāṇa, Apāna, and *Samāna* are responsible for the functions of the autonomic nervous system. *Vyāna* and *Udāna* are associated with the cerebro-spinal system.

touch, of tejas (fire) the organ of sight, of ap (water) the organ of taste, of pṛthivī (earth) the organ of smell. Because of the essence of sattva in them the organs of perception are illuminative. The rajas aspect of the five subtle elements, being combined, generates prāṇa, the life principle with its five main functions. The rajas aspect of the five subtle elements severally produces the five organs of action in succession. Thus, the rajas aspect of ākāśa (ether) produces the organ of speech, of vāyu (air) the hands, of tejas (fire) the feet, and so on. Because of the prevalence of rajas, the five prāṇas and the five organs of action have motive force.

10. *The continuity of the evolutionary process from the lowest to the highest order of life without the transformation of one species into another. Evolution presupposes involution.*

The five gross elements constitute the entire physical universe. All inanimate objects and the gross or physical bodies of all animate beings are composed of them. Every living creature, including the plant, is a jīva, an embodied soul. Each has a threefold body more or less developed. There are four kinds of jīvas with four kinds of physical bodies according to birth: (1) those born of the mother's womb, such as men, quadrupeds, etc.; (2) those born of eggs, such as birds, reptiles, etc.; (3) those born in moisture, such as lice, mosquitoes, etc.; and (4) those that spring from earth, such as trees, creepers, etc. Plants not only live but feel also. Wherever there is livingness there is sentiency. Among all animate beings there is the least manifestation of consciousness in plants.[52] These are designated as nonmoving (sthāvara) and the rest as moving (jaṅgama).

In the Vedantic view varieties of living forms exist from the beginning. The different types of animate beings arise when and where the conditions are favorable to their existence; just as many living things that disappear in winter emerge with the advent of spring. Truly, there is no conclusive proof of the beginning of life. "As to the origin of living things on the earth we know nothing," says Johnston.[53] The Vedantic idea of evolution supports the views held by some modern biologists that "all living things are derived from living things and are not generated from nonliving things" and there is no unbridgeable gap between the plant and the animal life.

[52]Cf. MS XII:13.

[53]James Johnston, *The Essentials of Biology,* New York, Longmans Green, 1932, p.274.

Each jīva assumes higher and higher physical form with the evolution of his inner nature. In fact, it is his subtle body that develops the gross body. He leaves the gross body at death but not the subtle body. Strictly speaking, the continuity of the jīva's evolution is in his subtle body; because he retains the same subtle body all along until he attains the final Liberation, absorption in Nirguṇa Brahman. His gross body does not evolve in the same sense. He leaves the physical body at death and is reborn in another. He successively attains new physical forms. In course of time he passes from the physical form of one species into that of another. Each time he is born in a particular species he gets the physical body from parents belonging to the species. For instance, a jīva in the ape form acquires, after many births in higher and higher physical forms, the competence for taking on the human form. As his subtle body rises by slow stages from the subhuman to the human level, he secures the seed of a human body from human parents. This is how Vedanta envisages the evolution of an individual jīva. It is not that the very ape-body develops into a human body in successive generations. One species is not transformed into another by the slow process of procreation in course of time.

Vedanta agrees with the biological evolutionists that heredity and environment can modify a species, but it holds neither of the two to be the basic cause of the evolution of a living organism. The secret of evolution is, in its view, in the organism itself. A similar idea is noticeable in modern biological thought. According to the psychobiological conception of the living organism creativeness is innate in its psychophysical system, particularly the psychical.[54] According to the Doctrine of Emergence, however, the cause of evolution is the creativity of life.[55] But neither of the two views account for the persistent development of higher and higher forms of life. The evolutionary process involves not only the mystery of *continued change,* but also the mystery of *continued progress.* Darwin wisely confessed: "Our ignorance of the laws of variation is profound."[56]

In the Vedantic view the cause of evolution is much deeper. It is the innermost urge of the living organism for the realization of the true nature of the self, which is intrinsically pure, free and perfect.

[54]Ralph Stayner Lillie, *General Biology and Philosophy of Organisms,* University of Chicago Press, 1945, pp. 22,87.

[55]C.E.M. Joad, *Guide to Modern Thought,* London, Faber and Faber, 1933, p.138.

[56]See Patrick Geddes and J. Arthur Thomson, *Evolution,* New York, Henry Holt, 1911, p.140.

Involution precedes evolution. As observed by Swami Vivekananda:

> From the lowest protoplasm to the most perfect human being, there is really but one life. Just as in one life we have so many various phases of expression, the protoplasm developing into the baby, the child, the young man, the old man, so, from that protoplasm up to the most perfect man, we get one continuous life, one chain. This is evolution; but each evolution presupposes an involution. The whole of this life — which slowly manifests itself, evolves itself from the protoplasm to the perfected human being, the Incarnation of God on earth — the whole of this series is but one life, and the whole of this manifestation must have been involved in that very protoplasm. This whole life, this very God on earth was involved in it, and slowly came out, manifesting itself slowly, slowly, slowly.[57]

Beginning from the plant life there has been greater and greater manifestation of the Self successively.

11. *The jīva's spiritual self does not evolve but has greater and greater manifestation with the evolution of the psychophysical organism.*

It is the jīva's psychophysical constitution composed of the gross and the subtle body that evolves. There is no evolution in the indwelling spirit, the real self, which is changeless. But there is greater and greater manifestation of the spiritual self as wisdom, mastery, and so forth, with the evolution of the jīva's psychophysical system from the lowest to the highest.[58] It is in human incarnation that the greatest manifestation of inner consciousness becomes possible. Plants may feel, lower animals may cognize, but humans can think. Man is the only animal that possesses reason, in Aristotle's view.[59] Not only that; self-knowledge attains its culmination in human life. According to Hindu tradition a jīva (from the stage of a protozoan, perhaps) attains competence for a human body after undergoing 8,400,000 births. Of all the sentient beings man alone has definite self-awareness. He knows himself as a distinct individual. He has the power to distinguish the self from the not-self. He can discriminate the innermost self from its adjuncts — the body, the organs, and the mind. Self-preservation is an instinct common to all living things, but striving for Self-knowledge is the special privilege of human life.

[57]CW II, p. 228.

[58]See BS I:3.30, S. com.

[59]*Politics,* 1, 2, 1253a 10, in *The Works of Aristotle: II, Great Books of the Western World,* University of Chicago, 1952, no. 9, p. 446.

The development of a jīva's psychophysical constitution is due to his innate urge for Self-realization. His spiritual self is intrinsically divine. The spirit requires better and better vehicles of expression. The manifestation of the spiritual self is effected by the removal of obstructions to it from the psychophysical system, which evolves in consequence. This leads to the transformation of a jīva's body from one species into another. As stated by Patanjali:

> The change of the body from one species into another is caused by the inflowing of [the jīva's] nature. Good and bad deeds are not the direct causes of its transformation. They act as breakers of obstacles to the inflow of nature, just as a farmer breaks down obstacles in a water course to let water flow of itself.[60]

Swami Vivekananda aptly remarks:

> Perfection is man's nature, only it is barred in and prevented from taking its proper course. If anyone can take the bar off, in rushes nature. . . . The two causes of evolution advanced by the moderns, *viz.,* sexual selection and survival of the fittest, are inadequate. Suppose human knowledge to have advanced so much as to eliminate competition, both from the function of acquiring physical sustenance and of acquiring a mate. Then, according to the moderns, human progress will stop and the race will die. . . . But the great ancient evolutionist, Patañjali, declares that the true secret of evolution is the manifestation of the perfection which is already in every being, that this perfection has been barred and the infinite tide behind is struggling to express itself. These struggles and competitions are but the results of our ignorance, because we do not know the proper way to unlock the gate and let the water in. This infinite tide behind must express itself; it is the cause of all manifestation. . . . Even when all competition has ceased this perfect nature behind will make us go forward until everyone has become perfect. Therefore, there is no reason to believe that competition is necessary to progress.[61]
>
> In the animal kingdom we really see such laws as struggle for existence, survival of the fittest, etc., evidently at work. Therefore Darwin's theory seems true to a certain extent. But in the human kingdom, where there is the manifestation of rationality, we find just the reverse of those laws. . . . The highest evolution of man is effected through sacrifice alone. A man is great among his fellow beings in proportion as he can sacrifice for the sake of others; whereas in the lower strata of the animal kingdom, that animal is the strongest which can kill the greatest number of animals. Hence the struggle theory is not equally

[60]YS IV:2,3.
[61]*Ibid.* com., CW I, p. 292.

applicable to both kingdoms. Man's struggle is in the mental sphere. A man is greater in proportion as he can control his mind. When the mind's activities are perfectly at rest, the Ātman manifests Itself.[62]

12. *The role of Hiraṇyagarbha (the cosmic soul) in the cosmic process.*

Let us turn to the order of creation. According to the *Vedānta-paribhāṣā,* it is through the direct agency of Parameśvara (the Supreme Lord) that the subtle and the gross elements originate, that Hiraṇyagarbha's subtle body — the cosmic intelligence — and his gross body — the physical cosmos — arise, and that the subtle bodies of all individual jīvas emerge. In the production of the jīvas' gross bodies and the rest of the physical universe His agency is indirect, being through the medium of Hiraṇyagarbha.[63] Evidently, Hiraṇyagarbha works on the gross elements provided by Parameśvara and gives them specific forms by compounding them. Since he is the first embodied being and is instrumental in providing all individual jīvas with physical bodies he is called Prajāpati, progenitor of living beings. He is also the first teacher of mankind. After creating Brahmā (Hiraṇyagarbha) the Supreme Lord imparted to Him the Vedic lore.[64] The Vedic lore has been transmitted to humanity through a succession of teachers beginning with Hiraṇyagarbha. Beyond Him the line of teachers does not extend.[65] Having as His limiting adjunct the cosmic intelligence, which is extremely pure, Hiraṇyagarbha is far above all individual jīvas and is close to the Supreme Self.

The Hindu conception of the physical cosmos testifies how well impressed the ancient sages of India were by the immensity of the space-time continuum. It has no limit spatially or temporally. Without beginning and without end, it continues to pass from the potential to the manifest state and from the manifest to the potential state. The order of Creation is an eternal process. The physical universe open to our view — with the living and the nonliving, with the sun, the moon, the stars and the planets — is but one of the innumerable world-systems that compose the cosmos. Throughout eternity the world-systems severally and the cosmos as a whole pass through the three consecutive stages of projection (sṛṣṭi), preserva-

[62]CW VII, p. 154-55.
[63]See VP VII.
[64]Sv.U. VI:18.
[65]Br.U. II:6.2.

tion (sthiti), and dissolution (pralaya), which form a complete cycle.[66]

Each world-system is the domain of a Brahmā or Hiraṇyagarbha. Having arisen from the embryonic stage induced by Brahmā (Īśvara as the Creator)[67] it is called Brahmāṇḍa (lit. the egg of Brahmā). It is composed of the same five gross elements (mahābhūtas), of which the gross bodies of all living creatures and also their food and drink are made. The world-system to which the earth belongs comprises fourteen major spheres (lōkas or bhuvanas), one situated above another according to the grade. All of them are said to be inhabited by jīvas. Seven of them are below the earthly level, the terrestrial region. Beginning with the lowest these are Atala, Vitala, Sutala, Rasātala, Talātala, Mahātala, and Pātāla. The seven upper spheres are Bhurlōka (the earth), Bhuvarlōka or Antarikṣa lōka (the celestial sphere with the sun, the moon, the planets, and the stars), Svarlōka or Mahendralōka (the first heaven of the righteous), Maharlōka (the higher heaven of the deified mortals), Janalōka, Taparlōka, and Satyalōka.[68]

These seven spheres are accessible to human beings according to their development. The last three are the gradations of Brahmalōka, the domain of Brahmā or Hiraṇyagarbha. Satyalōka is the highest plane in the relative order. It is the abode of Brahmā or Hiraṇyagarbha. Those who worship Saguṇa Brahman with whole-souled devotion reach there after death and live in full awareness of their essential unity with the Divinity. Being released from the round of births and rebirths, they do not return to the mortal plane. At the close of the cycle, when, on the expiry of Hiraṇyagarbha's term of life, "the basic dissolution"[69] takes place, then they (the worshippers of

[66]It has been stated above (see sec.2) that in the basic or the causal dissolution (prākṛta pralaya) the manifest world resolves into undifferentiated prakṛti, the potential cause, from which it rises again in the beginning of a new cycle. When a person attains final Liberation by realizing Brahman, the entire objective universe with its root cause, ajñāna, ceases to exist for him. But the world continues as an object of experience for all other jīvas. Since the jīvas are innumerable, the subject-object correlation never ends as a whole. This is the view of Patañjali as explained by Vyāsa and Vācaspati (YS II:22, *Tattva-vaiśāradī*). So the absolute dissolution of the universe, in which prakṛti or māyā vanishes altogether, is, according to them, improbable. Such a possibility has, however, been conceived by the Vedantic teachers in general. As stated in the *Vedānta-paribhāṣā* (sec. VII), the absolute dissolution (ātyantika pralaya) follows from the Liberation of all the jīvas on the realization of Brahman; according to the theory of single jīvas it is simultaneous, according to the theory of multiple jīvas it is gradual.

[67]See footnote 1, p. 110.

[68]See VS 16; VP VII; YS III:26, S.com.

[69]The reversion of the manifest universe into undifferentiated nature (avyākṛta prakṛti), its basic cause. This is called *Prākṛta pralaya.*

Saguṇa Brahman who reach Satyalōka), realize the identity of the Self with Nirguṇa Brahman, and attain final Liberation along with Him.[70] Hiraṇyagarbha is succeeded by another embodied being qualified for the position.

Hiraṇyagarbha's lifetime spans one cycle of projection-preservation-dissolution of the world-system (Brahmāṇḍa). Its duration is one hundred years, which is equivalent to two hundred thousand billion human years. (We are now considering particularly the world-system to which the earth belongs.) On each day and night of Hiraṇyagarbha a certain part of the world-system passes through a similar cycle. His day brings about the manifestation of its three regions — Bhurlōka (the earth), Bhuvarlōka (the celestial region), and Svarlōka (the heaven), his night their absorption. The *Bhagavad-gītā* thus refers to this "diurnal" cycle:

> On the approach of the day (of Brahmā) all manifested objects proceed from the unmanifested and on the approach of the night they merge in the same causal state, called the unmanifested.[71]

The expression "all manifested objects" signifies the above lōkas, which are more familiar to human beings than the rest. The term *the unmanifested* (avyakta) in the present context refers to Brahmā's sleep state, and not to the undifferentiated nature (avyākṛta prakṛti).

Brahmā's day and night are equal. Each covers 4,320 million human years.[72] His day is his waking state and the night his sleep, so to speak. His sleep is the withdrawal unto himself of the three lōkas (Bhūḥ, Bhuvaḥ, Svaḥ), which rise again as he awakes. This withdrawal or dissolution for the time being is called *naimittika pralaya* (intermediary dissolution).[73] It is short and partial in relation to "the basic dissolution (prākṛta pralaya)," in which the entire world-system of Hiraṇyagarbha with the whole series of causes and effects becomes merged in the primary cause — the undifferentiated prakṛti.

[70]VP VII. This is the Nondualistic view.

[71]BG VIII:18.

[72]The measure of Brahmā's day is one thousand "four yugas." The four yugas (eras) are Satya, Tretā, Dwāpara, and Kali, which rotate in succession. The duration of Kali yuga is 432,000 years. Dwāpara is twice as long as Kali. Tretā is three times and Satya four times of Kali. So the four yugas extend over 4,320,000 years. Brahmā's day is, therefore, 4,320,000,000 — four billion three hundred twenty million human years. (BG VIII:17; *Bṛhannāradīya Purāṇam,* XXXII:86) Of the four yugas (eras), Satya is the best — the golden age, Kali is the worst — the iron age. Tretā can be counted as the silver age and Dwāpara as the bronze age.

[73]VP VII.

13. *The Supreme Being, the Prime Mover of the universe, ever shines in His transcendent glory. He is the Adorable Lord.*

But the cosmic process does not affect the Imperishable Brahman. So it is said: "But beyond this unmanifested (undifferentiated Nature, avyākṛta prakṛti) there is yet another Unmanifested Eternal Being who does not perish even when all beings perish."[74] Brahman is the sole source of the variegated world. Animate or inanimate, everything is in essence the Ultimate Being. The subject and the object, the self and the not-self, are aspects of the same Reality. All differences are due to name and form (nāma-rūpa), which have an apparent existence. The universe contains the features of Brahman and also of māyā.

Existence, manifestation, and agreeableness are the aspects of Brahman; name and form (nāma-rūpa) are the aspects of māyā.[75] The last two are at the root of individuation; they superimpose variety on Unity. Says Śaṅkara, "The variety of experience subsists in the Self (Ātman) as the [illusory] snake does in the rope."[76] The Self exists in and through everything. Behind the phenomenal plurality there is the absolute unity of Brahman. "One effulgent Being is hidden in all things. All-pervading, He is the inmost Self of all creatures. He presides over the law of karma. All beings abide in Him. He is the Witness. He is Pure Consciousness, free from the guṇas and transcendent."[77] He holds the manifold with but a fraction of His Being as its Internal Ruler. Śrī Kṛṣṇa says, "I exist pervading the entire universe by a portion of Myself."[78] The Supreme Lord is the creator and teacher of Hiraṇyagarbha. He is the giver of Self-knowledge. He is the sole refuge of the seeker of Truth, who says the following prayer:

> Seeking Liberation I take refuge in that effulgent Being who in the beginning created Brahmā and delivered to him the Vedas, who is the revealer of Self-knowledge, who is indivisible, beyond activity, tranquil, faultless, stainless, who is the supreme bridge of immortality and resembles the blazing fire that has burnt all fuel [destroyed the seeker's ignorance].[79]

[74]BG VIII:20.
[75]Cf. *Dṛg-dṛśya-viveka (Vākya-sudhā),* 20.
[76]BS III:2.22, S.com.
[77]Sv.U. VI:11.
[78]BG X:42.
[79]Sv.U. VI:18,19.

CHAPTER VII

THE CREATION FROM THE WORD

1. *This is an ancient view prevalent in varying forms among the Indo-Aryans, the Greeks, the Hebrews, and the Christians.*

That "the universe arises from the Word (śabdāt prabhavati jagat)" has been declared by the Vedas from the earliest days.[1] As observed by Śaṅkara, the fact that the Word precedes creation (śabdapūrvikā sṛṣṭiḥ)[2] is held both by the *Śruti* and the *Smṛti.*[3] In the Vedas we find such statements as:

> Verily, in the beginning Prajāpati (the Creator, lit. the Lord of creatures) alone existed here. (Prajāpatirvai idam agre āsīt eka eva.)[4]
>
> Verily, Prajāpati alone was this universe. With Him was only vāk (the Word), as His own, as a second. (Prajāpatirvai idam eka āsīt. Tasya vāg eva svam āsīd vāg dvitīyā.)[5]
>
> Vāk (the Word) is coextensive with Brahman. (Yāvat Brahman tiṣṭhati tāvatī vāk.)[6]
>
> Verily, vāk (the Word) is the unborn one. It was from vāk (the Word) that the Maker of the universe produced creatures. (Vāgvai ajā vāchō vai prajāḥ viśvakarmā yajāna.)[7]

A similar view is expressed by St. John in the opening lines of the *Fourth Gospel:*

> In the beginning was the Word and the Word was with God and the Word was God.

[1]BS I:3.28, S.com.

[2]*Ibid.*

[3]As defined by Manu, "By Śruti is meant the Veda and by Smṛti the Dharmaśāstras (scriptures for the regulation of life)." (MS II:10) In a wide sense Smṛti includes all scriptures subordinate to the Vedas. Literally, Śruti means that which is heard (revelation); Smṛti means that which is remembered (tradition). (See Chap.I, sec.3)

[4]Sat.Br. VII:5.2.6.

[5]*Pañcaviṁśa Brāhmaṇa* XX:14.2, (also called *Tāṇḍya-Mahābrāhmaṇa* of the *Sāma Veda*).

[6]Rg.V. X:114.8.

[7]Sat.Br. VII:5.2.21.

The same was in the beginning with God.
All things were made by him; and without him was not any thing made that was made.

Thus, according to both Hinduism and Christianity the whole creation has proceeded from Vāk (the Word). The conception of the Word (Hebrew *Memra,* Greek *Logos*) as the creative principle was prevalent in varying forms among the ancient Hebrews and the Greeks. In the *Old Testament* we read:

And God said, Let there be light; and there was light.[8]

By the word of the Lord were the heavens made; and all the host of them by the breath of his mouth.[9]

The primary meaning of *Logos* (from *lego,* to speak) is "meaningful word." It connotes "active reason." The Stoics conceived Logos as the creative reason *(logos spermatikos)* that unfolds and sustains the manifold. It is the seed of the universe.

According to many eminent writers, St. John, the author of the *Fourth Gospel,* got the idea from Philo, the Jewish philosopher of Alexandria, and adapted it to the personality of Jesus Christ as the Saviour.[10] Philo Judaeus, known as "the Jewish Plato" lived in the late first century B.C. and the early first century A.D. He was thus a senior contemporary of Jesus Christ. He sought to harmonize the

[8]*Genesis* 1.3.

[9]*Psalms* 33.6.

[10]Cf. *Encyclopaedia Britannica,* 1948 edn., s.v. "Logos":

"Among the influences that shaped the Fourth Gospel that of the Alexandrian philosophy must be assigned a distinct, though not an exaggerated importance. There are other books in the New Testament that bear the same impress, the Epistles to the Ephesians and the Colossians, and to a much greater degree the Epistle to the Hebrews. The development that had thus begun in the time of Paul reaches maturity in the Fourth Gospel, whose dependence on Philo appears (1) in the use of the allegorical method, (2) in many coincident passages, (3) in the dominant conception of the Logos.

"The writer narrates the life of Christ from the point of view furnished him by Philo's theory. True, the Logos doctrine is only mentioned in the prologue to the Gospel, but it is presupposed throughout the whole book. The author's task indeed was somewhat akin to that of Philo, 'to transplant into the world of Hellenic culture a revelation originally given through Judaism.'

"This is not to say that he holds the Logos doctrine in exactly the same form as Philo. On the contrary, the fact that he starts from an actual knowledge of the earthly life of Jesus, while Philo, even when ascribing a real personality to Logos, keeps within the bounds of abstract speculation, leads him seriously to modify the Philonic doctrine . . . What John thus does is to take the Logos idea of Philo and use it for a practical purpose — to make more intelligible to himself and his readers the divine nature of Jesus Christ."

speculative philosophy of Greece, particularly Stoicism and Platonism, with the tenets of Judaism and developed his doctrine of the Logos. In the words of Dr. Radhakrishnan:

> In Alexandria, which was the meeting-place of East and West, Philo developed his new interpretation of the Jewish scriptures. It is the systematic attempt to combine Jewish teaching with Hellenic ideas, to express the religious conceptions of the Jewish prophets in the language of the Greek philosophers. He tried to bring together under the inspiration of his personal experience the dogmas of the Jewish revelation and the results of Greek speculative wisdom. The central and the determining feature of Philo's system is the doctrine of the Logos.[11]

2. *The significance of Vāk (the Word) in the Vedic texts quoted above.*

What does the Sanskrit *Vāk* (English *Word,* Greek *Logos*) signify in this context? The word *vāk* is from the root *vach,* to speak. Literally, it means voice (Latin *vox*). It signifies the word, uttered or written, which has a meaning. Some idea, thought, or reason is implicit in *vāk*. In fact, the Sanskrit *Vāk* and the Greek *Logos* (from *lego,* to speak) have the same etymological sense. Synonymous with *Vāk* is the Sanskrit term *śabda* (sound or word). A word is the verbal symbol of a concept. It connotes a class or a species. The concrete material form denoted by a word, such as *chair,* is the object perceived by the senses. But the word *chair* does not imply the percept, but the concept of chair. It signifies chair in general and not any particular chair. An object, its class name, and the concept are closely related. An individual thing or being represents a universal, or a type, which is signified by a corresponding name or word. There being a natural relation between the manifest object and the word embodying the concept, the religious view that the word precedes creation is not without reason. As observed by Prof. Max Müller:

> The word is the manifestation of thought; every word, we must remember, expresses a concept, not a percept. *Tree* is not meant for this or that tree, it is the general concept of all trees; and if every individual thing is the realization of an ideal type or thought or word, if every man, for instance, is the realization of the divine thought or word of man, or of manhood, we need not be startled when we find in India

[11] S. Radhakrishnan, *Eastern Religions and Western Thought,* 2nd edn., London, Oxford University Press, 1940, p. 191.

as well as in Greece a belief that God created the world by the logos or by the word, or by many words, the logoi, the ideas of Plato, the species or types of modern science.[12]

According to Vedanta the cosmic process continues endlessly in the cyclic order of projection, preservation, and dissolution. At the dissolution of the cosmic order (prākṛta pralaya) the whole variegated universe antecedent to the event reverts to the undifferentiated prakṛti, the māyā-śakti of Īśvara. Even Brahmalōka, the highest sphere of the cosmos, is dissolved. Hiraṇyagarbha, its ruler, and the free souls dwelling there, become disembodied and attain final Liberation in the supreme state of oneness with Brahman. The bound jīvas lie dormant with their causal bodies merged in undifferentiated prakṛti.

In due course, of incalculable duration, their karma, the latent impressions of past actions and experiences, become ready to bear fruit. Then Īśvara plans the creation in accordance with their merits and demerits and the unfoldment of their consciousness. In the words of Śaṅkara: "He reflected concerning the order and arrangement of the world to be created. Having thus reflected he created the universe with time and space, as required by the karma and other conditions of the living beings. This is the universe that is being experienced by all creatures in all states according to their perception."[13]

Evidently, the new creation is the development of the physical cosmos in conformity with the psychical realm, the inner nature of the jīvas. In fact, it is a readjustment of the natural to the moral order. The purpose is to lead the jīvas through experience to Liberation beyond the realm of experience.

The Vedic texts declare consistently that Īśvara "saw" or "viewed" before the creation:

He viewed: may I be many, may I be born variously.[14]

He willed: let Me be many, let Me be born variously.[15]

His activity consists in His knowledge or thought (yasya jñānamayam tapaḥ).[16] He makes no effort. He manifests the universe by His ideation and will. Like an architect, the Maker of the universe conceives the whole creation. But while the human architect depends

[12]F. Max Müller, *The Vedanta Philosophy,* Calcutta, Susil Gupta, 1955, pp.76-7. (Three lectures delivered at the Royal Institution, London, in March 1894, first published in London in 1894.)

[13]Tai.U. II:6, S.com. [14]Ch.U. VI:2.3. [15]Tai.U. II:6. [16]See Mu.U. I:1.9.

on external means to carry out his plan, the Divine architect needs nothing extraneous, i.e., outside Himself. He needs no preexistent material to work on. The manifold comprising the living and the nonliving is contained potentially in His māyā-śakti (prakṛti), the creative energy, inclusive of the power of will and the power of knowledge.

His will, ever associated with the sattva aspect of prakṛti, affects Him in no way. He wills not out of necessity, but out of freedom. Wisdom and joyousness are implicit in His will. His thought and action are invariably attended with reason. The fact that He needs no external means to accomplish His plan bespeaks its inherent potency and spontaneity. He starts the cosmic process, as it were, by glancing over prakṛti, the causal potentiality of the universe. It is worthy of note that although the new cosmos is primarily the manifestation of the potential cause, yet it is not a replica of the preceding one in all particulars. Every seed grows differently from the tree of its origin.

It is Īśvara's plan of creation, in other words, the cosmic ideation of Saguṇa Brahman on the eve of the creation, that is meant by the term *Vāk* in the Vedic texts quoted above. The Greek *Logos* and the English *Word* as used by St. John in the beginning of the *Fourth Gospel* also point to this. The Sanskrit term *śabda* is also used in this sense. Though the Hellenic conception of the Logos has varied in the course of time, yet the basic idea that the universe is rooted in the Divine thought or the cosmic reason has been, more or less, associated with it.[17]

[17]Cf. *Dictionary of Philosophy,* edited by Dagobert D. Runes, New York, Philosophical Library, 1960, "Logos."

"In its most important sense in philosophy it [Logos] refers to a cosmic reason which gives order and intelligibility to the world. In this sense the doctrine first appears in Heraclitus, who affirms the reality of a Logos analogous to the reason in man that regulates all physical processes and is the source of all human law.

"The conception is developed more fully by the Stoics, who conceive of the world as a living unity, perfect in the adaptation of its parts to one another and to the whole, and animated by an immanent and purposive reason. As the creative source of this cosmic unity and perfection the world-reason is called the seminal reason (logos spermatikos), and is conceived as containing within itself a multitude of *logoi spermatikoi,* or intelligible and purposive forms operating in the world.

". . . In Philo of Alexandria, in whom Hebrew modes of thought mingle with Greek concepts, the Logos becomes the immaterial instrument, and even at times the personal agency, through which the creative activity of the transcendent God is exerted upon the world. In Christian philosophy the Logos becomes the second person of the Trinity and its functions are identified with the creative, illuminating and redemptive work of Jesus Christ. Finally the Logos plays an important role in the system of Plotinus, where it appears as the creative and form-giving aspect of Intelligence (Nous), the second of the three Hypostases."

3. Vāk *(the Word) as the origin of the universe.*

As the creative ideation of Īśvara *Vāk* is the first move towards the manifestation of diversity in unity. It is the source of all ideas representing the types of objects. Words and ideas are inseparable. The idea is the subtle aspect of a word. One implies the other. We cannot conceive an idea without a word. Every word must express an idea. So the Divine Word signifies the Divine Ideation or the creative thought of God. It is next to God, as it were, in the order of creation and is united with Him. Hence it is said, "With Him (the Creator) was only *Vāk* (the Word) as His own, as a second." Īśvara and His creative thought or word are inseparable. As the matrix of all ideas and words, this is also designated *para vāk* or *para śabda* (supreme word). Since each new plan of creation follows the beginningless pattern of the universe latent in His māyā-śakti, God and His Word are coeternal. Even when the whole cosmos is dissolved, *śabda* (Word) as God's creative idea or knowledge stays in the potential state. It holds the archetype of the universe, which is implicit in every new design of the world order.

The Divine Word is intermediate between the unity of God and the plurality of creation. It forms the link between the One and the many. It is beyond the dichotomy of the subject and the object, the self and the not-self. Īśvara is above the distinction of "I" and "thou." He is the all-inclusive Reality. The creation in all its phases is contained in His māyā-śakti, the inscrutable power, which is the causal potentiality of the universe. Māyā manifests the manifold without causing any change in the unity and the fullness of the Supreme Being. Vedanta maintains not only the unity of God but also His sole reality. Nothing but He really exists. He alone exists in the absolute sense. The manifold exists because of Him. In itself it is unreal, being an appearance. He permeates every form of existence. He is the one Self of all. Undiversified He holds all diversities. Though immanent, He is all-transcendent.

In the Vedantic view the entire variegated universe is characterized by *nāma* and *rūpa* (name and form). All diversification is due to them. *Nāma* means the particular class or species to which an object belongs; *rūpa* means the specific form or structure which differentiates or separates it from every other object. *Nāma* and *rūpa* constitute the principle of individuation. Each and everything, e.g., a book, a desk, a tree, a house, a bird, a meadow, a lake, a mountain has these two distinctive marks. When different objects are made out of wood, such as a chair, a table, a shelf, a box, a door, a post, it is *nāma* and *rūpa* that make all differentiation in one and the same material cause. What we call wood is the outcome of another material cause, tree, under different name and form. Thus, each and everything in the universe is the product of a preceding material cause inscribed with new name and form.

The basic or the primal cause is never known to us. All that we deal with are only the effects, the primal cause of which ever remains hidden under a succession of names and forms. The ultimate causal substance is beyond our grasp. This, as declared by Vedanta, is Pure Being, Brahman. Underlying all diversities is the same fundamental Reality, Brahman; variations result from the modification of *nāma* and *rūpa* emerging from His māyā-śakti responsible for the world-appearance. The starting point of the whole array of *nāma* and *rūpa* is *Vāk,* the creative ideation of Saguṇa Brahman, the initial step towards the projection of the manifold.

From the Divine Word (Vāk) issue all names and forms that apparently differentiate the undifferentiated One. The Upaniṣad states thus:

> Of such names Vāk is the source, for all names arise from it. This is their common basis, for it is general in all names. It is their self, for it sustains all names.[18]

All finite objects have names and forms as the conditions of their manifestation. As stated in the same Upaniṣad:

> This universe was then undifferentiated. It differentiated into name and form — it was called such and such and was of such and such form. So to this day it is differentiated into name and form — it is called such and such, and is of such and such form.[19]

Every object is but the apparent modification of the Supreme Reality, Brahman, which is the sole causal substance of the manifold. Being an effect, it is not self-subsistent. Its reality depends on the Supreme Cause. In itself it is a mere name.[20] Its emergence depends on name and form proceeding from the Word.

Variety in unity is the principle of creation. The process of individuation starts with the rise of name and form, as Īśvara "sees" or views them. Says Śaṅkara:

[18]Br.U. I:6.1. [19]*Ibid.* I:4.7. [20]See Ch.U. VI:1.4-6.

> What then is the object to which the knowledge of Īśvara is related prior to the origin of the world? Name and form, we reply, which are indefinable either as identical with or as different from Brahman, unevolved but about to be evolved.[21]

The cosmic ideation initiates all differentiation through name and form.

4. *The monosyllabic word Ōm as the symbol of Vāk. Its significance.*

Being the matrix of all names and forms *para vāk* (lit. superword, the word of words) is the potent seed of the manifold. As the immediate source of the creation it is called Nāda-Brahman or Śabda-Brahman, that is, Sound-Brahman, indicative of its first movement or vibratory motion towards the manifestation of the universe. Its most appropriate verbal symbol as such is the mystic word *Ōm*. As explained by Swami Vivekananda:

> All this expressed sensible universe is the form, behind which stands the eternal inexpressible sphōṭa, the manifester as Logos or Word. This eternal sphōṭa, the essential eternal material of all ideas or names, is the power through which the Lord creates the universe; nay, the Lord first becomes conditioned as the sphōṭa, and then evolves Himself out as the yet more concrete sensible universe. This sphōṭa has one word as its only possible symbol, and this is the Ōm. And as by no possible means of analysis can we separate the word from the idea, this Ōm and the eternal sphōṭa are inseparable; and therefore it is out of this holiest of all holy words, the mother of all names and forms, the eternal Ōm, that the whole universe may be supposed to have been created.
>
> But it may be said that, although thought and word are inseparable, yet as there may be various word-symbols for the same thought, it is not necessary that this particular word Ōm should be the word representative of the thought, out of which the universe has become manifested. To this objection we reply, that this Ōm is the only possible symbol which covers the whole ground and there is none other like it. The sphōṭa is the material of all words, yet it is not any definite word in its fully formed state. That is to say, if all the peculiarities which distinguish one word from another be removed, then what remains will be the sphōṭa; therefore this sphōṭa is called the Nāda-Brahman (the Sound-Brahman).

[21]BS I:1.5, S.com.

> Now, as every word-symbol, intended to express the inexpressible sphōṭa will so particularize it that it will no longer be the sphōṭa, that symbol which particularizes it the least and at the same time most approximately expresses its nature, will be the truest symbol thereof; and this is the Ōm, and the Ōm only; because these three letters A,U,M, pronounced in combination as Ōm, may well be the generalised symbol of all possible sounds . . . If properly pronounced, this Ōm will represent the whole phenomenon of sound-production, and no other word can do this; and this, therefore, is the fittest symbol of the sphōṭa, which is the real meaning of the Ōm. And as the symbol can never be separated from the thing signified, the Ōm and the sphōṭa are one.[22]

It is worthy of note in this context that Swami Vivekananda's interpretation of the term *sphōṭa* (that which manifests the meaning) differs from that of the Grammarian philosophers, who advocate the sphōṭa-theory.[23] He does not refer to their *pada-sphōṭa* or *vākya-sphōṭa* (the unitary medium underlying a word or a sentence to convey its meaning). Nor does he refer to the ultimate sphōṭa, which is maintained by some Grammarians as pure, eternal, uncompounded, primary Word, without beginning or end, underlying the universe as its primal Cause.[24] By *sphōṭa* he signifies *para vāk,* Īśvara's cosmic ideation, in which Word and Idea are indistinguishable. It is the Idea of ideas and the matrix of all words as well. From this emerge all particularized ideas representing types of species and also the corresponding words composed of letters.

The Mīmāṁsā philosophers view this as the original Word, the potent seed of all articulate words, particularly the Vedic words, and thus maintain the eternity of the Vedas. They recognize a natural relation between the word and its meaning, that is, the type or the species signified by it. The word is ever associated with its meaning and the meaning is ever associated with the word; the two are inseparable. None of the six Vedic systems of philosophy, except the Yōga of Patañjali, supports the Grammarian philosophers' theory of sphōṭa. Śabara-swāmī has refuted the theory in his commentary on the *Pūrva-mīmāṁsā-sūtra* (I:1.5). So has Śaṅkara in his commentary

[22]*Bhakti-yōga,* CW III, pp. 57,58.

[23]The theory of sphōṭa has been discussed by the author in his *Methods of Knowledge,* London, George Allen and Unwin, 1965; reprint edn., Mayavati, India, Advaita Ashrama, 1974; pp. 185-87.

[24]See Bhartṛhari's *Vākya padīya* (Brahma-kāṇḍa), Kashi Sanskrit Series 124, Varanasi. Also Mādhavācāryya's *Sarvadarśana-saṁgraha,* and Madhusūdan Sarasvatī's *Prasthāna Bheda,* Anandashrama Sanskrit Series, Vol. 51, 1950.

on the *Brahma-sūtras* (I:3.28). The proponents of sphōṭa do not quite agree on their views of it.

It may be mentioned here that the significance of the verbal symbol *Ōm* is not restricted to Nāda-Brahman or Śabda-Brahman. It has a still wider and deeper import; being intermediary between the Supreme Being and His manifestation, Ōm represents Him in all His aspects. It signifies Saguṇa Brahman associated with every phase of existence, the causal, the subtle, and the gross, and also points to Nirguṇa Brahman beyond all distinction. The very sound Ō-m — prolonged and tapering like the peal of a distant bell — represents a movement from the grossest to the subtlest, from the finite to the Infinite, the all-pervading Self beyond all limitations. Consequently, this is the most comprehensive of all the verbal symbols. It signifies Supreme Consciousness that is all-embracing. As such Ōm is the embodiment of spiritual consciousness in concentrated form and is regarded as its potent seed. It develops mystical awareness of the inmost Self through repeated utterance with devout contemplation on its meaning.

It is to be noted that as a symbol of thought or idea every word is a form of inner consciousness and has the power to evoke the same. In Yōga as well as in Vedanta Ōm is commended as the most potent and purifying name of God.[25] (For detailed account of the symbol *Ōm,* see the author's book *Methods of Knowledge,* Chap. 12, particularly secs. 9, 10.)

5. *The manifestation of the Vedas and the role of the Vedic words in creation.*

According to the orthodox view the Vedic words as well as their meanings, that is, the ideas represented by them, are without beginning and without end. In the state of the cosmic dissolution they exist potentially in Īśvara's power of knowledge, of which Vāk is the first manifestation. From Vāk arise all the Vedic words with their meanings. So Vāk is said to be "the mother of the Vedas (Vedānām mātā)."[26]

The Vedic words were exhaled by Īśvara, so to speak, with ease like the exhalation of air by man, which is effortless. The spontaneous manifestation of the Vedas from the Supreme Being is thus described by Yājñavalkya to his wife, Maitreyī: "As from a fire kindled with a

[25]YS I:27,28; Ka.U. I:2.15-17; Ma.U.I, II; Tai.U. I:8; and so on.
[26]Tai.Br. II:8.8.5.

wet faggot diverse kinds of smoke issue, so my dear, the *Ṛg-Veda, Yajur-Veda, Sāma-Veda, Atharvāṅgirasa,* history, mythology, arts, Upaniṣads, verses, aphorisms, elucidations, and explanations are like the breath of this Infinite Being; they are like the breath of this, the Supreme Self."[27] The last eight items (history, mythology, etc.) are included in the Brāhmaṇa section of the Vedas. The first four constitute the Mantra or Saṁhitā section. As pointed out by Śaṅkara, only the Mantras and the Brāhmaṇas of the Vedas are meant here.[28]

In the beginning the Supreme Lord (Īśvara) brought into being the cosmic soul (Hiraṇyagarbha, Brahmā) and imparted to him the Vedic words.[29] It was with the help of the Vedic words that Hiraṇyagarbha created spheres of various orders and also countless varieties of natural phenomena and living beings with their respective functions.[30] As declared by the *Śruti,* "Uttering the word 'bhūḥ (the earth)' he (Hiraṇyagarbha, also called Prajāpati) created the earth."[31] This means that Prajāpati shaped the worlds, such as bhūḥ, etc., from the Vedic words bhūḥ, which, with their meanings, became manifest in his mind. The point is, the words as subtle ideas called forth the gross manifestations of the species of things that existed during the period of dissolution in potential state in Īśvara's māyā-śakti, the creative energy that is the causal potentiality of the universe.

So says Manu: "In the beginning, it is from the words of the Vedas that Hiraṇyagarbha developed the respective names and forms of all beings and their duties as well."[32] Śaṅkara remarks: "It has been observed by all of us that when a person wants to make a desired thing he first remembers the word signifying the object and then sets to work. So we conclude that before the creation the Vedic words became manifest in the mind of Prajāpati the creator, and he created things corresponding to those words."

That the creation of the diversified universe followed the manifestation of the Vedas is also affirmed by the *Mahābhārata:* "At the outset the self-existent Brahmā uttered[33] the divine and eternal Vedic words, having no beginning or end, from which all norms of

[27]Br.U. II:4.10.

[28]*Ibid.,* S.com.

[29]Sv.U. VI:18.

[30]See Chap. VI, "The Process of Creation," sec. 7; VP VII.

[31]Tai.Br. II:2.4.2.

[32]MS I:21 (Kullūka's com.), quoted by Śaṅkara in BS I:3.28, S.com.

[33]As noted by Śaṅkara, the term "uttered" is indicative of the institution of the oral transmission of the Vedas by the preceptor to the pupil. BS I:3.28, S. com.

actions proceeded. . . . Verily, the Lord of all creatures, in the beginning, created all things from the words of the Vedas. . . . Upon the expiration of his night [the period of intermediary dissolution][34] Brahmā created from the prototypes that existed before all things, which were, indeed, well made by him."[35]

It is a well-known fact that in order to create something a person has to conceive it first in his mind and that it is some word or words signifying the type of the object that conveys the idea to him. Hence it is reasonable that Hiraṇyagarbha conceived the diversified universe before he produced it and that it is the eternal words of the Vedas which provided him with the ideas of the different worlds and species of things and beings to be created. A word is inevitably connected with the idea of the object it denotes. It signifies thought and also the object of thought. But it does not refer to a particular object but the type, class, or species of the object. A word, whether it denotes substance, attribute, or action, always signifies the species or the type of what is denoted. While the individual objects vary, their species or type remains constant. Śaṅkara observes:

> And it is with the species or the type (ākṛti) that a word is related and not with the individual objects, which being innumerable and varied, its relation with the particulars is absurd.[36]

6. *The instrumentality of Vāk in creation.*

Every object represents the species of the type to which it belongs and which is signified by its name. This is why by knowing a single object of a class a person can recognize any other object of the same class. For instance, by knowing one chair a person can recognize any other chair in spite of differences in particularities. The object *chair* as well as the word denoting it acquaints him with the concept "chairness." The idea that underlies the word also underlies the object denoted by it. The word (śabda), its meaning (pratyaya), and the object (artha) are interconnected. The essence of the word is the idea implicit in it. In the origination of an object the word serves as the prototype and not as its material cause.

The following remarks of Śaṅkara in the present context are significant:

[34]See Chap. VI, sec. 12.
[35]Mbh., Śānti-parva, 232: 24-26.
[36]BS I:3.28, S. com.

> The origination [of the world] from the Word is spoken of not in the sense of the origination [of the world] from Brahman as its material cause. In what sense then? There being the eternal word with the potency of conveying the meaning and ever related to the eternal species of objects, the accomplishment of an individual object to which the word is applicable becomes possible. In this sense it is said to have originated from the word.[37]

The point is that in the origination of the world the Word (Vāk) does not serve as its material cause but as its instrumental or contributory cause.

It is to be noted that in the production of an object Advaita Vedanta recognizes only two kinds of cause: (1) material cause (upādāna kāraṇa), and (2) instrumental cause (nimitta kāraṇa).

For instance, when a pot is made out of clay, its material cause is clay, which constitutes its essence or substance; the instrumental cause includes all other factors that contribute to its production, such as the potter, the wheel, the rod for turning the wheel, the idea of the pot. The shape (ākṛti) of the pot that inheres in clay is included in the material causes. It would not be possible to make a pot out of clay, had not clay the potency of being shaped into a pot. None can make a clay pot out of sandy earth or dust. So the shape of the pot is included in clay as the material cause. Thus, the instrumental cause has several varieties. Among them the potter is the efficient cause, the rest are subsidiary to it.

According to Advaita Vedanta, Brahman is the material as well as the efficient cause of the universe. (See Chap. IV, sec. 3.) As subsidiary to the efficient cause the Word is included in the instrumental cause.

The manifest Veda, the assemblage of words, is not all that the Veda means. In the last analysis it is identical with Vāk, the cosmic ideation of Saguṇa Brahman, in which all particular ideas and the corresponding words naturally related to them exist potentially and are indistinguishable. As the immediate source of creation Vāk is called Śabda-Brahman or Nāda-Brahman (lit. Sound-Brahman), which is also an epithet of the Veda.[38] Nāda-Brahman represents the first movement or the vibratory motion of Vāk towards the manifestation of the universe and is symbolized by the monosyllabic word *Ōm*. We quote below the pertinent remarks of Swami Vivekananda in the course of a conversation with a lay disciple:

[37]BS I:3.28, S. com. [38]BG VI:44.

The Veda is essentially the word (śabda), that is to say, the idea. It is but the aggregate of innumerable ideas. The old Vedic meaning of śabda (word) is the subtle idea, which becomes manifest in gross form later on. Hence at the dissolution of the cosmos the subtle seeds of future creation become involved in the Veda. . . . Even when the whole universe is dissolved the idea of the cosmos or the totality of the subtle forms of the concrete things exists in Brahman in potential state.

. . . On the eve of the creation Brahman at first becomes manifest as the Word (śabda) and next assumes the form of "Nāda" or "Ōm." Then numerous particular words or ideas that existed in previous cycles, such as "bhūḥ (the earth)," "bhubaḥ (the next higher world)," "svaḥ (heaven)," "cow," "man," "pot," begin to issue from "Ōm." As these ideas successively appear to Brahman [manifest as Brahmā or Hiraṇyagarbha] of unfailing will, the corresponding concrete things also emerge and gradually the diversified universe becomes manifest. Now you see how the word is the source of the creation.[39]

7. *The Vedantic conception of the Word compared with that of Philo and of St. John.*

We have tried to explain from the Vedantic viewpoint the significance of Vāk (the Word) in the cosmic process and the way it brings forth the manifold. So far as the origination of things and beings in general is concerned Vedanta agrees with St. John, who says:

All things were made by him [the Word] and without him was not anything made that was made.[40]

But St. John also speaks of the special creation or manifestation of the Word. He affirms that Jesus Christ is the Word incarnate in human form:

And the Word was made flesh, and dwelt among us (and we beheld his glory, the glory as of the only begotten of the Father) full of grace and truth.[41]

He identifies Jesus Christ with the Word as the only begotten Son of God:

No man hath seen God at any time; the only begotten Son, which is in the bosom of the Father, he hath declared *him*.[42]

[39] *Swāmi-Śiṣya-samvāda* (Conversations between the Master and the Disciple, Calcutta, 1897) Calcutta, Udbodhan Office, 1955, p.82.

[40] St. John 1:3. [41] *Ibid.* 1:14. [42] St. John 1:18.

In the *Revelation* (of St. John the Divine) Jesus Christ is called "the first begotten."

> And [peace] from Jesus Christ *who is* the faithful witness *and* the first begotten of the dead, and the prince of the kings of the earth. Unto him that loved us, and washed us from our sins in his own blood.[43]

Long before St. John some Alexandrian philosophers, especially Philo, conceived the Word (the Logos) as the first born Son of God. Max Müller says:

> I only wanted to prove once more what had been proved long ago by Greek and Indian philosophers, namely, that language and thought are one, and that in that sense the creative thoughts of the Supreme Being were called *logoi,* and, if conceived as one, the Logos of God. It was the same Logos that was called by Philo and others, long before St. John, the *huios monogenes,* that is, the only begotten Son of God, in the sense of the first ideal creation or manifestation of the Godhead.[44]

Evidently, Philo and some of his predecessors in Alexandria called the Logos "the only begotten Son of God" figuratively.[45] They did not conceive the Logos as a mode of the being of God. By "Son of God" they did not mean one of the three persons in one Godhead, a person in the Trinity. Nor did they use the expression "the only begotten Son of God" with reference to any living personality. Never did Philo identify the Logos with the Messiah. In all probability St. John got the allegorical expression "the only begotten Son of God" from Philo. But instead of using it figuratively he hypostasizes the Word (the Logos) as the second person of the Godhead and declares historical Jesus as the Word incarnate in human form.[46]

[43]Rev. 1:5.

[44]*The Vedanta Philosophy,* by Max Müller — Three lectures on Vedanta philosophy delivered at the Royal Institution in March, 1894, Calcutta, Susil Gupta, 1955, p.76.

[45]Cf. Alfred Weber, *History of Philosophy,* Eng. trans. by Frank Thilly, New York, Charles Scribner's Sons, 1925, p.124, note 1.
"In order to reconcile Scripture with the philosophy of his century he [Philo] had recourse to allegory, like the Stoics. His theory of the Logos (the Word, as the revelation of God, the Son of God, the second Son) has passed into Christianity."

[46]Cf. Charles Bigg, *The Christian Platonists of Alexandria,* Eight Lectures before the University of Oxford in 1886; Oxford, Clarendon Press, 1886, p. 24.
"It is probable that Philonism colored the New Testament itself, and it is certain that it largely affected the after development of Christian doctrine. . . . But there can be little doubt that St. John acquired from Alexandria that conception of the Word, which first brought Christian theology within the sphere of metaphysics."

According to Vedanta, Vāk (the Word) is not of the essence of God. It is the first expression of His creative knowledge, a phase of His māyā-śakti that belongs to Him as an adjunct or attribute distinct from His Being.[47] As the first and ideal manifestation of His creative knowledge Vāk can be figuratively called the first born Son or the first begotten Son of God, but cannot be considered a hypostasis of the Supreme Being. The cosmic ideation of Saguṇa Brahman is not an embodiment of His essence. It is a mode of God's attribute, but not of His being. As we have noted above, Vāk, according to Śaṅkara, is neither the material nor the efficient cause of the universe, but a subsidiary cause.[48]

Philo's view of the Logos is in some respects similar to the Vedantic view of Vāk. He conceives the Logos as an intermediary between the all-perfect Godhead and the imperfect world. Dr. Radhakrishnan thus explains the status of the Logos according to Philo:

> In mediating the relation between the godhead and the universe Philo develops his conception of the Logos and the intermediate powers. He looks on the latter sometimes as personal beings, at other times as impersonal attributes. In one sense the Ideas are identical with God, for, through them, the finite is able to participate in the deity; in another they are different, for the supreme, in spite of this participation, remains free from all contact with the world. God touches matter not through His essence but through His powers. The cosmic process does not add to or take away from the perfection of God. The thoughts are in a sense objective to God, independent of His essential subjectivity, but they are not separate from Him. They are modes of His energy, eternally and inseparably dependent on Him.[49]

8. *The Christian and the Vedantic view of the Divine Incarnation.*

But St. John has a different conception of the Word (the Logos). The same Word, which is the source of all things and beings, from which the world order with all its imperfections proceeds, is comprehended by him as the Second Person of the Trinity, who became incarnate in human form as Jesus Christ the Redeemer. God the Son, God the Father, and God the Holy Ghost are fundamentally One. As God the Son, Jesus Christ is the manifestation of the same essential being of God that is said to be responsible for the creation of

[47]See Sv.U. VI:8.

[48]Sec. 6; BS I:3.28, S.com.

[49]Radhakrishnan, *Eastern Religions and Western Thought,* p. 194.

the variegated world. In the Christian view historical Jesus is the first and last incarnation of the Divine Being. He is the sole Saviour of mankind. Man has his chance for salvation only in one life. If he loses this opportunity he faces eternal damnation.

Vedanta upholds the doctrine of the Incarnation of God in human form. It is the descent of the Supreme Being from the transcendental plane to the human level. So the Divine Incarnation is called *avatāra* (lit. descent). It is not the manifestation of Vāk in a psychophysical frame. Out of compassion and love for the bound souls the Supreme Lord assumes the human body and imposes apparent limitations on Himself, for their guidance and liberation. So His power of action and knowledge remains intact. It is like a monarch's inspection of his kingdom in disguise, as Sri Ramakrishna puts it. Śrī Kṛṣṇa clarifies his position as Divine Incarnation:

> Though I am birthless, essentially immutable, and the Lord of all created things and beings, yet, subjugating My prakṛti [manifest as the psychophysical frame], I appear embodied through My māyā [the inscrutable power that apparently limits the limitless].[50]

Further, according to Vedanta, God becomes incarnate in the form of man whenever the human situation demands it. Unredeemed man is reborn and gets a chance for liberation in as many lives as he needs for the eradication of his ignorance of the real nature of the self and the cultivation of the true knowledge. The Divine Incarnation is not a lone incident of the world-process that takes place in the history of mankind once for all. It is the Benign Lord's periodic move for the preservation of the world-order. It is not confined to any particular age, country, race, or religious body. The All-beneficent Ruler of the universe lives among mortals as one of them whenever necessity arises. Śrī Kṛṣṇa says:

> Whenever, O Bhārata [Arjuna], righteousness declines and unrighteousness prevails, I incarnate myself. For the protection of the righteous and the punishment of the evildoers and for the establishment of the moral and spiritual order, I am born from age to age.[51]

Because of the outgoing force of the creative process, the inner spirit of religion declines in course of time, although its outer forms often continue to flourish. Ostentatious rites and ceremonies,

[50] BG IV:6.
[51] *Ibid.* IV:7,8.

gorgeous temples and pageantry, exhaustive paraphernalia, powerful organizations with stringent rules and regulations cannot compensate for the lack of spiritual ardor nor check the consequent moral decay. The world requires a new adjustment for its spiritual regeneration, for turning human minds Godward — towards the One Goal of all. This necessitates the advent of a Divine Teacher. The founders of the world's major religions, whether they are adored by their followers as prophets, or messengers of God, or as Divine Incarnations, all come from above. They are the Saviours of human souls. Their sole mission is to lead human beings from the unreal to the Real, from darkness to Light, from death to Immortality.

To conclude: Vāk is instrumental in the creation of the world-order, but its preservation needs God's direct action — His protective care, guidance and grace.

PART THREE

THE QUEST FOR GOD, REALITY OF REALITIES

CHAPTER VIII

THE SEARCH FOR THE ONE IN THE MANY

1. *It is man's innate tendency to seek the ideal in the real.*

The multiform universe we experience, howsoever real it may appear to be, does not appeal to us as the ultimate or the ideal reality. Even though we try to be content with it and make the best of it, ignoring the beyond, the actual never approximates the ideal. Invariably the ideal proves to be unattainable in the world perceivable by the senses. Time and again there has prevailed in man's mind a misgiving as to the validity of this world of incessant change and interdependence. It does not answer to his innate vision of an ideal existence, but proves to be a panorama of motley events, a medley of opposites — such as life and death, light and darkness, growth and decay, harmony and disharmony, love and hate, virtue and vice, joy and sorrow. From the earliest days the human mind has called to account the world of experience and investigated its true nature. It is perhaps his dissatisfaction with the sensible universe, rather than fancy, wonder, or curiosity, that has led man to metaphysical speculation as well as religious inquiry.

Be that as it may, man conceives the Ideal Existence or Supreme Reality, though he may not believe in its actuality, as something that endures forever, that never fails, that is undying, undecaying, unchanging, that is beyond duality and relativity, that is limitless, flawless, all-free, all-good. But his senses cannot reach nor can his thoughts grasp It. He vaguely imagines, or assumes, or infers the Supreme, but has no distinct knowledge of the same. What he experiences after all is the perishable and not the Imperishable, the changeful and not the Changeless, the finite and not the Infinite, the conditioned and not the Unconditioned, multiplicity and not Unity. The Supreme Reality is beyond his ken. Consequently, there have been among men doubts and disputes with regard to this. The pantheists identify It with the manifold. The agnostics acknowledge It as the underlying existence, unknown and unknowable. The positivists ignore It. The atheists deny It. The sceptics neither affirm nor deny It. The theists and the deists hold that the Supreme is distinct from the world. Advaita Vedanta upholds none of these views. It affirms the Ultimate Reality as absolutely One.

Whether man acknowledges the Supreme Being or not, he has a natural tendency to seek the permanent in the impermanent, the unlimited in the limited, the perfect in the imperfect. This is the intrinsic urge that motivates his thoughts and activities. So he cannot rest satisfied with anything finite, however great or grand it may be. Just as every water-course is constantly struggling to reach the ocean by straight or crooked ways, so is man, knowingly or unknowingly, rightly or wrongly, ever seeking the Eternal, the Infinite, the Perfect, the Divine. Of all his pursuits this is the one ultimate end. Religion provides the direct means to its attainment. It is man's avowed approach to the highest good, the absolute value.

While other pursuits of life are particularly concerned with the temporal, religion is the only pursuit that is concerned specifically with the Eternal. The essential purpose of every true religion is to lead man to the Supreme Being, his highest ideal of perfection. Spiritual life begins with the deliberate search for the Supreme as the highest end. Deep within the heart of man there is a cry for the Real, the Eternal, the All-perfect One. His innermost feeling has found expression in such a prayer as: "Lead me from the unreal to the Real, lead me from darkness to Light, lead me from death to Immortality." (Br.U. I:3.28) Is man's vision of eternal existence, unfailing light, and unending bliss an illusion? Or even though the goal be real, is his effort to attain it a hopeless quest?[1]

2. *That the Ideal Reality can be attained is evidenced by great spiritual leaders' experiences, words, and deeds.*

[1]Cf. Alfred North Whitehead, *Science and the Modern World,* New York, Macmillan, 1962, p. 275. "Religion is the vision of something which stands beyond, behind, and within, the passing flux of immediate things; something which is real, and yet waiting to be realized; something which is a remote possibility, and yet the greatest of present facts; something that gives meaning to all that passes, and yet eludes apprehension; something whose possession is the final good, and yet is beyond all reach; something which is the ultimate ideal, and the hopeless quest."

The most illustrious of the world's great personages, such as Śrī Kṛṣṇa, Zoroaster, Moses, Lao Tzu, the Buddha, and Christ — have been the seekers and discoverers of the Supreme Being. Their teachings are the most valued treasure of mankind. Their message of enlightenment, of complete freedom from bondages of ignorance, delusion, misery, and death is the beacon of the benighted world. Their exemplary lives, radiant with divine wisdom, purity, power, love, and joy have provided humanity with the noblest ideals. Indeed, they are the greatest benefactors of mankind.[2] They declare in one voice that to seek and reach the Supreme Being is the highest purpose of human life, because this is the only way to freedom from all bondages and sufferings, to absolute peace and blessedness. Throughout the ages the same message has been proclaimed by the seers and saints of the world, who realized the self-existent, self-luminous Divine Being and became free forever from errors, bondages, and sufferings. Rolling down the vista of centuries comes the clarion call of the Vedic seer echoed and re-echoed in countless human hearts:

> Hearken, o ye, the children of immortal bliss and ye that dwell in celestial regions. . . . I have realized this Great One, resplendent as the sun, beyond all darkness. It is by knowing Him that man overcomes death. There is no other way of escape from the cycle of births and deaths.[3]

The seers' pronouncements on the reality of the Divine Being have been substantiated by their whole-souled devotion to, and dependence upon Him, by their marvelous self-sacrifice for His sake, and their spontaneous joyousness at the very thought of Him. Not only did they realize the Truth themselves, but they also laid definite courses for the unillumined to attain Illumination. In the present age the greatest explorer into the unknown Beyond was Sri Ramakrishna.[4] He rent asunder the veil of darkness and saw the Light beyond. The ever-shining bedrock of Reality, Supreme

[2]Cf. Arnold J. Toynbee, *Civilization on Trial,* New York, Oxford University Press, 1948, p.156. "Now who are the individuals who are the greatest benefactors of the living generation of mankind? I should say: 'Confucius and Lao-tse; the Buddha; the Prophets of Israel and Judah; Zoroaster, Jesus, Muhammad, and Socrates.' "

[3]Sv.U. II:5; III:8.

[4]See *The Gospel of Sri Ramakrishna according to "M,"* Eng. trans. by Swami Nikhilananda, New York, Ramakrishna-Vivekananda Center, 1942; also Swami Saradananda, *Sri Ramakrishna, the Great Master,* Eng. trans. by Swami Jagadananda, Madras, India, Sri Ramakrishna Math, 1952.

Consciousness, the Light of lights, the purest of the pure, the fountainhead of all blessedness, was constantly manifest to him. His illustrious, potent, blissful, stainless, and beneficent life testifies to the validity of his supraconscious experiences.

Had the manifold — characterized by pairs of opposites and mutability — been all that exists, had there been no ideal existence beyond, then man's innermost longing for perfection, his constant struggle for freedom, his aspiration after true knowledge must have remained unfulfilled and without meaning. Not only that: there would have been in that case no escape for a human being from the round of birth and death, rise and decline, hope and fear, pleasure and pain, but through loss of consciousness or total annihilation of his existence. Further, even though there might be the transcendent Reality, but beyond man's reach, unknown and unknowable, it would leave him in the same predicament.

3. *Vedanta declares the Ideal Reality to be the Goal attainable by all.*

Vedanta not only affirms the Ultimate Reality as the Ideal, as the very perfection of existence, but also declares It to be the Highest End, attainable by all human beings through appropriate methods. It stresses the fact that the fundamental Reality is the very basis and being of the manifold. As such It underlies every form of existence. While the forms undergo incessant changes their inmost essence ever remains the same. All that we deal with are the fleeting forms and not the substance. The forms appear to be real in themselves because of the underlying Reality, the finest of all existences. It is identical with Consciousness pure and simple, *Vijñāna-ghana* in the Upaniṣadic term.[5] As such, It is self-manifest, real to Itself, and manifests all that appear to exist. As a matter of fact, It is the One All-pervading Self of the universe.

What is innermost in the universe is innermost in each one of us. The Supreme Self shines within every individual as the inmost self. Just as at the back of every wave in the ocean there is the entire ocean, similarly at the back of each center of finite consciousness there is Infinite Consciousness. By knowing the indwelling self man finds himself in God. He realizes his essential unity or even identity with the Divinity. Thus the direct way to the Supreme Being is an inner approach. It is stated in the *Kaṭha Upaniṣad:*

[5] Br.U. II:4.12.

> Rare is the self-controlled man who, desirous of immortality, discerns the inmost Self with the eyes closed [turning the vision inward].[6]

As we have mentioned before, the real self of man is the central principle of consciousness, ever manifest without subject-object relation. It appears as the knower being in contact with the object. There is but one knower within every individual. That one and the same knower cognizes the external objects, and also the conditions of the physical body, the conditions of the different organs and the conditions of the mind. That very knower is the experiencer of the waking, dream, and deep sleep states. While the objects cognized are multifarious and mutable, the knower is constant, invariable in the midst of the variable. Says the sage Pippalāda:

> It is he, the indwelling self of the nature of consciousness who sees, touches, hears, smells, tastes, thinks, and ascertains. He is the knower, he is the doer. He becomes established in the Immutable Supreme Self [on the removal of ajñāna].[7]

Being associated with the psychophysical adjunct, the one and the same knower has many different functions. So a man can say, "I see," "I hear," "I taste," "I speak," "I work," "I sit," "I stand," "I sleep," "I walk," "I breathe," "I think," "I doubt," "I ascertain the truth," and so forth. The same knowing self is responsible for the operations of the body, the organs, and the mind. Being identified more or less with the not-self, such as the body, the organs, and the mind, the self appears as the ego characterized by "I-ness," a particular modification of the mind. The ego assumes varied forms in the waking state as well as in the dream state. But behind all these guises shines the same changeless self.

While the objects of knowledge, internal as well as external, are devoid of consciousness, the knower is ever self-aware, pure and free. The knowing self is beyond birth and death, beyond growth and decay, beyond hunger and thirst, beyond pain and pleasure, beyond love and hate. Yet, the indwelling self, although aware of its own existence, being veiled by ajñāna or avidyā — a peculiar ignorance — does not recognize its true nature. Not only that; it misapprehends itself as a psychophysical being. Ajñāna or avidyā is at the root of this inapprehension and misapprehension; but it does not affect the true

[6] Ka.U. II:1.1.
[7] Pr.U. IV:9.

nature of the self. Like fire behind smoke the luminous self ever shines in its pristine glory behind the veil. The case is somewhat similar to that of a monarch who under the spell of amnesia fails to recognize his royal status and mistakes himself for a commoner and behaves as such.

Nevertheless by proper disciplinary courses man can eliminate ajnana and its effects, realize the Self, and be free forever. Truly speaking, the Self is ever attained. But as long as a man is not aware of Its true nature, due to ignorance, It is unattained to all intents and purposes. The "attainment" of the self therefore means the recognition of the true nature of the indwelling self and its unity with the Supreme Self, consequent on the removal of the veil of ignorance (ajñāna). An earnest seeker can realize the self even through prayer. Sri Ramakrishna remarks:

> Let me assure you that a man can realize his Inner Self through sincere prayer. But to the extent that he has the desire to enjoy worldly objects, his vision of the Self becomes obstructed.
>
> Let me tell you that the realization of the self is possible for all without any exception.[8]

As declared by the *Kaṭha Upaniṣad:*

> Smaller than the small, greater than the great is the self located in the heart of every being. A man who is free from desires beholds the glory of the self through the purification of the organs and the mind and goes beyond grief.
>
> The wise man who ascertains the self as bodiless in the midst of the bodies, as steady in the midst of the unsteady, as vast and all-pervading, does not grieve.
>
> The Self cannot be attained by the study of the Vedas, or by intellect or by vast learning. The Self the seeker yearns for is attainable through that (yearning). To him the Self reveals Its own being.
>
> He who has not refrained from wicked deeds, whose senses are not under control, whose mind is not settled, nor tranquil, cannot attain the self through intuitive knowledge.[9]

That the realization of Brahman is the only gateway to immortality, peace and blessedness has been unreservedly declared by Vedanta:

[8]GSR, p. 256.
[9]Ka.U. I:2.20,22-24.

> There is the One Supreme Ruler, the innermost Self of all, who makes the One Being manifold; eternal happiness belongs to the wise who perceive Him within themselves, and not to others. There is One Being, the Eternal in the midst of the non-eternal, who is the consciousness of all conscious beings, and who, single-handed, dispenses the fruits of actions of many; eternal peace belongs to the wise who perceive Him within themselves and not to others.[10]
>
> There is the One destroyer of ignorance in the universe. He alone is the fire dwelling in water. By knowing Him alone one overcomes death.[11]
>
> When men shall roll up the sky like leather, then only there will be the end of misery for them without realizing the effulgent Being.[12]

4. *The Vedantic view of the manifold is not illusionism or pantheism.*

According to Advaita Vedanta multiplicity has only an apparent existence but no ultimate reality. The Supreme One exists transcendentally — exclusive of all multiplicity, duality, and relativity. Beyond time, space, and causality is the One Undivided Absolute Being without difference or distinction of any kind. That is the subtle essence of every form of existence. That One is perceived as the manifold by the unillumined through ignorance (ajñāna).[13] This multiform universe, physical and mental, is essentially That. It is real not as it appears but as the Supreme Being. The unchanging, undiversified, nondual Absolute (Brahman) is the sole ground and being of the apparent manifold consisting of ever-changing names and forms. It is said in the *Muṇḍaka Upaniṣad:*

> That eternal Brahman is before, that Brahman is behind, that Brahman is to the right, that Brahman is to the left. That Brahman permeates all above and below; this universe is that absolute Brahman alone.[14]

[10]Ka.U. II:2.12,13.
[11]Sv.U. VI:15.
[12]*Ibid.* VI:20.
[13]The term *ajnāna,* usually translated as "ignorance" means, basically, the ignorance of the Supreme Reality. It indicates that the unillumined have no knowledge. With all their knowledge of the manifold they are ignorant of the ultimate nature of things. Not only are they unaware of the Ultimate Reality, but know It differently from what It is. So, with reference to Truth, they have only false knowledge. *Ajnāna* is not mere absence of knowledge. It is not non-entity, but something positive that has two distinct functions: (1) to hide Reality and (2) to present It as other than what It is. Ajnāna is at the root of all appearances of Reality. It includes all relative knowledge as well as all forms of ignorance. It has different names — avidyā, māyā, prakṛti —indicative of its different aspects.
[14]Mu.U. II:2.11.

Brahman is the reality of all that appears to be real. So in the Vedantic view the world is not just an illusion, but a misreading of Brahman.

Nor should the Vedantic view of the world be confused with pantheism, as is often done by some modern thinkers. The difference between the two has been very well pointed out by Swami Vivekananda:

> The Vedantist [Advaitist] says, "the universe is not real, it is only apparent. Nature is God seen through nescience." The Pantheists say, "God has become nature or this world." The Advaitists affirm that God is appearing as this world, but He is not this world.[15]

The following remark of Professor Hiriyanna is pertinent:

> It is now usual to represent the monism of the later mantras and the Brāhmaṇas as pantheistic; but it is not correct to do so, since the term as applicable to this teaching connotes the idea not merely of immanence but also of transcendence.[16]

As stated by Dr. Radhakrishnan:

> Pantheism is the view which identifies God with the sum of things and denies transcendence. If the nature of the absolute is exhausted completely by the course of the world, if the two become one, then we have pantheism. In the Upaniṣads we come across passages which declare that the nature of reality is not exhausted by the world-process. The existence of the world does not take away from the perfection of the absolute.[17]

Two of the Upaniṣads thus declare the Supreme Being to be both immanent and transcendent:

> Just as the sun which helps all eyes to see is not tainted by the defects of the eyes or the external objects revealed by it, even so the same undiversified innermost Self is not contaminated by the misery of the world, being beyond it.[18]
>
> One effulgent Being is hidden in all creatures, He is all-pervasive and is the innermost self of all. He presides over the law of karma and all beings reside in Him. He is the Witness and He is Pure Consciousness transcendent and free from relativity.[19]

[15]"Inspired Talks," CW VII, p.48.

[16]M. Hiriyanna, *The Essentials of Indian Philosophy,* London, George Allen and Unwin, 1949, p.16.

[17]S. Radhakrishnan, *Indian Philosophy,* I:202.

[18]Ka.U. II:2.11. [19]Sv.U. VI:11.

5. *The world of experience keeps man in bondage, whereas the knowledge of the Reality beyond the relative leads him to Freedom.*

Man remains in bondage as long as he ignores the Supreme One and holds to multiplicity as real in itself. Life and death, growth and decay, weal and woe, betide him as a matter of course. Since differences are quite real to him, he cannot help being seriously affected by such opposites as beauty and ugliness, plenty and poverty, gain and loss, love and hatred, honor and dishonor. Led by attachment and aversion he continues to toss on the waves of duality in the death-bound ocean of multiplicity. Not by wealth, nor by scholarship, nor by rank, nor by fame can he get rid of "the dual throng." Try howsoever he may, he cannot find true rest, security, or peace in the region of the finite, the perishable. Like a weather-beaten bird fluttering its broken wings, he makes vain efforts to soar into the realm of enduring light, joy, and freedom. But there is no escape from the bondage of duality in the relative order. The monarch in his royal mansion is no less subject to it than the peasant in his humble cottage. Whoever accepts diversity as real in itself must have dual experiences, no matter how glorious and prosperous he may become, because in every new situation, there will be a change in his standard of valuation, he will face order and disorder, the great and the small, the high and the low, in short, the agreeable and the disagreeable.

On the contrary, the man who recognizes the Imperishable One to be the Supreme Reality becomes free from attachment to the perishable. So he remains unperturbed under the varying conditions of life. With whole-souled devotion he seeks the Supreme Being as the one Goal and Abode. Śrī Kṛṣṇa observes: "I am the origin of all, from Me everything proceeds; knowing this the wise worship Me with ardent devotion."[20]

Though *in* the world, the seeker of the Supreme Being is not *of* the world. He cares for worldly power and possessions not for their own sake but for the sake of God-realization. Yet he makes the best use of everything because he lives for the highest and best. Since he sees the all-pervasive One as the sole Reality, he is above the plane of duality. He faces the pairs of opposites with complete self-possession. He finds peace and security in life because his mind rests on the Imperishable One and not on the perishable. Being free from worldliness he lives safely in the world like a boat that floats in water

[20]BG X:8.

but does not allow water to get into it. When he realizes the Supreme Being he becomes completely free. As the Upaniṣad says:

> A man becomes free from all fetters on realizing the blissful and effulgent One who pervades the whole universe and is hidden in all beings as the extremely subtle essence finer than cream.[21]

An illumined person, although he sees the falsity of the manifold, is not in any way callous to the weal and the woe of mankind. He works out of compassion for the guidance and the enlightenment of the unillumined, inasmuch as he can view things from their standpoint as well.

Śaṅkara says in his *Viveka-cūḍāmaṇi* (The Crest-Jewel of Discrimination):

> There are pure souls, calm and magnanimous, who do good to the world spontaneously as does the spring, and who, having themselves crossed the dreadful ocean of life, help others also to cross it, without any motive whatsoever.
>
> It is the very nature of the great-souled to move of their own accord towards removing others' troubles, even as the moon voluntarily soothes the earth parched by the flaming rays of the sun.[22]

It is also evident from Śrī Kṛṣṇa's words to Arjuna that a knower of the Self should work in order to set an example to the unillumined, even though work is not necessary for himself:

> O Bhārata, as the unwise perform action being attached to it, even so a wise man should work, but without attachment, in order to set them on the right path.
>
> A wise man should not unsettle the minds of the unwise who are attached to work. He should keep them engaged in all work, himself performing it with Self-knowledge.[23]

Thus, it is through the performance of work that the unillumined have to go beyond work.

An adult, although he does not require toys himself, takes interest in them for the sake of the children, who value them and need them. It is through the use of the toys that the children outgrow the necessity for them. Similarly, until a person attains illumination the world is real to him; to realize its unreality he has to work his way through this "real" world to Enlightenment. The point is, the dream-experience is

[21]Sv.U. IV:16. [22]VC 37,38. [23]BG III:25,26.

real to the dreamer as long as he dreams; he can see its falsity only when he wakes up. Śaṅkara says: "It is proper to perform temporal duties and religious rites until one attains to the knowledge that the self is identical with Brahman."[24]

6. *The quest of the many is the way of ignorance, the quest of the One is the way of knowledge.*

To find the Ultimate One is the goal of human knowledge. To quote Swami Vivekananda:

> Knowledge is nothing but finding unity in the midst of diversity. Every science is based upon this; all human knowledge is based upon the finding of unity in the midst of diversity; and if it is the task of small fragments of human knowledge, which we call our sciences, to find unity in the midst of a few different phenomena, the task becomes stupendous when the theme before us is to find unity in the midst of this marvellously diversified universe, where prevail unnumbered differences in name and form, in matter and spirit — each thought differing from every other thought, each form differing from every other form.[25]

Yet this is the task that the Vedantic teachers have faced.

There is no denying the fact that with all our knowledge of the manifold universe we are groping in darkness. The mysteries of life and death, of the physical and the psychical nature, of the real self of man, of the eternal Being, are hidden from us. The more we know, the more we realize our ignorance. With the extent of the known, the extent of the unknown expands. Howsoever varied, extensive, or deep our knowledge of the phenomenal existence may be, we cannot get out of darkness and delusion; we cannot gain complete knowledge until we can find the ultimate One, which undiversified comprehends all diversities, unchanging sustains and integrates all changing forms, unmoving becomes the origin, the support, and the goal of the manifold. The knowledge of the many must culminate in the knowledge of the One.

When we know the all-pervasive Being, the one Self of all, then we know everything. "The Self being known, all this is known," says Yājnavalkya,[26] for then the essential nature of everything becomes known. The One that penetrates everything through and through must be all in all. Nothing exists beyond the Self (Ātman). So it is said

[24] BS II:1.14, S.com. [25] CW III, pp. 397-98. [26] Br.U. II:4.5; IV:5.6.

in the *Muṇḍaka Upaniṣad,* "Know that nondual Ātman alone and give up all other talk."[27] Until we know the Supreme One we are in ignorance. "To know many things is ignorance. To know that God dwells in all beings is knowledge," says Sri Ramakrishna.[28] "See the One in all; it is the other that misleads," says Kabir.[29] "From the second comes fear," declares the Upaniṣad.[30]

Human intellect is ever tending towards the One. In every sphere of life the explanation of the many is in the one. To understand diversity anywhere we have to find unity in it. Until we can do that we say, "What is all this about?" In his thirst for knowledge man is constantly seeking unity in plurality, identity in difference, harmony in disharmony, relation in the apparently unrelated. Knowledge implies classification, generalization. All sciences, all branches of knowledge, seek unities in their respective fields. Science means ordered knowledge. Laws of nature are but uniformities or regularities discerned in natural phenomena. It is the function of philosophy, the science of sciences, to find the unity of all unities.[31] Philosophical inquiry attains fulfillment only when it reaches the ultimate One, the common ground of all. Without the oneness of existence no universal knowledge would be possible; metaphysical investigation would be meaningless. The One which is the culmination of human knowledge, the One which the human mind invariably seeks, the One in which human aspirations attain fulfillment cannot but be the ultimate Reality.

7. *The Vedantic view of the Ultimate One. Its consistency with empirical knowledge.*

We see the many, but not the One. Yet in view of the facts stated above, we cannot deny the One. How can the many and the One be harmonized? Both cannot be real in the same sense, for even the vastest of the coordinate existences can be only one of the many and not the nondual, absolute One. So, if the Fundamental Reality be

[27]Mu.U. II:2.5.

[28]GSR, p.911.

[29]A Hindu saint (mystic and poet) of the early part of the fifteenth century.

[30]Br.U. I:4.2.

[31]Cf. Henry Sidgwick, *A Memoir,* Appendix 1. "It is the primary aim of philosophy to unify completely, bring into clear coherence all departments of rational thought, and this aim cannot be realized by any philosophy that leaves out of its view the important body of judgments and reasonings which form the subject-matter of ethics." (Quoted by A.N. Whitehead in *Science and the Modern World,* New York, Macmillan, 1960, p. 204.)

absolutely one, then multiplicity must be apparent and hence unreal. Or, if multiplicity be ultimately real, then oneness of existence must be false, for it would be no more than an aggregate of separate entities. Nor can multiplicity form the parts of the Supreme Reality like branches and leaves of a tree or waves and foam of the ocean, because anything that is composed of parts must be liable to change, decay, and disintegration like all other compounds. Then again, the parts of an organic whole must be similar in nature despite their differences; otherwise there can be no interrelation and no unity is possible. If there be essential unity among them, then the unifying principle must be the basic reality, the differences being only in name and form.

So the Supreme Reality cannot be both the one and the many. It has been observed by Śaṅkara: "Were multiplicity and unity both real, then how could the knowledge of the manifold be overcome by the knowledge of unity?"[32] It is a fact that the seers experience the Nondual Being. According to Vedanta the Supreme Reality is pure, simple, homogeneous existence. It has no component parts. It is not a system. It is not a process. It is flawless, stainless.[33] It excludes dependence. Therefore the many cannot belong to the absolute Being even as dependent existences.

Further, if multiplicity be the effects or actual modifications of the One cause, then oneness of existence no longer persists. Vedanta views multiplicity only as apparent modifications of the One Being. The Supreme One, without undergoing any change whatsoever, appears as multifarious to those who are under the spell of ignorance (ajnāna). In reality there is one undiversified, immutable Being. This is not the synthesis of the changeful and the changeless. "The changefulness and the changelessness of the same Brahman cannot be maintained," says Śaṅkara.[34]

Though the order of becoming rests in Brahman from the empirical standpoint, it does not inhere in It. The point is that appearance in no way forms an integral part of Reality. There cannot be "absolute appearances" or "relative absolutes," these being self-contradictory. Attempts have been made by some philosophers to reconcile the contraries in the Absolute. Apart from the question of logical consistency, no synthesis of opposites, comprehensive though it may be, can be regarded by the human mind as the ideal Reality or

[32]BS II:1.14, S. com.
[33]See Sv.U. VI:19.
[34]BS II:1.14, S. com.

the perfection of existence. To go beyond duality, beyond contradiction, beyond finiteness, is the constant endeavor of man. All contradictions must be absorbed in ultimate Oneness. Any half-way harmony will be far from the Goal.

It may be noted here that unlike Śaṅkara, Bradley is a concrete absolutist. He says:

> The Real is qualified by all plurality. It owns this diversity while in itself it is not plural. And a reality owning plurality but above it, not defined as against it but absorbing it together with the one-sided unity which forms its opposite — such a reality in its outline is certainly a positive idea.[35]

Again,

> The Reality itself is nothing at all apart from appearances.[36]

According to Śaṅkara there cannot be appearance without Reality; but Reality is not dependent on appearance either for Its existence or for Its experience. It is self-existent, self-effulgent, self-sufficient. Appearance is to Reality as smoke is to fire. There can be no smoke without fire; but there can be fire without smoke.

The fact that the senses present to us only the appearances of Reality and not the Reality Itself is acknowledged by modern science as well. The nature of the Ultimate Reality is, truly speaking, beyond its province. So physical science is conscious of its own limitation. It has been aptly noticed by Sir James Jeans:

> We see that we can never understand the true nature of reality. Our studies can never put us into contact with reality; we can never penetrate beyond the impressions that reality implants in our minds.[37]

"The frank realization that physical science is concerned with a world of shadows is one of the most significant of recent advances," observes Eddington.[38] This trend of modern science is also recognized by Needham: "The world as seen by science is not the world as it really is."[39]

[35]F.H. Bradley, *Appearance and Reality*, Oxford, Clarendon, 1930, p. 461.
[36]*Ibid.* p.489.
[37]Sir James Jeans, *Physics and Philosophy*, New York, Macmillan, 1946, p.15.
[38]A.S. Eddington, *The Nature of the Physical World*, The Gifford Lectures, 1927, New York, Macmillan, 1948, intro.
[39]Joseph Needham, *The Sceptical Biologist*, London, Chatto & Windus, 1929, p. 245.

This, however, does not falsify science, because the world exists to all appearance. It is not as false as "the son of a barren woman" or "the horns of a hare." It is real for all practical purposes until the vision of the Supreme Reality is attained. Vedanta denies the absolute reality of multiplicity but not its empirical reality, which persists for all but the illumined experiencing the Absolute.

While the knowledge of multiplicity keeps man in bondage, the knowledge of the One makes him free, because the former is the false and the latter the right perception. Just as delusion creates bondage, so enlightenment leads to Freedom. To see "the apparent" as real is delusion; to see the real as *real* is enlightenment or right knowledge. Hence multiplicity is only apparently real; the nondual Being is the Supreme Reality. As the absolute One is realized, multiplicity disappears. Thus the Upaniṣads say: "By the purified mind alone the Supreme Being is to be realized; then one does not see in It any multiplicity whatsoever. He goes from death to death who sees in It multiplicity, which is a mere appearance."[40] It is said in the *Bhagavad-gītā,* "That (the ultimate One) which is night to ordinary beings is as clear as day to the awakened sage. That (multiplicity) in which ordinary beings are awake is the night to the sage who sees."[41]

The truth is that the manifold universe is real to the unillumined; but to the illumined the nondual Being alone shines. The sun, which is ever stationary and ever resplendent, appears as rising or setting, as bright or dim, to those who are on the earth, but from the position of the sun all these movements and changes have no meaning, there being all along the same glorious, steady sun. Just as the mirage cannot moisten a single grain of sand in the desert, just as to mistake a rope for a snake produces no change in the rope, just as the apparent movements of the sun do not affect the sun in any way; even so the manifold universe perceived through ignorance (ajñāna) makes no difference in the absolute One. Truly, *That* alone shines in full glory ever the same. There is no trace of multiplicity in the Absolute. The ever shining One casts no shadow of appearance.

[40] Ka.U. II:1.11; Br.U. IV:4.19.
[41] BG II:69.

CHAPTER IX

WHAT IS REALITY? THE OBJECTIVE AND THE SUBJECTIVE APPROACH

1. *Reality defined. Pure existence underlies all changing forms. It is invariable and undeniable.*

In the Vedantic view, that is real in the true sense which *in all ways is,* which is uncaused, which undergoes no change, which is not dependent on or contradicted by anything. The real is self-existent. It is unconditioned by time, space, and causality. It prevails at all times, in all places, in all events. It is also beyond time, beyond space, beyond the chain of cause and effect, beyond all distinctions, external or internal. Reality is eternal, infinite, absolute existence. Vedanta identifies reality with being. Whatever fails *to be* has but apparent existence and is, therefore, unreal. "That which exists not in the beginning or in the end exists not even in the middle,"[1] says Gauḍapāda, because it is a mere appearance like a mirage. What is fleeting is unreal. What is constant is real. It is said in the *Bhagavad-gītā,* "Of the unreal there is no *being,* of the real there is no *nonbeing.*"[2] The meaning is this: the unreal is a mere form or appearance without *being*; it appears and disappears; the real never goes out of existence, being absolute existence.

Does it follow then that Vedanta views the world of experience, where nothing can be considered permanent, as a mere appearance without *being,* a shadow without substance? No. Vedanta is not nihilistic. Vedanta does not view the world as a nonentity. Rather it contradicts the theory of void (śūnyavāda) advocated by the Buddhist Nihilists (Vaināśikas).[3] In the Vedantic view there is no void; it is all *being.* The aim of Vedanta is not to prove the unreality of the objective universe, but to maintain the supreme reality of the absolute Being underlying it. The world of appearance, no doubt,

[1]MK II:6; IV:31.
[2]BG II:16.
[3]BS II:2.26, S.com.

obscures our vision of the ultimate Being and Its nature; yet we have a faint gleam of its presence in every object of experience. In truth, whatever we experience is characterized by *being*. Everything is perceived as existing — the sun exists, the sky exists, the earth exists, the tree exists, light exists, darkness exists, man exists, cloth exists, a pot exists, and so on.

Had nonbeing or nonexistence been the fundamental nature of things, then "isness" would not be a constant factor in all that we perceive. Even when we say, "there is nothing," we acknowledge the existence of space by the word *there*. Indeed, existence is the one fundamental fact that we face in each and every act of perception, and so whatever we experience appears to be real. To quote Swami Vivekananda, "All that we see and feel about things is pure and simple existence, *isness*."[4] No one ever perceives anything, be it mirage or dream, as nonexistent. Any illusion is real to the experiencer. Its unreality is an afterthought.

Existence should not be considered a mere abstraction achieved by intellect or imagination, because it is patent in all that we perceive. For instance, a pot and its existence are inseparable, but not indistinguishable. They are not, however, two distinct realities related to each other as substance and attribute, as in the case of a blue lotus. A lotus can be without blueness, and blueness can be without a lotus. But there can be no pot without existence, although there can be existence without a pot. Apart from existence a pot has no reality. In fact, it is one existence that is manifest under various names and forms, such as the sun, sky, earth, tree, man, light, shadow. While names and forms change and are therefore unreal, existence ever remains the same and is therefore real.

Nor can it be maintained that existence inheres in objects as a universal feature. Truly speaking, distinctive forms, universal or particular, adhere to being; being does not adhere to forms. We recognize the impermanence of the different aspects of an object but not the impermanence of its being. While the aspects change, its being endures. Otherwise, there could be no relation of cause and effect. We can dismiss all distinctive forms, but not the being which sustains them. We can think away the modes of existence, whether in the form of an object, or an attribute, or an action, but not existence itself. The cognition of existence persists some way or other, whether any objective form subsists or not. We cannot conceive absolute

[4]"Inspired Talks," CW VII, p. 53.

nonexistence. We cannot deny anything without positing something. The truth is that the one and the same substratum, existence, is the reality in all distinctive forms. Our cognition of distinctive forms fails, but the cognition of existence remains constant. It follows, therefore, that the distinctive forms are finite and fleeting, whereas existence is invariable and all-pervasive. "Know that to be imperishable by which all this is pervaded," says Śrī Kṛṣṇa.[5]

Noncontradiction is the mark of reality, according to Vedanta.[6] The real is that which does not contradict itself nor is contradicted by anything else. Any object of experience is subject to a twofold contradiction. It falsifies itself and is also falsified by another. Things seem to be independent and self-sufficient. Actually they are dependent and relative. No finite object can account for itself. For instance, an earthen pot has no existence apart from earth. It is all earth; the pot is merely name and form. Even as such it is confined to a particular space, a particular time, and a particular state of consciousness, namely, waking. As we know, our waking experience is contradicted by our dream-experience, and our dream-experience again is contradicted by the experience of dreamless sleep. Similarly, what we call earth is also but name and form. Thus, in the last analysis, all concrete objects prove to be mere names and forms, pure existence being the only reality underlying them. As observed by Swami Vivekananda, "Existence is the very ultimate generalization which the human mind can come to."[7]

The distinction between the real and the unreal is thus pointed out by Śaṅkara:

> Every act of experience involves a twofold consciousness, the cognition of the real and the cognition of the unreal. Now, that is said to be real which never drops out of our cognition; and that to be unreal which does drop out. Thus, the distinction between reality and unreality depends upon our cognition . . . The cognition of an objective form, such as a pot, is fleeting; therefore its content is unreal. The cognition of existence, on the other hand, is constant; therefore its content is real.[8]

That is to say, objective forms are unreal, the all-pervasive existence alone is real. Thus, there is one Reality in all that we

[5]BG II:17.
[6]See Pd. III:29, "Satyatvaṁ bādharāhityaṁ."
[7]"Reason and Religion," CW I, p. 371.
[8]BG II:16, S. com.

experience.[9] It is the thing itself. We vaguely apprehend it as mere existence even though our senses fail to discern it as it is. It strikes our thought as something abiding and sets us to the search for Truth. There cannot be any quest of the absolutely unknown.

Thus Vedanta recognizes one immutable, immovable, indivisible existence or pure Being as the ground of all multiplicity and movement. It is the ultimate principle that supports and sustains all shifting forms both physical and mental. Diversities and changes are related to forms and are therefore apparent. The supreme cosmic principle is the sole reality. The world is real not as it appears but as pure Being. The reality of light is not in its appearance as light but in pure Being. The reality of the sun is not in its appearance as the sun but in pure Being. The reality of beauty is not in its appearance as beauty but in pure Being. The reality of virtue is not in its appearance as virtue but in pure Being. The reality of thought is not in its appearance as thought but in pure Being. Thought exists because of pure Being. It is that which makes thought possible. It is the innermost essence of all that appears.[10] Vedanta calls this *Ātman* (Self), the all-pervasive principle. From this originate all objects, physical and mental.[11] So Vedanta does not view the Ultimate Reality as an objective entity external to thought.

2. *The order of becoming cannot be real in itself.*

Evidently, the Vedantic view of reality is quite the reverse of the Heraclitean, which denies being and upholds the process of becoming as reality itself. According to Heraclitus (535-475 B.C.), reality is a condition of unrest. "Into the same rivers we step and do not step; we are and we are not," observes the Greek philosopher, who envisages the universe as an endless alternation of being and nonbeing.[12] In the view of the Buddhist teacher, Nāgasena, who lived in India about 300 years later, there is nothing permanent in the entire physical and psychical universe, since everything, sentient or insentient, is only becoming and has strictly no being. So he says to the Greek King

[9]It is interesting to note that modern science is gradually recognizing the fact that there is one fundamental reality behind the world of phenomena. Einstein's Generalized Theory of Gravitation points to such an underlying unity. (See Dr. Albert Einstein's *The Meaning of Relativity,* Appendix II, and his article in *Scientific American,* April, 1950.)

[10]See Ch.U. VI:8.6,7.

[11]See Tai.U. II:1-3.

[12]*Heraclitus on the Universe,* LXXXI, (Hippocrates, Vol. IV, New York, The Loeb Classical Library, 1931).

Milindā (Menander): "That, which has not been, becomes; as soon as it has begun to become it dissolves away again."[13] A staunch advocate of the philosophy of change in the modern age is Henri Bergson, who says, "Things and states are only views, taken by our mind, of becoming. There are no things, there are only actions. . . . In vain shall we seek beneath the change the thing which changes . . . the reality is movement."[14]

In the human mind, however, the idea of reality is ever associated with stability and permanence. What is changeful and perishable is regarded as unreal. What is constant and durable is regarded as real. Is this innate view of man without basis of truth? Is it quite contrary to fact? There must be a correspondence between reality and the universal idea of it. On the contrary, if reality is conceived as ceaseless change or movement, then the question arises: "How can there be a continuous flow of impermanent events without a permanent background?" Continuity implies a connection, a relation between the preceding and the succeeding occurrence. If the antecedent vanishes before the subsequent arises, how can there be a relation? The sequence of cause and effect cannot hold in case everything is momentary. The seed must persist when the sprout grows in order to be its cause. This means that the seed undergoes change at the time in certain aspects but does not cease to exist altogether; its being endures. Otherwise, we shall have to hold that anything can come out of anything, because nonexistence precedes the effect in every case. Further, as observed by Śaṅkara, in case the things are momentary, they cannot have any existence beyond origination and destruction, so the two processes must be identical. Now, if there is any difference between the two, then it must be admitted that a thing lasts at least more than one moment. Therefore the theory of momentariness falls to the ground.[15]

If both the physical universe and the mental universe are in a state of flux, one can pertinently ask: "Do the ever shifting elements sustain themselves? Do they not require an eternal basis to sustain and integrate them?" Certainly, there must be something abiding and self-sustaining to sustain all that are fleeting. Moreover, movement is possible only in relation to something less moving or relatively

[13]Milindā Panhā, II:3.3, *The Questions of King Milindā,* The Sacred Books of the East, Vol.35.

[14]Henri Bergson, *Creative Evolution,* New York, The Modern Library, 1944, pp.270-1, 327-8.

[15]See BS II:2.20, S. com.

unmoving. The series of the relatively unmoving will lead ultimately to the absolutely unmoving. Therefore the ever changing universe of mind and matter must have an unchanging background.

3. *What is objectively known as pure Being is subjectively found to be Pure Consciousness. So by realizing the inmost self one can realize That.*

If the world order is held to be an appearance, then also its basis of reality cannot be denied. How can there be an appearance without a base? Appearance means something appears as other than what it is, as in a mirage the desert appears as a lake. It is the rope that appears as the snake in the rope-snake illusion. "No illusory perception is possible without a substratum," says Śaṅkarācārya.[16]

So the entire world of phenomena has one ultimate Being as its ground and basis. This appears as manifold. This is the sole immutable essence of all changing forms, physical and psychical. But it is not a dark, dead, material entity, nor a dry, dull, stark abstraction. It is the Ideal Reality and can be realized as such. As the very being of the universe, pure existence is man's innermost self. What is innermost in an atom must be innermost in man. By realizing one's true self one can realize That. Indeed, the innermost self of man is the only unchanging principle in this universe of change. It is the sole witness of all physical and mental events. Changes can be known only by an unchanging observer. Being the knower *per se* the self cannot be known as an object. Still one can realize the self, inasmuch as it is of the nature of consciousness and self-shining. So says Vidyāraṇya in *Pañcadaśī,* "Though not an object of knowledge still the self can be directly experienced because it is self-luminous."[17]

Several Western philosophers beginning with Parmenides have acknowledged an immutable being in the order of becoming. Their views regarding the Absolute Being and the mode of reaching It, however, differ from those of the Vedic sages. According to some, the Absolute is to be assumed or believed but cannot be known. Some others say the Absolute can be an object of knowledge. But very few of them regard the Absolute as the Supreme Ideal attainable by man. Being identical with the self of man, it cannot be objectified. It becomes manifest on the removal of the veil of ajnana associated with the self.

In the *Chāndōgya Upaniṣad*[18] we find the sage Uddālaka teaches

[16]MK II:33, S.com. [17]Pd. III:28. [18]Ch.U. VI:1-12 (abridged).

his son, Śvetaketu, how one can know everything by knowing pure existence and how one can know pure existence by knowing the self. Having studied the Vedas with his teacher for twelve years Śvetaketu returned home at the age of twenty-four. The father noticed that the son was very proud of his learning and said to him, "Śvetaketu, did you ask for that instruction by which what is unheard becomes heard, what is unthought of becomes thought of, and what is unknown becomes known?" "How can there be such an instruction, sir?" inquired Śvetaketu.

Uddālaka: Just as, my child, by knowing a single lump of clay all that is made of clay becomes known, since all modifications are mere names arising from speech, the truth being that all this is clay; just as, my child, by knowing a nugget of gold all that is made of gold is known, since all modifications are mere names arising from speech, the truth being that all this is gold; similarly, by knowing the One we know all. Such is that instruction, my child.

Śvetaketu: Surely, my venerable teachers did not know about this. For, if they had known it, they would have told me about this. Kindly tell me about this, sir.

Uddālaka: Be it so, my child. In the beginning it was Existence only, One without a second. Some say in the beginning there was nonexistence only and from nonexistence the universe arose. But how could that be? How could existence be born of nonexistence? No, my child, in the beginning there was Existence only, One without a second. . . . Of all these created things and beings, my child, pure existence is the origin, pure existence is the support, pure existence is the end. . . . In that subtle essence all this has its being. That is Reality. That is the Self. Thou art That, O Śvetaketu.

Śvetaketu: Kindly explain to me further, sir.

Uddālaka: Be it so, my son. . . . Bring a fruit from this nyagrodha tree.[19]

Śvetaketu: Here it is, sir.

Uddālaka: Break it.

Śvetaketu: It is broken, sir.

Uddālaka: What do you see there?

Śvetaketu: These tiny seeds, sir.

Uddālaka: Split one of them.

Śvetaketu: It is split, sir.

Uddālaka: What do you see there?

Śvetaketu: Nothing, sir.

[19]Indian fig-tree, banyan *(ficus Indica).*

Uddālaka: My son, that is the subtle essence of the seed which you do not see. From that very essence this great nyagrodha tree grows and has its existence. Whatever part of the tree loses the subtle essence withers. Believe it, my son. That which is the subtle essence, in That all this has its being. That is Reality. That is the Self. Thou art That, O Śvetaketu.

Therefore man can realize That by knowing his own self.

4. *The inmost self of man is uncontradicted Being-Consciousness-Bliss.*

The Vedantic view of Reality does not rest as much upon an inquiry into the external universe as on an investigation into the inner nature of man. The fundamental difference between the subject and the object, between the knower and the known, has been the clue in its search for reality. The principal method of investigation has been the discrimination between the knower and the known, rather than the observation of the objects known, internal as well as external. Just as the external things, including the physical body, fall into the category of the object, so does the mind. The mind is not the knower within, for its movements are observed by the self, the knower *per se*. The knowing self (ātman) is beyond the body, the organs, and even the mind, since the knower must be distinct from the known. Consciousness is intrinsic in the knower and not in the known. So, unlike the mind, the self is self-intelligent, that is to say, has consciousness as its very essence. However, the distinction between the self and the mind has not been noticed by many thinkers of the West.

Though the subject and the object, the knower and the known, are related to each other, yet the object is not real in the sense in which the subject is. The object is variable; the subject is constant. The self remains one and the same despite all the variations of the objects, which include not only external things and beings, but also the knower's own body, the organs, and the mind. Being distinct from all objects of experience, external and internal, it is uncontaminated by their changing conditions. So the self is beyond birth, growth, gain, loss, pain, pleasure, decay, death.

As in the waking state, so in the dream state diverse objects appear and disappear before the self, their observer, without tainting it in the least. In dreamless sleep also the self is untarnished by the state of inapprehension or unspecified ignorance, of which it is the witness.

So says Bhāratī Tīrtha: "The luminous self neither rises nor sets. It does not wax or wane. It shines of itself and illumines all else without any aid."[20] In the superconscious state the transcendental self prevails, beyond egoism, beyond the duality of the self and the not-self. Even after the objects disappear the self persists being identified with undivided pure Consciousness, the sole Reality. Everything but the self fails. The self stays throughout. It does not contradict itself nor is it contradicted by anything.

Every form of existence presupposes the knowing self. Without postulating the self-intelligent knower nothing can be affirmed or denied. While the subject is self-aware, the object is bereft of all consciousness. It is the subject that manifests the object. Being self-luminous the subject is self-evident. Who ever doubts his own existence? A person may doubt or deny the existence of everything else, including God, but not of himself. Even in denying himself he has to affirm himself. So the innermost self, the witness, is the first thing real. And we have seen that it is beyond contradiction. So the self is self-existent, and consequently identical with pure existence, the supreme cosmic principle. Again, consciousness is not an attribute or a function or a state of the self, but its very nature; the self is pure consciousness, awareness itself. So it follows that pure existence is identical with pure consciousness. Śaṅkara observes:

> Many and diverse are the genera with their species, sentient and insentient. Through successive stages they are all included in one Supreme Existence, Pure Intelligence.[21]

The self is the dearest of all. In the words of the Upaniṣad: "This self is dearer than a son, dearer than wealth, dearer than everything else and is innermost."[22] Anything that is dear is dear for the sake of the self. Says Yājñavalkya to his wife, Maitreyī:

> It is not for the sake of the husband, my beloved, that the husband is dear, but for the sake of the self he is dear. It is not for the sake of the wife, my beloved, that the wife is dear, but for the sake of the self she is dear. It is not for the sake of the sons, my beloved, that the sons are dear, but for the sake of the self they are dear. It is not for the sake of wealth, my beloved, that wealth is dear, but for the sake of the self it is dear. . . . It is not for the sake of anything, my beloved, that anything is dear, but for the sake of the self it is dear.[23]

[20] *Dṛgdṛśya-viveka* (Discrimination of the seer and the seen) 5.
[21] Br.U. II:4.9, S.com. [22] Br.U. I:4.8. [23] Br.U. II:4.5.

The self is the dearest of all, because it is the one source of all joy. That which gives joy is dear to man. So the self is all-bliss. Thus we find that pure Existence is identical with pure Consciousness and pure Bliss. The supreme Reality is Existence-Consciousness-Bliss (Sat-cit-ānanda). By realizing the self one realizes That. So adds Yājñavalkya:

> The self, my dear Maitreyī, should be realized — should be heard of, reflected on, and meditated upon. By the realization of the self, my dear, through hearing, reflection, and meditation, all this is known.[24]

Man can know God if he can know himself. "Seeking the 'I', you discover 'Thou'," [25] says Sri Ramakrishna.

5. *The three orders of existence.*

From the viewpoint of the Absolute, Nondual Brahman is all that exists. From the viewpoint of the embodied self under the spell of ajñāna, the universe of multiple beings and things and its Ruler (Īśvara) have a relational existence, which prevails until he realizes his identity with Brahman. All relativity, multiplicity, and difference belong to the realm of appearance, being superimposed on Brahman through ajñāna. They disappear when Brahman, their substratum, is realized, just as the illusory snake disappears when the rope, mistaken for the snake, is found. Brahman is the substratum of the manifold from the viewpoint of appearance.

As far as the finite self is concerned, Vedanta recognizes the apparent reality of the manifold and also degrees of that reality. There is a difference in the realm of appearance between the waking and the dream state, even though from the standpoint of the Absolute both are entirely false. There is a difference in the realm of appearance between the illusory snake and the snake that can bite, even though from the standpoint of the Absolute both are entirely false. As observed by Śaṅkara: "Relative to the illusory objects, such as mirage, actual water and the like are real."[26] Thus Vedanta considers three main orders of existence:[27]

(1) Absolute existence (pāramārthika sattvam) — Nondual Brahman. The One without a second.

[24]*Ibid.* [25]GSR, p. 819. [26]Tai.U. II:6, S.com. [27]See VP II.

(2) Empirical existence (vyavahārika sattvam) — the world of experience marked by space, time and causality which persists for the embodied self until he realizes Nondual Brahman.

(3) Illusory existence (prātibhāsika sattvam) — such as a mirage, which is erroneous and occasional. It serves no practical purpose and disappears when its base is cognized.

The last two belong to the realm of appearance. The empirical existence is no less real than the empirical self, and both depend on Īśvara, the all-encompassing Ruler of the subjective and the objective. The empirical existence is universal. The illusory existence is due to the erroneous perception by the embodied self concerned. Unlike the empirical existence it is usually individual. It is not false as the son of a barren woman or the horn of a hare, which do not exist at all, and never appear.

CHAPTER X

THE DIRECT AND THE INDIRECT KNOWLEDGE OF THE SUPREME BEING

1. *The close relation between the two.*

The Vedantic view of God, the Supreme Being, is based primarily on the experiences of the seers and not on mere speculative knowledge. The Sanskrit word for philosophy is *darśana,* which means view or vision of Truth. Both philosophical and scriptural knowledge attain their fulfillment in the immediate apprehension of Truth (aparōkṣānu-bhūti). The authoritative spiritual teacher, according to Vedantic tradition, should be versed in the Vedic studies (śrōtriya), and also established in the experience of Brahman (Brahma-niṣṭha). He should have both *jñāna* (indirect knowledge) and *vijnāña* (direct knowledge), as Sri Ramakrishna points out. Indeed, the highest religious personalities are the *seers* of Truth. They gain their knowledge of the beyond not simply from scriptural texts or ratiocination but from actual perception. Their experiences are the authentic proof of the existence of God and the Soul (Ātman). They verify what the scriptures declare. Once a person asked Swami Brahmananda, "Sir, what is the proof of the existence of God?" "The saints say, 'We have realized Him and you will also realize Him if you follow the way,' " was the answer.

The following remark of Swami Vivekananda is pertinent:

> The greatest proof that we have of the existence of a God is not because our reason says so, but because God has been seen by the ancients and by the moderns as well. We believe in the soul not only because there are good reasons to prove its existence, but, above all, because there have been in the past thousands in India; there are still many who have realized, and there will be thousands in the future who will realize, and see their own souls.[1]

Even philosophical investigation cannot be complete unless it

[1]"The Common Bases of Hinduism," CW III, p. 378.

takes into account the data of the mystical experience. The philosophical study in Vedanta is based not only on the facts of the three ordinary states of human experience — waking, dream, and dreamless sleep — but also on the facts of the supraconscious state or samādhi. It is generally recognized that many of the world's great saints and sages, ancient and modern, Eastern and Western, such as Śukadeva, the Buddha, Lao Tzu, Pythagoras, Philo, St. Paul, Plotinus, Śaṅkara, Jalāluddīn Rūmī, St. Bernard, Eckhart, Ruysbroeck, Sūfī Al-Ghazzāli, Kabīr, Tulsīdās, Mīrabāi, St. Theresa, Jacob Boehme, Nanak, Rāmaprasād, Sri Ramakrishna — to mention just a few — had mystical awareness, in which they found supreme satisfaction.

Facts are the materials that reason has to use for conceptual construction. It cannot deny or ignore facts. Nor can it create them. No argumentation, however subtle, can make the nonexistent existent. No reasoning can make God real. Reason may prove or disprove God's existence, but His existence or nonexistence does not depend on this. What reason concludes may or may not be a fact. "The highest demonstration of reasoning that we have in any branch of knowledge can only make a fact probable, and nothing further," says Swami Vivekananda.[2] There is a gulf between idea and reality. Philosophy of religion has to be built on the perception of suprasensuous facts. The truth of religion cannot rest mainly on sense-perception and reason.

Swami Vivekananda rightly observes:

> All argument and reasoning must be based upon certain perceptions. Without these there cannot be any argument. Reasoning is the method of comparison between certain facts which we have already perceived. If these facts are not there already, there cannot be any reasoning. If this is true of external phenomena, why should it not be so of the internal? The chemist takes certain chemicals and certain results are produced. This is a fact; you see it, sense it, and make that the basis on which to build all your chemical arguments. So with the physicists, so with all other sciences. All knowledge must stand on perception of certain facts, and upon that we have to build our reasoning.
>
> But, curiously enough, the vast majority of mankind think, especially at the present time, that no such perception is possible in religion, that religion can only be apprehended by vain arguments. . . . There are certain religious facts which, as in external science, have to be perceived, and upon them religion will be built.[3]

[2] "My Master," CW IV, p.163. [3] "Realization," CW II, pp. 162-63.

So in Vedanta we find that philosophy and mysticism, reason and intuition are closely allied. Philosophical inquiry starts with the systematization of the truths of suprasensuous experience as well as sense-perception. But it does not stop with mere speculative knowledge of Reality. The seeker of Truth is urged to verify the verdict of reason by actual experience, for which he has to undergo special discipline. While speculative knowledge awaits the evidence of intuitive perception, intuitive perception needs rational interpretation for its universal acceptance. The close connection between philosophical reason and intuitive experience has been aptly noted by N.K. Brahma in his *Philosophy of Hindu Sadhana:*

> It is the task of philosophy to try to translate and understand analytically in terms of thought or conceptual thinking what has been presented in the living experience of intuition. It must start from experience and it must recognize experience to be the goal of all philosophy. Philosophy cannot give us an experience of the actual — it attempts to show what is possible, not what *is* but what *may be*. The merely possible demands a verification or rather an actualization in concrete experience. This is supplied by intuition. A philosophy that does not base itself on this solid footing of perfect experience is a merely barren speculation that moves in the sphere of ideas alone, detached from Reality. This is what distinguishes Hegel's Idea from Śaṅkara's Brahman. The latter is a concrete experience in ecstatic intuition, while the former is only the highest achievement of reason.[4]

2. *The gulf of difference between the two types of knowledge — the direct and the indirect.*

It goes without saying that the knowledge of the Supreme Reality can be either mediate (parōkṣa) or immediate (aparōkṣa). Metaphysical investigation leads to mediate or indirect knowledge, which gives the seeker some idea of the existence and the nature of the Supreme Reality but does not unveil It to him. Mediate knowledge, therefore, lacks in definiteness and certitude which characterize the immediate or direct apprehension of Reality. Hence it fails to dispel the seeker's doubts and misconceptions regarding Truth. This vagueness or indecisiveness is the mark of all speculative or inferential knowledge. For instance, when we infer the presence of fire from the sight of smoke, we cannot form an accurate idea of the fire in question. Inasmuch as inference is incapable of giving us a

[4]N.K. Brahma, *Philosophy of Hindu Sadhana,* London, Kegan Paul Trench, Trubner and Co., p. 167.

definite knowledge of things perceptible by the senses, far more inadequate it must be to give us the precise knowledge of suprasensuous verities.

The knowledge of the Supreme Being derived from the study of the scriptures is similarly mediate. So it cannot remove delusions and fears rooted in ignorance (ajñāna) and reveal Truth. However, to the seeker whose mind is properly disciplined mediate knowledge — inferential as well as scriptural — conveys an assurance of Truth that enables him to strive after its realization. Only the immediate knowledge of Reality eradicates his ignorance (ajnāna), the root of all errors, fears, sufferings, and bondages, and makes him free forever. It is said in the *Muṇḍaka Upaniṣad:*

> The knots of the heart are broken, all doubts are dissolved, the deposits of karma are destroyed when He is beheld who is transcendent and immanent.[5]

Hence in Vedanta the spiritual culture for the immediate apprehension of the ultimate Reality is called *the supreme knowledge* (parā-vidyā), and the cultivation of its mediate apprehension *the subsidiary knowledge* (aparā-vidyā).

In the following story the *Muṇḍaka Upaniṣad* distinguishes the "supreme" from the "subsidiary" knowledge. Śaunaka, the great householder, duly approached the sage Aṅgiras and said: "Revered sir, what is that by the knowing of which all this becomes known?" Aṅgiras replied,

> Two kinds of knowledge have to be cultivated — this is what the knowers of Brahman say. These are *the supreme knowledge* (parā-vidyā) and *the subsidiary knowledge* (aparā-vidyā). Of these two, *the subsidiary knowledge* (aparā-vidyā) is gained from the *Ṛg-Veda,* the *Yajur Veda,* the *Sāma Veda,* the *Atharva Veda,* śikṣā (phonetics), kalpa (rituals), vyākaraṇa (grammar), nirukta (etymology), chandas (metre), and jyōtis (astronomy);[6] and *the supreme knowledge* is that by which the Imperishable One is realized; it is that by which the wise perceive Brahman everywhere, which otherwise cannot be seen or grasped, which has no cause or attributes, no eyes or ears, no hands or feet, which is eternal, undecaying, all-pervasive, and extremely subtle, which dwells in all beings and is the origin of all.[7]

[5]Mu.U. II:2.8.

[6]Śikṣā (phonetics) . . . jyōtis (astronomy) — these six are called the six Vedāṅgas, aids to the study of the Vedas.

[7]Mu.U. I:1.3-6.

In his commentary on the above passage Śaṅkarācārya remarks: By the expression *parā-vidyā* is here meant especially the direct knowledge of the Imperishable Brahman taught by the Upaniṣads and not their verbal contents. But the term *Veda* usually denotes its verbal contents. Even after the mastery of the verbal contents one cannot attain the Imperishable Brahman without further efforts, such as approaching a qualified teacher, practice of renunciation, and so forth; hence is the differentiation of the attainment of Brahman as *parā-vidyā.*

By reading a treatise on milk, though a man may know all about milk, yet he does not know milk as it is until he can secure it and drink it; similarly by studying the Vedas, though an aspirant may know all about Brahman, still he does not actually know Brahman until he realizes It by requisite methods.

The Upaniṣads themselves declare that the study of the revealed texts do not reveal Brahman to the seeker. After knowing about Brahman from the scriptures he should put them aside and cultivate intuitive knowledge by spiritual practice:

> The Self cannot be attained by the study of the Vedas, or by intellect, or by vast learning. The Self the seeker yearns for is attainable through that (yearning). To him the Self reveals Its own being.[8]
>
> The intelligent seeker of Brahman, after knowing about this very Self [from the teacher and the scriptures] should cultivate intuitive knowledge. He should not dwell on too many words, because it is particularly tiresome to the organ of speech.[9]
>
> Of what use are the Vedas to him who does not know that indestructible Being, all-pervading like ākāśa, and the highest of all, wherein the Vedas and all the gods are sheltered. Only those who know That as such attain self-fulfillment (Supreme Bliss).[10]
>
> Know that nondual Self alone and give up all other talk.[11]

Indeed, the immediate apprehension (aparōkṣānubhūti) of Brahman is the central theme of Vedanta. That which is real must be a fact of experience.

3. *The imperative need of internal discipline for the realization of Brahman.*

We cannot be quite sure of the reality of the Ultimate One until we

[8]Ka.U. I:2.23; Mu.U.III:2.3.
[9]Br.U. IV:4.21.
[10]Sv.U. IV:8.
[11]Mu.U. II:2.5.

perceive That. "We have to sense God to be convinced that there is a God," says Swami Vivekananda.[12] No amount of reasoning but our own perceptions can make things real to us. As we perceive the world, so it is real to us. As it is real to us, so we evaluate it. As we evaluate it, so we become attached or averse to its objects and beings. Whoever loves or hates a trifle? Now, both attachment and aversion create bondages. Therefore, until we can perceive the Imperishable One and know It to be the sole Reality we cannot see through the falsity of multiplicity and be free from its fetters. It is the mission of Vedanta to direct men and women to this ultimate Goal. All its teachings, theoretical and practical, center on the realization of Brahman. It has developed well-defined spiritual courses (yōgas) to prepare human minds of different types for the attainment of Illumination.

In fact, the Vedantic culture comprises various disciplines. But none of these — belief, or intellectual comprehension, or ecstasy, or equanimity, or righteousness, or scriptural lore, or the observance of religious rites and ceremonies, or charity, or austerity, or performance of duties or humanitarianism — is regarded as an end in itself. Each of them has a distinct place in *parā-vidyā* as contributory to the experience of the Supreme Being. Until the mind is wholly pure and calm one cannot have the vision of Truth. Metaphysical investigation, scriptural study, moral observances, social duties, austerities, rites and ceremonies — any one or more of these cannot effect adequate inner purification and tranquility necessary for the purpose. Hence the imperative need in spiritual life for such internal disciplines as faith, discrimination between the real and unreal, yearning for Truth, dispassion, self-resignation, ardent devotion to the Supreme Being, contemplation, and meditation. The *Muṇḍaka Upaniṣad* affirms:

> Brahman is not reached by the organ of vision or of speech or by any other organ; nor is this attained by austerity or by work. Being pure-hearted through the purification of the understanding a person sees the Impartite One by the practice of meditation.[13]

4. *To realize Brahman is the supreme purpose of human life.*

Vedanta proclaims the realization of Brahman, Saguṇa or Nirguṇa, to be the Goal of life. A man can attain this even in his lifetime and live in this world as a free soul. To reach this stage is the

[12]"My Master," CW IV, p. 163. [13]Mu.U. III:1.8.

blessed privilege of human life. The realization of Brahman is not the exclusive right of a particular person or a body of persons. It is possible for any man or woman to attain this supreme end. The Vedantic literature resounds with the commendation of the direct experience of the Supreme Being: This is the highest Good. This is the attainment of perfection. This is the culmination of knowledge. This is the consummation of peace and joy. This is the most covetable treasure. This is the fulfillment of all desires. This is the cessation of all sorrows and fears, all doubts and delusions, all sins and sufferings, all weaknesses and limitations. This is the ecstatic end of life's weary journey. This is the portal to eternal life, light and bliss.

We quote below a few relevant passages:

> The knower of Brahman attains the Highest (Brahman).[14]
>
> He who knows the Bliss of Brahman has nothing to fear.[15]
>
> If a man realizes Brahman here then the very purpose of his life is fulfilled. If he does not, then utmost misery awaits him. Having perceived Brahman in every being the wise depart from the world and become immortal.[16]
>
> Verily, the Imperishable, Supreme Being he attains who knows that Pure, Imperishable One free from darkness, free from adjuncts, free from attributes. He becomes all-knowing, he becomes all.[17]
>
> Verily the highest joy attends the yōgī whose mind is perfectly tranquil, whose passions are calmed, who is free from stain and has become one with Brahman.[18]
>
> Those who have perfected themselves in indirect and direct knowledge attain to My Supreme State. Since the knower cherishes Me through his knowledge, therefore he is the most beloved of Me. Austerity, pilgrimage, repetition of the mantra, charity, and whatever else is sacred cannot improve that perfection which follows from even a gleam of realization.[19]
>
> That is the Goal, that is the abode of Peace, that is the Supreme Good, the Bliss eternal. He who finds rest there once is not deluded again.[20]

5. *Nothing less than the direct knowledge of Brahman can make man sorrowless.*

[14]Tai.U. II:1.1.
[15]*Ibid.* II:9.
[16]Ken.U. II:5.
[17]Pr.U. IV:10.
[18]BG VI:27.
[19]SB XI:19.3,4 (Śrī Kṛṣṇa's message to Uddhava).
[20]*Yōgavāśiṣṭha Rāmāyaṇa,* Upaṣama-prakaraṇa, 54 sarga, stanza 70.

The fact that no other knowledge but the immediate apprehension of the Supreme Being can give man complete satisfaction is illustrated by the story of a seer and a seeker of Truth in the *Chāndōgya Upaniṣad.*[21]

Nārada approached venerable Sanatkumāra with the words, "Revered sir, give me instruction."

Sanatkumāra: Tell me what you have already learnt, then beyond that I will teach you.

Nārada: Revered sir, I have studied the Ṛg-Veda, the Yajur-Veda, the Sāma Veda, the fourth — the Atharva Veda, the fifth — annals and mythology, grammar, rites for manes, mathematics, the science of portents, economics, logic, ethics and politics, etymology, the six Vedāṅgas,[22] physics, the science of warfare, astronomy, snake-charming, and the fine arts. I have studied all these. Yet I have learnt only the letter. I am not the knower of Ātman (the all-pervasive Self). I have heard from the sages like you that the knower of Ātman goes beyond sorrow. So I am in grief. Take me, revered sir, beyond grief.

Sanatkumāra: Whatever you have learnt is mere name.[23] . . . you meditate on name. He who meditates on name as Brahman goes freely as far as name can go.

Nārada: Revered sir, is there anything greater than name?

Sanatkumāra: Yes, power of speech is greater than name. . . . you meditate on speech. He who meditates on speech as Brahman goes freely as far as speech can go.

Nārada: Revered sir, is there anything greater than speech?

Sanatkumāra: Yes, thought is greater than speech. . . . you meditate on thought as Brahman. He who meditates on thought as Brahman goes freely as far as thought can go.

Nārada: Revered sir, is there anything greater than thought?

Sanatkumāra: Yes, will is greater than thought. . . . you meditate on will as Brahman. He who meditates on will as Brahman goes freely as far as will can go.

Nārada: Revered sir, is there anything greater than will?

Sanatkumāra: Yes, intelligence is greater than will. . . . you meditate on intelligence. He who meditates on intelligence as Brahman goes freely as far as intelligence can go.

[21]Ch.U. VII:1-26 (adapted).

[22]These are the auxiliaries to the Vedas — phonetics, prosody, grammar, etymology, astrology, ritual.

[23]Because all effects are mere names, being the apparent modifications of the ultimate Cause; they have no reality apart from the ultimate Cause.

Thus Sanatkumāra directed Nārada's mind to higher and higher truths until he came to the all-pervasive vital principle, prāṇa. Then he said, "It is prāṇa (the life principle) that has become all these; the knower of prāṇa, pondering this, determining this, and seeing this, becomes a declarer of the truth beyond (ativādī). On hearing this Nārada considered prāṇa to be the ultimate Truth and kept quiet. So in order to instruct him on the ultimate Truth Sanatkumāra added, "But he indeed is 'the declarer of the truth beyond' who declares the ultimate Truth, the Truth of truths."

Nārada then said, "Revered sir, I want to be a 'declarer of the truth beyond' in this sense."

Sanatkumāra: Then you must seek the right knowledge of the ultimate Truth.

Nārada: Revered sir, I want to have the right knowledge of the ultimate Truth.

Sanatkumāra: Then you must know about the realization of the ultimate Truth.

Nārada: Revered sir, I want to know about the realization of the ultimate Truth.

Sanatkumāra: Realization needs reflection. Reflection needs faith. Faith needs reverence. Reverence needs self-discipline. Self-discipline is not possible without joy.

Nārada: Revered sir, I want to know about joy.

Sanatkumāra: The Infinite Itself is joy. There is no joy in the finite. The Infinite alone is joy.

Nārada: Revered sir, I want to know about the Infinite.

Sanatkumāra: That is the Infinite where one sees nothing else, hears nothing else, knows nothing else. But where one sees something else, hears something else, knows something else, that is finite. That which is Infinite is immortal; that which is finite is mortal.

Nārada: Revered sir, in what does the Infinite rest?

Sanatkumāra: In Its own greatness, or not even in that. That alone is below, That above, That behind, That before, That to the right, That to the left; That alone is all this. . . . I am That. I am below, I am above, I am behind, I am before, I am to the right, I am to the left, I am all this. . . . The Self alone is below, the Self is above, the Self is behind, the Self is before, the Self is to the right, the Self is to the left, the Self is all this. . . . So it is written: "He who sees the Infinite Self sees not death, nor disease, nor sorrow. He sees all as the Self and obtains all in every way." When the sense-perceptions are

> purified, then the heart is purified; when the heart is purified, then there is continuous remembrance of the Self. When there is continuous remembrance of the Self, then there is complete deliverance from all bonds.

Thus the venerable Sanatkumāra showed Nārada of purified heart the Truth beyond darkness.

6. *Inner purity is an essential prerequisite for the direct knowledge of Brahman.*

Evidently, it was Nārada's eagerness, sincerity, and purity of heart that made him especially fit for the attainment of the ultimate Truth. Indeed, pure-mindedness is the essential prerequisite for the cultivation of the direct knowledge of Brahman (parā-vidyā). "Blessed are the pure in heart: for they shall see God," says Jesus Christ.[24] The seeker's mind should be purged not only of passions and prejudices, not only of sense-desires, just and reasonable though they may be, but also of subtle attachment to power, position, fame, or learning. He should not even cherish moral goodness or social work as an end in itself. "As long as there is a single fibre sticking out, the thread will not pass through the eye of the needle," says Sri Ramakrishna.[25] Released from all alien thoughts, feelings, and proclivities the seeker's entire mind should turn to the attainment of Truth and Truth alone. The point is that real longing for Truth does not grow in the heart until it is free from every other desire. The story of Naciketā in the *Kaṭha Upaniṣad* illustrates the fact that a seeker of Truth has to give up all desires for earthly possessions and celestial enjoyments, and desire nothing but Truth in order to receive the knowledge of Truth.

That spiritual illumination is not possible without purity of thought, word, and deed is an axiomatic truth in the Vedantic tradition. In the Upaniṣadic view of life, unless a person acquires virtue (dharma), he cannot even gain the insight and the aptitude necessary for the cultivation of "the supreme knowledge (parā-vidyā)." The practice of virtue must precede the pursuit of Truth. For spiritual culture special emphasis has been laid on truthfulness, continence, desirelessness and calmness of mind. Time and again the Upaniṣads remind the aspirant after Truth of the importance of self-mastery and the necessity of constant watchfulness:

[24] Matthew 5:8.

[25] GSR, p. 178.

> This Ātman (Self), luminous and pure, whom the stainless Sannyāsins see within the body, is attainable by the continuous practice of truthfulness, austerity, right knowledge, and continence.[26]
>
> The Ātman (Self) cannot be attained by him who is devoid of strength, or where there is lack of vigilance, or where there is knowledge without renunciation. But if a wise man endeavors by these methods, his self enters the Abode of Brahman.[27]
>
> He who has not abstained from evil ways, or whose senses are not subdued, or whose mind is not calm, or whose heart is not peaceful, cannot gain the right knowledge by which the Self is attained.[28]
>
> Through purified mind alone It (Brahman) is to be realized.[29]
>
> Therefore, he who knows it as such becomes Self-controlled, calm, indrawn, enduring, and contemplative, and sees the Self in his own self and sees all as the Self.[30]
>
> The Self is thus perceived in the self by him who looks for the Self again and again by means of truthfulness, self-control, and absorption of mind.[31]

7. *The ways of the illumined ones.*

How does he who realizes Brahman live in this world? He becomes perfect. He enjoys infinite Bliss. He also leads people to Bliss infinite. His life becomes a blessing to mankind, a shining light in the benighted world. Who but the seer of Truth can guide the unwise, the misguided, to sure Light? Who but the free can make the bound free? The world needs the seer, the man of vision, for its leadership. A million blind people getting together cannot have eyesight and guide a single man, while a single man with vision can find the way and lead a million blind men. It is he who has solved the mystery of life, who can teach others the meaning of life and give right direction to all. The silent influence of his pure, blissful, exemplary life uplifts human minds, not to speak of his words and deeds. Sri Ramakrishna did not preach any social gospel; yet his life has been the chief source of inspiration for numerous social and cultural organizations.

And what is the basic need of the world other than the development of man's moral and spiritual nature? Is any progress possible without these? Is material prosperity ever secure without inner goodness? A man of realization is filled with all-embracing love, because he sees the Self in all. To do good to all beings is his very nature. Śrī Kṛṣṇa states in the *Bhagavad-gītā:*

[26]Mu.U. III:1.5.
[27]Mu.U. III:2.4.
[28]Ka.U. I:2.24.
[29]Br.U. IV:4.19.
[30]Br.U. IV:4.23.
[31]Sv.U. I:15.

The knowers of the self look with an equal eye on a Brāhmaṇa endowed with learning and humility, a scavenger, a cow, an elephant, or a dog.

With imperfections exhausted, doubts dispelled, senses controlled, engaged in the good of all beings, the seers obtain absolute freedom.

Since seeing the Lord equally existent everywhere, he injures not the Self by the self and so goes to the highest goal.[32]

These truths have been exemplified in the lives of the Buddha, Jesus, Śaṅkara, Rāmānuja, Śrī Caitanya, Ramakrishna, Vivekananda, and others who saw the Light of lights. Who has done greater good to mankind than its spiritual leaders? The effective solution of the world problems is always to be found in their lives and teachings. What the world needs is the application of their guiding principles to man's life under varying conditions. The laws of human nature after all remain the same, so the fundamental principles of life always hold good; they never become obsolete. Spiritual idealism has always proved to be the greatest cultural force. To reach the Highest from where he is, the seeker has to pass through many intermediary stages of inner development.

It is true that all the illumined souls are not the knowers of Brahman in the same sense. Broadly speaking, some attain the union of the self with Brahman, some its identity with Brahman. That is to say, some are the knowers of Brahman as Saguṇa (possessed of attributes, i.e., God Personal); some are the knowers of Brahman as Nirguṇa (beyond attributes, i.e., God Impersonal). The nondualistic school of Vedanta holds that a seer can be free from the bondages of life by realizing either his union or his identity with the Supreme Being, but does not consider union to be the consummation. On the other hand, monotheistic schools of Vedanta which maintain some forms of distinction between the finite self and the Supreme Being as ultimate, regard union and not identity as the final beatitude.

[32]BG V:18; V:25; XIII:28.

CHAPTER XI

REALITY AS AFFIRMED BY THE SCRIPTURES AND EXPERIENCED BY THE SEERS

1. *The ultimate One is a fact of experience.*

The Nondual Reality (Brahman), as realized by the seer, is not only a fact but the sole fact. It alone exists. "The Reality is One (ekam sat)," declares the *Ṛg-Veda.*[1] When the seer's ignorance (ajñāna) is dispelled by spiritual enlightenment multiplicity disappears. The knower, withdrawn from all limiting adjuncts, such as the body, the senses, the mind, and the ego — the products of ajñāna — realizes the essential infinitude of the self. The individualized self becomes identified with the Limitless One, the Self of all. The knower becomes merged in the Knowable, all distinction between the two vanishes, and one integral, undivided Consciousness beyond subject-object relation alone shines. Relational knowledge culminates in non-relational Consciousness. The Absolute, the ultimate One, which is the Goal of knowledge, must be beyond duality, beyond relativity. So long as there is difference between the knower and the known, so long as the subject is known in relation to the object and the object in relation to the subject, the culmination of knowledge has not been reached.

In the transcendental experience (nirvikalpa samādhi) there is no such gap as exists between idea and reality, between thought and fact, between the subject and the object, because the two coalesce in unitary Consciousness. This is pure awareness of the self-shining (svayaṁprakāśa) Reality without the process of knowledge. The tripartite division of the knower, the known, and the knowledge that marks all relational cognition is altogether absent in nirvikalpa samādhi.

The fundamental Reality, which is absolute Consciousness, is real to Itself. It is self-evident. In the state of samādhi, however, the mind of the seer does not dissolve. But it becomes so tranquil and

[1]See footnotes 1-5 on page 40.

transparent, and so permeated with the light of Pure Consciousness, that its individualizing function — egoism — completely drops. It is egoism rooted in ignorance (ajñāna) that falsely limits the finite consciousness by a semblance of separation from the Infinite. So the realization of Brahman is complete in the state of nirvikalpa samādhi, when the finite consciousness becomes free from all limitations as the ego of the seer disappears.

The words of Sri Ramakrishna, who speaks from his own experience, bear out this truth:

> Reaching this plane of consciousness, the mind merges in Brahman. The individual soul and the Supreme Soul become one. The aspirant goes into samādhi. His consciousness of the body disappears. He loses the knowledge of the outer world. He does not see the manifold any more. His reasoning comes to a stop . . . the aspirant does not attain the knowledge of Brahman as long as he is conscious of his ego . . . true knowledge is impossible without samādhi.
>
> In samādhi man becomes one with God . . . then, for him, the forms or attributes of God disappear altogether. Then he does not feel God to be a person. Then he cannot describe in words what God is. And who will describe it? He who is to describe does not exist at all; he no longer finds his "I." To such a person Brahman is attributeless. In that state God is experienced only as Consciousness by man's inmost consciousness. He cannot be comprehended by the mind and pure intelligence.[2]

It is said by Śaṅkara:

> The truth of Brahman is clearly and decisively realized by nirvikalpa samādhi, and not by any other way, in which it is apt to be mixed up with alien ideas because of the fluctuation of the mind.[3]

An illuminating account of this nondual experience is given by Yājñavalkya in the course of his instruction to his wife, Maitreyī:

> Just as a lump of salt dropped into water dissolves as water mingles in water and no one is able to pick it up, but from whatever part one takes that water it tastes salty, even so, my dear, this immense, endless, boundless Reality is but Pure Consciousness. The finite self that arises because of the elements constituting its limiting adjuncts disappears with their disappearance. When freed from them it no longer has [individualized] consciousness. This is what I say, my dear.

Then Maitreyī said:

[2]GSR, pp. 245, 430, 767, 859. [3]VC 365.

> Just here you have confused me, sir, by saying that the self, when freed from the limiting adjuncts, no longer has consciousness.

Yājñavalkya answered:

> Certainly, I am not saying anything confusing, my dear; the Nondual Reality is quite capable of consciousness. When there is the appearance of duality then one smells something, one sees something, one hears something, one speaks something, one thinks something, one knows something. But when to the knower of Brahman everything has become the Self, then what should one smell and through what, what should one see and through what, what should one hear and through what, what should one speak and through what, what should one think and through what, what should one know and through what? Through what should one know that because of which all this is known, through what, O Maitreyī, should one know the Knower?[4]

2. *The realization of Nondual Brahman as Pure Consciousness.*

Transcendentally, "One only without a second," the Nondual Reality, is absolute Consciousness. As immanent in the universe, It is the all-pervasive Self, the one ground of all experience, of all knowledge. From the grossest physical object to the highest metaphysical concept, all become manifest through It. So there is no question of Its ever being bereft of consciousness; only It has no individualized or particularized consciousness, because It is beyond all duality and distinction. It is the essence of all specific forms of consciousness. The fact that the seer does not lose consciousness in the state of samādhi or supraconscious experience has been well vindicated by Sri Ramakrishna. Referring to his own samādhi he once remarked, "Some say that this state of mine is a malady. I say to them, 'How can one lose consciousness by thinking of Him whose consciousness has made the whole world conscious?' "[5]

Supraconscious means beyond ego-consciousness. In samādhi consciousness transcends the limitations of the ego. Indeed, to seek God is to seek the very source of consciousness; to realize God is to be united with Pure Consciousness. There is no consciousness anywhere but in God, the Self of all. The Self alone is self-aware.

Essentially consciousness is not a mental state or process. It is awareness itself. All cognitions, feelings, and volitions are varied expressions of inner Consciousness through different modes of the mind. As a matter of fact, mental states are not conscious in

[4]Br.U. II:4.12-14. [5]GSR, p. 256.

themselves. They are illuminated by the light of the luminous Self, just as charcoal becomes aglow when permeated by fire. Absolute Consciousness is Reality Itself. Immanent in the manifold, It is the immutable Being, the all-pervasive Self, the transcendental Witness, of the ever-changing universe, physical and psychical. Every form of existence presupposes consciousness. It is the ground of all experiences and of all assumptions. One cannot posit or negate anything without consciousness. It is the precondition of all thoughts, beliefs, and imaginations. It determines existence and nonexistence. It is the basic fact. Nothing but Pure Consciousness can be the foundational Reality. Nothing else is self-existent (svayaṁ-siddha) and self-effulgent (svayaṁ-prakāśa). Nothing else is real to itself or by itself.

Man daily experiences three different states: waking, dream, and dreamless sleep. They come to him naturally. No one ever gets out of the bondage of life through them. Being rooted in ignorance (ajnāna) they disguise the true nature of the Self. Only the transcendental experience unveils the Self. This is the state of Self-realization. One cannot attain it without proper discipline. It is the fourth state, altogether different from the other three — waking, dream, and dreamless sleep. Truly speaking, this is the sole state native to the Self, yet it is called the fourth (turīya) only in relation to the other three, which are superimposed on It through ignorance (ajñāna) and are therefore adventitious.

An illuminating portraiture of the sublime Self exempt from the three extrinsic states of waking, dream, and dreamless sleep has been presented by the *Māṇḍūkya Upaniṣad:*

> The wise know that to be the fourth (turīya), which is not inwardly conscious [as in dream], nor outwardly conscious [as in the waking state], nor conscious both ways [as in a state intermediary between waking and dream], which is not a mass of dormant conscious processes [as in profound sleep], nor omni-consciousness, nor unconsciousness; which is ungraspable, imperceptible, indeterminable, uninferable, inconceivable, undefinable; which is pure Self-awareness, which endures after the negation of the manifold; which is nondual, calm, and blissful. That is the Self. That is to be realized.[6]

The realization of the Self as Pure Consciousness is fully convincing and satisfying. It is its own proof. It is self-validating. The Self can be known only by the Self (sva-saṁvedya). The Self is the

[6]Ma.U. VII.

knower of everything. "By what shall one know the Knower?" says Yājñavalkya.[7] Being of the nature of consciousness, the Self is awareness itself. Just as light requires no other light to show itself, so the Self shines by Its own right. No wonder that the realization of the self as Supreme Consciousness, the Light of lights, which removes all darkness, all delusions, all doubts forever, should be an evidence for itself! Once perceived, that Light is never lost sight of. "Verily, for him (the knower of Brahman) the sun neither rises nor sets. He who thus knows the secret of the Vedas for him there is perpetual day," says the Upaniṣad.[8] The seer who returns to the plane of multiplicity after samādhi sees that Light shining in and through everything. He becomes self-luminous because he has realized his oneness with Supreme Consciousness. He finds all beings in the Self and the Self in all beings. He is no longer subject to error or aversion.

As the *Īśa Upaniṣad* declares:

> He who sees all beings in the Self and the Self in all beings has no reason for hatred. When to the seer all things have verily become the Self; what delusion, what sorrow, can there be for him who beholds that oneness?[9]

3. *Pure Being is Pure Consciousness and Pure Bliss.*

In the state of samādhi the seer experiences ineffable joy. He is merged, as it were, in an effulgent ocean of bliss. The Supreme Reality (Brahman) is Pure Bliss as well as Pure Consciousness (Vijñānam Ānandaṁ Brahma).[10] Being is Consciousness Itself and Bliss Itself. Pure Being, Pure Consciousness, Pure Bliss are one and the same. They are not the aspects or attributes of Brahman. Brahman is Being-Consciousness-Bliss (sat-cit-ānanda).[11] The Bliss that the enlightened one experiences is not just the negation of sorrow, but a positive Entity. Liberation is defined in Vedanta as the cessation of all misery and the attainment of absolute Bliss.[12] Unlike the Sāṁkhya system, Vedanta views happiness or pleasure as a positive attainment, not as mere negation of pain. All joys have but one source, Brahman. "The Infinite Itself is joy. There is no joy in the finite. The Infinite alone is joy," says Sanatkumāra to Nārada.[13] "On a particle of this very Bliss other beings live," says Yājñavalkya.[14] "He

[7]Br.U. II:4.14; IV:5.15.
[8]See Ch.U. III:11.3.
[9]Is.U. 6,7.
[10]Br.U. III:9.28.7.
[11]NPT.U. I:6; NUT.U. VII:5.
[12]Cf.VP VIII.
[13]Ch.U. VII:23.1.
[14]Br.U. IV:3.32.

is Joy Itself. By attaining that joy the finite being becomes joyful," says the *Taittirīya Upaniṣad.*[15]

While the illumined ones experience unlimited, unalloyed Bliss, the joys of the unillumined are limited and alloyed. As stated in the *Vedānta-paribhāṣā:*

> Joy is of two kinds — relative and absolute. Of these, relative joy is a certain expression of a particle of Bliss through variations in the mental mode due to contact with objects. . . . Absolute Bliss is Brahman alone.[16]

All the joys of life are included in the Bliss of Brahman. Therefore he who attains Brahman loses none. On the contrary, all happiness that people hanker after in life through sense enjoyment, through intellectual pursuit, or through aesthetic culture, the knower of Brahman gains in an infinite degree and in the purest form. So says the Upaniṣad: "Whatever good is acquired by people all are united in him (the enlightened Raikva)."[17] "To the enlightened Brāhmaṇa all the Vedic rituals are of as much use as a pond when the entire region is flooded."[18] Once a man tastes that Supreme Bliss, the highest pleasures of the relative existence lose all charm for him. They become quite insipid. "He who drinks rock-candy syrup cares not for molasses,"[19] remarks Sri Ramakrishna.

After the experience of the Bliss of Brahman in samādhi an aspirant thus gives expression to his feelings, as stated by Śaṅkara in his *Viveka-cūḍāmaṇi* (The Crest Jewel of Discrimination):

> My mind fades away and its functions cease as I realize the identity of the self and Brahman. I do not know either this or not-this; nor what or how much is the immeasurable joy. The majesty of the ocean of Supreme Brahman filled with the nectar of Its own Bliss is quite impossible to express in words or comprehend by the mind. In the minutest portion of this my mind melted and merged like a hail-stone dropped and dissolved in the ocean, and is now satisfied with the essence of Bliss. Where is the universe gone, by whom is it removed, and wherein is it merged? Just now it was seen by me; has it ceased to exist? It is exceedingly strange. In the ocean of Brahman filled with the nectar of absolute Bliss what is to be rejected and what to be accepted? What is other, what is different? I do neither see, nor hear nor know anything in It. I exist as the ever blissful Self of a distinctive nature.[20]

[15]Tai.U. II:7.
[16]VP VIII.
[17]Ch.U. IV:1.4.
[18]BG II:46.
[19]GSR, p. 671.
[20]VC 481-85.

4. *The meaning of "The One only without a second."*

The Ultimate Reality is absolutely One. As declared by the *Chāndōgya Upaniṣad,* It is "The One only without a second."[21] This means that Brahman is free from all limitations and distinctions. Every created thing is limited in three ways — in space, in time, and as a particular object. In the first place, it occupies a certain space; it cannot exist everywhere; so it is subject to space-limitation (deśa-pariccheda). Secondly, it exists for the time being, it did not exist before its origin and will not exist after its destruction; so it is subject to time-limitation (kāla-pariccheda). Thirdly, it is distinguished from every other object. It is just what it is, and not anything else. Being thus confined to itself, it is under object-limitation (vastu-pariccheda). Brahman precludes all the three limitations. Being all-pervasive, It is beyond space-limitation. Having no beginning or end, growth or decay, It is beyond time-limitation. Being the Self of all, It is beyond object-limitation. In fact, It is all that appears to exist, because It is the one immutable Being of all apparent modifications. "Verily all is Brahman," declares the Upaniṣad.[22] Beyond space and time, and without differentia, Brahman is limitless (ananta) in every way. So it is said, "Brahman is Truth, Consciousness, and Infinitude."[23] Being infinite or limitless, It is the perfection of existence, in other words, All-Bliss.

The expression "The One only without a second" also means that Brahman is free from the three kinds of distinction. These are: (1) the distinction of an object from every object of a different class, just as a tree is different from everything that is not a tree (vijātīya-bheda); (2) the distinction of an object from all other objects of the same class, just as a tree is different from all other trees (svajātīya-bheda); (3) the distinction in the object itself, just as a tree has different parts and qualities, such as trunk, branches, leaves, size, shape, color, etc., (svagata-bheda).[24] As there is no entity different from Brahman, such as Nature or finite being, It is free from the first kind of distinction. As there is no other Brahman, It is free from the second kind of distinction. Being one and the same throughout (ekarasam), It is free from the third kind of distinction. In Brahman there is no such distinction as that of the whole from the parts, of substance from attributes, of the subject from the object.

"Being impartite, Brahman cannot be at the same time the knower

[21]Ch.U. VI:2.1.
[22]Ch.U. III:14.1.
[23]Tai.U. II:1.
[24]Pd. II:20.

and the known" says Śaṅkara.[25] It is one whole simple Being, formless, featureless, partless, actionless, attributeless. Yet It is not a substance without attributes but something beyond the distinction of substance and attribute. It is neither the subject nor the object, nor the synthesis of both. It is not that Brahman as the subject is conscious of Itself as the object. Brahman is not a self-conscious personality. It is processless Pure Consciousness, self-effulgent. The light of Consciousness does not shine Itself, but shines of Itself. Luminosity is not Its attribute, but Its very nature. It may be noted that Śaṅkara's Brahman is different from Hegel's Absolute, in which the distinction between the subject and the object prevails. Hegel's Absolute has consciousness of the object evolving from and abiding in Itself. The ultimate principle, according to Śaṅkara, is *simple* unity, but, according to Hegel, *complex* unity.

5. *The ultimate One beyond the range of thought and speech is betokened by negatives.*

Truly speaking, Brahman has no distinguishing mark. It is indefinable. It cannot be expressed in words. As observed by Śaṅkara,[26] every word used to denote a thing conveys the meaning by indicating a certain genus, or act, or quality, or relation. For example, the words *cow, horse,* indicate genus; *cook, teacher,* indicate action; *white, black,* indicate quality; *wealthy, cattle-owner,* indicate relation. Brahman has none of these. It belongs to no genus. It has no quality. It is actionless. It is unrelated.

Transcendentally, "One only without a second" Brahman is beyond the world of appearance. As immanent in the universe, Brahman is the Self of all. Therefore, It cannot be objectified by the senses or the mind. "It is the Ear of the ear, the Mind of the mind, the Speech of speech, the Life of life."[27] "The eye does not go there, nor speech, nor the mind."[28] It sees through the eyes; the eyes cannot see It. It hears through the ears; the ears cannot hear It. It speaks through the mouth; the mouth cannot express It. It works with the hands; the hands cannot grasp It. It knows through the mind; the mind cannot know It. "You cannot see That which is the witness of vision; you cannot hear That which is the hearer of hearing; you cannot think That which is the thinker of thought; you cannot know That which is the knower of knowledge."[29] "It is different from the known; and

[25]Tai.U. II:1, S.com.
[26]BG XIII:12, S.com.
[27]Ken.U. I:2.
[28]*Ibid.* I:3.
[29]Br.U. III:4.2.

again, It is above the unknown."[30] How can words denote That, "Wherefrom words along with ideas turn back unable to reach It?"[31]

Therefore, the only way to indicate Brahman is to say "what It is not" rather than "what It is." So Brahman is disclosed by excluding as "not this," "not this" (neti, neti) all adjuncts that one might be inclined to associate with It. What remains after the negation of all superimpositions is Brahman. In the *Bṛhadāraṇyaka Upaniṣad* Brahman is spoken of as "without prior or posterior, without interior or exterior."[32] Again, as declared by the same Upaniṣad, "There is no other or more appropriate mode of expression with regard to Brahman than this 'not this.' Reality of realities is Its name." Śaṅkara remarks in this context:

> By setting aside all differentia owing to adjuncts, the negative expressions indicate something which is undifferentiated by name, or form, or function, or diversity, or species, or attribute. It is through one or other of these that words signify things. But none of these distinguishing marks exists in Brahman. Therefore It cannot be specified as, "It is such and such," in the same way as people can point out a cow by saying, "there moves a white cow with horns." Brahman is expressed by means of name, form, and function superimposed on It, in such terms as "Knowledge-Bliss-Brahman," "Pure Intelligence," "Brahman," and "Ātman." When, however, one intends to express Its essential nature divested of all distinctions due to adjuncts, then one cannot do it by direct means. Then this is the only way: to indicate It as "not this," "not this," thus eliminating all specifications that might be ascribed to It.[33]

Indeed, the seer's experience of Brahman is like the tasting of a delicious food by a dumb person (mūkāsvādanavat), who cannot say what it is like but can give some indication of it by gesture. Śaṅkara mentions a significant story: Being asked by Bāṣkali about Brahman, Bādhva kept quiet. "Instruct me, sir," said Bāṣkali a second time, a third time. Then Bādhva said, "I am answering, but you do not understand. Silence is the Self."[34] Indeed, Silence is the name of Brahman. "What Brahman is cannot be expressed in words," says Sri Ramakrishna. "All things in the world — Vedas, the Purāṇas, the Tantras, the six systems of philosophy — have been defiled, like food that has been touched by the tongue, for they have been read or uttered by the tongue. Only one thing has not been defiled in this way,

[30]Ken.U. I:4.
[31]Tai.U. II:4.1.
[32]Br.U. II:5.19.
[33]*Ibid.* II:3.6, S.com.
[34]BS III:2.17, S.com.

and that is Brahman. No one has ever been able to say what Brahman is."[35] How can the seer describe Brahman? In samadhi his ego disappears. Sri Ramakrishna illustrates this truth by a parable. "Once a salt doll went to measure the depth of the ocean. It wanted to tell others how deep the water was. But this it could never do, for no sooner did it get into water than it melted. Now who was there to report the ocean's depth?"[36]

6. *Similarity between the Vedantic and the Neo-Platonic view with regard to the Ultimate Reality.*

It is interesting to note in this context the resemblance between the Vedantic and the Neo-Platonic view as expressed by the mystic philosopher, Plotinus. He holds that the Supreme Reality is all-transcendent, beyond the duality of the knower and the known, and indefinable; neither speech nor thought can reach It; only by ecstasy (samādhi) can we attain It.[37] Observes he with regard to the Ultimate One and Its experience:

> The One is in truth beyond all statement: any affirmation is a thing; but "all-transcending, resting above even the most august divine Mind," possesses alone of all true being, and is not a thing among things; we can give it no name because that would imply predication: we can try to indicate, in our feeble way, something concerning it: when in our perplexity we object: "Then it is without self-perception, without self-consciousness, ignorant of itself" we must remember that we have been considering it only in its opposites. (The Enneads, V:3.13)
>
> The One can be indicated only in negations: — How can we make such a statement about It, seeing that all else we say of It is said by negation. (The Enneads, VI:8.11)
>
> In our self-seeing There, the self is seen as belonging to that order, or rather we are merged into that self in us which has the quality of that order. It is a knowing of the self restored to its purity. No doubt we should not speak of seeing; but we cannot help talking in dualities, seen and seer, instead of, boldly, the achievement of unity. In this seeing, we

[35]GSR, p. 102. [36]*Ibid.*, p. 103.

[37]It is evident from Porphyry's account of the life of Plotinus that he had mystical experience four times in his life, and that Porphyry himself had it once. " 'There was shown to Plotinus the Term ever near': for the Term, the one end, of his life was to become Uniate, to approach to the God over all; and four times, during the period I passed with him, he achieved this Term, by no mere latent fitness but by the ineffable Act. To this God, I also declare, I Porphyry, that in my sixty-eighth year I too was once admitted and entered into Union." *Plotinus: The Ethical Treatises* (The Enneads), Vol. I, trans. by Stephen Mackenna, Boston, Charles T. Branford, 1916, p.24.

> neither hold an object nor trace distinction; there is no two. The man is changed, no longer himself nor self-belonging; he is merged with the Supreme, sunken into it, one with it; centre coincides with centre, for on this higher plane things that touch at all are one; only in separation is there duality; by our holding away, the Supreme is set outside. This is why the vision baffles telling; we cannot detach the Supreme to state it; if we have seen something thus detached we have failed of the Supreme which is to be known only as one with ourselves . . . There is thus a converse in virtue of which the essential man outgrows Being, becomes identical with the Transcendent of Being. (The Enneads, VI:9.10,11)[38]

7. *The Real is the Ideal.*

Vedanta emphasizes the fact that Brahman is All-Bliss, that the Supreme Reality is also the supreme value. Therefore one should seek Truth for the sake of Truth, one should love God for the sake of God. The discrepancy between the actual and the Ideal which persists in the relative existence, does not prevail in the Absolute. Brahman is the perfection of existence, where the Real and the Ideal are identified with each other. It is an end in itself. It is the Supreme Goal, beyond which there is nothing to attain, nothing to know, nothing to desire.

The attainment of Brahman is complete self-fulfillment. It is related in the *Taittirīya Upaniṣad* that Bhṛgu approached his father, Varuṇa, for the knowledge of Brahman. As instructed by his father, he practiced one course of meditation after another and finally knew through higher and higher truths that "Bliss is Brahman. It is from Bliss that all beings are born; by Bliss all that are born are sustained; into Bliss they return and re-enter."[39]

When a person realizes Brahman, then only does he become absolutely free from fear. Everywhere else there is fear in some form or other. So the same Upaniṣad declares: "When the aspirant gains secure position in imperceptible, formless, indefinable, unsupported Brahman, then he becomes fearless. He who knows the Bliss of Brahman, wherefrom words along with ideas turn back unable to reach It, has nothing to fear."[40]

As long as the self is confronted by the not-self there is fear. So by

[38] *Plotinus, The Ethical Treatises* (The Enneads), trans. by Stephen Mackenna, Boston, Charles T. Branford, 1916. See also *Plotinus, The Enneads,* trans. by Stephen Mackenna, London, Faber and Faber (containing Porphyry's account of *The Life of Plotinus and the Arrangement of his Work).*

[39] Tai.U. III:6.

[40] Tai.U. II:7,9.

realizing the Infinite Self one becomes free from fear. "The Infinite alone is joy."[41] "When the aspirant sees the all-pervasive, self-luminous Brahman, the Origin, the Maker, and the Lord of the Universe, then the seer shaking off good and evil becomes stainless and attains perfect unity."[42] "This (the Self) is his supreme Goal; this is his supreme Wealth; this is his supreme Abode; this is his supreme Bliss."[43]

[41]Ch.U. VII:23.
[42]Mu.U. III:1.3.
[43]Br.U. IV:3.22.

PART FOUR

REALIZATION OF GOD, THE ALL-PERFECT SUPREME BEING, THE IDEAL ONE, IS THE ULTIMATE GOAL

CHAPTER XII

BRAHMAN, ALL-TRANSCENDENT AND IMMANENT

1. *Defining the Indefinable.*

As the Supreme Principle immanent in the universe, Brahman, the Ultimate One, is apparently differentiated. It has many aspects. But in Itself Brahman is absolutely undifferentiated. It is "One only without a second" (see Ch. XI, sec. 4) and cannot, therefore, be designated even as the substratum (adhiṣṭhāna) of appearance, which does not endure. Free from all limitations and distinctions, the nondual Absolute is "beyond the range of speech and thought." This is called *Para Brahman* (Supreme Brahman) and the other *Apara Brahman* (Subordinate Brahman).[1]

Human language is fitted to the world of difference and relativity. Words imply distinction in some form or other. Definition means determination by inclusion and exclusion. It must include what is intended and exclude what is not intended. This involves differentiation. There is nothing else from which the All-transcendent Absolute, "the One only without a second," can be distinguished. Unrelated to any other, the Ultimate One in Itself is incomprehensible and indescribable. Such epithets as the Self (Ātman), the Witness (Sākṣī), the Ruler (Īśvara), the Cause (Karaṇa) do not describe the All-transcendent Supreme Being (Para Brahman); they only suggest It by

[1]See Pr.U. V:2.

implication. Nor, in true accuracy, can It be called "the Omnipresent," "the Omniscient," "the Omnipotent," because all such terms relate It to something other than Itself.

The All-transcendent Supreme Being (Para Brahman), the Ultimate Reality, is unlike anything we experience in the manifold universe. It cannot be expressed in terms of the phenomenal world. It excludes all that we perceive by the senses or comprehend by the mind. Hence, the Upaniṣads indicate the nature of the All-transcendent Supreme Being (Para Brahman), the Ultimate Reality, by negations, such as:

> It is neither massive nor minute, neither short nor long, neither red (like fire) nor moist (like water). It is neither shadow nor darkness, neither air nor ether. Unrelated, It is without savor or odor, without eyes or ears, without the vocal organ or the mind, without lustre or life. Without mouth, measureless, without interior or exterior, It does not eat anything nor is eaten by anything.[2]
>
> Tell me That which you see as other than righteousness and unrighteousness, other than cause and effect, other than what has been and what is to be.[3]
>
> One becomes free from the jaws of death by realizing That which has no sound, no touch, no form, no taste, no smell, which is undecaying, immutable, without beginning, without end, beyond the Cosmic mind and immovable.[4]

Even the positive terms, such as *one, eternal, calm, steady,* when used with reference to the All-transcendent Reality (Para Brahman), have negative connotations. *One* (eka) means nondual; *eternal* (nitya) means timeless, changeless; *calm* (śānta) means motionless, unchanging; *steady* (dhruva) means immovable, immutable. Similarly, the expression "Being-Consciousness-Bliss (sat-cit-ānanda)" indicates Para Brahman indirectly by negating the opposite. *Being* (sat) excludes the idea of nonbeing, *consciousness* (cit) the idea of materiality or unintelligence, and *bliss* (ānanda) the idea of sorrow, limitation, or imperfection, with regard to Brahman. The constant use of the negative expressions is likely to create in the mind of the seeker the erroneous notion that Brahman is a non-entity, a void. To counteract this the term *sat* (being) is used. Even then the seeker may think that, though a positive entity, Brahman is a material, unintelligent principle; to counteract this the term *cit* (consciousness), that which is self-manifest, is used. Finally, to show that

[2]Br.U. III:8.8. [3]Ka.U. I:2.14. [4]*Ibid.* I:3.15.

this Consciousness is entirely without imperfection the term *ānanda* (bliss) is used.

Indeed, All-transcendent Brahman is beyond all the categories of the relative existence. Unconditioned by space, time, and causality, It is neither here nor there; It is neither born nor unborn; It is neither cause nor effect; It is neither subject nor object. It is neither known nor unknown. It is even beyond the triad of the jīva (living being), jagat (inanimate world), and Īśvara (their Ruler). "Still the seers see It constantly as if with the eyes wide open unto the sky."[5] "The Light that is Brahman, the Light that is clear as daylight, the Light that is eternal, the Light that is the source of the world, the knowers of Brahman see that Superb Light everywhere."[6] Just as blind people living and moving in the full blaze of the midday sun have no knowledge of the splendor of sunlight, similarly, the unillumined are unaware of the Light of Brahman, even though living and moving and having their being in It.

2. *Nondual Brahman can be comprehended and expounded as well in relation to the apparent manifold as its substratum. Extrinsic and intrinsic marks of Reality.*

However, in the state of ignorance (ajñāna), while the world of appearance persists, we can comprehend Brahman only in relation to it, just as we can comprehend the world in relation to Brahman. We have to know the One with reference to the manifold as we have to know the manifold with reference to the One. Brahman is the reality underlying all diversity and relativity. It is immanent in the whole universe. We have to find the Absolute through the manifestation.

When Bhṛgu approached his father Varuṇa for the knowledge of Brahman, the father said to him, "The body, the vital principle, the eye, the ear, the mind, the vocal organ — these are the instruments for the realization of Brahman." Then he added, "Seek That from which all these beings are born, by which all that are born are sustained and into which they return and re-enter. That is Brahman."[7]

The sage Śāndilya gives the following instruction on Brahman:

> All this [the sensible universe] is [essentially] Brahman, because of its origin, end, and sustenance in It. Therefore one should calmly meditate on Brahman. Man is as his determination is. As his

[5] See Rg V. I:22.20. [6] Ch.U. III:17.7. [7] Tai.U. III:1.

determination is in this life, so will he be after death. Hence he must have a determination. Verily he will attain Brahman who has right determination and unshaken faith like this:

"He who acts or rests through the mind [the seat of volition], who dwells in the subtle body [the seat of cognition], who is self-intelligent, whose will is unfailing, who is formless like the sky, who holds all actions, all desires, all smells, and all tastes, who pervades all this, who has no organs and no interest; He is my Self within the heart, smaller than a grain of rice, or barley, or mustard, or śyāmāka corn, or its kernel. He is my Self within the heart, greater than the earth, greater than the sky, greater than heaven, greater than all these worlds. His work is all this; all desires are His; all smells are His; all tastes are His. He pervades all this. He has no organs, and no interest. He is my Self within the heart. He is Brahman. I will attain Him on departing from this world."[8]

In accord with the Upaniṣads, the *Brahma-sūtras* tersely define Brahman as "That from which are the origin and so forth of this (the world)." It means, as explained by Śaṅkara, "Brahman is the Omniscient and Omnipotent Cause, from which proceed the origin, the sustenance, and the dissolution of the universe, which is manifest through name and form, which includes innumerable sentient beings as doers and experiencers, which contains actions and their results conditioned by time, space, and causality, and the nature and the plan of which cannot be conceived even by the mind."[9]

Here Brahman is defined by extrinsic marks (taṭastha lakṣaṇa), such as the origin, the sustenance, and the dissolution of the universe. These do not belong to Him intrinsically, and yet indicate Him by characterizing Him as the omniscient and the omnipotent Cause of the universe, distinct from anything else that may be imagined as its Cause, such as the primordial unintelligent nature (prakṛti), time, accident, necessity, void. When the seeker is able to comprehend Brahman as the omniscient, omnipotent, all-pervading Cause of the universe, then he can possibly conceive Him as the Ultimate Reality beyond all diversity.

Without grasping unity in multiplicity one cannot grasp unity beyond multiplicity. Without understanding the concrete expressions of consciousness one cannot understand it as a transcendental principle. Without finding the basis of the panorama of cause and effect one cannot know the One. Without knowing the substratum of the world of appearance one cannot reach the

[8]Ch.U. III:14.1-4.
[9]BS I:1.2, S.com.

Absolute. In such terse expressions as "Brahman is Truth, Consciousness, Infinitude,"[10] "Brahman is Consciousness, Bliss,"[11] the Upaniṣads indicate Brahman by intrinsic characteristics (svarūpa lakṣaṇa), which inhere in It. The intrinsic mark of some thing forms its essential nature. It lasts as long as the thing lasts. The extrinsic mark is not an essential part of a thing, and yet distinguishes it from other things. It may or may not last as long as the thing lasts. In the expression, "the hexagonal temple with the flag," the term "hexagonal" denotes the intrinsic, and the term "with the flag" denotes the extrinsic mark of the temple.

3. *Brahman as immanent in the universe.*

Brahman, the omniscient and omnipotent Cause of the universe, is immanent in it as its innermost Self. As the one all-pervading Self of the phenomenal world, Brahman holds, sustains, integrates, illumines, enlivens, and regulates it. The Upaniṣad states:

> This (the innermost) Self is the ruler of all beings, and the king of all beings. Just as all spokes are fixed to the hub and the rim of a chariot-wheel, so are all created things, all gods, all worlds, all organs, and all these finite selves fixed in this Self.[12]

Indeed, the Omnipresent Self controls everything from within.

About this Internal Ruler Yājñavalkya thus speaks to Gārgī in answer to her question in a debate on Brahman:

> Under the mighty rule of this Imperishable One, O Gārgī, the sun and the moon keep to their positions; under the mighty rule of this Imperishable One, O Gārgī, heaven and earth are held in their places; under the mighty rule of this Imperishable One, O Gārgī, moments, hours,[13] days and nights, fortnights, months, seasons, and years roll on; under the mighty rule of this Imperishable One, O Gārgī, some rivers run eastward from the White Mountains, others flowing westward continue in that direction, and still others follow their respective courses; under the mighty rule of this Imperishable One, O Gārgī, men praise them that give, the gods depend on those that offer sacrifice, and the manes on a special oblation.

[10]Tai.U. II:1.
[11]Br.U. III:9.28.7.
[12]Br.U. II:5.15.
[13]The Sanskrit text uses the term *muhūrtā,* which is equivalent to about 48 minutes.

> He who in this world, O Gārgī, without knowing this Imperishable One offers oblations in fire, performs sacrifices, practices austerities, even though for many thousands of years, gains no lasting results. He who departs from the world, O Gārgī, without knowing this Imperishable One, is wretched. But he who departs from this world, O Gārgī, after knowing this Imperishable One, is a knower of Brahman.
>
> This Imperishable One, O Gārgī, is never seen but is the Witness; It is never heard, but is the Hearer; It is never thought, but is the Thinker; It is never known, but is the Knower. There is no other witness than This, no other hearer than This, no other thinker than This, no other knower than This. By this Imperishable One, O Gārgī, ākāśa [the finest and the most pervasive of all the elements] is permeated.[14]

As immanent in the manifold universe, the same Brahman has different phases. It is the one immutable substance of all changing forms. Everything exists because of It. "In that subtle Essence all this has its being."[15] Brahman is the sole support of all. "In That all the worlds are contained."[16] "In That is the triad (living beings, inanimate nature and their Ruler)."[17] (See Chap. V.) Brahman manifests the universe. "Through Its effulgence all this shines."[18] "It is the Light of lights."[19] Brahman is the Omnipresent Divine Being "who is in fire, who is in water, who is in the plants, who is in the trees, who pervades the whole universe."[20]

Brahman is the Almighty Ruler, the Protector of the universe, the Benign Father, the Adorable Lord, the Giver of Self-knowledge, the Sole Refuge of the seekers of Liberation. Brahman as Providence regulates the results of all actions. "From Him are the fruits of actions; for that is reasonable."[21]

Brahman is the finite self dwelling in the heart of each and every living creature. Indeed, One effulgent Being is the Soul of all souls. "With hands and feet everywhere, with eyes, heads, and mouths everywhere, with ears everywhere in the universe That exists encompassing all — shining by the functions of all the senses, yet without the senses; unattached, yet sustaining all; beyond the senses, yet their experiencer."[22] "Brahman that is immediate and direct, That is the self within all."[23] "The senses do not perceive That, no one can see That with the eye. Those who know That through the purified mind as thus seated in their heart, become immortal."[24]

[14]Br.U. III:8.9-11.
[15]Ch.U. VI:14.3.
[16]Ka.U. II:3.1.
[17]Sv.U. I:7.
[18]Ka.U. II:2.15.
[19]Mu.U. II:2.9.
[20]Sv.U. II:17.
[21]BS III:2.38.
[22]BG XIII:13,14.
[23]Br.U. III:4.2.
[24]Sv.U. IV:20.

4. *Though immanent, Brahman is All-transcendent.*

Essentially formless, featureless, attributeless, Brahman assumes forms, features, and attributes in association with the phenomenal world that prevails for the finite self. That which is undiversified becomes diversified, That which is Impersonal becomes Personal, That which is static becomes dynamic, through adjuncts (upādhi) superimposed, without undergoing any change whatsoever, just as pure light appears variegated through a multicolored medium. Therefore, the Upaniṣads teach two distinct aspects of Brahman: the Transcendent (para) and the Immanent (apara). The one is free from the adjuncts (nirupādhi) and the other with the adjuncts (sōpādhi); the one is undifferentiated (nirviśeṣa) and the other differentiated (saviśeṣa); the one is beyond attributes (nirguṇa) and the other with attributes (saguṇa). So says Śaṅkara:

> Two kinds of Brahman are stated: the one having as its adjuncts the diversities of the universe, the modifications of name and form; the other, its contrary, completely free from all adjuncts.[25]

In some passages of the Upaniṣads both the aspects are presented side by side:

> Just as the sun which helps all eyes to see, is not tainted by the defect of the eyes or the external objects revealed by it, even so the same undiversified innermost Self is not contaminated by the misery of the world, being beyond it.[26]
>
> It moves and It does not move. It is far and It is also near. It is inside all this and It is also outside all this.[27]
>
> One effulgent Being is hidden in all creatures. He is all pervasive and is the innermost Self of all. He presides over all actions and all beings reside in Him. He is the Witness and He is Pure Consciousness free from the guṇas.[28] And He is all by Himself.[29]

Śrī Kṛṣṇa thus speaks of the twofold aspect of Brahman:

> All this world is pervaded by Me in my unmanifested form . . . All beings exist in Me; but I do not abide in them. Nor do the beings abide in Me. Behold My divine mystery! My being, which is the substance and the sustenance of all, does not abide in them.[30]

[25]BS I:1.11, S.com.
[26]Ka.U. II:2.11.
[27]Is.U. 5.
[28]See footnote 13 on the three guṇas, p. 42.
[29]Sv.U. VI:11.
[30]BG IX:4,5.

There are references to the two aspects of Brahman in the *Ṛg-Veda:*

> The whole universe is His glory. He (the Cosmic Being) is, indeed, greater than His glory. All beings existing in the past, the present, and the future form only a quarter of Him. The other three quarters remain in the immutable and luminous state.[31]

5. *Intrinsically undifferentiated Brahman is apparently differentiated.*

The purport of these teachings, however, is not that Brahman is dual in character. The same Brahman cannot be intrinsically both undifferentiated and differentiated, because these are contradictory modes. In presenting Brahman in two different aspects, the undifferentiated and the differentiated, the Upaniṣads intend that the one is true in the absolute sense, the other is true only with relation to the world of appearance. When the seeker of Truth goes beyond darkness and attains true knowledge, he realizes Brahman as undifferentiated, free from all adjuncts, which are due to multiplicity prevailing through his ignorance (ajñāna). So according to the Upaniṣads, Brahman is essentially undifferentiated, absolutely One. In Itself It is neither differentiated, nor both differentiated and undifferentiated.[32]

The Nondual Brahman being manifested as differentiated in relation to the world of names and forms suffers no change, just as a crystal appearing red in association with a red object, a crimson flower for instance, does not actually become red. As the crystal retains its intrinsic purity in spite of its apparent redness, so does Brahman ever remain undifferentiated. That the apparent existence of the manifold makes no difference in the absoluteness or infinitude of Brahman has been pithily expressed in the following Peace Chant of the *Śukla Yajur-Veda:* "That (the Absolute Brahman) is infinite. This (the universe) is infinite [in its essential nature as Brahman]. From the Infinite (Absolute Brahman) emerges the infinite (the universe), on seeing the infinitude of the infinite (the universe), the Infinite (Absolute Brahman) alone remains (whether the universe appears or not)."[33] The whole order of phenomena is essentially the Absolute Brahman, being Its manifestation through names and forms, which are insubstantial and seemingly existent. The Undiversified Infinite One exists throughout apparent diversities.

[31] Ṛg V. X:90, Puruṣa Sūktam; see also Ch.U. III:12.6.
[32] See BS III:2.11, Śaṅkara's com.
[33] Br.U. V:1.1.

Through all the descriptions of Brahman as differentiated the Upaniṣads intend to lead the mind of the seeker from the differentiated to the undifferentiated Brahman.[34] While the manifold universe prevails, the seeker can at best conceive the Absolute Brahman as its all-pervasive Self supporting it, sustaining it, and shaping its course from within. So the Upaniṣads try to help the aspirant after Truth in finding the One in the many, the Imperishable in the perishable, the Infinite in the finite — in seeing the Creator of the created, the Ruler of the ruled, the Knower of the known. For this purpose different methods of meditation on Brahman with symbolic forms and figures have also been prescribed. Brahman is envisaged as the Cosmic Person with thousands of heads, with thousands of eyes, with thousands of legs, who covers the whole universe and also exists beyond.[35]

Again the universe is conceived as the body of the Cosmic Self: "The heavens are His head; the sun and the moon His eyes; the quarters, His ears; the revealed Vedas, His speech; the wind is His breath; the universe, His heart. From His feet is produced the earth. He is indeed, the inner Self of all beings."[36] To help aspirants to comprehend the oneness of existence, the unity of man and the universe, of the microcosm and the macrocosm in various aspects, has been stressed.[37] The Upaniṣads have further instructed the seekers to contemplate the luminous sun — the source of life and light, the all-pervasive sky (ākāśa), the all-comprehensive word "Ōm,"[38] and the mind — the ruler of the senses, as symbols of Brahman. Meditation on Brahman within the heart, the locus of the self, has also been recommended.

6. *A true knower of Brahman sees Brahman in both the aspects.*

His knowledge is complete who sees Brahman as transcendent

[34]This is the view of the Nondualistic Vedanta. Other schools of Vedanta, however, maintain the ultimacy of the Differentiated Brahman in some form or other. According to Rāmānuja, the chief exponent of Qualified Nondualism, "Undifferentiated" (nirviśeṣa or nirguṇa) means 'absolutely free from all blemishes' and "Differentiated" (saviśeṣa or saguṇa) means 'characterized by all blessed qualities.' (See BS III:2.11, S.com.) But in the view of Śaṅkara this is not the true import of the Upaniṣadic teachings.

[35]See Rg V. X:90, Puruṣa Sūktam; Sv.U. III:14.

[36]Mu.U. II:1.4.

[37]See Ma.U.

[38]For the significance of the symbol "Ōm," see Chap.VII, sec.4.

and also as immanent, who knows that the same Brahman which is essentially undifferentiated appears differentiated as multiple existences. Underlying all the diversities of name and form there is one undiversified Being, Brahman. Of all the orders of existence from the highest to the lowest, Brahman is the immutable essence. Indeed, the whole universe with all its ramifications is but the manifestation of Brahman.

So says Sri Ramakrishna:

> At first one discriminates, "not this, not this," and feels that God alone is real and all else illusory. Afterwards the same person finds that it is God Himself who has become all this — the universe, māyā, and the living beings. First negation and then affirmation. . . . One should attain Sat-cit-ānanda (Being-Consciousness-Bliss) by negating the universe and its living beings. But after the attainment of Sat-cit-ānanda one finds that Sat-cit-ānanda Itself has become the universe and the living beings. . . . First of all reach the indivisible Sat-cit-ānanda, and then, coming down, look at the universe. You will then find that everything is Its manifestation. It is God alone who has become everything. The world by no means exists apart from Him.[39]

After realizing the undifferentiated Absolute Brahman in samādhi, when the seer comes back to the normal plane of consciousness, he sees the universe existing in the nondual Self like a city reflected in a mirror, so to speak. The reflection has only an apparent existence, the mirror is all that exists.[40]

Though appearing as many, Brahman is transcendentally "One only without a second." Śrī Kṛṣṇa says:

> It is within and without all beings. It is the unmoving and also the moving. It is incomprehensible, because It is subtle. It is far away, and yet It is near. It is indivisible, and yet It is, as it were, divided among beings. That Brahman, the Goal of knowledge, is the Sustainer of all beings, and also their Devourer and Generator.[41]

Therefore, he has not the right knowledge who knows Brahman as differentiated, as one and manifold, as conditioned by names and forms, as possessed of attributes, as divided in each body as an individual doer and experiencer. In his view, the diversities form an

[39] GSR, p. 395.

[40] See Śaṅkara's hymn of eight stanzas on the benign preceptor — the embodiment of grace and compassion — called "Dakṣiṇā-aṣṭakam." Included in the collection of Śaṅkara's Works in the original, Vol. XI, Sri Rangam, S. India, Vanivilas Press.

[41] BG XIII:15,16.

integral part of Brahman. He imagines Brahman to be like an ocean, so to speak, with currents, eddies, waves and other variations as its essential features. By knowing Brahman as such and not knowing anything of Its true nature beyond, one cannot get out of the bondage of life. One may attain certain good results by meditating on Brahman as differentiated but cannot be free from ignorance (ajnāna) and attain immortality.

In the *Bṛhadāraṇyaka Upaniṣad* there is a story illustrating this point: Bālāki Gārgya (a Brāhmaṇa of the Gārgya family) was a good speaker, but very proud. Once he approached Ajātaśatru, the King of Benares, and said to him, "I will speak to you about Brahman." The King said, "For this very proposal I present you a thousand cows."

Gārgya:	The being who is in the sun I meditate on as Brahman.
Ajātaśatru:	Please don't talk about him. I meditate on him as all-surpassing, as the head of all beings and as resplendent (since he is manifest in the sun as the source of life, light, and joy of the living creatures). He who meditates on him as such becomes all-surpassing, the head of all beings and resplendent.
Gārgya:	That being who is in the moon I meditate on as Brahman.
Ajātaśatru:	Please don't talk about him. I meditate on him as great, white-robed and radiant (being manifest in the silvery moon, whose smooth rays influence plants and herbs). He who meditates on him as such has abundant food and drink.
Gārgya:	That being who is in lightning I meditate on as Brahman.
Ajātaśatru:	Please don't talk about him. I meditate on him as powerful. He who meditates on him as such becomes powerful, and his progeny too become powerful.
Gārgya:	This being who is in the ether I meditate on as Brahman.
Ajātaśatru:	Please don't talk about him. I meditate on him as full and steadfast. He who meditates on him as such is filled with progeny and cattle, and his progeny is never extinct from this world.
Gārgya:	This being who is in air I meditate on as Brahman.
Ajātaśatru:	Please don't talk about him. I meditate on him as all-controlling, irresistible, and as the unvanquished army. He who meditates on him as such ever becomes victorious and invincible, and conquers his enemies.

In this way King Ajātaśatru refuted Gārgya's conceptions of Brahman one after another. As a matter of fact, Gārgya identified Brahman with Prāṇa, the all-pervasive vital principle manifesting itself as psychical and physical forces, which he conceived as the ruler and illuminator of the physical cosmos and also as the doer and experiencer in each individual body. With his knowledge of Brahman exhausted, Gārgya kept quiet, with his head bowed.

Ajātaśatru:	Is this all?
Gārgya:	This is all.
Ajātaśatru:	By knowing this much one cannot know Brahman.
Gārgya:	I approach you as a student.
Ajātaśatru:	It is contrary to custom that a Brāhmaṇa (priest) should approach a Kṣatriya (ruler) for the knowledge of Brahman. However, I shall teach you.

On seeing Gārgya abashed the King took him by the hand and arose. They came to a man who was asleep in a part of the palace. Then the King addressed the sleeping man by the special names of prāṇa, the vital principle. But the man did not wake up. Then the King pushed him and the man was awake.

When the man was asleep, prāṇa, the vital principle, was still functioning in his body. Had this prāṇa actually been the experiencer in the body, then it would have responded when called by its special names. But it did not. From this it was evident that the vital principle which Gārgya conceived as Brahman was not the experiencer in the sleeping man. As the man did not respond, the King had to push him to wake him up. In case this aggregate of body and organs was the very experiencer, then this aggregate remaining the same, in sleep and waking, pushing or not pushing would not make any difference as regards awaking.

Śaṅkara remarks in this context:

> Therefore it was proved — that which awoke through pushing, blazing forth, as it were, flashing, as it were, and coming from somewhere, as it were, rendering the body different from what it was, endowing it with consciousness, activity, a different look, and so forth — is an entity other than the body and different from the types of Brahman advocated by Gārgya.[42]

Ajātaśatru: "When this man, a conscious being, was thus asleep, where was he, and whence did he thus come?" Gārgya did not know that.

[42]Br.U. II:1.15, S.com.

Ajātaśatru: "When this man, a conscious being, is in deep sleep, he absorbs at the time the functions of the organs through his own consciousness and lies in the Supreme Self, which is his own nature and transcendent."

It means that, in deep sleep, an individual, the finite self, withdraws himself from the limiting adjuncts, such as the body, the organs, the mind, the vital principle, and egoism, and, wrapped in primal ignorance (ajñāna), remains absorbed in Brahman, undifferentiated Consciousness, which is his very being.

Ajātaśatru concludes:

> As a spider moves along the thread (it produces), and as from fire tiny sparks fly in all directions, so from this Self emanate all organs, all worlds, all gods, and all beings. Its secret name is "The Truth of truth." The vital principle is truth, and It is the Truth of that.[43]

7. *The distinction of the Ultimate One as transcendent and immanent is also recognized by other mystical religions.*

To maintain the distinction of the Supreme One as transcendent and immanent or as attributeless and possessed of attributes is not, however, a specialty of Vedanta. A similar distinction is noticeable in the metaphysical views of some other religions and philosophical systems. In the opening lines of the *Tao Te Ching* Lao Tzu recognizes the two aspects of the indefinable Absolute One:

> The Tao[44] that can be trodden is not the enduring and unchanging Tao. The name that can be named is not the enduring and unchanging name. (Conceived of as) having no name, it is the Originator of Heaven and Earth. (Conceived of as) having a name, it is the Mother of all things.
>
> Always without desire we must be found, if its deep mystery we would sound. But if desire always within us be, its outer fringe is all that we shall see.
>
> Under these two aspects, it is really the same; but as development takes place, it receives the different names.

[43]Br.U. II:1.1-20 (adapted).

[44]*The Tao* is usually translated as the way or course. Whatever its literal sense may be, the name signifies, as is evident from the treatment of the subject-matter, something above the world of becoming. This is the indefinable Absolute One, which is the Goal, rather than the Way. However, *The Tao* is also the Way, because it is by holding to It as the Ideal that one can reach It.

The transcendence and the immanence of The Tao (the indefinable Absolute One) are further expressed:

> There was something undefined and complete, coming into existence before Heaven and Earth. How still it was and formless, standing alone, and undergoing no change, reaching everywhere and in no danger (of being exhausted). It may be regarded as the Mother of all things. I do not know its name and I give it the designation of the Tao. Making an effort (further) to give it name I call it The Great.
>
> All-pervading is the Great Tao! It may be found on the left hand and on the right.[45]

In the conception of the three Kāyas (bodies or forms of the Buddha) in Mahāyāna Buddhism, Dharmakāya represents the Eternal Being, the Impersonal Absolute One, corresponding to the Undifferentiated Brahman of the Upaniṣads; Sambhōgakāya represents the all-pervading, all-powerful, all-knowing Ruler of the Universe, Īśvara, or Brahman with attributes; Nirmāṇakāya represents the Divine Incarnation (avatāra), such as the living, historical Buddha.

In Christianity the idea of the Transcendent Being without attributes and activities has been clearly expressed by some of the mystics. Meister Eckhart draws a distinction between Godhead (Deitas) and God (Deus), corresponding to the Impersonal and Personal God:

> God and Godhead are as distinct as heaven and earth. Heaven stands a thousand miles above the earth, and so the Godhead is above God. God becomes and disbecomes.
>
> Not the Godhead made this or that, but God first creates all things. Where God is the Creator, there He is manifold and knows multiplicity. But where He is One, there He is free from all works, and knows in such oneness nothing beyond what He is Himself.[46]

The dual aspect of the Divine Being is also recognized by Ruysbroeck:

> The Divine Persons who form one sole God are in the fecundity of their nature ever active; and in the simplicity of their essence they form

[45]Lao Tzu, *Tao Te Ching*, in The Texts of Taoism, Vol. I, James Legge, trans., Sacred Books of the East, F. Max Müller, ed., Vol. 39, 1891; reprint edn., New York, Dover Publications, 1962, pp. 47,67,76.

[46]See Rudolph Otto, *Mysticism East and West*, New York, Macmillan, 1932, pp.13-14.

> the Godhead and eternal blessedness. Thus God according to the Persons is eternal work; but according to the essence and Its perpetual stillness, He is eternal Rest.[47]

In Neo-Platonism also there are evidences of the two aspects of the Supreme Reality. We have seen that the Ultimate Being, according to Plotinus, is All-transcendent. It is beyond anything that the mind can conceive or words can express. It is above Plato's Idea, which is accessible to reason. It is the Absolute One without attributes of any kind. Plotinus calls It "the One," "the Good," "Pure Thought," but he admits that these terms are quite inadequate to express Its true nature. The first and direct emanation from the Absolute One is *nous*. Then there are succeeding emanations more and more imperfect. *Nous* has been translated by various terms, such as "Divine Mind," "Divine Intelligence," "Intellectual Principle," "thought," "intellect," "reason," "spirit." But none of these gives an adequate idea of what Plotinus means by it. *Nous* is at once the cause of the manifestation of the existence of the world of ideas, individual souls and bodies, and the sensible universe. It beholds and contains them all. It is one in many and many in one.

> *Nous* possesses all things at all times simultaneously. It possesses all things unchanged in identity.[48]

As far as we can see, *nous* is the Absolute immanent in the manifold universe as the self-intelligent Supreme principle, as the all-knowing, all-pervading, all-controlling innermost Self (Paramātman). *Nous* being the Supreme Self dwelling in all, it is through *nous* that the soul can realize the Transcendent One. So says Plotinus:

> Cleared of all evil in our intention towards the good, we must ascend to the Principle within ourselves; from many, we must become one; only so do we attain to knowledge of that which is Principle and Unity. We shape ourselves into that Intellectual Principle; we make over our soul in trust to Intellectual Principle, and set it firmly in That; thus what That sees the Soul will waken to see: it is through the Intellectual Principle that we have this vision of the Unity.[49]

In Sūfism *al Hagg* is the sole reality. It is the nondual Absolute

[47]See Evelyn Underhill, *Mysticism,* London, Methuen & Co., 1911, p. 521.

[48]*Plotinus, The Ethical Treatises,* The Enneads, V:1.4, trans. by Stephen MacKenna, Boston, Branford, 1916.

[49]*Ibid.* VI:9.3.

beyond all names and definitions. It is conceived as Light. It underlies and manifests the Personal God, *Allah.* The world is Its reflection. According to Sūfī monism, as observed by Professor Nicholson, "God is both Immanent in the sense that He appears under the aspect of limitation in the phenomenal forms, and Transcendent in the sense that He is the Absolute Reality above and beyond every appearance."[50]

8. *The two ways of viewing the all-pervading Supreme Being.*

The immanence or all-pervasiveness of the Supreme Being has a dual meaning: "One in all" and "All in One." In Christian doctrine the Omnipresence of God generally conveys the former sense. God as Supreme Spirit exists everywhere. He fills the whole universe. He is in all beings. To quote the Old Testament, "Do not I fill heaven and earth? saith the Lord."[51] In Vedanta, however, both the meanings endure, but the latter is prevalent. "In Him all the worlds rest."[52] "All this has its being in That."[53] The following utterance of St. Paul is, however, reminiscent of the Vedantic idea of immanence: "For in him we live, and move, and have our being."[54]

In the Vedantic view the Supreme One is, as it were, the warp and woof of the whole fabric of the diversified existence. He penetrates everything through and through. "Verily, He is all this."[55] So the seer beholds the Self in all and all in the Self.[56] Śrī Kṛṣṇa says, "He whose self is united with the Supreme Being through deep concentration of the mind, who perceives the same Being everywhere, sees the Self abiding in all beings and all beings in the Self."[57] This vision is akin to the perception of the undifferentiated Absolute Brahman.

9. *The unique position of Īśvara (the Lord of the Universe) in Nondualistic Vedanta.*

As the Supreme Principle immanent in the phenomenal world Saguṇa Brahman (God with attributes) is the one Self of all. He is the all-encompassing Ruler of the subjective and the objective. In fact, He is manifest as multiple beings and things and is their sole Master.

[50]Reynold A. Nicholson, *Rūmī, Poet and Mystic,* London, Allen and Unwin, 1964, p. 23.
[51]Jeremiah 23:24.
[52]Ka.U. II:2.8.
[53]Ch.U. VI:8.7.
[54]The Acts 17:28.
[55]Ch.U. VII:25.1.
[56]Is.U. 6.
[57]BG VI:29.

"All this is the Self," "The Self is all this," declare the Upaniṣads.[58] As the Lord of the Universe, Saguṇa Brahman has a unique place in Nondualistic Vedanta, according to which, the finite self (the experiencer), the world of experience, and their Internal Ruler, God (Īśvara), are the three distinct aspects of Brahman.[59] They form a triad (trayam). None of the three ever exists without the other two. They have no beginning in time. It is with their existence that time begins. Beyond them is the Timeless Absolute Brahman.

They are the manifestations of Brahman from the standpoint of the finite self, but not from the standpoint of the nondual Absolute; just as the rising and the setting sun are the appearances of the real sun from the viewpoint of those who are on the earth, but not from the position of the sun itself. All the three — the finite self, the world of experience, and God (Īśvara) have their being in Undifferentiated Brahman. In their essential nature as Brahman (Being-Consciousness-Bliss) they are absolutely real. But they do not inhere in Brahman as distinct entities. Being superimposed, their distinctive features do not adhere to nondual Brahman, just as the apparent movements of the sun do not adhere to the real sun. The relation is only seeming.

When an individual is able to overcome his ignorance (ajñāna) completely, then all the three, the finite self, the world of experience, and their Ruler, God, cease to exist for him, being merged in the nondual Brahman (Being-Consciousness-Bliss). That is to say, their distinctive forms disappear and they are realized in their essential nature as Undifferentiated Brahman. The finite being and the world are not ultimately real as distinct entities, neither is God their Ruler. Until an individual realizes the Absolute One all the three are real for him in their distinctive forms; none of them is unreal. They are interrelated. They constitute the relative order. With the finite self invariably exists the objective universe, in some form or other, and with them "the interpenetrating Sustainer of both — Īśvara" invariably exists. Even in cosmic dissolution when all finite beings and things, including the earth and the heavenly bodies, remain absorbed in undifferentiated, primordial Nature (Prakṛti), God is there.

To regard the finite being and the objective world as real and at the same time to dismiss God their Ruler (Īśvara) as unreal or imaginary, as some do, is far from the intent of Vedanta. The

[58]Br.U. II:4.6; Ch.U. VII:25.2.
[59]Sv.U. I:12.

following remarks of Swami Vivekananda on this point are illuminating:

> True it is that we cannot have any idea of Brahman which is not anthropomorphic, but is it not equally true of everything we know? The greatest psychologist the world has ever known, Bhagavan Kapila,[60] demonstrated ages ago that human consciousness is one of the elements in the make-up of all the objects of our perception and conception, internal as well as external. Beginning with our bodies and going up to Īśvara we may see that every object of our perception is this consciousness plus something else, whatever that may be; and this unavoidable mixture is what we ordinarily think of as reality. Indeed it is, and ever will be, all of the reality that is possible for the human mind to know.
>
> Therefore to say that Īśvara is unreal, because He is anthropomorphic, is sheer nonsense. It sounds very much like the occidental squabble on idealism and realism, which fearful looking quarrel has for its foundation a mere play on the word "real." The idea of Īśvara covers all the ground ever denoted and connoted by the word "real," and Īśvara is as real as anything else in the universe; and after all, the word "real" means nothing more than what has now been pointed out. Such is our philosophical conception of Īśvara.[61]

10. *He is the Adorable One.*

In the Vedantic view God (Īśvara) is the highest reality in the relative order of existence. He is the greatest and best manifestation of Sat-cit-ānanda Brahman (Being-Consciousness-Bliss) through Māyā in its purest form. Māyā is the mysterious principle determining all appearance of differences in Undifferentiated Brahman. As it has no absolute existence, it is not real; yet it is not unreal like the son of a barren woman. It is neither real nor unreal. The same is true of all the appearances determined by it. Māyā is at the root of the relative existence. It is a complex positive something. Like pure light having different expressions through a multiform medium, Absolute Brahman (Being-Consciousness-Bliss) has through the agency of Māyā various manifestations from the highest to the lowest, from the finest to the grossest, from the largest to the smallest. Thus God, the world, and myriad finite beings and things of numerous types and orders have come into existence. Until an individual is fully free from his ajñāna (ignorance), which is a product of Māyā, all these will be there for him.

[60] Bhagavan Kapila, author of Sāṁkhya System of Philosophy.
[61] *Bhakti-Yoga,* CW III, p. 42.

In the manifestation of Brahman (Being-Consciousness-Bliss) as the objective universe, being (sat) is more or less implicit. In the manifestation of Brahman as the finite self (the experiencer), being and consciousness (cit) are more or less implicit. In the manifestation of Brahman as God there is full expression of Being-Consciousness-Bliss (Sat-cit-ānanda). So God is the Omnipresent, Omnipotent, Omniscient Eternal Ruler of the universe and also the All-blissful, All-merciful Deliverer of the finite beings. The God of justice (Īśvara) is the God of grace (Bhagavān) as well. He is the supreme object of knowledge, love, and adoration. Man can reach Him through His grace by whole-souled devotion.[62] Loving worship and knowledge of Him lead to Liberation.

God (Īśvara, Bhagavān) is ever aware of His supreme state as Pure Being-Consciousness-Bliss where Māyā does not exist. At the same time He is the transcendental Witness of the ever changing universe, which He knows to be an appearance. As the knower of Māyā, he controls Māyā, which cannot control Him. By means of Māyā as His power, He guides the course of the cosmos continuously through each cycle of its emergence, manifestation, and reabsorption in the causal state.[63] He is the Sole Ruler of all sentient beings, including Brahmā (the cosmic soul) from their dormant state in primordial nature (Prakṛti) till their final emancipation on the attainment of nondual Brahman. There is no other agency of Rulership.[64]

A liberated soul can realize his identity with Undifferentiated, Absolute Brahman, but can never be God the Ruler of the universe. Freed from the bondage of Karma, a worshipper of God may reach the highest realm of relative existence and have vast powers, but can never wield the power of the projection, the preservation, and the dissolution of the universe, which belongs to Īśvara and Īśvara alone.[65] Swami Vivekananda rightly observes:

> You and I are very low manifestations (of the Impersonal), and the Personal God is the highest of which we can conceive. Nor can you or I become that Personal God. When the Vedanta says you and I are God, it does not mean the Personal God. To take an example, out of a mass of clay a huge elephant of clay is manufactured, and out of the same

[62]See BG VIII:22; X:8-11.
[63]See Rg V. X:190.3; BS I:3.30, Śaṅkara's com.
[64]See Sv.U. VI:16,17.
[65]BS IV:4.17-21.

> clay, a little mouse is made. Would the clay mouse ever be able to become the clay elephant? But put them both in water and they are both clay; as clay they are both one, but as mouse and elephant there will be an eternal difference between them. The Infinite, the Impersonal, is like the clay in the example. We and the Ruler of the Universe are one, but as manifested beings, men, we are His eternal slaves, His worshippers.[66]

Rare are the spiritual aspirants who can reach the Impersonal Absolute Being directly. Most of them have to approach the Impersonal through devotion to the Personal God. Śrī Kṛṣṇa says to Arjuna, "Harder is their struggle whose minds are set on the Impersonal; for the ideal of the Impersonal is difficult to attain for those who are attached to the body as if it were the self."[67]

Even the free souls, the knowers of Nirguṇa Brahman, like Śaṅkara and Sri Ramakrishna, have loving devotion to the Personal God. It is said in the *Bhāgavatam:* "Such are the blessed qualities of the Lord that even the sages whose sole delight is in the Self and who are free from all fetters love Him of superb greatness for love's sake."[68] Indeed, the worship of God as the Master, the Protector, the Father, the Mother, the Friend, the Child, the Lover, the Refuge, the Goal, the Abode, as All-in-all, is a very remarkable feature of the Vedantic approach to Saguṇa Brahman. Vedantic literature, nondualistic as it is, is replete with meditations and prayers in adoration of Brahman with attributes. We conclude the topic with a prayer for the realization of Brahman with attributes (saguṇa) and without attributes (nirguṇa).

> He appears as the universe. From Him all creatures proceed. After the practice of meditation on that Adorable Effulgent Being as dwelling within the heart, a person can realize Him as the Primordial Being presiding over Māyā [the cause of the identification of the self and the not-self] and also as the Transcendent One beyond the three divisions of time and without parts.
>
> He moves the cycle of the manifold universe. He is beyond death. He is the bestower of virtues, the destroyer of sin, the master of all excellences, and the abode of all things and beings. When one knows Him as the Self within, He is perceived as different from, and as transcending the tree of the world with time and form.
>
> May we realize the Adorable Lord of the universe, who is the Supreme Ruler over all the rulers, the Supreme Deity over all the deities, the Supreme Master over all the masters, and who is all-transcendent.

66"Reason and Religion," CW I, p. 378. 67BG XII:5. 68SB I:7.10.

He has neither body nor organs. No one is found equal or superior to Him. As revealed in the Vedas, His great power is verily manifold and His knowledge, strength, and action are effortless.

No one in the universe is His master. No one has any control over Him. There is no sign by which He can be determined. He is the Cause of all. He is the Ruler of the ruler of the senses (the finite self). No one is His originator or ruler.

May the Effulgent Being, who veils Himself with the products of Nature (Prakṛti), just as a spider covers itself with the threads drawn from its self, grant us identity with Brahman (Being-Consciousness-Bliss).[69]

[69]Sv.U. VI:5-10.

CHAPTER XIII

KARMA-YŌGA — THE STEPPING STONE TO THE SPIRITUAL PATH

1. *Karma which binds a man to the continuous rounds of birth and rebirth, leads him to full freedom and infinite joy when done in the spirit of yōga or perfect equanimity.*

Karma-yōga reconciles the conflicting calls of social and secluded life and leaves the spiritual aspirant free to pursue the practical course. It combines in a single process his inner and outer growth and widens the scope of spiritual practice. It does not confine spirituality within the walls of a cell, cloister, or temple, but installs it even in the open market place. By spiritualizing the common duties of life Karma-yōga does away with the superficial distinctions of the secular and the spiritual deeds. It makes the spiritual life accessible to persons of all ranks and positions. From the prerogative of certain privileged classes it turns spiritual culture into a common heritage of men and women of all spheres of life.

By endowing karma with a spiritual outlook Karma-yōga teaches the worker efficiency in work. He is not to consider the kind of work as much as the spirit in which the work is done. The humblest work done earnestly with the right attitude produces the greatest good. Having no ulterior motive, a Karma-yōgī can devote his whole attention to the work itself. He is unconcerned with the pleasures and pains entailed in the work. But this does not mean any indifference to work, as we are prone to think. A Karma-yōgī does his work neither mechanically nor in a mood of abstraction but with full attention and devotion. As he directs his whole mind to whatever work he takes up, he learns the secret of detachment. He is hardly engrossed with things that do not concern him at the time. A great difficulty in practical life is preoccupation. The powers of attachment and detachment, which are the secret of concentration and the key to all excellence in life, are the *sine qua non* of Karma-yōga.

There is another obstructive element in active life which also does not affect a Karma-yōgī. This is the worker's self-consciousness. Being free from personal considerations, the thought of being at work creates no adverse feeling in a Karma-yōgī. He does not make much of the work done by him, nor does he worry about the work to be done. Constant thinking of the worker's own self, or of the hardship undergone by himself, is a great impediment to the progress of work and tires the worker sooner than the work itself.

2. *Karma-yōga is not mere unselfish work or ethical deeds.*

Although Karma-yōga includes unselfish work, all unselfish work does not necessarily come under Karma-yōga. Man lives in the world with the avowed object of securing pleasure and avoiding pain. There are people who seek happiness even at the expense of others. There are some who endeavor to make themselves happy, but refrain from doing harm to others. Some, again, while looking after their own well-being try to help their fellow-beings at the same time. Then, there are a few others who do not care for their own joys and sorrows, but find delight in doing good to people at large. There have been many scientists and philanthropists who have sacrificed their personal interests for the betterment of the world. Are such self-denying persons to be entitled Karma-yōgīs? No. Not until they have a spiritual outlook on life; not until they seek the eternal, the spiritual Reality beyond the transitory. Karma-yōga is not just a moral discipline. It is a spiritual course.

One essential condition of Karma-yōga is that work should be done without attachment to the temporal, for the sake of the eternal, for the supreme Good, beyond relative good and evil. A Karma-yōgī should not look for any secular gain here or hereafter. Whatever is done with a secular end in view, leaves an impression (saṁskāra) on the mind; good work yields good impressions as merits, evil work evil impressions as demerits. These, being accumulated, fructify in due course as favorable and unfavorable situations here and hereafter, both of which create bondages of the soul. Thus good and evil work make the soul pass from birth to death and from death to birth experiencing happiness and misery alternately. Good and evil are inevitably associated with each other on the relative plane. One does not exist without the other. There is no pleasure that is not followed by pain. There is no rise without fall, no life without death. In fact, there is nothing which is wholly good or wholly evil. So in order to be really free from both one must go beyond the relativity of good and evil. Any situation in the relative order, whether agreeable or disagreeable, is a state of bondage. Consequently, there is no freedom merely through good work.

Can we not give up work altogether and escape both good and evil? No, that is not possible. We cannot live without work. Our very nature compels us to act. Our very existence requires it. A man may give up work externally, but internally he will be dwelling on the objects of desire. Such a person is called *mithyācāra,* a hypocrite. One cannot abstain from work by force. Reaction is bound to come. Therefore, a man has to work and work in such a way that it will not create any bondage for him. This method is Karma-yōga. It means that a seeker of liberation should perform worldly duties without any attachment to their fruits. As a result, his work will not produce new impressions (saṁskāras) in his mind, but on the contrary will gradually eliminate the old impressions accumulated therein.

3. *Preparation for Karma-yōga. (See Chap. II, sec. 10.)*

In order to be a Karma-yōgī a person has to realize the dual character of things. The relativity of good and evil is to be apprehended by him not as a theory but as a fact of the deepest concern. He should feel its iron grip and strive to get free from it. This is the first mark of spiritual awakening. This demarcates the spiritual life from the secular. In fact, a Karma-yōgī is not simply an ethical man, but a spiritual aspirant. To a Karma-yōgī, the relative world appears as a mass of contraries, made up of pairs of opposites, such as life and death, growth and decay, heat and cold, pleasure and pain, love and hatred, good and evil. He who is not disillusioned of the duality of good and evil, who is not prepared to face it boldly and determined to get over it, though working for the benefit of mankind even at personal risk, cannot be counted a Karma-yōgī.

The crucial point is: Does he realize the impermanence of the sense-world? Does he feel that Reality is beyond all phenomena? Does he see through the glamor of all temporal interests and yearn for the eternal? Is he aware of the spiritual reality underlying the ephemeral? That is to say, has he a spiritual outlook? Unless he has this, unselfish though he may be, he is not a Karma-yōgī. All yōgas, karma not excepted, imply a hankering for the realization of God, the Supreme Self, the Soul of all souls, who alone is eternal. Devoid of this hankering, none can be a yōgī. And indeed, until we feel the transitoriness and the insubstantiality of the phenomenal existence, we cannot yearn for the eternal.

Thus there are two kinds of unselfishness, two different attitudes with which good work can be done in the world. The one is of the kind we usually know, which is without any spiritual background; that is to say, without the realization of the dual character of life and the world, and the longing for the eternal. The other is the spontaneous outcome of such realization. This is the unselfishness of Karma-yōga.

It should not be supposed that because a Karma-yōgī does not care for the result of action for himself, he works without any consideration of good and evil. A Karma-yōgī gives up all attachment to the fruits of work, since he knows this to be the binding element in work. This does not indicate that he must not discriminate between right and wrong deeds. He knows that certain acts are right and promote happiness, while certain acts are wrong and bring about misery. He finds the cause of bondage in both. But he is not blind to their relative worth. As he has to work, he must choose the right work. There is another reason why a Karma-yōgī cannot work indiscriminately. It is selfishness which impels a man to wrong deeds. No one will harm others unselfishly. A Karma-yōgī, having no selfish motive, cannot do misdeeds. His very nature directs him to the right path.

A person can practice Karma-yōga only at a certain stage of moral development. He alone who has done sufficient good work in this life and in previous lives, who has as a result experienced the blessings of the relative existence, can realize their dual nature and inherent shortcomings. Only those in whom good tendencies prevail, as a consequence of the impressions of evil work being overcome by the impressions of good work, can be disillusioned of duality. Thus a Karma-yōgī has a natural inclination to do good work. But, while doing good work, his mind is set not upon the result of the work but upon its performance. As soon as the work is chosen, his thoughts are concentrated on doing it in the best way possible. To do good work is to him a blessing in itself. He is not elated by success or depressed by failure.

Thus, we see that a great deal of preparation is necessary for the practice of Karma-yōga. Many of those who read the *Bhagavad-gītā* and find Karma-yōga to be the secret of work, feel inclined to practice it at once. Their attempt often results in failure or pretense. This is why not a few of them undergo lifelong internal conflict and can make neither temporal nor spiritual progress. The point is, an average human individual cannot be free from sense desire, unless he first works with desire. So long as he hankers after possessions and pleasures, he must work with the object of securing them. He cannot discard them until he can experience them and realize their hollowness. It is then that he outgrows the desires for the temporal.

Work with desires rightly performed leads to work without desires. This is why the seekers of material well-being have been instructed to perform work with secular desires keeping firm on the path of virtue. While advocating Karma-yōga the *Bhagavad-gītā* approves of this measure. Says Śrī Kṛṣṇa:

> The Prajāpati having in the beginning created mankind together with Yajña (sacrificial rite), said: "By this shall ye multiply; this shall be the milch cow of your desires. Cherish the Devas (gods) with this, and may those Devas cherish you: thus cherishing one another, ye shall gain the highest good. The Devas cherished by Yajña, will give you desired-for objects." So, he who enjoys objects given by the Devas without an offering to them (in return), is verily a thief.[1]

Work with desire is certainly better than no work or pretense of nonattachment.

4. *The practice of Karma-yōga — the common basis of all the other yōgas.*

To be free from the desire for the fruits of actions, a person has to renounce his egoism as the doer of action. From the idea "I have done the work" arises the idea, "I must have the fruits of the work." It is the claim of the work that leads to the expectation of its result. This is how karma produces its effect on the doer, that is, how it reacts on him. The ego as the doer of an action turns into the ego as the experiencer of its fruits. A Karma-yōgī must not have such egoistic idea as "I am the doer of the work, therefore, I have the right to its fruit." He should try to be free from "I-ness" and "My-ness." There should not be any feeling of vanity or humiliation in him for doing a deed howsoever great or humble. Impersonality is an essential characteristic of a Karma-yōgī. Even the pleasure derived from the consciousness of performing a good deed does not affect him in any way.

The well-known maxim, duty for duty's sake, as it is commonly understood, does not represent Karma-yōga. Here also the same difference as we noted between merely unselfish action and Karma-

[1]BG III:10-12.

yōga has to be recognized. Unless there is a spiritual outlook, the sense of duty is merely a form of bondage. But being endowed with it, duty becomes transformed into Karma-yōga. Oftentimes, our lack of spiritual understanding makes us glorify our life of bondage as something inviolable and unavoidable. Due to worldly attachment we usually consider ourselves as performing duty for duty's sake.

Practiced with the appropriate mental attitude, Karma-yōga can be preparatory to the yōgas of knowledge, meditation, and devotion, known respectively as Jñāna-yōga, Dhyāna-yōga and Bhakti-yōga. The various attitudes of Karma-yōga corresponding to different yōgas have been indicated by Śrī Kṛṣṇa in the *Bhagavad-gītā.* A Karma-yōgī of the devotional type makes an offering of his work to God. Whatever he does, he does for the sake of the Lord. He does not care for his own happiness or misery. He resigns himself to the will of God and feels himself to be an instrument in His hands. He knows that he has no claim to the deeds or the fruits thereof. As he forsakes all claim to the actions, they create no impressions in his mind as merits or demerits. So it is said in the *Bhagavad-gītā:*

> He who does actions, offering them to God, abandoning attachment, is not tainted by sin as a lotus-leaf is not tainted by water.[2]

Therefore, Śrī Kṛṣṇa asks Arjuna to dedicate all work to God without any reservation:

> Whatever thou doest, whatever thou eatest, whatever thou offerest in sacrifice, whatever thou givest away, whatever austerity thou practicest, O son of Kuntī, do thou as an offering unto Me.[3]

The selfsame principle of the dedication of work has been stated in the *Śrīmad-bhāgavatam,* the most luminous exposition of divine love and divine knowledge:

> Whatever a person does by the body, by the organs, by word, by thought, by will, by intellect, or due to natural tendency, he should offer them all to the Supreme Being.[4]

A Karma-yōgī who is inclined to self-introspection, whose ideal is to withdraw the self from the not-self — comprising the body, the organs, and the mind — maintains the attitude of a witness towards

[2]BG V:10.
[3]BG IX:27.
[4]SB XI:2.36.

all their activities. As their constant observer the self is intrinsically conscious and aloof from them all. The body, the organs, the mind, and the external objects are the products of prakṛti, the primordial nature, which is devoid of consciousness. They are the transformations of the guṇas — sattva, rajas, and tamas — the primal constituents of prakṛti.[5] All activities belong to them, but are falsely ascribed to the changeless, luminous self. He who knows the self to be aloof from prakṛti is not affected by the work done by the transformations of the guṇas. The idea is thus expressed in the *Bhagavad-gītā:*

> The guṇas of Prakṛti [in the form of the body, the organs, and the mind] perform all actions. With the understanding deluded by egoism, a man thinks, "I am the doer." But one with true insight into the domains of guṇa and karma, knowing that the guṇas as senses merely rest on the guṇas as objects, does not become attached.[6]

A Karma-yōgī whose aim is to attain Liberation through the realization of the identity of the individual self with the Supreme Self, looks upon all activities as superimposed on the self through ajñāna, nescience. It is because of ajñāna that a person identifies the self with the body, the organs, and the mind, to which action and the cessation of action truly belong. Intrinsically changeless and static, the self neither undertakes nor withdraws. The psychophysical system

[5]Like a three-stranded rope, prakṛti is composed of three substantive energies — sattva, rajas, and tamas, each of which is called a *guṇa* in the sense of "strand," and not in the sense of "attribute," which is the usual meaning of the term. The three guṇas are inseparable. They form a triad, in which each has a tendency to overcome the two others. Sattva is the principle of calmness conducive to purity, knowledge, and joy. Rajas is the principle of motivity leading to activity, desire, and restlessness or pain. Tamas is the principle of inertia resulting in inaction, dullness, and delusion.

Before the creation the three guṇas are in a state of equilibrium. Then prakṛti is undifferentiated. The Supreme Self, the Lord of prakṛti, holds it as His creative power. As He wills creation and reflects on it, nonconscious prakṛti receives the animation of consciousness. Then the equilibrium of the guṇas is lost and differentiation starts. It is the preponderance of one or another of the three guṇas over two others in varying degrees that brings about all varieties of objects, while the Supreme Lord watches and directs the cosmic process. From prakṛti evolve the five basic elements, mind, vital principle (prāṇa), the ten organs, the physical body of every living being, and all inanimate objects. They are but the products of the guṇas. All movements, all transformations are in prakṛti, the domain of the guṇas. The Self is ever unaffected as their witness.

The Supreme Self is apparently divided into countless individual selves. Being identified with the mind, the organs, and the body, an individual is deluded with the idea, "I am the doer." But a man of discrimination never gets attached to the work and its results, which belong to the effects of the guṇas.

[6]BG III:27,28.

functions simply due to its radiance. Action and inaction or the cessation of action are attributed to it through the false egoistic notions, "I work," "I rest." He who has no such egoistic idea, though engaged in action, is really inactive. Again, a man may be inactive, but, if he is led by the egoistic idea that he has abstained from work, then he is not inactive, because he ascribes the withdrawal from action to the self. In the words of the *Bhagavad-gītā:*

> He who can see inaction in action, and also action in inaction is wise among men. He is settled on the Self and has finished all action.[7]

One common feature of the different forms of Karma-yōga mentioned above is equanimity. A man of dynamic nature who has no marked tendency towards jñāna (knowledge), dhyāna (meditation), or bhakti (devotion), but who works with mental equipose, in spite of success and failure, in spite of joy and sorrow, can be regarded a Karma-yōgī. Equanimity is the yōga, says Śrī Kṛṣṇa:

> Being steadfast in yōga, O Dhanañjaya, perform actions, abandoning attachment, remaining unconcerned as regards success and failure. This evenness of mind is known as yōga.[8]

This is Karma-yōga pure and simple. It can be adopted even by a person who has no theistic belief or conception but who finds egoistic attachment to be the root of all miseries and tries to get rid of it completely. A Buddhist can practice this type of Karma-yōga.

It should be noted here that the verses quoted above represent the ideal states of Karma-yōga. These attitudes are natural only with the adepts. An initiate endeavors to cultivate any one of them, according to his aptitude. The very ideal is adopted by him as the means. He attains this fully through persistent efforts. Practice is but the gradual realization of the ideal.

5. *Karma-yōga paves the way to the practice of other yogas through the purification of the mind.*

When the mind is disciplined through Karma-yōga, then it is adapted to the practice of the yōgas of knowledge, devotion, and meditation. We have seen that in order to be a Karma-yōgī a person

[7]BG IV:18.
[8]*Ibid.* II:48.

has to realize the inherent inadequacy of all temporal values here and hereafter. He should be prepared to go beyond relative evil as well as relative good. Even though he realizes that it is his attachment to sense-objects that makes him run after them, and even though he tries to get rid of this attachment completely, yet it does not leave him easily. Being firmly and deeply rooted in him, the sense desires cling persistently to his mind. He has to struggle hard and long to overcome them. Though he does not seek possessions or pleasure as before, yet he has to perform work. Work he must, but at the same time he has to keep constant watch over himself so that no secular desire can dominate his mind and no egoistic attitude can prevail in his consciousness. As he goes on this way, the force of desire grows less and less, and a time comes when it disappears altogether. Then his mind is no longer swayed by any prospect of enjoyment here or hereafter. The outgoing tendencies of the mind cease and a natural longing for the eternal develops. This is what is meant by *cittaśuddhi* (the purification of the mind). This struggle to get rid of the deep-seated worldly desires through work is generally regarded as Karma-yōga proper.

Karma-yōga is preparatory to the practice of Bhakti-yōga, the path of devotion. It also prepares the ground for the practice of Jñāna-yōga, the path of Self-knowledge.

Śrī Kṛṣṇa says to Uddhava in the *Bhāgavatam:*

> In order to confer supreme good on human beings I have spoken of three yōgas. These are the yōga of Self-knowledge, the yōga of work, and the yōga of devotion. There is no other way than these anywhere.
>
> The way of Self-knowledge (Jñāna-yoga) is for those who have become disenchanted of worldly activities and have renounced them. For those who have not lost interest in worldly activities and desire their fruits, there is the path of work (Karma-yōga).
>
> But for the man who has somehow got veneration for listening to tales about Me and such other things, who is neither disenchanted of activities nor who is grossly interested in them — the path of devotion (Bhakti-yōga) is the way.[9]

A spiritual aspirant must continue the practice of Karma-yōga until he develops a natural interest in devotional practices or until an apprehension of the true nature of the Self grows within him.

It is worthy of note that Śrī Kṛṣṇa mentions only three yōgas as the means to the attainment of the Supreme Good. He does not

[9]SB XI:20.6-9.

mention Rāja-yōga. The reason is this: the practical methods of Patañjali's Rāja-yōga are adapted by Vedanta to both Jñāna-yōga and Bhakti-yōga. Vedanta does not recognize the metaphysical background of Patañjali, which is dualistic. The practical aspects have some common features and cannot be strictly alienated. Vedanta recognizes one ultimate Reality while Patañjali accepts two ultimate Reals, Puruṣa and Prakṛti.

CHAPTER XIV

THE INTERRELATION OF THE FOUR YŌGAS

1. *That Karma-yōga is preparatory to the practice of Jñāna-yōga as well as Bhakti-yōga is expressly stated by Śrī Kṛṣṇa in the* Bhāgavatam *as noted at the end of the last chapter.*[1]

The goal of Jñāna-yōga is Nirguṇa Brahman and the goal of Bhakti-yōga is Saguṇa Brahman. Nirguṇa means "attributeless" or "Impersonal";Saguṇa means "possessed of attributes" or "Personal." To the Advaitins Brahman is essentially Nirguṇa, but appears as Saguṇa in association with māyā. According to them, Bhakti-yōga or the path of devotion (the worship of Saguṇa Brahman) is an indirect method of the realization of Nirguṇa; Jñāna-yōga is the only direct method. To the Vaiṣṇavas, who follow the path of devotion, Saguṇa Brahman is all-in-all. The jīva (individual soul) and prakṛti (the matrix of the objective universe) belong to Him. Though distinct, these have no existence independent of Īśvara (Saguṇa Brahman). This is monotheism[2] altogether different from the dualism of the Sāṁkhya system which recognizes two ultimate Reals. According to the Vaiṣṇavas, the advocates of monotheism, the ardent love for God is an end in itself. Patañjali's Rāja-yōga is based on the Sāṁkhya system, which affirms puruṣa (the conscious self) and the non-conscious prakṛti to be the dual existences independent of each other. But unlike Sāṁkhya, Rāja-yōga admits a Personal God in the form of the First Teacher.

When the aspirant attains inner purification through Karma-yōga subsidiary to Bhakti-yōga (the path of devotion), he feels a natural longing for God. With him bhakti is no longer a conventional observance of rites and duties, but a spontaneous feeling of devotion to the Supreme Lord. As a result, the aspirant engages himself more

[1]SB XI:20.6-9.

[2]See *Methods of Knowledge* by the author, Appendix B, sec. 5, "The Vedānta Philosophy; its Triple Basis and Different Schools."

and more in the loving worship and the contemplation of God. It is through ritualistic devotion (vaidhī bhakti) that he attains ardent devotion (rāgānugā bhakti). Then he gets more and more absorbed in God and finds delight in the practice of contemplation and meditation on Him and in listening to discourses on Him. Says Śrī Kṛṣṇa in the *Bhāgavatam:*

> One should perform work, until one has dispassion towards results of work, or until one has developed a real interest in listening to talks about Me and the like.[3]

2. *Through Karma-yōga, an aspirant of Dhyāna-yōga acquires the two prerequisites of the meditative life: nonattachment and calmness of mind.*

He perceives his aloofness from prakṛti and is not disturbed by its operations. He is now in a fit position to give up external activities and practice concentration on the real self. So says Śrī Kṛṣṇa:

> For the wise man who aspires after meditation Karma-yōga is the way; but when he gains the capacity for meditation, then for him the cessation of work is the way.[4]

When a seeker of jñāna (Self-knowledge) attains purity of mind through Karma-yōga, he finds himself in possession of the four essential prerequisites of Jñāna-yōga. These are: firstly, the six assets of *śama* (control of internal organs), *dama* (control of external organs), *titikṣā* (endurance), *uparati* (renunciation), *śraddhā* (faith) and *samādhāna* (concentration); secondly, discrimination between the real and the non-real; thirdly, freedom from desire for the fruits of action in this and other worlds; and fourthly, longing for Liberation. He is convinced of the innate purity and blissfulness of the self (ātman). His eagerness for Self-realization is true and intense. Now he is capable of renouncing work and cultivating Jñāna-yōga, which consists of *śravaṇa* (hearing about the identity of the self with Brahman), *manana* (reflecting on the identity) and *nididhyāsana* (meditation on the same). That Karma-yōga paves the way to jñāna (Self-knowledge) has been aptly expressed by Sureśvarācārya in his *Naiṣkarmyasiddhi:*

[3]SB XI:20.9.
[4]BG VI:3.

> Actions [free from desires] develop an inwardness of the mind by purifying it, and then, their purpose being served, they disappear like clouds after the rains.[5]

Hence we see that Karma-yōga invariably precedes the life of contemplation. One is entitled to retire from active life only when one has developed a natural inwardness of the mind. When the mind is indrawn, external activities cease of themselves. This does not indicate, however, that after the purification of the mind (cittaśuddhi) the spiritual aspirant cannot perform work. Of course, when engaged in actual practice of the yōga of devotion or of Self-knowledge, for which he has qualified himself, he has to abstain from work. Or, if he be so intensely meditative that his spiritual exercises absorb his whole thought and energy, then he cannot possibly direct any attention either to work for social good or for his own living. At this stage the aspirant has a natural inclination for meditation and contemplation and tries to devote as much attention to their practice as possible. So when an aspirant resorts to higher yōgas after cittasuddhi, external activities are no longer necessary for his inner development. But this does not mean that he should by all means give up work or that his mental disposition does not permit him to do any external work. Had it been so, Śrī Kṛṣṇa would not have commended a sage's actions in such terms as:

> So should the wise act desirous of setting an example to the world.[6]
>
> Though engaged in action, he does not do anything.[7]
>
> Though acting he is not tainted.[8]
>
> Those who worship Me resigning all actions in Me, regarding Me as the supreme Goal, meditating on Me with exclusive devotion, to them whose minds are thus absorbed in Me, verily, I become before long, the saviour from the ocean of transmigratory existence beset with death.[9]

These statements show that karma is not incongruous with the yōgas of jñāna, dhyāna, or bhakti.

3. *Śaṅkara's view of jñāna and karma are not self-contradictory.*

But Śaṅkarācārya categorically denies the coordination of jñāna and karma. Yet his view is not contrary to the teachings of the *Gītā*.

[5]NS I:49.
[6]BG III:25.
[7]*Ibid.* IV:20.
[8]*Ibid.* V:7.
[9]*Ibid.* XII:6.

Why, we shall explain. It has been repeatedly asserted by him that the two — jñāna and karma — cannot be practiced by an individual simultaneously. At the outset of his commentary on the *Bhagavad-gītā* he observes:

> It is not, therefore, possible for anybody to show that the Gītā-śāstra teaches a conjunction of knowledge with any work whatsoever enjoined in the Śruti or in the Smṛti.[10]

There is no denial of the fact that kāmya-karma (work done with desire) is incompatible with jñāna and that no work whatsoever is possible in the state of Brahma-jñāna, when all distinctions of instrument, object, and the agent, the threefold basis of action, melt away. But that is not Śaṅkara's only point of contention. According to him, the very yōgas of jñāna and karma are mutually exclusive. As stated by him in his commentary on the *Gītā:*

> The two paths, the one of knowledge and the other of (selfless) action are respectively intended for two distinct classes of aspirants.[11]

The point is that Śaṅkara uses the term karma in a very restricted sense. Whatever is done with the egoistic idea "I am the doer" is, according to him, karma. All work done after sattva-śuddhi (purification of the mind) he includes in jñāna, because the doer of work, being established in the knowledge of the immutable witness-self, no longer thinks of himself as the doer. Śaṅkara does not deny that a person, steadfast in the path of jñāna, can continue the performance of work. But he calls such a performer of action a Jñāna-yōgī or Jñāna-niṣṭhā, and not a Karma-yōgī or Karma-niṣṭhā. Any work done by him who is ever aware of the transcendental self beyond all actions and their results is, according to Śaṅkara, a form of knowledge and cannot be regarded as karma.

So in Śaṅkara's view no conjunction of jñāna and karma is possible; they represent two contrary mental attitudes. In his introductory remarks on the very first ślōka with which he begins his commentary on the *Bhagavad-gītā* he states:

> Now a person, who having been first engaged in work owing to ignorance and worldly attachment and other tendencies, and then having attained the purification of mind by sacrificial rites, gifts,

[10]BG II:11, S. com.

[11]BG III:3, S. com.

> austerity, etc., arrives at the knowledge of the grand truth that "all is one — Brahman, the Absolute, the non-agent," may continue performing work in the same manner as before for setting an example to the masses, though neither actions nor their results attract him any longer. This semblance of active life on his part cannot constitute that course of action with which knowledge is sought to be conjoined as a means of attaining mōkṣa (Liberation).[12]

Again in his commentary on ślōka 20, Chapter IV, he observes:

> Finding that for some reason he cannot abandon work, a wise man may continue doing work as before in order to set an example to the world at large; being devoid of attachment to work and its result, and therefore having no selfish end in view, such a man really does not work.[13]

Thus, according to Śaṅkara, Karma-yōga is a stepping-stone to Jñāna-yōga. It is a remote aid to the attainment of mōkṣa with which it has no direct connection. It leads to perfection, as he says, "through the purification of mind, concentration, and the attainment of knowledge (sattva-śuddhi-yōga-jñāna-prāpti-dvāreṇa)."[14] By "the attainment of knowledge" he means the realization of the oneness of the self (ātman) with Brahman. This he holds to be the immediate cause of Liberation, because bondage is due to the ignorance of the identity of the self with Brahman. He states in his *Viveka-cūḍāmaṇi* (The Crest Jewel of Discrimination):

> Neither by restraining the modifications of the mind, nor by the discrimination [of the self from prakṛti], nor by righteous deeds, nor by learning, but by the realization of one's identity with Brahman that Liberation is possible, and by no other means.[15]

The same view is expressed by him in his commentary on the *Gītā:*

> Therefore, the conclusion of the Gītā is that Liberation is attained by knowledge (of Truth) alone and not by that conjoined with work.[16]

The term *yōga* used by Śaṅkara in the expression "sattva-śuddhi-yōga-jñāna-prāpti-dvāreṇa" implies meditation leading to jñāna. The threefold path of śravaṇa (hearing of the identity of the self with Brahman), manana (reflection on it), and nididhyāsana (meditation) is regarded as Jñāna-yōga proper. The way of sāṁkhya (discrimination) characterized by the disengagement of the self from the guṇas as

[12]BG II:11, S. com.
[13]*Ibid.* IV:20, S. com.
[14]*Ibid.* XII:10, S. com.
[15]VC 56.
[16]BG II:11, S. com.

their witness, and the way of devotion, consisting in the meditation on the Supreme Lord (Parameśvara), are considered by him as conducive to jñāna, the knowledge of the identity of the self with Brahman. Hence in his view Jñāna-yōga is the sole means of the attainment of mōkṣa (Liberation). There is no alternative course. Thus, he refutes samuccaya (conjunction) of jñāna and karma as well as their vikalpa (alternation).

4. *No actual contradiction between Śaṅkara and Swami Vivekananda.*

But Swami Vivekananda, the greatest exponent of the Advaita Vedanta in the modern age, has expressed a view of Karma-yōga, which is evidently contradictory to that of Śaṅkara. In his *Karma-Yōga* he says:

> Each one of our yōgas is fitted to make man perfect even without the help of the others, because they have all the same goal in view. The yōgas of work, of wisdom, and of devotion are all capable of serving as direct and independent means for the attainment of mōksha (Liberation).[17]

But the contradiction, though so marked, is only apparent in so far as the philosophical basis is concerned. The point is, Swami Vivekananda uses the term *karma* not in the same restricted sense as Śaṅkara. He makes quite a free and wide application of it. By *karma* he means not only the work done with dispassion before citta-śuddhi (the purification of the mind), but also that performed after the attainment of the competence for Jñāna-yōga or Bhakti-yōga. In case an aspirant continues to work in the world after being established in the path of knowledge (jñāna), subjectively considered he is a Jñāna-yōgī, but objectively considered, he is a Karma-yōgī. Śaṅkara views his position subjectively and calls him a Jñāna-yōgī. But Swamiji chooses to call him a Karma-yōgī instead of a Jñāna-yōgī. So in his view Karma-yōga reaches as near the goal as Jñāna-yōga. The one leads to mōkṣa (Liberation) in the same way as the other through "the knowledge of the identity of the self with Brahman."

That the knowledge of one's identity with Brahman is the immediate cause of mōkṣa by the destruction of primal ignorance,

[17] *Karma-Yōga,* CW VI, p. 91.

has also been maintained by Swami Vivekananda. He remarks:

> The various methods of spiritual practice that have been laid down in the scriptures are all for the attainment of the knowledge of ātman. Of course, these practices vary according to the qualifications of different aspirants. But they also are a kind of work, and so long as there is work, the ātman is not discovered. The obstacles to the manifestation of the ātman are overcome by practices as laid down in the scriptures, but work has no power of directly manifesting the ātman; it is only effective in removing some veils that cover knowledge. Then the ātman manifests by its own effulgence.[18]

That Bhakti-yōga attended with karma is effective of Freedom through supreme knowledge (samyak-darśana), has also been acknowledged by Śaṅkara. He thus expounds ślōka 26, Chap. XIV of the *Gītā:*

> A Sannyāsin or even a man of work (karmin) who serves Me — the Īśvara, Nārāyaṇa — dwelling in the heart of all beings, with a never-failing Bhakti-yōga, crosses beyond the three guṇas mentioned above and is fit to become Brahman, that is, to attain mōkṣa.[19]

Annotating on this passage, Ānandagiri remarks:

> Bhakti-yōga is that supreme love (parama-prema) which leads to communion with the Supreme. To serve God in Bhakti-yōga means to constantly contemplate Him by completely withdrawing the mind from all external objects, from the not-self. By virtue of the Divine grace he is imbued with right knowledge. Thus enlightened, he becomes Brahman while still alive.

5. *Thus, the contradiction between Śaṅkara and Swami Vivekananda can be said to be mostly verbal.*

There is no real disagreement as regards the philosophy of Karma-yōga in the basic conceptions, though different results follow as regards practice from their different view-points. It seems that from Swami Vivekananda's viewpoint of Karma-yōga the following ślōkas of the *Gītā* admit of more natural interpretation than given by some classical commentators:

> Children, not the wise, speak of knowledge and performance of action as distinct. He who is rightly devoted to even one obtains the fruits of both.[20]

[18]CW VII, p. 176. [19]BG XIV:26, S.com. [20]BG V:4.

By meditation some behold the Self in the self by the self, others by Jnāna-yōga, and others by Karma-yōga.[21]

Hence karma, as conceived by Swami Vivekananda, is capable of being performed in conjunction with jñāna, and is a direct means of Liberation. As a matter of fact, the definition of the yōgas depend on the way they are viewed. Their distinction is due to the predominance of one or another of the three elements — karma, bhakti, and jñāna, which are closely associated. They are not quite exclusive of one another. So Swami Vivekananda's affirmation of the conjunction of the yōgas, which is in accord with the facts of life, does not in any way contradict Śaṅkara's view that karma can never be reconciled with jñāna.

In his *Karma-Yōga* Swami Vivekananda says: "But you must at the same time remember that these divisions are not very marked and quite exclusive of each other. Each blends into the other. But according to the type which prevails we name the divisions. It is not that you can find a man who has no other faculty than that of work, nor that you can find men who are no more than devoted worshippers only, nor that there are men who have no more than mere knowledge."[22]

6. *The difference of viewpoints with regard to jñāna and karma naturally find different expressions in Śaṅkara and Swami Vivekananda.*

Their different interpretations of Karma-yōga are perhaps due to the difference of environments in which they lived and worked. Śaṅkara had to contend with the Mīmāṁsakas, whose vindication of karma as a means of mōkṣa was not in keeping with the highest Vedic ideal. So he makes jñāna more prominent than karma. He directs the whole attention to the inner spirit of renunciation rather than the actual performance of work. To him work counts little. But Swami Vivekananda had to face a different situation. He had to deal with the present active, busy, complex life of intellectual triumph and material achievements — a life which cannot be readily turned into primitive simplicity or meditative quietude. The age, therefore, demanded of him some spiritualizing principle of karma, which would serve as a pivot for its maddening course of activity. Then, there were others

[21] *Ibid.* XIII:24.
[22] *Karma-Yōga* VIII, CW I, p. 106.

who were immersed in tāmasika passivity under the pretense of sāttvika quiescence. They had to be roused to action with a fresh and sublime vision of the life of karma. Consequently Swami Vivekananda had to present Karma-yōga with a broad and lofty outlook. He laid greater stress on renunciation *in* work than renunciation *of* work. In fact, the inner spirit of renunciation is far more important than the outer abandonment of work. With *ātmanō mōkṣartham* (for the emancipation of the self) he added *jagaddhitāya* (for the good of the world). "For the good of the many and for the happiness of the many is your life," he was never tired of reminding his adherents.

It should not, however, be supposed that the Swami did not find any necessity of karma-sannyāsa (renunciation of work) for this age. The bliss and glory of the reposeful life of a recluse had a peculiar charm for him. It had for him a value all its own. His heart often cried for complete absorption in the meditation on Brahman in the Himalayan solitude. Even in his *Karma-Yōga* he states:

> The highest kind of men silently collect true and noble ideas, and others, the Buddhas and Christs, go from place to place preaching them and working for them.[23]

Swami Vivekananda has further widened the scope of Karma-yōga by allowing it a position independent of theistic faith and metaphysical views: "The Karma-yōgī need not believe in any doctrine whatsoever. He may not believe even in God, may not ask what his soul is, nor think of any metaphysical speculation. He has got his own special aim of realizing selflessness, and he has to work it out himself. Every moment of his life must be realization, because he has to solve by work, without the help of doctrine or theory, the very same problem to which the jñānī applies his reason and inspiration and the bhākta his love."[24]

Here perhaps the Swamiji has in his view the Buddhist conception of karma as a means of Nirvāṇa. Buddha was actuated by practical consideration rather than by speculative spirit. He viewed life as it is and took his start from where man stands. The primary object of all human efforts is to overcome misery. The root of all sufferings is evidently sense desire. This, he points out, originates with the egoistic self. So in order to go beyond all sufferings, one has to abnegate the ego completely. This can be done through selfless karma as well. By

[23] *Karma-Yōga* VII, CW I, p. 103.
[24] *Ibid.* VIII, CW I, p. 109.

"Nirvāṇa" Buddha means the extinction of the empirical or the apparent self and the flames of desire associated with it. He did not deny the metaphysical self, though he did not actually avow it. Let the individualized existence, the source of all miseries, be destroyed, and then what remains, if any, will assert itself — this perhaps was the implication of his silence regarding the ultimate Truth, which is beyond mind and speech as declared by the Vedanta.

Vedantic Karma-yōga has also adopted the same negative method of self-denial. It also aims at Liberation by eradicating individuality, the offspring of ignorance. Perfect nonattachment is but the culmination of self-abnegation. This point of contact between Buddhism and Vedantism has provided Swami Vivekananda with sufficient ground for holding the above view of Karma-yōga. Unlike Buddhism, Vedantism has added to this negative process a positive conception of ātman or the inmost being as the ultimate ground of all knowledge and experience.

7. *In one respect Swami Vivekananda has made a distinct contribution to the conception of Karma-yōga.*

We have seen that work done as an offering to God results in the highest Good. It is said in the *Gītā:*

> From whom is the evolution of all beings, by whom all this is pervaded, worshipping Him with his own duty, a man attains perfection.[25]

Swami Vivekananda brings out the full significance of this teaching of the *Gītā* and presents it in a new light. To do one's duty surrendering the fruits of actions to God is, no doubt, an indirect form of worship. The Swamiji turns this into a direct method of worshipping Him. He shows that a person can worship God directly through service to his fellow-beings. He calls upon men and women to look on all beings as veritable manifestations of God and serve and worship Him in them:

> From the highest Brahmā (the cosmic being) to the yonder worm,
> And to the very minutest atom,
> Everywhere is the same God, the All-Love;
> Friend, offer mind, soul, body at their feet.

[25]BG XVIII:46.

These are His manifold forms before thee,
Rejecting them, where seekest thou for God?
Who loves all beings, without distinction,
He indeed is worshipping best his God.[26]

Look upon every man, woman, and every one as God. You cannot help anyone; you can only serve; serve the children of the Lord, serve the Lord Himself, if you have the privilege. If the Lord grants that you can help any one of His children, blessed you are; do not think too much of yourselves. Blessed you are that that privilege was given to you, when others had it not. Do it only as a worship.[27]

This is his clarion call to the modern age. The fact that the sages find God in all beings and love them as such, has been again and again declared by the Upaniṣads and later Hindu scriptures. The Swamiji exhorts us to embody in our daily practices this supernal vision, the apex of spiritual life. The very end is recommended to the aspirant as the means. The Swamiji's genius lies in the widest possible application he made of the sublime Upaniṣadic truth in the common life of man.

One may doubt the Swamiji's originality in this, in view of the fact that similar principles of conduct have been previously enunciated by the Śāstras. In the *Taittirīya Upaniṣad* we find the following instruction:

Let thy mother be to thee a god; let thy father be a god to thee; a god let thy teacher be unto thee, and (so also) let thy guest be unto thee a god.[28]

But a little attention to the trend of the lessons will bring home to one that these have the nature of moral precepts rather than spiritual disciplines. These instructions are given by the preceptor to the pupil at the close of his educational career, on the threshold of his life as a householder. On returning home the pupils are required to serve their parents and other persons deserving respect with as much veneration as is due to a god. But Swami Vivekananda asks men and women to serve the Supreme Lord through one and all. In the former case the idea of father, mother, etc., is predominant in the worshipper's mind, and in the latter case, the consciousness of God reigns supreme. The two attitudes are, however, so related that one may ultimately lead to the other.

[26]CW IV, p. 429.
[27]*Ibid.* III, p. 246.
[28]Tai.U. I:11.2.

8. *Swami Vivekananda's message is the logical conclusion of the teachings of the Upaniṣads and the* Gītā.

Truly speaking, it is not a new message. In the *Śrīmad-bhāgavatam* Śrī Kṛṣṇa urges Uddhava to see God in all beings and regard them as such.

> With a pure mind one should observe in all beings as well as in oneself only Me, the ātman, who am both inside and out, and all-pervasive like space.
>
> This looking upon all beings as Myself in thought, word, and deed is, to My mind, the best of all methods of worship.[29]

But the application of this method of worship in the lives of the spiritual aspirants in general for the alleviation of all kinds of miseries of mankind is Swami Vivekananda's special contribution to this age.

With the progress of thought and the triumph of science a new consciousness of man's inherent greatness has dawned upon humanity. The Divinity of man has been a fact of more general recognition than ever before. Mankind has been drawn close together in inseparable ties of fellow-feeling and cooperation. None can live isolated or grow at the expense of others. A synthetic vision of the widest expanse has opened unto man in all directions. World-culture, world-religion, world-state, and world-peace have become the crying needs of the day. The disastrous effects that are produced by the perversion of man's inner and outer resources, have also been sadly watched. The necessity of a spiritual outlook on life is being keenly felt in all quarters as the panacea for all evils. The spirit of the age has consequently given birth to a universal regulative principle, which can be adopted by the majority of mankind, irrespective of color, creed, caste, or position, which is calculated to foster the utmost love, good-will, and respect between man and man, and which harmonizes tremendous practicality with profundity of feeling and sublimity of vision.

[29]SB XI:29.12,19.

CHAPTER XV

BHAKTI-YŌGA, THE WAY TO THE REALIZATION OF SAGUṆA BRAHMAN

1. *The threefold distinction of Reality, according to Advaita Vedanta. The goal of Bhakti-yōga and the goal of Jñāna-yōga.*

Bhakti-yōga is the path of devotion. It is the direct approach to Saguṇa Brahman, the Supreme Being in relation to the universe constituted of the three guṇas.[1]

The Ultimate Reality, according to Vedanta, is verily "the One without a second," beyond thought, beyond word. Mind fails to think of That and speech fails to express That, yet That is not nonentity or void, but Pure Existence, Absolute Being. Nor is That Being a material entity bereft of consciousness. That Being is Consciousness Itself. That is to say, That is real to Itself. That Pure Being which is Pure Consciousness is Bliss Itself. This means That is the ideal reality, perfection itself. So the Ultimate Reality according to Vedanta is pure Being-Consciousness-Bliss (Sat-cit-ānanda).[2]

That Reality, "the One without a second," designated Nondual Brahman, is immanent in this apparent manifold. Though immanent, that is all-transcendent, not at all affected by diversities. As immanent in the universe that is Saguṇa, being related to the universe constituted of the three guṇas. As all-transcendent, that is Nirguṇa, unaffected by the guṇas. The same Supreme Being, Nondual Brahman, is both Saguṇa and Nirguṇa. While Bhakti-yōga is the approach to Saguṇa Brahman, Jñāna-yōga is the approach to Nirguṇa Brahman. The one leads to the realization of unity with the Supreme Being, Saguṇa Brahman; the other leads to the realization of identity with the Supreme Being, Nirguṇa Brahman — the watchword of the one is "I am His"; the watchword of the other is "I am He," or "I am That."

[1]See Chap. II, footnote 13 on the three guṇas, p. 42.
[2]"Satcidānandam Brahma" NPT.U. I.6.

Śrī Kṛṣṇa thus refers to Himself in the *Bhagavad-gītā:*

> Through devotion, one knows Me in truth what and who I am. Then knowing Me in truth he forthwith enters into Me.[3]

He, the Supreme Being, is the Goal of both Bhakti-yōga and Jñāna-yōga.

The threefold distinction of Reality is thus noted in the *Śrīmad-bhāgavatam:*

> The knowers of Truth declare that to be the Truth — the ultimate reality, which is nondual consciousness. As all-transcendent that is called Brahman; and as immanent in the universe, that is called *Paramātmā* (the all-pervading Self) and *Bhagavān*[4] (the all-gracious God worshipped by the devotees).[5]

2. *Bhakti-yōga as related to Karma-yōga and Jñāna-yōga.*

As the mind is purified by the practice of Karma-yōga the aspirant develops the understanding that in this world of transitory things and beings, pleasures and possessions, family, home, race, country, there is nothing that man can hold to as his own but God, who alone is eternal, omnipresent, all-knowing, omnipotent, and all-gracious. With the dawning of this consciousness, the aspirant becomes eligible for Bhakti-yōga. Yet devotion to God does not grow within him simultaneously. Our thought and feeling hardly grow *pari passu* (at the same rate). The more the devotee thinks of God's love, sweetness, and grace, the greater is the possibility of his mind turning towards Him. He is the one source of all beauty, all goodness, all love, all joy.

Preparation for meditation in Bhakti-yōga means the progressive development of devotion to the Supreme Being. The more the devotion grows the more the mind turns towards Him. The mark of the growth of devotion is the constant remembrance of Him by the devotee. This constant remembrance also can be counted as the very beginning of meditation. We cannot afford to forget Him to whom we are devoted, whom we love. Just as the mariner's compass turns invariably to the magnetic pole wherever the ship may go, similarly

[3]BG XVIII:55.

[4]Bhagavān is a favorite term with the devotees. Etymologically, it means the possessor of Bhaga, the six assets each in its fullness. These are glory, valor, fame, beauty, knowledge and renunciation.

[5]SB I:2.11.

the heart of a devotee turns persistently towards God wherever he may be.

When a Karma-yōgī becomes eligible for Bhakti-yōga, he may still continue his external duties as before if the situation requires it; but his actions are no longer to be counted as expressions of Karma-yōga but of Bhakti-yōga. Such Bhakti-yōga also leads to the realization of God.

Bhakti-yōga is also recognized by the followers of Jñāna-yōga, the seekers of Nirguṇa Brahman. They hold that the direct approach to Nirguṇa Brahman is very difficult for most aspirants. After realizing Saguṇa Brahman through devotion, the seeker can approach Nirguṇa Brahman. Says Śrī Kṛṣṇa in the *Bhagavad-gītā:*

> Greater is the difficulty of those whose minds are set on the all-transcendent Being beyond manifestation. The goal of the unmanifested One is very hard to reach for the seekers who are not free from the body-idea [who identify themselves with the body].[6]

3. *Two distinct stages of devotion: (1) Preparatory, and (2) Spontaneous.*

Broadly speaking, the path of devotion has two distinct stages. The one is the preparatory stage when the devotee has to go through rites and ceremonies — practical courses —physical, verbal, and mental; the other is the stage of spontaneous devotion. Whatever you do for the sake of the Lord with the physical body, or the organ of speech, or the mind will help you to develop devotion to Him. Of all the preparatory courses, association with the devotees of God is counted to be the most efficacious. Blessed are they who are devoted to the devotees of God.

In the *Adhyātma Rāmāyaṇa*[7], Śrī Rāmacandra has specifically mentioned the following nine courses for the cultivation of devotion:

1. Association with My devotees.
2. Talking about Me.
3. Expounding My attributes.
4. Elucidation of My utterances and service to the preceptor with earnestness whenever possible looking upon him as My representative.
5. Practice of virtue along with the observance of:

[6]BG XII: 5. [7]Araṇya-kāṇḍa Ch.10.

   a. Yama (nonviolence, truthfulness, nonstealing, continence, noncovetousness).
   b. Niyama (cleanliness, contentment, self-control, reading of scriptures, surrendering the fruits of actions to God).
6. Daily worship of Me with steadfastness.
7. Repetition of My sacred word or formula with the pertinents, such as the use of the rosary.
8. a. Special service to My devotees while looking upon Me in all beings.
   b. Dispassion to sense-objects with the serenity of mind.
9. Discussion on spiritual truths.

Śrī Rāmacandra further mentions in this context that any human individual whose mind turns to God is eligible for practicing these courses. He adds that whoever will persistently follow as many as possible of these courses will develop spontaneous devotion to God regardless of sex, caste, color, social status, and so forth. This statement has been corroborated by the lives of saints and seers throughout the ages.

From the Vedic times up to the twentieth century there have been numerous seers and sages, among women as well as among men, who have been well known for their self-dedication to spiritual idealism and for their devotional fervor.

Truly, man is a born devotee of God; all his life he is seeking God knowingly or unknowingly.

"The cultivation of devotion means the manifestation of the innate devotion ever existent within man," remarks a Vaiṣṇava sage.

The *Śvetāśvatara Upaniṣad* concludes with an eulogy of fervent devotion:

> The truths related in this text become manifest to those great ones who develop supreme devotion to God and as much devotion to the preceptor as to God.

With the development of ardent devotion the devotee feels closer and closer to the Supreme Being. He contemplates more and more on His sweetness, beauty, graciousness, love and less and less on His splendor, might, knowledge, immensity, and so forth.

4. *Marks of spontaneous devotion: closer and closer relationship with God.*

In the beginning the devotee approaches Him with serene attitude marked with awe and veneration; the Lord of the universe is held to be far away. As he progresses in the path of devotion he feels a closer and closer relationship with Him. This develops according to the inner constitution of the devotee. The different types of relationships can be noted as follows:

1. The relationship between the Ruler and the ruled; the Preserver of the universe preserves him as well.
2. The relationship between the Master and the servant.
3. The relationship between the Parent and the child; this is twofold:
   a. The relationship between the Father and the child.
   b. The relationship between the Mother and the child.
4. The relationship between Friend and friend. God is held to be the sole dependable friend.
5. The devotee's love becomes so intimate and deep that he approaches God with the affectionate attitude of a parent. He or she looks upon God as the Divine Child. A male devotee looks upon God as the divine Child and himself as the father. A woman devotee thinks of herself as the mother and God as the Divine Child. (For instance, Śrī Kṛṣṇa's mother treated the Child Kṛṣṇa with motherly affection even though she was not unaware of the child's divinity. The Madonna affectionately treated the child, Jesus, even though she was more or less conscious of His divinity.)
6. The relationship wherein the devotee looks upon God as the most beloved (sweetheart).

These relationships prevail more or less in all religions. Not a few Christian mystics held the sweetheart attitude towards God. Through the development of any one of these relationships the devotee can realize God. The validity of all these relationships have been testified in the life of Sri Ramakrishna, who saw God through each one of them.

A person should try to hold constantly to any relationship that appeals to him, whatever duty he may have to perform, or wherever he may have to go.

By cultivating any one of these relationships, according to his inner constitution, the devotee recognizes the truth that God is all in all. He is not just the Ruler, or just the Master, or just the Father, or just the Friend, and so forth. He is all these and even more, beyond definition. Then the devotee embraces God with all his heart, with all his soul, with all his mind. No longer does he look upon God as the Omnipotent, Omnipresent, Omniscient, Originator, Ruler, Sustainer of the universe, but as his Sole Refuge, his Sole Benefactor, his Sole Friend, his Sole Support, his Sole Goal. There is nothing else anywhere he can hold to with assurance.

5. *Whole-hearted devotion is the greatest treasure of human life. The development of spiritual insight.*

Whole-souled devotion is the greatest asset of human life. It is the source of incessant joy and makes man free forever.

It is said in the *Śrīmad-bhāgavatam:*

> Getting the first and foremost requisite, the human body, which is like a strong boat, so difficult to secure, yet within easy reach — with the teacher as his helmsman, and propelled by Me (God) as a favorable wind, with such means as these the man who does not strive to cross the ocean of worldly existence verily commits suicide.[8]
>
> The wise man having after many births obtained this extremely rare human body, which, though frail, is yet conducive to man's supreme good, should quickly strive for liberation, before the body, which is always subject to death, chances to fall; for sense-enjoyments are available in any body.[9]

Earnest devotion is the golden chain by which God can be tied. If God cares for anything it is the spontaneous devotion of the human heart.

Just as the devotee approaches God so also God approaches the devotee.

Says Śrī Kṛṣṇa in the *Bhagavad-gītā:*

> Persons who, giving up all other thoughts, worship Me with their mind constantly fixed on Me, I carry to them what they do not have and guard what they already have.[10]

With the development of fervent devotion to God the devotee gains a clear understanding of the true nature of God. He comes to recognize the fact that God is not away from us. He is the finest of all existences — Pure Consçiousness. As such He is the innermost

[8]SB XI:20.17. [9]*Ibid.* XI:9.29. [10]BG IX:22.

Reality, the One Self of all. The Soul of the universe is the Soul of his soul, his inmost self, the indwelling consciousness.

Then he can meditate on God within the heart. At this stage he needs the help of a preceptor, and God's grace also descends on him.

6. *Of all the means for the development of devotion, association with holy men is most efficacious. Divine grace descends through them. The devotee should continue his efforts without relaxation.*

There are higher and higher stages of ardent devotion. Even after reaching the stage of spontaneous devotion the devotee is expected to continue such practices as association with holy men, hearing about God, talking about God and the repetition of some name signifying Divinity, and meditation on the corresponding form as far as possible. As stated by Nārada, "Devotion is attainable by continuous spiritual practice."[11]

Of all these means, association with holy men is readily efficacious. Says Śrī Kṛṣṇa in the *Bhāgavatam:*

> He who worships Me, attaining devotion to Me through association with sages easily realizes My state taught by the sages.
>
> O, Uddhava, there is almost no other efficient way except the Bhakti-yōga due to the association with sages for I am the goal of the sages.
>
> It was through the association with the saints, O stainless one, that many who were of ambitious or indolent nature attained Me in different ages.[12]

Nārada is of the opinion that devotion to God is attained primarily through the grace of a true devotee of God or through a modicum of God's grace.[13]

Devotion to God is purificatory. Nothing else can cleanse the mind as effectively. As the alloy in gold cannot be extracted by any such means as washing, wiping or polishing, but through the process of smelting it, even so a man's subtle impressions of past karma buried in the subsoil of the mind cannot be eradicated by any physical, mental or moral method, but by the generation of devotion within his heart.

Says Śrī Kṛṣṇa in the *Bhāgavatam:*

[11] *Bhakti-sūtras,* Aphorism 36.
[12] SB XI:11.25, 48; 12.3.
[13] *Bhakti-sūtras,* Aphorism 38.

> As gold smelted by fire gives up its dross and gets back its real state, so the mind by means of systematic devotion to Me winnows off subtle impressions of past karma and attains to Me.[14]

As the mind is purified more and more devotion grows. Śrī Kṛṣṇa strongly recommends single-minded devotional practice.

> If even a wicked person worships Me to the exclusion of all else, he should be regarded as righteous for he is rightly resolved.
>
> Forthwith he becomes pious and attains abiding peace. O, Arjuna, you can proclaim that my devotee never perishes.[15]

There are many words in Vedantic scriptures signifying the Divine Being, such as Viṣṇu, Nārāyaṇa, Hari, Bhagavān. They have different shades of meaning. Each word fits the particular inner attitude of a devotee. The preceptor chooses the word for the devotee according to his inner constitution.

By repeating that word the devotee generates devotion suited to his or her mental make-up. With the repetition of the word Vedanta prescribes some form corresponding to the word. Each word represents an inner idea, as does the form. The word is not just a mere sound or a combination of a few letters. Along with the word, the preceptor prescribes the form corresponding to the word. While repeating the word or formula the devotee meditates on the corresponding form.

It has been stated by Nārada, "Devotion is the source of inexpressable joy and peace."[16] As devotion grows within, the devotee continues the practice more and more.

7. *The worship of God is the universal duty of all human beings.*

"Worship [of God] is a duty for all," says Śrī Kṛṣṇa in the *Bhāgavatam*. He continues:

> He who thus worships Me constantly and exclusively, through the performance of his duties, knowing My presence in all beings, soon attains to steadfast devotion to Me.
>
> O Uddhava, through his undying devotion he comes to Me, the great Lord of all beings, the originator and destroyer of all, their cause, the Brahman.

[14]SB XI:14.25. [15]BG IX:30,31. [16]*Bhakti-sūtras*, Aphorism 60.

> Having his mind thus purified by the performance of his duties, and knowing My Divinity, he becomes endowed with knowledge and realization and soon attains to Me.
>
> All this duty, consisting of specific rites, of those belonging to the castes and orders of life, if attended with devotion to Me, becomes supreme and conducive to liberation.[17]

As devotion grows the worshipper acquires a greater and greater power of concentrating the mind on the form representing Divinity. For example, when a fowler aims at a bird seated on a tree he sees nothing but the bird. Gradually the worshipper develops the power of concentrating his mind on the divine form within himself and on its meaning as well.

8. *Even by practicing meditation on God through an image the devotee can realize Him as an Omnipresent Being.*

Śrī Kṛṣṇa relates to Uddhava how by meditating on God through an image a devotee can realize God as pure Consciousness dwelling within him and all-pervading.

> One should meditate on this form concentrating the mind on all the features. The man of self-control should withdraw the organs from the sense-objects with the help of the mind, and with the intellect [the determinative faculty] as guide, direct the mind to the entire form. Then he should concentrate the mind — distributed all over the form — on one part and think of the smiling countenance alone and nothing else.
>
> Drawing the mind which is concentrated on that, one should fix it on the Supreme Cause [the Lord as projecting the universe]. Then leaving this too one should rest on Me [Brahman as all-pervading Consciousness] and think of nothing whatsoever. With one's mind thus absorbed one sees God alone in one's self and sees oneself united to Him, the Self of all — the Light united to Light [state of samādhi].[18]

9. *God's grace descends upon the devotee with his self-surrender. Śrī Kṛṣṇa also mentions how one realizes God through His grace.*

As greater devotion grows within the devotee, he surrenders himself to God more and more. With self-surrender God's grace descends upon him. As long as a person holds to his own egoistic will

[17] SB XI:18.44-47.
[18] SB XI:14.42-45.

he is under the law of karma. He receives Divine Grace when he surrenders the ego to God's supremacy.

Śrī Kṛṣṇa mentions in the *Bhagavad-gītā* how a devotee worships God with whole-souled devotion knowing Him to be the One Self of all, how God's grace descends upon him, and how He reveals Himself unto him.

> I am the origin of all, from Me everything evolves; knowing this the wise worship Me with loving consciousness.
>
> With their minds wholly in Me, with their senses absorbed in Me, enlightening one another, and always speaking of Me, they rejoice and are delighted.
>
> To them, ever steadfast and serving Me with affection, I give that Buddhi-Yōga by which they come unto Me.
>
> [Buddhi-Yōga — clear grasp with the mind of My true nature as all-pervading Consciousness dwelling within as the inmost self.]
>
> Out of mere compassion for them, I, abiding in their hearts, destroy by the luminous lamp of knowledge the inner darkness born of ignorance.[19]

(Luminous lamp of knowledge, etc.: When through the grace of God the mind of the devotee apprehends the Supreme Being as the Self, being identical with the indwelling self, then the light of the Supreme Being shines in the mental mode, which serves as the shining lamp that removes the underlying ajñāna (the darkness of inapprehension that hides the Supreme Being). When this ajñāna is removed then the Supreme Being becomes self-revealed in samādhi. See Madhusūdana Saraswatī's commentary.)

10. *The devotee who realizes God within himself also sees Him in all beings.*

He who realizes God within also sees God in all beings. Just as God is worshipped in an image even so he can be worshipped in a living being as the indwelling self. In his last message Śrī Kṛṣṇa speaks highly of this form of worship. In the *Bhagavad-gītā* He has thus praised this spiritual outlook:

> With the heart concentrated by Yōga, with the eye of evenness for all things, he beholds the Self in all beings and all beings in the Self.

[19]BG X:8-11.

He who sees Me in all things, and sees all things in Me, he never becomes separated from Me, nor do I become separated from him.

He who being established in unity, worships Me, who am dwelling in all beings, whatever his mode of life, that Yōgī abides in Me.

He who judges of pleasure or pain everywhere, by the same standard as he applies to himself, that Yōgī, O Arjuna, is regarded as the highest.[20]

Says Śrī Kṛṣṇa to Uddhava:

With a pure mind one should observe in all beings as well as in oneself only Me, the Ātman, who am both within and without, and all-pervasive like space.

O great soul, he who, taking his stand on pure knowledge, thus regards and honors all beings as myself, who has the same attitude towards a low born one as to a Brāhmaṇa, towards a thief as to a supporter of the Brāhmaṇas, towards a spark of fire as to the sun, and towards a ruffian as to a kind man; he is considered a sage.

Ideas of rivalry, jealousy, pity and egoism quickly depart from a man who always thinks of Me in all men.

One should worship thus in thought, word, and deed till one comes to look upon all beings as Myself.

To such a man everything is Brahman [the Supreme Being] owing to the knowledge that comes of seeing the Ātman in all. Seeing Brahman everywhere, he becomes free from doubts and all attachment. This looking upon all beings as Myself in thought, word, and deed is, to My mind, the best of all methods of worship.

Herein lies the wisdom of the wise and the acumen of the intelligent, that in this very life they attain Me, the Real and Immortal, by means of that which is unreal and mortal.[21]

[20]BG VI:29-32.
[21]SB XI:29.12-15, 17-19, 22.

CHAPTER XVI

JÑĀNA-YŌGA, THE WAY TO THE REALIZATION OF NIRGUṆA BRAHMAN

1. *The goal of Jñāna-yōga is the realization of the identity of the individual self with the Supreme Self.*

Jñāna-yōga, the path of knowledge, is the way to the realization of the identity of the adherent's inmost self[1] with Nirguṇa Brahman. Finally the self merges in the Ultimate Reality, the One without a second, beyond thought, beyond word. By implication this is said to be Nondual Brahman, pure Being, Consciousness, Bliss.

As declared by the Upaniṣads:

Brahman is Truth, Consciousness, Infinite.[2]
Brahman is Consciousness, Bliss.[3]
Supreme Brahman is Being-Consciousness-Bliss.[4]

The manifold we experience has no Ultimate Reality. The fundamental one is the substratum of the apparent manifold, the playground of diversities. The apparent multiplicity does not affect the underlying Reality, just as mirage water does not moisten the sandy bed of the desert. Nondual Brahman is all-in-all. It interpenetrates each and every finite form of the living and the nonliving. Though immanent in the universe it is all-transcendent. As such it is called Nirguṇa Brahman, unaffected by diversities.

Verily, "All this is Brahman," declares the *Chāndōgya Upaniṣad.*[5] So says the *Muṇḍaka Upaniṣad:*

[1]Also called *Sākṣī-caitanya* (witness-self), and *Kūṭastha-caitanya* (rock-steady self).
[2]Tai.U. II:1.3.
[3]Br.U. III:9.28.7.
[4]NPT.U. I:6.
[5]Ch.U. III:14.1.

> The immortal Brahman alone is before, that Brahman is behind, that Brahman is to the right and to the left. Brahman alone pervades everything above and below; this universe is that Supreme Brahman alone.[6]

It is further said in the same Upaniṣad with regard to Brahman:

> That is all-pervasive and self-effulgent; and Its nature is inconceivable. It is subtler than the subtle. It shines diversely. It is further away than the far-off, and It is near at hand in this body. By the seers It is (perceived as) seated in this very body, in the cavity of the heart.
>
> This is not comprehended through the eye nor through the other senses; nor expressed by the organ of speech. Nor is It attainable through austerity or karma. When one becomes purified in mind through the clarity of understanding, then can one see that indivisible Self through meditation.[7]

The all-transcendent Supreme Being — Nirguṇa Brahman — underlying the apparent manifold is the One Self of the multiform universe and of every individual thing and being. The existence of each and everything is due to that Basic Reality, Being-Consciousness-Bliss. It penetrates each and every finite form, living and nonliving. It is specially manifest in the sentient; above all in human beings. Each and every individual is essentially That. The Supreme Being — pure Being-Consciousness-Bliss — is the inmost self of every human being. This is why the self is the dearest of all. Whatever is loved is loved for the sake of the self. Man's inmost self is the central principle of consciousness in the psychophysical constitution, which cognizes not only the external objects but also the conditions and functions of the body, the organs, and the mind. It is beyond the ego. This is the first object of man's love and is identical with the universal Self. The supreme purpose of human life is to realize the identity of the indwelling self with the all-transcendent Supreme Being. Finally the individual self is known to be the Self of all.

2. *The importance of Self-knowledge. The triple method of its attainment.*

We recall in this context the anecdote of Yājñavalkya and Maitreyī in the *Bṛhadāraṇyaka Upaniṣad*:[8]

[6]Mu.U. II:2.12.
[7]*Ibid.* III:1.7,8.
[8]Br.U. IV:5.1-15.

Yājñavalkya had two wives: Maitreyī and Kātyāyanī. Of these, Maitreyī was conversant with the knowledge of Brahman, while Kātyāyanī had an essentially feminine outlook. One day Yājñavalkya, when he decided to embrace monastic life, said:

"Maitreyī, my dear, I am going to renounce this life [to become a monk]. Let me make a final settlement between you and Kātyāyanī."

Maitreyī said: "Venerable Sir, if indeed the whole earth full of wealth belonged to me, would I be immortal through that or not?"

"No," replied Yājñavalkya, "your life would be just like that of people who have plenty. Of immortality, however, there is no prospect through wealth."

Then Maitreyī said: "What should I do with that which would not make me immortal? Tell me, venerable Sir, of that alone which you know [to be the only means of attaining immortality]."

Yājñavalkya replied: "My dear, you have been my beloved [even before], and [now] you have resolved [to know] what is after my heart. If you wish, my dear, I shall explain it to you. As I explain it, meditate [on what I say]."

"Verily, not for the sake of the husband, my dear, is the husband loved, but he is loved for the sake of the self [which, in its true nature, is one with the Supreme Self].

"Verily, not for the sake of the wife, my dear, is the wife loved, but she is loved for the sake of the self.

"Verily, not for the sake of the sons, my dear, are the sons loved, but they are loved for the sake of the self.

"Verily, not for the sake of wealth, my dear, is wealth loved, but it is loved for the sake of the self.

"Verily, not for the sake of the animals, my dear, are the animals loved, but they are loved for the sake of the self.

"Verily, not for the sake of the brāhmin, my dear, is the brāhmin loved, but he is loved for the sake of the self.

"Verily, not for the sake of the kṣatriya, my dear, is the kṣatriya loved, but he is loved for the sake of the self.

"Verily, not for the sake of the all, my dear, is the all loved, but it is loved for the sake of the self.

"Verily, my dear Maitreyī, it is the Self that should be realized — should be heard of, reflected on, and meditated upon. By the realization of the Self, my dear, through hearing, reflection, and meditation, all this is known.

• • •

"Thus you have the instruction given to you. This much, indeed, is [the means to] immortality."

After giving the instruction Yājñavalkya left home.

3. *The fourfold requisite for Self-knowledge with which the pupil should approach a competent teacher.*

As a result of the practice of Karma-yōga subsidiary to Jñāna-yōga (which we have discussed in a previous chapter), the aspirant develops the following four prerequisites for the attainment of Self-knowledge.

1. The discrimination of the Real and the unreal: That is Real which never goes out of existence, what is unreal has no existence. Also the consequent conviction that Brahman is real; the manifold is unreal, it only appears to exist.
2. Aversion to the enjoyment of the fruits of actions here and hereafter.
3. Six assets: (i) Serenity of the mind; (ii) Self-control; (iii) Fortitude; (iv) Dispassion; (v) Faith in the words of the scriptures and the preceptor; (vi) Having the Goal constantly in mind.
4. Longing for Liberation.

A competent seeker of Self-knowledge has to go invariably to a proficient teacher. The necessity of approaching an adept teacher on the part of a qualified spiritual aspirant has been very much emphasized in the Vedantic literature.

It is said in the *Muṇḍaka Upaniṣad:*

> Thoroughly investigating into the realms attainable by work the seeker of Self-knowledge should be dispassionate. The eternal cannot be the product of work. In order to realize the Truth he should positively approach with faggots in hand [a mark of humility and readiness to serve] the teacher who is well versed in the Vedas and established in the knowledge of Brahman.[9]

(Śaṅkarācārya remarks in this context that even though possessed of knowledge of the scriptures the pupil should not independently seek the direct knowledge of Brahman.)

Śrī Kṛṣṇa says in the *Bhagavad-gītā:*

> Know that (the Truth), by prostrating thyself, by queries, and by servicefulness; the wise, who have realized the Truth, will instruct thee in that knowledge.[10]

[9]Mu.U. I:2.12. [10]BG IV:34.

Says Śaṅkarācārya in his *Viveka-cūḍāmaṇi* (The Crest-Jewel of Discrimination):

> The inquirer about the truth of the Ātman who is possessed of the above-mentioned four means of attainment [see previous page] should approach a wise preceptor, who is capable of deliverance.
>
> Who is versed in the Vedas, taintless, unsmitten by desire and a knower of Brahman par excellence, who is settled in Brahman, is calm like fire that has consumed its fuel, who is a boundless reservoir of mercy by nature and a benefactor of all good people who prostrate themselves before him.[11]

Even a scholar well versed in the Vedic texts often fails to grasp the central truths declared by them. For the profitable study of the Vedas the pupil must get acquainted not only with the core of the Vedic teachings but also must be convinced of their rationality. Above all, he has to adopt practical methods to realize the spiritual truths. For all these purposes the guidance of an efficient spiritual teacher is indispensable. The teacher points out the central teachings, convinces the pupil of their reasonableness by arguments, and also instructs the pupil on the practical courses for realizing the truth. For this threefold reason particularly, the necessity for the guidance of an adept has been emphasized in Vedanta.

It is said in the *Kaṭha Upaniṣad:*

> Many there are who do not have the chance to hear of Ātman. Though hearing of Ātman, many cannot comprehend That. Wonderful is the expounder and rare is the hearer; rare indeed is the experiencer of Ātman, being taught by an able preceptor.
>
> Ātman when taught by an incompetent person, is not easily comprehended, because It is diversely regarded by disputants.
>
> But when It is taught by him who has become one with Ātman, there can remain no more doubt about It. Ātman is subtler than the subtlest and not to be known through argumentation.[12]

4. *The identity of the individual self and the Supreme Self is the quintessence of the Vedic knowledge.*

In each of the four Vedas there is a terse sentence delivering this knowledge. This is called "Mahāvākya," lit. the Great Saying. It points to the identity of the individual self with Nirguṇa Brahman, and not with the Ultimate Reality, beyond thought, beyond word

[11]VC 32,33. [12]Ka.U. I:2.7,8.

(avāṅgmanasōgōcaram), which is beyond all characterization. (See Chap. II, sec.2, para.3.)

In the *Aitareya Upaniṣad* of the *Ṛg-Veda* the Mahāvākya is "Consciousness is Brahman." The meaning is that the indwelling consciousness in an individual is identical with Brahman, the Supreme Being.[13]

In the *Bṛhadāraṇyaka Upaniṣad* of the *Yajur-Veda,* the Great Saying is "I am Brahman." One's inmost self is Nirguṇa Brahman.[14]

In the *Chāndōgya Upaniṣad* of the *Sāma-Veda,* the Great Saying is "That Thou Art."[15] The sage Uddālaka imparted the lesson to his son, Śvetaketu, that everything in the universe is permeated by One Self, the All-pervading Consciousness. So every individual is essentially That.

In the *Māṇḍūkya Upaniṣad* of the *Atharva-Veda* the Great Saying is "This self is Brahman." One's innermost self is essentially Nondual Consciousness.[16]

"This supreme Vedic teaching [Mahāvākya] imparts a twofold knowledge attainable by no other means: on the one hand, by affirming ātman as Brahman, it removes man's deep-rooted misconception regarding himself, namely, that he is bound, finite, imperfect, and mortal, and points to his true self as self-existent, self-shining, ever-pure and ever-free. On the other hand, by proclaiming Brahman as ātman it removes man's equally indomitable misconception regarding the Supreme Being, namely, that He is remote, unattainable, hidden, if not nonexistent and reveals Him as the innermost Self, ever-manifest, immediate and direct. Thus, what is conceived as the farthest is revealed as nearer than the nearest, what appears to be unattainable as already attained, what is ever hidden as self-manifest."[17]

Each of these terse sentences declares the identity of the individual consciousness and the universal or all-pervading consciousness, and points to the sole reality of Nondual Consciousness that Brahman is. Hence, this great teaching (Mahāvākya) is said to be akhaṇḍārthabōdhaka (indicative of the undivided Absolute Being free from all distinctions).

We recall in this context Śaṅkarācārya's hymn *Nirvāṇa-ṣaṭkam* (Six stanzas on Nirvāṇa). This is also called *Ātma-ṣaṭkam* (Six stanzas on the Self).

[13]Ai. U. III:1.3.
[14]Br.U. I:4.10.
[15]Ch.U. VI:8.7, *passim* (here and there).
[16]Ma.U. II.
[17]See the author's *Methods of Knowledge*, pp. 200-201.

Ōm, I am neither mind, nor intellect, nor ego, nor citta;[18]
Neither ears nor tongue nor the senses of smell and sight;
Nor am I ether, earth, fire, water, or air:
I am Pure Consciousness and Bliss: I am Śiva! I am Śiva!

I am neither the prāṇa nor the five vital breaths;
Neither the seven elements of the body nor its five sheaths;
Nor hands nor feet nor tongue, nor the organs of sex and
elimination:
I am Pure Consciousness and Bliss: I am Śiva! I am Śiva!

Neither loathing nor liking have I, neither greed nor delusion;
No sense have I of ego or pride, neither dharma nor mōkṣa;
Neither desire of the mind nor object for its desiring:
I am Pure Consciousness and Bliss: I am Śiva! I am Śiva!

Neither virtue nor vice am I, neither pleasure nor pain;
Nor the mantra, the sacred place, the Vedas, the sacrifice;
Neither the act of eating, the eater, nor the food:
I am Pure Consciousness and Bliss: I am Śiva! I am Śiva!

Death or fear I have none, nor any distinction of caste;
Neither father nor mother nor even a birth have I;
Neither friend nor comrade, neither disciple nor guru:
I am Pure Consciousness and Bliss: I am Śiva! I am Śiva!

I have no form or fancy; the All-pervading am I;
Everywhere I exist, yet I am beyond the senses;
Neither salvation nor bondage have I, nor anything that
may be known:
I am Pure Consciousness and Bliss: I am Śiva! I am Śiva!

5. *How Brahman is realized through meditation as the Self within.*

For the practice of meditation on the Ātman, as identical with Brahman, it is absolutely necessary for the seeker of Truth to have the previous knowledge of the Ātman and of Brahman from a reliable source, that is to say, from the scriptures and the words of the preceptor. Next he should form a clear idea of the nature of both (Ātman and Brahman) by contemplation. Then he has to be convinced of the Truth of their identity through reasoning. When he forms a definite idea in his mind of Nirguṇa Brahman, then he can meditate on the Self as Brahman with firm conviction. The practice of meditation is an attempt to make the mental mode conform with Reality. The more the mental mode conforms with Reality the more the light of Reality shines in the mental mode. Realization comes with

[18]These are responsible for four different functions of the cognitive aspect of the mind (antaḥkaraṇa): 1) Deliberation, 2) Determination, 3) I-ness, 4) Recollection.

the full conformity of the mental mode with Reality as the light of Reality shining in the mental mode removes primal ajnāna underlying it. The threefold method by which this is achieved is known as: (1) Hearing (śravaṇa), (2) Contemplation (manana), and (3) Persistent Practice of Meditation (nididhyāsana).

So it is said in the *Muṇḍaka Upaniṣad:*

> That Brahman is vast, self-luminous, inconceivable, subtler than the subtle. That shines forth. That is far beyond what is far, and yet here very near at hand. That is seen here, dwelling in the cave of the heart of conscious beings. Brahman is not grasped by the eye, nor by the organ of speech, nor by other organs or senses, nor by penance nor by righteous deed. Being pure-minded through the purity of understanding, as a person practices meditation, thereby he beholds Him, who is whole and without component parts.[19]

We conclude with the citation of the following two verses from the *Śvetāśvatara Upaniṣad:*

> Just as a lump of gold stained by dirt being purified by fire shines brightly, similarly the embodied being by realizing the truth of ātman becomes united with the Supreme Self, attains self-fulfillment and goes beyond sorrows.
>
> When the ardent seeker of Self-knowledge recognizes the truth of Brahman through the perception of the true nature of the self shining within the body, then by realizing the effulgent Self, eternal, changeless, beyond the modifications of Prakṛti, he becomes free from all fetters.[20]

[19]Mu.U. III:1.7,8.

[20]Sv.U. II:14,15.

APPENDIX I

THE FIRST AND THE LAST MESSAGE OF ŚRĪ KṚṢṆA, THE PIONEER TEACHER OF THE PRACTICAL PHASE OF VEDANTA (SMṚTI-PRASTHĀNA)

Śrī Kṛṣṇa delivered his message, as is evident from literary records, on two significant occasions: (1) on the eve of the war of Kurukṣetra, and (2) on the eve of his departure from the world. The first message, well-known as the *Bhagavad-gītā* (or *Gītā* for short), was delivered to his friend and disciple Arjuna, on the very battlefield. The other message, which is evidently his second and last, was delivered to another devoted friend and disciple, Uddhava, not in a field of contest, but in a secluded and sacred place called Prabhasa, near the seacoast of Gujarat, north of Bombay. The *Bhagavad-gītā,* literally the "Song of God," though widely circulated as an independent book, is actually a small but pithy section of the voluminous Sanskrit epic the *Mahābhārata,* a poetical work of ninety thousand couplets, perhaps the world's largest, being about seven times the size of Homer's *Iliad* and *Odyssey* put together.

The Last Message of Śrī Kṛṣṇa, which has not gained much circulation as an independent treatise, forms a part of one of the most authoritative Sanskrit scriptures, *Śrīmad-bhāgavatam* (Section XI, Chaps. 6-29). This sacred book (called the *Bhāgavatam* for short), dwells specifically on the love of God and the knowledge of God. Sri Ramakrishna used to remark that the *Bhāgavatam* is fried in the butter of divine knowledge and soaked in the syrup of divine love. The Vaiṣṇavas—the worshipers of Viṣṇu, the Omnipresent Preserver, who is all-love and all-bliss—hold this book in great veneration and consider it as authoritative as the Vedas. A small compendium of this book in lucid English, called *The Widom of God,* has been brought out by my brother disciple, Swami Prabhavananda, and is widely read by seekers of God, with much interest and profit.

There is no fundamental difference between the first and the last

(See p. 36 for the three stages of Vedanta.)

message so far as the central theme is concerned. But there is a difference in the methods of its presentation and the emphasis laid on certain aspects. Both messages center on the topics of the Highest Good and the means of its attainment. The Highest Good is defined by Vedanta as the cessation of all sufferings and the attainment of Supreme Bliss. This is the goal for which all are striving knowingly or unknowingly, directly or indirectly. Man is constantly struggling to overcome evil by good in some form or other. All human activities are directed to this end. What is the ultimate aim of this struggle? The removal of all evil and the attainment of the Supreme Good. After long, long experience in this world of dualities a person realizes that the unalloyed joy and the unmixed blessing that he has been seeking all along is not to be found anywhere in the relative order, where good and evil coexist. Then he is convinced that the supreme object of his search is God and God alone; it is He who is all-good beyond the pairs of opposites, such as birth and death, growth and decay, pain and pleasure, knowledge and ignorance, virtue and vice; it is by attaining Him that there remains nothing more to attain, it is by knowing Him that there remains nothing more to know.

Indeed, the attainment of the Highest Good means the realization of God, in whom is the culmination of knowledge, the fulfillment of all desires, and the consummation of joy. When a person realizes God he discovers his essential unity with Him. He finds himself in Him. He is restored to his intrinsic divine nature. He is reinstated in his innate perfection. A seer does not see God apart from himself not even as the greatest of all. God is not one of the many, but the inmost Self of one and all. He is the Reality underlying each and every phase of the manifold. He, the all-pervading Supreme Self, Pure Being-Consciousness-Bliss, is the unobserved observer of the order of phenomena. The imperfect world has perfection as its very basis and being. Though hidden in all physical objects, the self-effulgent Supreme Consciousness that God is shines even in the lowest orders of life more or less as sentiency, as the light of cognition. Consciousness is coextensive with livingness according to most biologists. It is the light that belongs solely to the cognizing self, the subject, and by no means to any part of the objective universe, physical or psychical. In human individuals the same Supreme Consciousness is clearly manifest as the knowing self distinct from the psychophysical system. This is why man alone is capable of realizing Him in the depth of his heart as the inmost Self beyond all limitations.

It is true that a devotee can see God in a particular form that represents divine power, love, or knowledge, or beauty, and is chosen by him to worship the Adorable One. God actually appears to him in the form of his Chosen Ideal. Such God-vision is not therefore a case of imagination or hallucination on the part of the devotee. Yet this is not the realization of God in the true sense. For after the vision, God may again disappear from the devotee's sight. But once a person realizes God as his very Self, as the Soul of all souls, he never loses sight of Him. Says Śrī Kṛṣṇa to Arjuna:

> He who sees Me in all things and sees all things in Me never becomes separated from Me, nor do I become separated from him.[1]

But even momentary God-vision can be a prelude to the timeless transcendental experience.

Though the ultimate goal is the same for one and all, yet the ways differ according to seekers' tendencies, capacities, and situation in life. Śrī Kṛṣṇa has enunciated to Uddhava a triple means to the attainment of the Highest Good: the yōga of work (karma), the yōga of devotion (bhakti), and the yōga of knowledge (jñāna) — the threefold way to God-realization. The word *yōga* properly means spiritual discipline— a method of God-realization, in other words, Self-realization. None but a spiritual aspirant, none but a seeker of the Highest Good is eligible for the practice of yōga in the true sense. Śrī Kṛṣṇa thus speaks of the efficacy of the three yōgas and their suitability for different grades and types of spiritual aspirants:

> The yōgas of love, knowledge and work have been given by me to men for their Highest Good. Except through these, there is no way to attain freedom. Of these, the yōga of knowledge is for those who desire nothing; for they, knowing every desire to be fraught with evil, have renounced work. Those who still have desires, and who are attached to work must follow the yōga of work. The yōga of love is successfully followed by those blessed mortals who take delight in Me and My word.[2]

Those who are dutiful and virtuous and live a happy and contented life usually discern the inherent limitations of all temporal possessions and pleasures and turn to the search for the eternal. It is on them that Śrī Kṛṣṇa enjoins the practice of Karma-yōga. Such spiritual aspirants as have worldly desires but are convinced of their

[1]BG VI:30. [2]SB XI:20.6-8.

futility and want to get rid of them and attain the Supreme Good, must practice the yōga of work (karma). They should try to do their duties, domestic and social, without the ego-idea, surrendering the self to God, and giving up all claim to work and its results. It is the yōga of selfless work that prepares the mind for the practice of the yōga of devotion and the yōga of knowledge. It removes worldly attachment and intensifies the desire for the Supreme Good. As the mind is purified by the practice of Karma-yōga, the spiritual aspirant develops, according to his aptitude, a real interest either in the loving worship of the Personal God, or in the cultivation of Self-knowledge (that is, in the realization of the identity of the individual self with the Supreme Self). In the one case he acquires the competence for the practice of Bhakti-yōga (the path of devotion), and in the other for the practice of Jñāna-yōga (the path of knowledge). Without the necessary preparation through Karma-yōga none can follow the path of devotion or the path of knowledge effectually. So says Śrī Kṛṣṇa to Uddhava:

> Work one must until the heart has become tranquil and free from desires. Work must be performed until one has come to love Me and to take delight in My word. By doing one's duties for the sake of duty and performing them as services unto Me, having no selfish end in view, one becomes free from both the good and evil effects of work. The yōga of work frees the mind from all evil tendencies and purifies the heart. Being thus purified one attains pure knowledge or pure devotion to Me.[3]

As indicated by Śrī Kṛṣṇa, Bhakti-yōga and Jñāna-yōga are the two direct ways to the realization of God; Karma-yōga is preparatory to either of them. Bhakti-yōga is the approach to Saguṇa Brahman, the Personal God, possessed of all blessed qualities, who, though without form, has special manifestations in forms as well. This is the path of devotion, characterized by the seeker's feeling of a loving relationship with the Divinity. Jñāna-yōga is the approach to Nirguṇa Brahman, the attributeless impersonal Absolute Being. This is the path of knowledge, characterized by the seeker's apprehension of the essential identity of the individual self with the Supreme Self. It is a steep course. It does not suit the average spiritual aspirant, in whom the body-idea prevails. After the realization of Saguṇa Brahman through Bhakti-yōga, it is not so difficult for him to realize the same as Nirguṇa if he desires it.

[3]SB XI:20.9-11.

It is to be noted that Bhakti-yōga is not wholly an emotional approach nor is Jñāna-yōga purely an intellectual method. There is ample scope for intellect in Bhakti-yōga, just as there is ample scope for emotion in Jñāna-yōga. Yet the one is called the way of devotion because devotion is predominant in it, and the other is called the way of knowledge, because intellect is predominant in it. Unaided by reason and understanding, devotion is liable to misconception, prejudice, error, and bigotry. Similarly, the path of knowledge without the love for Truth lacks animation and turns into a dry mechanical process. There must be an ardent longing in the seeker's heart for the realization of the Truth grasped by the intellect. Unless the heart moves with the intellect, his search for God will prove to be similar to academic research. Without whole-souled devotion to Truth the mind of the seeker cannot be tranquil and transparent enough for its revelation or immediate apprehension.

A follower of the path of devotion (bhakti) or a follower of the path of knowledge (jñāna) does not necessarily have to give up his duties, although they are no longer imperative for his inner purification. Along with the practice of the yōga of bhakti or the yōga of jnāna he can continue to perform them with complete self-renunciation. Karma in such a case is a form of devotion or knowledge. It promotes the aspirant's love for God and his knowledge of God and thus becomes a means of liberation. So says Śrī Kṛṣṇa:

> He who worships Me constantly and exclusively, through the performance of his duties, knowing My presence in all beings, soon attains to steadfast devotion to Me. O Uddhava, through his undying devotion he comes to Me, the great Lord of all beings, the originator and destroyer [re-absorber] of all, their cause, the Brahman. Having his mind thus purified by the performance of his duties, and knowing My Divinity, he becomes endowed with knowledge and realization and soon attains to Me. All this duty, consisting of specific rites, of those belonging to the castes and orders of life, if attended with devotion to Me becomes supreme and conducive to liberation.[4]

Evidently, Śrī Kṛṣṇa does not consider Rāja-yōga as a means of God-realization, since he clearly states that except through these three — the yōgas of karma (work), bhakti (devotion), and jñāna (knowledge) there is no way to attain freedom. But actually he does not exclude Rāja-yōga from the methods of God-realization,

[4]SB XI:18.44-47.

inasmuch as its practical courses are included in the three other yōgas mentioned by him. Patañjali's yogic method is based on the Sāṁkhya system of philosophy with minor differences. So far as the philosophical background of his Rāja-yōga is concerned, Vedanta disagrees on many points. But its practical methods of self-realization are mostly adopted to the Vedantic disciplines. Indeed, the eight steps of Rāja-yōga are in a sense the common features of the moral and spiritual courses followed by the seekers of God in most religions.

In both the messages Śrī Kṛṣṇa delineates the three methods of God-realization—the yōgas of karma, bhakti, and jñāna, which cover all the spiritual disciplines prevalent in different religions. As such, both messages have universal significance. But in the one he lays emphasis on Karma-yōga, while in the other on Bhakti-yōga. The reason is this: the first message was delivered to Arjuna, who was fit for the practice of Karma-yōga, while the last message was delivered to Uddhava, who was capable of practicing Bhakti-yōga. Though both messages are intended for all types of spiritual aspirants, yet the direct appeal of the one is to a follower of Karma-yōga, while the direct appeal of the other is to a follow of Bhakti-yōga. The different yōgas suit spiritual aspirants of different grades as well as tendencies. They can therefore be practiced by the same spiritual aspirant according to his stage of development.

The Vedantic teachers impart spiritual as well as moral instruction in view of the pupils' capabilities and situation in life. Their aim is to lead every individual at whatever level of life to the highest goal by progressive courses suited to his inner resources and environmental conditions. It may be asked in this context—Why does Śrī Kṛṣṇa take pains to explain to either disciple other yōgas than what he is ready for? The answer is: In order to fully explain the meaning and the application of any one of the yōgas it is necessary to define its exact position in man's spiritual life in relation to other yōgas. Moreover, these were occasions for the Divine Teacher to promulgate his message for different types of spiritual aspirants wherever they might be.

Arjuna was a man of heroic nature, distinguished for his valor. He was the third of the five sons of King Pāṇḍu. As a leading member of the ruling (kṣatriya) class, it was his primary duty to uphold justice, to subdue the wicked, to protect the virtuous, and to maintain peace and order. Accompanied by his four brothers, he had come to the battlefield as the commander-in-chief of the Pāṇḍava army in order to restore their kingdom forcefully seized by their wily and powerful cousins, the Kauravas. As he surveyed the huge array of troops of the belligerent powers ready to strike, he noticed on both sides his kinsmen and elders prepared to sacrifice their lives for the sake of the paltry kingdom. Commiseration for their lives on the one hand and, on the other, the stern call of duty to wage a just war regardless of their lives, created a conflict in Arjuna's mind.

But grief combined with sentimentality, proceeding from his attachment to his kith and kin and the venerable ones, prevailed over his sense of duty. Bewildered, he wanted to quit the battlefield and don the garb of a mendicant, not knowing how it would misfit his warlike heroic disposition. At this juncture he laid aside his weapons and begged instruction of Śrī Kṛṣṇa, who had assumed the role of his charioteer. The Divine Teacher pointed out his mistake and urged him to fight as a Karma-yōgī, while explaining to him the full significance of each of the three yōgas. After receiving the message Arjuna engaged in battle, free from all doubts and fears.

But the case of Uddhava was different. He was of a saintly disposition. He functioned as a state counselor, and not as a warrior. Moreover, he had outgrown all worldly attachment and developed pure devotion to God. He was capable of living the contemplative life of a devotee dedicated to the realization of the Divine Being, the one Self of all. His problem was not, as in the case of Arjuna, whether to fight or not to fight, but how to get free from all bondages and attain the Supreme Goal. While Arjuna was urged to fight against the wrongdoers, Śrī Kṛṣṇa instructed Uddhava to follow the principle of nonresistance to evil and even illustrated this with a story. To quote him in part:

> Even though scolded by the wicked, or insulted, ridiculed, calumniated, beaten, bound, robbed of his living or spat upon, or otherwise abominably treated by the ignorant — being thus variously shaken and placed in dire extremities, the man who desires his well-being should deliver himself by his own effort [through patience and discrimination].[5]

Śrī Kṛṣṇa recognizes Uddhava's devotional nature and recommends to him the way of a lover of God:

> Compassionate, with enmity to no creature, forbearing, with truth as his strength, of an unimpeachable mind, the same to all, benefactor of

[5]SB XI:22.57,58.

all beings; with his intellect unsullied by desires, a master of his organs, mild, pure, without possessions, without outward activity, with measured diet, a master of his mind, steady, having Me as his refuge, and meditative.

Ever alert, of a balanced mind, with fortitude, a master of the sixfold evil [hunger and thirst, grief and infatuation, decay and death], seeking no name, yet giving honor to others, expert, friendly [to those who are happy], merciful [to those who are in misery], and illumined.

He who knowing the merits and demerits [of duty and its opposite] gives up all his formal duties even as sanctioned by Me, and worships Me, is also the best among sages.[6]

Throughout his last message Śrī Kṛṣṇa emphasizes the path of devotion. After hearing him Uddhava, with all his doubts dispelled, with his misconceptions cleared, and fears chased away, repairs, as instructed by the teacher, to a remote and sacred place in the solitude of the Himalayas, called Badarikasrama. It is situated near the source of Alakananda, the second tributary of the Ganges in the high mountain ranges.

To Uddhava, Śrī Kṛṣṇa describes in detail the various practical courses for the cultivation of devotion. These form, broadly speaking, three distinct modes of worship: (1) physical, (2) verbal, and (3) mental. The physical methods of worship consist of service to the temple, service to the devotees of God, making pilgrimages, obeisance to the altar and to men of God, worshiping the Deity with offerings of flowers, incense, light, food, etc., the observance of festivals, and so forth. The verbal methods include speaking about God, reading and writing about Him, hearing about Him, chanting His glory, singing devotional songs, recounting the lives and deeds of the divine incarnations, saints, and seers, and the repetition of a sacred word or formula over and over again (inaudibly, semiaudibly, or audibly). The mental methods have such forms as remembering God at all times, self-surrender to the Divine will, contemplation of God whenever possible, and the regular practice of meditation on Him. Physical and verbal methods prepare the ground for the mental method. They make the worshipper God-minded. No worshipper can very well remember God, or resign himself to God, or contemplate on Him, or can ever truly meditate on Him until he develops genuine interest in God as the sole and supreme object to love and worship.

Even a single method of worship followed by a seeker of God

[6]SB XI:11.29-43.

steadily from day to day, according to his capacity and condition of life, will invariably generate devotion within his heart. The cultivation of devotion is but the manifestation of love for God that is latent within man. Each individual is a potential lover of God. He is a born seeker of Him and Him alone. Through his search for prosperity, for power, for happiness, for knowledge, or beauty, or love, a man is seeking, knowingly or unknowingly, rightly or wrongly, the very source of these, the Ultimate One, where is the perfection of all that the human mind aspires after. What man really seeks is not something limited or imperfect, but its very perfection. Where else but in God, the Ideal, the Perfect One, does this exist? It is but the love for Him that, being misdirected, finds expression as greed or lust.

Of the various methods for the cultivation of devotion to God, the most efficacious is the association with the holy. He who gains devotion through holy association finds no difficulty in realizing God, declares Śrī Kṛṣṇa:

> He who worships Me, attaining devotion for Me through association with sages, easily realizes My state taught by the sages.
>
> O Uddhava, there is almost no other efficient way except the bhakti yōga due to the association with sages, for I am the goal of the sages.
>
> It was through the association with saints, O stainless one, that many who were of an ambitious or indolent nature attained Me in different ages.[7]

Thorough cleansing of the human mind is not possible by any other means than through devotion to God. Says Śrī Kṛṣṇa:

> As fire kindled into a blaze burns the faggots to ashes, so, O Uddhava, devotion to Me totally destroys all sins.
>
> I, the dear Self of the pious, am attainable by devotion alone, which is the outcome of faith. Devotion to Me purges even the low-born of their congenital impurity.
>
> Piety joined to truthfulness and compassion or learning coupled with austerity, never wholly purifies a mind which is devoid of devotion to Me.[8]

As the alloy in gold cannot be extracted by any such means as washing, wiping or polishing it but through the process of smelting it, even so a man's subtle impressions of past karma buried in the subsoil of the mind cannot be eradicated by any physical, mental, or moral

[7]SB XI:11.25,48; 12.3.   [8]SB XI:14.19,21,22.

method but by the generation of devotion within his heart. In the words of Śrī Kṛṣṇa:

> As gold smelted by fire gives up its dross and gets back its real state, so the mind by means of systematic devotion to Me winnows off subtle impressions of past karma and attains to Me.[9]

Śrī Kṛṣṇa praises the path of devotion and exhorts Uddhava to follow it:

> O Uddhava, neither yōga, nor knowledge, nor piety, nor study, nor austerity, nor renunciation captivates Me so much as a heightened devotion to Me.
>
> O pure-minded one, I have already expounded the philosophy of devotion to thee, but since thou hast special liking for it, I shall again describe the chief means to the attainment of devotion to Me.
>
> That religion is called the best which makes for devotion to Me; knowledge is the realization of the unity of Self.
>
> Whatever is acquired through works, austerities, knowledge, dispassion, yōga, or charity, or through any other means of well-being, My devotee easily attains to it through devotion to Me—aye, even heaven, or liberation, or My abode, should he care to have it.[10]

Śrī Kṛṣṇa instructs graphically how a devotee by practicing meditation on God with form can realize the Formless One:

> One should meditate on this form, concentrating the mind on all the features. The man of self-control should withdraw the organs from the sense-objects with the help of the mind, and with the intellect as guide direct the mind to My whole body. Then one should concentrate the mind—distributed all over My body—on one part, and think of the smiling countenance alone and nothing else.
>
> Drawing the mind which is concentrated on that, one should fix it on the Supreme Cause [the Lord as projecting the universe]. Then leaving that too, one should rest on Me [Pure Brahman divested of all attributes] and think of nothing whatsoever [state of samādhi]. With one's mind thus absorbed, one sees Me alone in oneself and sees oneself united to Me, the Self of all—like light united to light.[11]

It is a rare privilege to be born as a human being. Self-realization is not possible in any other life. Śrī Kṛṣṇa stresses the importance of human life and its blessings:

[9]SB XI:14.25.
[10]SB XI:14.20; 19.19,27;20.32,33.
[11]SB XI:14.42-45.

> Getting the first and foremost requisite, viz. a human body, which is like a strong boat — so difficult to secure, yet attained somehow — with the teacher as its helmsman, and propelled by Me as by a favorable wind — with such means as these, the man who does not strive to cross the ocean of transmigration — the rounds of birth and rebirth — commits suicide.
>
> Obtaining a human body, which gives a glimpse of My nature, a man, by practicing the religion of love for me, realizes Me, the all-blissful Paramātman, who dwells in his heart.[12]

The culmination of devotion is in seeing and worshiping God in all living beings. Here devotion is united with supreme spiritual vision. The highest devotion is inseparable from the highest knowledge. It is said in the *Bhāgavatam:*

> He who sees the divine Self in all beings and all beings in the divine Self is the best devotee of God. He who bears love to God, friendship to His devotees, kindness to the ignorant, indifference to his foes, is of the second best type, and he who faithfully worships God only in the image, and not His devotees or others, is a novice.[13]

Just as God is worshiped in an image, even so He can be worshiped in a living being as the indwelling Self. In his last message Śrī Kṛṣṇa speaks highly of this form of worship, which has not been expressly stated by him in the *Bhagavad-gītā.* Says he to Uddhava:

> With a pure mind one should observe in all beings as well as in oneself only Me, the Ātman, who am both within and without, and all-pervasive like space.
>
> O great soul, he who, taking his stand on pure knowledge, thus regards and honors all beings as Myself, who has the same attitude towards a low-born one as to a Brāhmaṇa, towards a thief as to a supporter of the Brāhmaṇas; towards a spark of fire as to the sun; and towards a ruffian as to a kind man; he is considered a sage.
>
> Ideas of rivalry, jealousy, pity and egoism quickly depart from a man who always thinks of Me in all men.
>
> One should worship thus in thought, word, and deed till one comes to look upon all beings as Myself.
>
> To such a man everything is Brahman, owing to the knowledge that comes of seeing the Ātman in all. Seeing Brahman everywhere, he becomes free from doubts and all attachment.
>
> This looking upon all beings as Myself in thought, word, and deed is, to My mind, the best of all methods of worship.

[12]SB XI:20.17; 26.1. [13]SB XI:2.45-47.

> Herein lies the wisdom of the wise and the acumen of the intelligent, that in this very life they attain Me, the Real and Immortal, by means of that which is unreal and mortal.[14]

That this mode of seeing and worshiping God in all beings is natural with the seers and the lovers of God who attain illumination has been affirmed by the Upaniṣads and by later Vedantic literature. Rare individuals, highly advanced in spiritual life, have also carried this idea into actual practice. But so far the seekers of God in general have not adopted this way of worship as a spiritual discipline. Such a course has been recommended for the first time by Sri Ramakrishna in the present age. "No, not kindness to living beings," urges he, "but service to God dwelling in them." Further he remarks:

> It is God who exists in all forms, though His manifestations differ.
>
> If God can be worshiped through a clay image, then why not through a man?[15]

It was the genius of Swami Vivekananda to find new light in this precept of the Master and seek its practical application in modern life for the amelioration of man's condition in every sphere. He exhorts the worshipers of God to follow this method:

> Look upon every man, woman, and every one as God. You cannot help anyone; you can only serve; serve the children of the Lord, serve the Lord Himself, if you have the privilege. If the Lord grants that you can help any one of His children, blessed you are; do not think too much of yourselves. Blessed you are that that privilege was given to you, when others had it not. Do it only as worship.[16]
>
> You may invent an image through which to worship God, but a better image already exists, the living man. You may build a temple in which to worship God, and that may be good, but a better one, a much high one, already exists; the human body.[17]

In Swami Vivekananda's view all social work and the teaching of religion as well should be carried on in the spirit of worshiping God in man. For this purpose he established the Ramakrishna Math and Mission — a religious and philanthropic institution that has developed into a world-wide organization — the monastic and lay

[14]SB XI:29.12-15,17-19,22.
[15]GSR, p. 407.
[16]CW II, p. 246.
[17]CW II, p. 311.

members of which are urged to render service to the ignorant, the needy, the distressed, and the diseased as the veritable worship of God dwelling in them.

Some may hold that the message of Śrī Kṛṣṇa, which was delivered several millenniums ago, must be too old for the modern age; like many theories, views, and usages of former days, it must be antiquated. It is true that the world is progressing continually, particularly in physical and intellectual aspects. With the advancement of science and technology there have been tremendous changes in man's way of living and thinking. In this space-age we do not live in the same world as our forebears did. Naturally, one may ask, "How can the teachings that applied to life centuries ago be adequate for the present age?"

But the message of Śrī Kṛṣṇa is basically eternal and universal. It cannot be obsolete, being grounded on fundamental truths that ever remain the same. These can be stated as follows:

1. The ever-changing manifold is sustained by the Changeless One, the all-pervading Self, we call God.
2. Man's restive psychophysical system is regulated by a central principle, his conscious immortal Self.
3. There is a kinship or unity between the individual self and the Supreme Self.
4. To realize this kinship or unity is the goal of life.

Moreover, the message of Śrī Kṛṣṇa has for its setting the common background of human life that undergoes no change. This is the same old drama of smiles and tears, of love and hate, of union and separation, of success and failure, that is going on the world over. From the primitive to the modern life the same old tragi-comedy has continued to be enacted in the East, in the West, in the North, in the South, in every home from the king's palace to the farmer's cottage. Despite man's marvelous achievements, despite all distinctions of color, creed, culture, position, and power, human life is invariably a drama of birth, growth, decay and death. Notwithstanding this, there is within the heart of man a deep longing for the eternal, a constant cry for release from all confusion, all fear, all delusions, all bondage, all limitations. As long as this basic human situation remains unaltered, Śrī Kṛṣṇa's message will evoke irresistible response from the hearts of men and women at all times and in all places. It will serve as the beacon for erring human beings to find the way from darkness to light, from death to immortality, from bondage to freedom.

APPENDIX II

THE ABUNDANT LIFE

A person whose body is healthy and strong, whose senses are keen and vigorous, whose organs function properly, who can eat hearty meals without fearing the consequence, who sleeps soundly, enjoys the world through all the variety and richness of sense experiences, who has no worries of any kind — such a person is said to be full of life. But it would not be proper to say that his life is full or abundant, because he has developed only one side of it — the physical side. This is not the whole of life. He whose sole concern is to eat, sleep, and enjoy is no better than an animal. An animal also is healthy and strong, moves about freely, enjoys life, and seldom falls sick. True, some men's enjoyments are finer and richer than those of animals. Nevertheless, they are but a superior type of animal.

What is the difference between man and other animals? Man lives; animals, trees, and plants also live. Man has feelings; animals, trees, and plants also have feelings. The difference is this: animals and plants live and feel but cannot think. Man can think; man can have knowledge. Man not only sees things, but reads and interprets them; he can find out their meaning. Man can look far beyond the senses. It is man who discovers the laws of nature, unravels the secrets of life, probes into the deepest mysteries of existence; he is able to distinguish between the real and the unreal, the good and the pleasant, between right and wrong. And not only this, man can regulate his life by this knowledge. This is what other living creatures cannot do.

So with man the main point is not simply living but the *how* of living. The art of life is more important than the life itself. In human life there must be an ideal, a philosophy, a regulative principle. He who lacks this, he who never thinks of the meaning and the purpose of life but simply lives, his life is of no value. He is no better than a breathing machine; he breathes but does not live — just as the bellows of a blacksmith.

Thus, a human being has two distinct aspects of life, the physical and the psychical. The psychical aspect, if taken in the broadest sense, includes the intellectual, the moral, the aesthetic, and the spiritual life. So the psychical life or, I may say, the inner life, is much vaster, higher, and grander than the physical life, that is, the life on the sense plane. The physical life is only the outer rim of our being, the center of which is the inner life. Our thoughts, our imaginings, our moral ideas, our spiritual vision, all are great controlling forces in our physical life. It is true that the body influences the mind, but the body does not govern the mind; on the contrary, the mind governs the body. We cannot live the physical life in the right sense unless our inner life is sound. In order to keep the body healthy and fit we need to study the physical system, know the hygienic laws and observe them. Out of this need medical science has developed. You all know how much the knowledge of the physical universe has contributed to our material progress.

We require not only intelligence but moral principles as well to regulate the life on the physical plane. If there is violent emotional excitement or severe conflict within us, our nervous system is shattered. The body becomes a wreck. When anger, hatred, jealousy, or intolerance prevails in us, our social life, too, disintegrates; we find discord in all the fields of collective life. In order to live in peace and harmony we have to cultivate moral and spiritual virtues.

Now, it may be asked: Is the inner life to be developed for the sake of the physical life? Should scientific knowledge be cultivated only for the promotion of material welfare? Should our philosophy be guided by pragmatic considerations alone? Should religion, art, and ethics subserve the interest of the sense life?

Life on the physical plane is so predominant in our consciousness that compared with this the finer aspects of life seem insignificant. The sense objects appear so real, so charming to us that for their sake we do not hesitate to sacrifice the subtler realities. Our religion, our art, our ethics, our science, our philosophy, appear to be of no value if they do not advance the cause of the material life, the practical life, as we call it. In fact, we judge the inner powers and virtues by the standard of the material good we can derive from them — as if the material values were of greater consequence than the moral and spiritual values! This confusion of values in the modern age has brought the world to its present chaotic condition. It cannot be that we shall have inner development only for the sake of material well-being; rather our material life must be so regulated as to promote inner growth. The inner self is the ruler of the physical life. The spirit should utilize matter to its own advantage, not permitting matter to usurp the mastership.

The superiority of the inner life when compared with the physical is not difficult to perceive. Physical life may come to an end at any time. But what intellectual progress we make, what moral and spiritual worth we acquire in this life, persists even after the body drops, for this does not belong to the gross body but inheres in a vital part of our being that does not perish with the body. According to all religions the soul exists even after the separation from the body. From the biological standpoint also it does not seem reasonable that consciousness, which is the highest achievement of nature, which nature has developed in the course of countless ages, should be a mere servant of the physical organism and should not exist by its own right. This appears to be contrary to the principle of evolution.

It is also a fact of common experience that the inner life is of greater importance than the outer life. Suppose a man is living under very desirable conditions: he resides in a beautiful, richly furnished home; everything around him is in perfect order; everything outside is bright and charming; but within him all is darkness, all is chaos — there is no peace, no light. Would you think this to be an enviable state of affairs? Now think of a person who lives in very humble circumstances, satisfied with the bare necessities of life, free from worries, doubts, and fears, who has inner peace and joy in consequence of a true understanding of life. Which of the two lives would you prefer? "Certainly the latter," you will all say.

It is also found that the more a person advances culturally, the greater his interest in the inner life. A scientist will find greater delight in the solution of a problem than in the finest sense enjoyment. A philosopher relishes an intellectual discussion far more than his dinner. Persons of great culture always forego material gain for the attainment of inner greatness. "Plain living and high thinking" is their motto. Great personages the world over have sacrificed even their lives for the sake of knowledge, truth, and virtue.

This life of sense experience, however dear it may be to us, cannot be an end in itself. It is so uncertain, so unsatisfying. However successful, happy, or promising a life one may live, death may put an end to it most abruptly. There is no good here without concomitant evil. Pain comes in the guise of pleasure. Virtue suffers; vice prospers. Such is this life. It is not self-explanatory. There must be something beyond it to fulfill it. We can find meaning in this life only if we take it as a preparatory stage for a higher existence. To me this world appears to be a huge factory, where divine man is being manufactured out of brute man. If you enter a factory and see things in the process of being made, you cannot easily understand what is going on there. Similar is the case of the world. Life seems meaningless to a casual observer. In order to extract gold from ore, you have to take the ore to the smeltery, subject it to heat, dip it in water, batter it by hammering, and pass it through other processes before pure gold emerges out of the crude metal. Similarly, the animal man has to pass through many trials and struggles, successes and failures, hopes and fears, smiles and tears, before his spiritual self shines forth in its native purity, free from all the crudities of physical life.

So this sense life of ours is for the development of the spiritual life. First of all it builds the intellectual life by furnishing the mind with experiences. We are gaining experiences all our life. What is the ultimate experience or conviction we gain from this life? This: sense pleasures can never bring us true satisfaction. We must seek life's fulfillment elsewhere. What we seek is not to be found in material existence. We seek not the evanescent but the eternal. We seek the changeless, not the changeful. We seek the real, not the unreal. We seek the infinite, not the finite. We seek true light, true freedom, true joy. We seek the Absolute, the Perfect, the Divine. This is the knowledge that dawns upon the mind after it has passed through many, many, many experiences on the physical plane. Our intellectual life attains fulfillment when intellect presents to us this Supreme Ideal and the way to realize it, when it makes us aware of the presence of the Divine spirit within us as our inmost self; ever free, ever pure, ever blissful, self-illumined.

The intellectual life is much more expansive than this sense-bound life on the physical plane. Intellect broadens our vision, deepens insight, and opens before us higher and higher realms of existence. But intellect cannot lead us very far unless supported by the moral life. On the moral plane we feel still greater freedom and expansion of life. Intellect cannot free us from the thralldom of the senses. Even a highly intellectual person is found to be suffering from the weaknesses of the flesh, while a morally sound individual is immune to these weaknesses. This is why a morally advanced person is held in much greater esteem than a man of mere intellectual greatness. The moral life is closer to the soul than the intellectual life, being the expression of the higher mental plane, which is in direct touch with the soul. It is through the moral life that the soul finds self-expression on the intellectual and the physical planes. This is why morality is the *sine qua non* of spiritual life and spiritual knowledge.

An immoral man, however advanced intellectually, cannot have spiritual insight.

The basic principle of a moral life is unselfishness. No moral virtue can exist where selfishness rules. Anger, hatred, jealousy, lust, avarice, fear, pride, hypocrisy, and so forth, prevail in us because we are selfish. When we are unselfish, then only moral qualities, such as kindness, forgiveness, humility, purity, sincerity, honesty, and truthfulness can function within us.

Unselfishness seeks expression in the positive form of love. What is love? Love means self-expansion. When you have love, you are no longer confined within your body; you find yourself in others as well. Thus, as love develops more and more, you transcend the narrow limits of family, community, city, country, nation, race, creed, yea, even humanity; and eventually you identify yourself with all beings. This is self-expansion. And the more you expand, the more of life you have. We know from our own experience that when we perform any act of disinterested love, we feel free and full of life; but when selfishness takes hold of us, we feel cooped in, choked to death, as it were. It has been admirably said by Swami Vivekananda: "Expansion is life; contraction is death. Love is life and hatred is death."[1] Love is expansion, therefore love is life; hatred is contraction, therefore hatred is death. Here lies the secret of the abundant life.

But this is not all. The moral life attains its consummation in the spiritual life. The ultimate basis of morality is spirituality. Spirituality means the realization of one's own self as spirit, as soul: pure, illumined, free, blissful. At the present stage of life we have no knowledge of the soul, our real self. We are fully aware of the physical body and think of the body as our very self. Our thoughts and actions are dominated by this body-consciousness. But the body is not our real self. Our real self is spirit — immortal and divine. As the consciousness of this spiritual self dawns upon the mind, a person realizes himself more and more as a spiritual entity, becomes more and more united with the Divine in spirit, and his thoughts and actions proceed from that self-realization. This is what is meant by spiritual life.

With self-realization one transcends the material plane of multiplicity and enters the realm of universal Spirit. Spirit has neither form, nor color, nor sex, nor denomination. It is in unison with the Infinite. So through the realization of the spiritual self one realizes one's unity with the all-pervasive Divine Being that shines within us

[1]"Reply to the Calcutta Address," 1894, CW IV, p. 311.

as our inmost self. A man of the highest realization no longer thinks of his narrow individuality. He no more finds himself limited by form, place, and time. His self becomes so magnified that he sees himself in all. He experiences that he is in man, he is in woman, he is in the saint, he is in the sinner, he is in every living creature; he is in the sun, he is in the moon, he is everywhere; never did he not exist, he exists forever. This is the abundant life. There is no life anywhere but in spirit. Spirit alone lives — the Eternal, the Immutable. It is Spirit that enlivens the body, enlivens the mind, enlivens nature. Every being, everything in this universe, is mortal. Why? Because their life is borrowed. Spirit is the only reality, the very existence, the being-ness. Everything else has its being in Spirit. Without Spirit everything is but shadow. It is the life of Spirit that Jesus means when he said, "I came that they might have life and that they might have it more abundantly."[2] With regard to the sense life He declared, "Whosoever will save his life shall lose it."[3]

The universality of Spirit is not poetic imagination nor is it a metaphysical abstraction, but a truth demonstrated by the experience of great seers and saints in all climes and ages. All the great world-teachers were possessed of universal love, which was the outcome of their consciousness of the oneness of the Self. They loved all without distinction; reviled and persecuted they loved their enemies, because they found the Self in friend and foe alike; rather to them there was neither friend nor foe, only the One Self, existing in all.

As an illustration of the realization of the One Self in all I may cite an incident from the life of Sri Ramakrishna, the great mystic saint of modern India. One day in December, 1885, during his last illness, some of his young disciples prayed to him that for their sake he should prolong his earthly existence. They knew that he was a great yōgī; so if he willed, he could stay with them longer in the physical body. "How can that be?" replied Sri Ramakrishna. "My mind has been given to the Divine Mother once for all. Should I ask it back for the sake of this cage of flesh and bone?" "For our sake," implored the disciples. "Everything depends on the Mother's will," answered Sri Ramakrishna. "Your will and the Mother's will are the same," insisted the disciples. "If not, please ask the Divine Mother to spare you for some time longer in this human life." At last Sri Ramakrishna agreed. After a while one of the disciples came forward and inquired whether he had prayed to the Divine Mother. Sri Ramakrishna

[2]John 10:10.
[3]Matthew 16:25.

answered, "Yes, I was going to tell the Divine Mother: 'Mother, I cannot swallow food, let this body take some food.' Just then the Mother showed me as I am eating through so many mouths, what matters it if I do not eat through this one mouth?"

He who realizes the Self draws his power directly from the Self, that is, from the Omnipotent, Omniscient Divine Being. We are always drawing what energy, what vitality, what intelligence we possess from this One Source. But we draw feebly and indirectly. Our ignorance and egoism obstruct and obscure the course. We have forgotten our spiritual self; we have forgotten that we are eternally united with the Divine. Instead, we have taken the material adjuncts of the soul, the psychophysical complex, to be our very self. Neither the body, nor the mind, nor their compound constitutes our real being. With the knowledge of the Self, egoism vanishes; ignorance dies out as we realize our unity with the Divine. Then the floodgate of Divine Energy opens within us and the Divine Life overflows our entire being. This is why the great spiritual leaders of the world were dynamos of unlimited power, unlimited knowledge, unbounded love. Think of Buddha, Christ, Śaṅkara! What material resources did they have in life? None! What, then, was the secret of their power? This, that they drew from the very fountainhead of life. Within them was no barrier of ignorance or egoism. So they were perfect channels of the Divine Life, the Divine Light, the Divine Love. Within a few years of earthly existence they manifested life and light sufficient to guide humanity for centuries and centuries.

So in order to have true life and have it abundantly we must rise to the spiritual plane. We should so regulate this humdrum life of eating, drinking, dressing, talking, earning, and enjoying as to lead us to higher and higher levels of consciousness. In no case should we hold our moral and spiritual nature in fealty to the sense life. Do not fear that your practical life will be cramped if it is subordinated to the spiritual ideal. On the contrary, moral purity and spiritual wisdom will react on the material life and make it conducive to real good, real peace, and happiness. There is no dearth of material resources in the world at the present time; still the world is rushing headlong to a catastrophe! Why? Because there is no inner goodness nor true understanding to manipulate the material powers to the best advantage.

The spiritual life is the only life which knows no death, no decay, no darkness; because this is the life of Spirit, which is self-existent, self-luminous, self-fulfilled. When the Divine Life flows into a person, all weaknesses leave him; all darknesses vanish from his mind. His body, his senses, his mind, become so surcharged with the Divine Life that his thoughts, words, and deeds always rebound to the good of the world. No untruth passes over his lips. His very presence is an inspiration. Though apparantly living in the body, he is so far above the physical plane that those conditions to which the body is subject by its very nature cannot affect the inner flow of the spiritual life and light. He faces death with a smiling face, because he knows that for him there is no death. He is in the fullness of the Divine Life while in the body; he is one with the Divine Life when without the body.

APPENDIX III

LIFE HERE AND HEREAFTER

Life here and life hereafter form a continuous existence. They are, as it were, two stages in the development of an individual. They are so related that we cannot be interested in one to the exclusion of the other. We cannot afford to be either this-worldly or other-worldly. Yet there are some modern thinkers who consider a this-worldly attitude superior to the other-worldly attitude. They even condemn the Hindu view of life as other-worldly and fail to see that neither this-worldliness nor other-worldliness is the right approach to life. They do not recognize the fact that the Hindu view of life is neither this-worldly nor other-worldly. The Hindu mind has tried to visualize life as an integral whole. Every individual has a past, present, and future. A human being has many levels of life — physical, intellectual, aesthetic, moral and spiritual. A sound scheme of life must take into account all its aspects.

Evidently, the earthly life is not self-sufficient. It is full of anomalies. It does not satisfy our rational nature. Here we often see that the innocent suffer and the wicked prosper. Such unmerited sufferings and enjoyments cannot be accounted for without reference to the life beyond. Limited by birth and death this short span of life is not self-explanatory. Our unsatisfied sense of justice, unrequited labor, unrealized hopes and desires, unfulfilled love, all demand its continuation after death. This mortal life, so encumbered, must have its fulfillment elsewhere. Pairs of opposites in this life, such as birth and death, growth and decay, joy and sorrow, light and darkness, inevitably mark its course. It cannot satisfy our deepest longing for unmixed blessing, for unalloyed joy. Yet, curiously enough, many of us want to see this life complete in itself.

It may be said that we are not as sure of the "hereafter" as we are of the "here." Are we really sure of the life here? Can it not end any moment? Who knows when, how, or where death befalls a man? Without any warning whatsoever he can be snatched away from all that he holds near and dear. Yet he fondly relies on the unreliable and seeks security in the insecure. There is no sense in clinging desperately to this life as an end in itself. It is far from an ideal existence. It has no meaning unless directed to a transcendent goal. This earthly life, fragile as it is, can, however, serve as a raft to reach the shore of immortality.

This-worldliness follows from the conception of man as a physical or a psychophysical being. It ignores the soul, the immortal divine essence in him. This means the acceptance of death as the sole destiny of man. No matter what he does, what he achieves, what he aspires after, he has no prospect other than disintegration. This is not a hopeful situation! Moreover, the denial of the soul blinds the spiritual vision of human beings, stunts their moral growth and makes their material progress hollow and insecure. In the absence of spiritual insight sound moral life is not possible; and material well-being cannot rest secure on a shaky moral foundation.

With the conception of man as a physical or a psychophysical being our interest centers on the physical aspect of life. We rely on the senses and accept the sense world as the true type of reality. Even if the existence of the mind is acknowledged, it does not appear as real as the physical body, from which it is said to have derived. As a result, our inner nature — intellectual, aesthetic, or moral — becomes subordinate to the sense life; our science, philosophy, arts, and ethics subserve material interests. Sense desires are insatiable. With the prevalence of the sensuous outlook on life, greed takes hold of the human mind. It motivates selfishness, the root of all vices. Thus, a this-worldly attitude tends to degrade human beings.

It is true that despite sense desires man can exercise self-restraint and cultivate enlightened self-interest. As a rational being he can see that his interest is linked with the interests of others. He forms a social unit. He grows and declines with society. For his own welfare he has to care for the welfare of his fellow-beings. An individual's interest must conform to the weal of the community. Thus, ethical conduct can be based on the consideration of material and cultural interests common to all. It is to be noted, however, that this attitude of enlightened self-interest does not imply real selflessness or disinterested love. It cannot be a secure basis for man's ethical life. It has a tendency to slide down to expediency. A person's moral nature is not sound unless he becomes selfless for the sake of selflessness, unless he regards virtue as a value in itself. Moral values far outweigh the material values. The former can insure inner peace, wisdom, and freedom, while the latter cannot.

No human relationship based on common secular interests can develop disinterested love in us. It is the recognition of a spiritual kinship with our fellow-beings, irrespective of all differences of physical form, mental traits, property, rank, race, nationality, or ideology, that can make us unselfish in the true sense. We become selfless for the sake of selflessness only when we realize that our self-fulfillment is in self-effacement, in complete dedication of the ego to the Supreme Self, who abides in all. Like the waves belonging to the ocean each and every individual soul belongs to the all-pervading Spirit, the Soul of all souls.

The undivided luminous Being, Supreme Consciousness, has assumed countless forms. Being associated with various psychophysical systems, the one Self is apparently divided into myriad souls. He who is aware of his inner self as pure spirit, as the principle of consciousness witnessing all physical and psychical events, recognizes his essential unity with the Omnipresent Being. The more he realizes his unity with the Supreme Being, the deeper is his relationship with his fellow-beings. Not only does he look upon them as his brothers and sisters, but his inner self expands and enfolds them as his own. Again, the more a person realizes his spiritual relationship with his fellow-beings the deeper is his experience of unity with the Supreme Being.

Had there been no such relationship among men, disinterested love would have no place in human life. It is meaningful to us simply because we feel this relationship, however vaguely, even without spiritual knowledge. Such an imperceptible feeling may become intense in certain individuals and lead them to altruism. Without spiritual insight or feeling real self-expansion is not possible. Devoid of either of these, a person may identify himself with his family or community, or nation, or race, yet there will be no widening of his heart but only inflation of the ego. So it is very often found that tribal, communal, racial or national ego makes a greater devil of man than the individual ego.

Thus we find that moral life is not mature without spiritual insight. Since the material well-being of man depends on moral integrity, it needs a spiritual basis for its security. The this-worldly attitude, stressing secular values, is a great incentive to material progress, but cannot provide it with a sound moral basis. Any civilization lacking spiritual vision must have this inherent weakness. Ancient Greek civilization had this drawback. Notwithstanding its material power and prosperity, notwithstanding its glaring attainments in arts and philosophy, it collapsed because of moral decadence. It is the sense world that dominated the Greek mind. Man was viewed as a physical or a psychophysical being with no divine heritage, with no other master than himself. A similar outlook on life has prevailed in the modern age. Modern man is concerned with this sense world. He wants to make it self-sufficient. He is conscious of his tremendous power. His emphasis on secular values has been the cause of his success and failure as well. With his unprecedented intellectual advancement, with his marvelous scientific achievements that make this earth a progressive, prosperous, and safe place in which to live, he faces to his dismay growing discontent, despair, disharmony in individual and collective life, world-wide tension, confusion and mistrust, paving the way to global catastrophe.

Try howsoever we may, this earthly life lived as an end in itself, cannot succeed. It has to serve as a means to the life beyond. Its supreme purpose is to lead us from mortality to immortality, from the unreal to the real, from darkness to light, from the ever-changing psychophysical level to the realm of eternal Spirit. All its resources must develop with that end in view. All the values pertaining to earthly life — material, intellectual, aesthetic and moral — must subserve the ultimate spiritual objective. All temporal interests must be directed to the attainment of the Supreme Goal. This is world-affirmation in the true sense. To live for the highest and best is certainly not life-negation.

While this-worldliness makes man practical without spiritual vision, other-worldliness makes him a visionary without practical urges. He who neglects this world for the sake of the other world loses both. What we attain hereafter depends on how we live here. The present determines the future. The seen is the preparatory ground for the unseen. It is by right use of the means that we reach the goal. He who cares for the beyond must not disregard what is on hand. To ignore this world in order to reach a better world is but a delusion. Other-worldliness may even lead to greater darkness than this-worldliness.

In the Vedantic view, four main courses are possible after death in accordance with the life man lives on this earth. When a person dies he leaves behind only the physical shell; his mind, with all its contents, goes with him. The real man is not the physical body, not the mind, nor the body-mind complex, but the seer within, the one that perceives the psychical as well as the physical events. In the Upaniṣadic language, He sees through the eyes, but the eyes cannot see Him; He hears through the ears, but the ears cannot hear Him; He speaks through the mouth, but the mouth cannot express Him; He receives with the hands, but the hands cannot grasp Him; He knows through the mind, but the mind cannot know Him. Who can know the ultimate knower and by what? He is the one observer of all that is observed.

In fact, the organs of action and the organs of perception, as well, are his instruments. He is the indwelling spirit in the psychophysical system. The center of human personality is a spiritual principle, self-shining, pure, free, birthless, changeless, deathless. It is this which integrates the physical and the psychical elements into an organic whole. It is this which coordinates all the functions of the senses and the mind. At death the spiritual self departs, appareled with the mind and a fine physical vesture formed at the time to serve as a vehicle. Whither? Where his inner nature leads.

It is particularly the ethico-spiritual status of a person that determines his upward or downward course after death. The departing spirit carries whatever merit and demerit he has within the mind. His virtues and vices, his beliefs and disbeliefs, his talents and shortcomings, his wisdom and foibles, all go with him. His latent tendencies, capacities, desires, ideas and sentiments, right or wrong, never leave him. Equipped with all these psychical factors he sets out on his journey beyond. No external possession of any kind whatsoever can be taken by him. Of all his inner resources, his moral and spiritual attainments avail him most.

The lowest course after death awaits those who are lowest in the scale of self-development. There are human beings who live on the animal plane. Rational thinking, the distinctive mark of human nature, is lacking in them. Some are like brutes in human form. Impelled by animal instincts they perform diabolical deeds. Never do they hesitate to injure or ruin others for their gain, or mere pleasure. Because of the predominance of vice in their nature, they go after death to a nether region of darkness and misery or are reborn on the subhuman plane. In this degraded state they reap the bitter fruits of those wrong deeds which bring it about. But they cannot stay there indefinitely. As soon as the effects of the fructified karma are exhausted they return to human life. The force of karma being limited, there can be no eternal damnation. Entering into the lower sphere of existence is like going into a penitentiary. Its main purpose is to mend the inner life of the condemned through suffering. When the mending is over they become ready for regular growth on the human level. The penitentiary is not the place for normal development nor for fresh acquisition.

The next higher course is the way of reincarnation. It is for those who live normal human lives. These are the persons who rise above the animal plane and develop a rational nature. They discriminate between right and wrong, between good and pleasant. They try to control their sense appetities and observe moral principles. Their aim is to live honestly promoting others' interests as well as their own. In many of them good and evil become balanced, so to speak. Such persons, after leaving the body, do not usually go to any other region but are soon reborn as human beings. There are some in whom virtue preponderates, but who do not believe in the other-world. They, too, return to human life shortly.

The third course is the journey to the heaven-world (svargalōka). This is for those who lead virtuous lives but who lack in the spiritual sense. Not a few in this world worship God and perform meritorious deeds in order to be rewarded with greater happiness and prosperity here and hereafter. They do not realize the futility of sense desires, even though they recognize the facts that earthly possessions and pleasures are transitory and unreliable, and that the earthly life is short and marred by illness, old age, and mishaps. They do not see through the delusion of duality and do not seek liberation from its bondage. Consequently, they look for complete sense fulfillment after death in a paradise, where they can live for aeons as a result of their religious and virtuous life on this earth. But not all of them can reach such a heaven-world. It is accessible only to those few who acquire adequate merit for the purpose; the rest shortly return to human life or go to some intermediary sphere for the time being. None can, however, live in the heaven-world eternally. Those who go there experience for a long, long period the sweet and abundant fruits of their respective meritorious deeds which lead them there. But as soon as the effects of karma are exhausted they come back to the human plane for reincarnation.

This heaven-world or paradise is not the same as the Kingdom of God. It is but the realm of the highest sense-fulfillment. Eternal life, light, freedom, or joy is not to be found there. It does not even provide the opportunity for spiritual development. Consequently, none can go direct from the heaven-world to the Kingdom of God. Like a place of vacation it is meant for enjoyment and not for work. There they spend what they have earned in human life. Hardly is there scope for the exercise of will power and judgment. So, no special acquirement through self-culture is possible there. The denizens of the heaven-world are like some scions of wealthy families who lack in deep thinking but live the easy life of plenty and comfort. They are harmless beings who instinctively follow the path of virtue; evil is overpowered but not eliminated in their nature. In a certain sense they are higher than human beings and are called devas, the shining ones.

Human life is particularly the field of action. It is the battleground of good and evil forces. Such conflict does not exist on the sub-human or the suprahuman level. Man has to grow through right thinking and right living. He has the power to discriminate between the proper and the improper, between the pleasant and the beneficial, between the real and the apparent, between the relative and the absolute. Freedom of choice and freedom of action are the special privileges of human life. This is why on the human plane there is the greatest possibility for moral and spiritual development. So the great seers and saints always exhort us to avail ourselves of this unique opportunity. Says Śaṅkarācārya:

> Human birth, longing for Liberation, and the guidance of a sage — these three are rare assets due to divine grace.[1]

The realization of God is possible only in human life, and this is the way to immortality. A Vedic seer declares:

> I have known this Great Being, resplendent as the sun and beyond darkness. It is by knowing Him one goes beyond death. There is no other way of Liberation.[2]

The fourth course is the luminous path leading to the Kingdom of God. It is the way of liberation from the wheel of birth and rebirth. This is the only bright path, being followed by the illumined; the rest are all dark, being followed by the ignorant, the unillumined. He who goes this way never returns to the mortal plane. Only those who seek God for God's sake, who worship Him with whole-souled devotion as the sole goal and refuge and become freed from all attachments to the sense-world as such, depart by the bright path that leads to the Abode of God, Brahmalōka. Whether they expire in broad daylight or in the darkness of night, whether they leave the body in a temple or in a wilderness, whether any funeral is held over the corpse or not, they

[1]VC 3. [2]Sv. U. III:8.

enter into the luminous way and go straight to Brahmalōka.

This is the highest realm of the relative existence, where the devotees live in loving relationship with the Personal God, Saguṇa Brahman, in whatever form or aspect they worship Him. Because of the clearest manifestation of the all-encompassing Divine Presence, Brahmalōka is unaffected by the dualities of the relative order. It is beyond the range of the law of karma. Blessed are they that can reach it; there is no falling from this stage. But whenever the Lord wills, such free souls become incarnate in human form and live exemplary lives for the guidance and enlightenment of mankind. Even this sublime state of freedom and blessedness is not considered ultimate by nondualistic Vedanta. In due course, the worshipper of the Personal God, Saguṇa Brahman, fully realizes his essential identity with the impersonal, absolute Being, Nirguṇa Brahman, and attains final Liberation. So the way to Brahmalōka is called the path of gradual emancipation, krama-mukti.

Among spiritual personalities very few realize Nirguṇa Brahman while living in this world. Those few dwell in the consciousness of Brahman as the Supreme Self. They perceive the Self in all and all in the Self. They are regarded as the living-free, jīvanmukta. Having overcome ignorance, the limiting adjunct of the individual self, they realize their identity with the Absolute Brahman. At the time of death their soul does not actually depart from the body but becomes merged in the ultimate Being. For such illumined ones there is no course to follow after death. This is the way of direct emancipation, sadya-mukti. Declares the *Muṇḍaka Upaniṣad:*

> Just as the gliding streams, giving up their names and forms, merge into the ocean, so does the illumined one, being free from name and form, attain the effulgent all-transcendent Being. Verily he becomes Brahman who knows that Supreme Brahman.[3]

There are, however, exceptional cases of the knowers of Brahman who at the time of death do not merge themselves in Brahman, but retain their individuality for the good of mankind. On rare occasions, such free souls, being authorized by the Benign Providence, so to speak, come down to the human plane and play the role of spiritual leaders in the benighted world. They are called, in Vedantic terminology, ādhikārika puraṣas (persons with special authority or capacity).

[3]Mu U. III:2.8,9.

APPENDIX IV

AVAILABLE EDITIONS OF EXTANT VEDIC TEXTS

I. Ṛg-Veda

1. *Ṛg-Veda Saṁhitā,* together with the Commentary of Sāyaṇācārya. Edited by Max Müller (in 4 volumes). The Chowkhamba Sanskrit Series, Work No. 99. The Chowkhamba Sanskrit Series Office, Varanasi, India, 1966
2. *Ṛg-Veda Saṁhitā,* text with exhaustive Index. Edited by Sreepada Sarma Satavalekara.
   Svadhyaya-mandala, Paradi, Surat, India
3. *Ṛg-Veda Saṁhitā,* with the Commentary of Sāyaṇācārya (in 5 volumes — volume 5 contains various Indices to the Ṛg-Veda).
   Vaidika Samshodhana Mandala, Tilak Maharashtra University, Poona, India
4. *Aitareya Brāhmaṇa,* in Punthi form (loose pages).
   Nirnaya Sagar Press, Bombay, India (distributors)
5. *Aitareya Āraṇyaka,* with the Commentary of Sāyaṇa.
   Ananda Ashram, Poona, India

IIA. Kṛṣṇa (Black) Yajur-Veda

1. *Taittirīya Saṁhitā,* with the Commentary of Sāyaṇa (in 8 volumes).
   Ananda Ashram, Poona, India
2. *Taittirīya Brāhmaṇa,* with the Commentary of Sāyaṇa (in 2 volumes).
   Ananda Ashram, Poona, India
3. *Taittirīya Āraṇyaka,* with the Commentary of Sāyaṇa (in 2 volumes).
   Ananda Ashram, Poona, India
4. *Taittirīya Upaniṣad,* with the Commentary of Śaṅkara, and the Gloss of Ānandagiri, Dīpika of Śaṅkarānanda, and Taittirīyaka-vidyā-prakāśa of Vidyāraṇya. Edited and annotated by Dinker Vishnu Gokhale.
   Manilal Itcharam Desai (Publisher), The Gujarati Printing Press, Bombay, India, 1914
5. *Śvetāśvatara Upaniṣad,* with the Commentary of Śaṅkara, and the Gloss of Śaṅkarānanda and others.
   Ananda Ashram, Poona, India

IIB. Śukla (White) Yajur-Veda

1. *Yajur-Veda Saṁhitā,* Mādhyandina Recension, text with exhaustive Index. Edited by Sreepada Sarma Satavalekara.
   Svadhyaya-mandala, Paradi, Surat, India
2. *Yajur-Veda Saṁhitā,* Mādhyandina Recension, in Punthi form (loose pages) with Gṛhya-sūtra, Index, etc.

3. *Śatapatha Brāhmaṇa,* Mādhyandina Recension (in 5 volumes) — Volumes 1-4, with Vedārthaprakāśa of Sāyaṇācārya and the Commentary of Harisvāmin. Volume 5, with the Commentary of Shri Vasudeva Brahma Bhagwat.
Gangavishnu Shrikrishnadass (Publisher), Proprietor, Laxmi Venkateshwar Steam Press, Kalyan, Bombay, India, 1940
4. *Śatapatha Brāhmaṇa,* according to Mādhyandina Recension, with extracts from the Commentaries of Sāyaṇa, Harisvāmin, and Dvivedagangā. Edited by Albrecht Weber. The Chowkhamba Sanskrit Series, Work No. 96.
The Chowkhamba Sanskrit Series Office, Varanasi, India, 1964

III. <u>*Sāma-Veda*</u>

1. *Sāma-Veda Saṁhitā,* text with exhaustive Index. Edited by Sreepada Sarma Satavalekara.
Svadhyaya-mandala, Ananda Ashram, Paradi, Surat, India
2. *Tāṇḍya-Mahābrāhmaṇa* (or *Pañcaviṁśa,* with the Supplement Ṣaḍviṁśa), with the Commentary of Sāyaṇa (in 2 volumes). Edited with Notes, Introduction, etc. — Part I, by Pandit A. Chinnaswami Sastri. — Part II, by Pandit A. Chinnaswami Sastri and Pandit Pattabhirama Sastri "Mīmāṁsācārya." The Kashi Sanskrit Series (Haridas Sanskrit Granthamala) No. 105 (Veda Section, No. 6)
Jai Krishnadas-Haridas Gupta (Publisher), The Chowkhamba Sanskrit Series Office, Varanasi, India
3. *Sāmavidhāna Brāhmaṇa,* with Vedārthaprakāśa of Sāyaṇa and Padārthamātrāvivṛti of Bhāratasvāmin. Critically edited by Dr. B. R. Sharma, with a Foreword by Dr. V. Raghavan. Kendriya Sanskrit Vidyapeetha Series, No. 1.
Kendriya Sanskrit Vidyapeetha, Tirupati, India
4. *Devatādhyāya, Saṁhitōpaniṣad,* and *Vaṁśa Brāhmaṇas,* with Commentaries. Edited by Bellikoth Ramachandra Sharma. Kendriya Sanskrit Vidyapeetha Series, Nos. 2-4.
Kendriya Sanskrit Vidyapeetha, Tirupati, India
5. *Chāndōgya Brāhmaṇa,* with the Commentaries of Guṇaviṣṇu and Sāyaṇa. Edited by Durgamohan Bhattacharyya. Calcutta Sanskrit College Research Series, No. 1.
Sanskrit College, Calcutta, India

IV. <u>*Atharva-Veda*</u>

1. *Atharva-Veda Saṁhitā,* text with exhaustive Index. Edited by Sreepada Sarma Satavalekara.
Svadhyaya-mandala, Paradi, Surat, India
2. *Atharva-Veda (Śaunaka) Saṁhitā,* with the Pada-pātha and Sāyaṇācārya's Commentary (4 parts in 5 volumes). Edited by Vishva Bandhu. Vishveshvarananda Indological Series — 13-17.
Vishveshvarananda Vedic Research Institute, Hoshiarpur, India, 1964
3. *Gōpatha Brāhmaṇa,* in 2 parts. Edited by Rajendra Lal Mitra, with elaborate Introduction. A Bibliotheca Indica book.
Indological Book House, Delhi, India, 1972

V. Upaniṣads of the Four Vedas

1. *Ten Principal Upaniṣads*, with Śaṅkara's Commentary (in 2 volumes). Ashtekar & Co., Poona, India, 2nd ed., 1928
Volume I — *Īśa, Aitareya, Kaṭha, Kena, Chāndōgya, Taittirīya, Praśna, Māṇḍūkya, Muṇḍaka*
Volume II — *Bṛhadāraṇyaka*
2. *Twenty-Eight Upaniṣads*, text only. Nirnaya Sagar Press, Bombay, India
Single volume contains the following: *Īśa, Kena, Kaṭha, Praśna, Muṇḍaka, Māṇḍūkya, Taittirīya, Aitareya, Chāndōgya, Bṛhadāraṇyaka, Śvetāśvatara, Kaivalya, Jābāla, Garbha, Nārāyaṇa-atharvaśira, Nārāyaṇa, Bṛhajjābāla, Kauṣītakī, Sūrya, Kṛṣṇa, Hayagrīva, Dattātreya, Rudrākṣa, Mahāvākya, Kalisantaraṇa, Jābāli, Bahvṛca, Muktika*
3. *One Hundred and Eight Upaniṣads*, text only with various readings. Nirnaya Sagar Press, Bombay, India, 1932
Besides the above mentioned 28, a single volume contains the following: *Brahmabindu, Haṁ-saḥ, Āruṇika, Paramahaṁsaḥ, Brahma, Amṛtā-nāda, Atharvaśira, Atharvaśikhā, Maitrāyaṇī, Nṛsiṁha-pūrvatāpinī, Nṛsiṁha-uttaratāpinī, Kālāgni-rudra, Maitreyī, Subālā, Kṣurika, Yantrika, Sarvasāra, Nirālamba, Śuka-rahasya, Vajra-sūcikā, Tejōbindu, Nādabindu, Dhyānabindu, Brahmavidyā, Yōgatattva, Ātmabōdha, Nārada-parivrājaka, Triśikhi-Brāhmaṇa, Sītā, Yōga-cūḍāmaṇi, Nirvāṇa, Maṇḍala-Brāhmaṇa, Dakṣiṇāmūrti, Śarabha, Skanda, Tripād-vibhūti-mahānārāyaṇa, Advaya-tāraka, Rāma-rahasya, Rāma-pūrvatāpinī, Rāma-uttaratāpinī, Vāsudeva, Mudgala, Śāṇḍilya, Paiṅgala, Bhikṣuka, Mahā, Śārīraka, Yōga-śikhā, Turīyātīta, Sannyāsa, Paramahaṁsa-parivrājaka, Akṣamāla, Avyakta, Ekākṣara, Annapūrṇa, Akṣi, Adhyātma, Kuṇḍika, Sāviṭrī, Ātma, Pāśupata-Brahma, Parabrahma, Avadhūta, Tripurātāpinī, Devī, Tripura, Kaṭharudra, Bhāvanā, Rudra-hṛdaya, Yōgakuṇḍalī, Bhasmajābāla, Gaṇapati, Jābāladarśana, Tārasāra, Pañcabrahmā, Prāṇāgnihōtra, Gōpāla-pūrvatāpinī, Gōpāla-uttaratāpinī, Yājñavalkya, Varāha, Śāṭyāyanīya, Garuḍa, Saubhāgya-lakṣmī, Sarasvatī-rahasya*
4. *Ten Principal Upaniṣads in separate volumes*, with the Commentary of Śaṅkara and the Gloss of Ānandagiri, and elucidatory annotations.
Ananda Ashram Sanskrit Series. Ananda Ashram, Poona, India. *Īśa, Kena* (containing *Dīpika* of Śaṅkarānanda), *Kaṭha, Praśna, Muṇḍaka, Māṇḍūkya* (with the *Kārikā* of Gauḍapāda), *Taittirīya, Aitareya, Chāndōgya, Bṛhadāraṇyaka*
Also, *Bṛhadāraṇyaka Bhāṣya-vārttikam*, by Sureśvarācārya, with the Commentary of Ānandagiri (in three parts).

BIBLIOGRAPHY I

ENGLISH WORKS QUOTED FROM IN THIS BOOK

Aristotle — *Metaphysics.* Trans. by H. Tredennick. Aristotle Vol. II, The Loeb Classical Library. London: William Heinemann Ltd., 1933.

Aristotle — *Physics I.* Trans. by Rev. P. Wicksteed and F. M. Cornford. Aristotle Vol. I, The Loeb Classical Library. London: William Heinemann Ltd., 1929.

Aristotle — *Politics I.* In *Great Books of the Western World,* no. 9. Chicago: University of Chicago, 1952.

Bergson, Henri, *Creative Evolution.* New York: The Modern Library, 1944.

Berkeley, George, *The Principles of Human Knowledge.* Chicago: The Open Court Publishing Co., 1920.

The Holy Bible, edited by Rev. C. I. Scofield. New York: Oxford University Press, 1917.

The Holy Bible. Chicago: Spencer Press, Inc., 1947.

Bigg, Charles, *The Christian Platonists of Alexandria.* Eight lectures before the University of Oxford in 1886. Oxford: The Clarendon Press, 1886.

Bradley, F. H., *Appearance and Reality.* Oxford: The Clarendon Press, 1930.

Brahma, N.K., *Philosophy of Hindu Sadhana.* London: Kegan Paul, Trench, Trubner and Co., Ltd.

Dictionary of Philosophy, edited by Dagobert D. Runes. New York: Philosophical Library, 1960.

Eckhart, Meister, *Meister Eckhart: A Modern Translation.* Trans. and ed. by Raymond Blakney. New York: Harper & Brothers, 1941

Eddington, A.S., *The Nature of the Physical World.* The Gifford Lectures, 1927, intro. New York: The Macmillan Company, 1948.

Einstein, Albert, *The Meaning of Relativity,* Appendix II. Princeton, New Jersey: Princeton University Press, 1950.

Emerson, Ralph Waldo, *Representative Men.* In *The Complete Works of Ralph Waldo Emerson.* Boston: Houghton Mifflin, 1903.

Encyclopaedia Britannica, 1948 edn.

Geddes, Patrick, and Thomson, J. Arthur, *Evolution.* New York: Henry Holt, 1911.

The Gospel of Sri Ramakrishna according to "M". Eng. trans. by Swami Nikhilananda. New York: Ramakrishna-Vivekananda Center, 1942.

Green, T. H., *Prolegomena to Ethics.* Oxford: The Clarendon Press, 1906.

Heraclitus on the Universe. Hippocrates — Vol.IV. New York: The Loeb Classical Library, 1931.

Hiriyanna, M., *The Essentials of Indian Philosophy.* London: Allen & Unwin, 1949.

Jeans, Sir James, *Physics and Philosophy.* New York: The Macmillan Co., 1946.

Joad, C.E.M., *Guide to Modern Thought.* London: Faber and Faber Ltd., 1933.

Johnston, James, *The Essentials of Biology*. New York: Longmans Green and Co., 1932.

Kant, Immanuel, *Critique of Pure Reason*. Trans. by J.M.D. Meiklejohn. New York: Willy Book Co. 1781; revised 1787.

Lao Tzu, *Tao Te Ching*, The Texts of Taoism, Vol. I. Trans. by James Legge. Sacred Books of the East, ed. by F. Max Müller, Vol. 39. Oxford University Press: 1891; reprint edn., New York: Dover Publications, 1967.

Lillie, Ralph Stayner, *General Biology and Philosophy of Organisms*. Chicago: University of Chicago Press, 1945.

Müller, F. Max, *The Vedanta Philosophy*. Calcutta: Susil Gupta Ltd., 1955. (Three lectures delivered at Royal Institution in March, 1894, London)

Needham, Joseph, *The Sceptical Biologist*. London: Chatto & Windus, 1929.

Nicholson, Reynold A., *Rūmī, Poet and Mystic*. London: Allen & Unwin, 1964.

Otto, Rudolph, *Mysticism East and West*. New York: The Macmillan Company, 1932.

Plotinus — The Enneads. Trans. by Stephen Mackenna. London: Faber and Faber Ltd., 1930.

Plotinus — The Ethical Treatises (The Enneads). Trans. by Stephen Mackenna. Boston, Mass.: Charles T. Branford Company, 1916.

The Questions of King Milinda (Milinda Pañha, II:3.3). In *The Sacred Books of the East*, Vol.35, edited by F. Max Müller. London: Oxford University Press, 1925.

Radhakrishnan, S., *Eastern Religions and Western Thought*. London: Oxford University Press, 2nd edn., 1940.

Radhakrishnan, S., *Indian Philosophy*, Vols. I and II. London: George Allen & Unwin Ltd., 1931, 1940.

Saradananda, Swami, *Sri Ramakrishna, the Great Master*. Eng. trans. by Swami Jagadananda. Madras, India: Sri Ramakrishna Math, 1952.

Satprakashananda, Swami, *The Goal and the Way*. St. Louis: The Vedanta Society, 1977.

— *Meditation: Its Process, Practice and Culmination*. St. Louis: The Vedanta Society, 1976.

— *Methods of Knowledge*. London: George Allen & Unwin, 1965. First Indian edn. Mayavati, Himalayas: Advaita Ashrama, 1974.

Seal, Brajendranath, *The Positive Sciences of the Ancient Hindus*. Harlow, Essex: Longmans Green and Co. Ltd., 1915.

Sinha, Jadunath, *Indian Realism*. London: Kegan Paul, Trench, 1938.

Stutfield, Hugh E.M., *Mysticism and Catholicism*. London: Fisher Unwin, 1925.

Toynbee, Arnold J., *Civilization on Trial*. New York: Oxford University Press, 1948.

Underhill, Evelyn, *Mysticism*. London: Methuen & Co. Ltd., 1911.

Vivekananda, Swami *Complete Works*, vols. I-VIII. Mayavati, Almora: Advaita Ashrama, 1922-1951.

— *Inspired Talks*. Mylapore, Madras: Sri Ramakrishna Math, 1938. (*Complete Works*, Vol. VII)

— *My Master*. Calcutta: Advaita Ashrama, 1973.

— *Vivekananda — The Yogas and Other Works*. New York: Ramakrishna-Vivekananda Center, 1953.

Weber, Alfred, *Histogy of Philosophy*. Eng. trans. by Frank Thilly. New York: Charles Scribner's Sons, 1925.

Whitehead, A.N., *Science and the Modern World*. New York: The Macmillan Company, 1962.

BIBLIOGRAPHY II

SANSKRIT WORKS QUOTED FROM AND CONSULTED

Adhyātma Rāmāyaṇa (Araṇya-kāṇḍa) by Vālmīki. Gita Press, Gorakhpur, U.P., India

Ātma-bōdha

(1) *The Works of Śaṅkara,* vol. X. Sri Vanivilas Press, Srirangam

(2) (Bengali edn.) *The Works of Śaṅkara,* Pt. I. Text, trans., notes, and intro. compiled by Rajendranath Ghosh, Calcutta

(3) *Self-knowledge,* Eng. trans., notes, and intro. by Swami Nikhilananda. Ramakrishna-Vedanta Center, New York, 1946

Bhagavad-gītā (Śrīmad)

(1) (Sanskrit edn.) Text with Śaṅkara's commentary (with Ānandagiri's gloss) and the commentaries of Nīlakaṇṭha, Śrīdhara, Madhusūdana Sarasvatī, and two others. Nirnaya Sagar Press, Bombay, 1936

(2) Text with Eng. trans. of Śaṅkara's commentary by A. Mahadeva Sastry. Published by V. Ramaswamy Sastrulu & Sons, Madras, 1929

(3) Text with Eng. trans., comments & index by Swami Swarupananda. Advaita Ashrama, Mayavati, Himalayas, 1948

(4) Text with Eng. trans. and Eng. rendering of Śrīdhara's gloss by Swami Vireswarananda. Sri Ramakrishna Math, Mylapore, Madras, 1948

Bhāgavatam (Śrīmad) by Kṛṣṇa-dvaipāyana Veda-vyāsa (in Beng. character). Sanskrit text with Śrīdhara Swāmī's commentary "Bhāvārtha-dīpikā." Bangavasi Press, Calcutta, 1927

Brahma-sūtras of Bādarāyaṇa

(1) (Sanskrit edn.) with the commentary of Śaṅkara and the sub-commentaries — "Bhāṣya-ratnaprabhā," "Bhāmatī," and "Nyāya-nirṇaya" — of Śrī Gōvindānanda, Vācaspati, and Ānandagiri. Nirnaya Sagar Press, Bombay, 1934

(2) Text with Eng. trans., elucidation and introduction by Swami Vireswarananda. Advaita Ashrama, Mayavati, Himalayas, 1936

(3) Text with Eng. trans. of Śaṅkara's commentary by Swami Gambhirananda. Advaita Ashrama, Calcutta, 1965

Brahma-sūtras also called *The Vedānta Philosophy*

(1) (Beng. edn., in 4 parts) Sanskrit text with Śaṅkara's commentary, Vācaspati's *Bhāmatī* in the original, and explanation in Beng. by Durgacharana Samkhya-Vedanta-tirtha. Calcutta, 1951

(2) (Beng. edn., in 2 parts) The first four Aphorisms with Śaṅkara's commentary, Vācaspati's "Bhāmatī," Rāmānanda's "Bhāṣya-ratnaprabhā," and Amalānanda's "Śāstradarpaṇa," etc. in the original with Beng. trans. and explanation with notes by Mahamahopadhyaya Pramathanatha Tarkabhusana. Udbodhan Office, and Lotus Library, Calcutta

(3) (Beng. edn.) Text with Śaṅkara's commentary and "Vaiasika-nyāyamālā" (Reasoning Process of Vyāsa-sūtras in Verse) of Bhāratī Tīrtha; also Rāmānanda Sarasvatī's "Bhāṣya-ratnaprabhā" of the first four Aphorisms. Beng. trans. of all with the exposition "Bhāva-dīpikā" by Swami Visvarupananda, the compiler. Advaita Ashrama, Calcutta

Dṛg-dṛśya Viveka (Vākya-sudhā) by Bhāratī Tīrtha. Text with Eng. trans. and notes by Swami Nikhilananda. Sri Ramakrishna Ashrama, Mysore, 1931

Hymns of Śaṅkara (including *Dakṣiṇāmūrtyaṣṭakam* & *Māyā-pañcakam*), *The Works of Śaṅkara,* vol. XI. Sri Vanivilas Press, Srirangam

Mahābhārata of Kṛṣṇa-dvaipāyana Veda-vyāsa. Sanskrit Epic of eighteen parts (Parvas), trans. into Eng. by Pratap Chandra Ray. Bharata Press, Calcutta, 1893

Manu-smṛti (or *Manu-saṁhitā*) with Kullūka Bhaṭṭa's commentary "Manvartha-muktāvalī" and an alphabetical index to first lines of the couplets. Nirnaya Sagar Press, Bombay, 1929

Naiṣkarmya-siddhi by Sureśvarācārya

(1) with Jñānōttama's commentary "Candrikā" — revised edn. by M. Hiriyanna. Sanskrit and Prakrit Series, 38, Bombay, 1925

(2) (Beng. edn.) Text and trans. with notes and index by Swami Jagadananda. Udbodhan Office, Calcutta, 1953

Nārada Bhakti Sūtras

(1) Trans. by Hanuman Prasad Poddar. Gita Press, Gorakhpur, U.P. India

(2) Sanskrit text, word-for-word meaning, Eng. rendering of the text and elaborate explanatory and critical notes by Swami Tyagisananda. Sri Ramakrishna Math, Mylapore, Madras, 1955

(3) (Eng. edn.) *Narada's Way of Divine Love,* trans. with commentary by Swami Prabhavananda. Vedanta Press, Hollywood, 1971

Nirvāṇa-ṣatkam (Ātma-ṣatkam)

(1) *The Works of Śaṅkara,* vol. XI. Sri Vanivilas Press, Srirangam

(2) (Beng. edn.) *The Works of Śaṅkara,* Pt. I — Text, trans., notes, and intro. compiled by Rajendranath Ghosh, Calcutta

Pañcadaśī by Bhāratī-tīrtha Vidyāraṇya

(1) with the commentary of Rāmakṛṣṇa. Nirnaya Sagar Press, Bombay, 1935

(2) Text with Eng. trans. and notes by Swami Swahananda. Sri Ramakrishna Math, Mylapore, Madras, 1967

Puruṣa-sūktam (Ṛg-Veda X:90)

(1) with Sāyaṇa's commentary. Ananda Ashram Sanskrit Series, No. 3, Ananda Ashram, Poona

(2) (Beng. edn.) Text and Sāyaṇa's commentary with trans. by Swami Kamaleswarananda. Gadadhar Ashrama, Calcutta

Ṛg-Veda Saṁhitā

(1) with Sāyaṇa's commentary — Edited by F. Max Müller. Vols. I-IV. London, Oxford University Press, 1890

(2) with Sāyaṇa's commentary and exhaustive index. Edited by Sontakke, Kashikar, and others. Vols. I-V. Vaidika Samsodhana Mandala, Poona, 1933-51

(3) Text only with exhaustive index. Edited by Sreepada Sarma Satavalekara. Svadhyaya Mandala, Paradi, Surat, India.

Sāṁkhya-darśana (Sāṁkhya-sūtras) of Kapila, with Vijñāna-bhikṣu's commentary "Pravacana-bhāṣya." Vacaspatya Press, Calcutta, 1936

Sāṁkhya-kārikā of Īśvarakṛṣṇa, with Vācaspati Miśra's commentary "Tattvakaumudī" and explanatory notes by Pundit Rajesvara Sastri Dravida. Chowkhamba Sanskrit Series, Chowkhamba, Varanasi, 1932

Sarvadarśana-saṁgraha by Mādhavācārya, together with Madhusūdana Sarasvatī's *Prasthāna-bheda.* Ananda Ashram Sanskrit Series, Ananda Ashram, Poona, 1950

Śatapatha Brāhmaṇa (of the *Śukla Yajur-Veda)* Mādhyandina Recension

(1) with "Vedārthaprakāśa" of Sāyaṇācārya and the commentary of Harisvāmin, in five vols. Laxmi Venkateshwar Steam Press, Kalyan, Bombay, 1940

(2) with extracts from the commentaries of Sāyaṇa, Harisvāmin, and Dvivedagaṅgā. Edited by Albrecht Weber. The Chowkhamba Sanskrit Series, Chowkhamba, Varanasi, 1964

(3) (Eng. edn.) Eng. trans. by Julius Eggeling. Sacred Books of the East, vol. IX, Oxford University Press, London, 1900

Siddhānta-leśa-saṁgraha by Appaya-dīkṣita

(1) Intro., trans., and copious notes in Hindi. Acyuta-granthamala, Varanasi, 1927

(2) (Beng. edn.) Beng. trans. and notes by Swami Gambhirananda. Udbodhan Office, Calcutta

Swāmi-śiṣya-samvāda (Conversations between Swami Vivekananda and his Disciples, Calcutta, 1897) (Beng. edn.) Udbodhan Office, Calcutta, 1955

Taittirīya Āraṇyaka (of the *Kṛṣṇa Yajur-Veda*) — see Appendix IV

Taittirīya Brāhmaṇa (of the *Kṛṣṇa Yajur-Veda*) — see Appendix IV

Tāṇḍya-Mahābrāhmaṇa (Pañcaviṁśa Brāhmaṇa) (of the *Sāma-Veda*) — with the commentary of Sāyaṇa, in two vols. Edited with notes, intro., etc. by Pandit A. Chinnaswami Sastri. The Kashi Sanskrit Series, no. 105, Chowkhamba, Varanasi

Upaniṣads — Sanskrit edns.

(1) *Ten Upaniṣads* — Text with Śaṅkara's commentary. Pt. I includes *Īśa, Aitareya, Kaṭha, Kena, Chāndōgya, Taittirīya, Praśna, Māṇḍūkya,* and *Muṇḍaka.* Pt. II includes *Bṛhadāraṇyaka.* Ashtekar and Co., Poona, 1927-29

(2) The above ten Upaniṣads — each a separate volume with Śaṅkara's commentary and Ānandagiri's gloss. Ananda Ashram Sanskrit Series, Ananda Ashram, Poona

Bṛhadāraṇyaka — Sanskrit text with Eng. trans. of Śaṅkara's commentary by Swami Madhavananda. Advaita Ashrama, Mayavati, Himalayas, 1934

Bṛhadāraṇyakōpaniṣad-bhāṣya-vārttikam — by Sureśvarācārya with Ānandagiri's commentary "Śāstra-prakāśikā" — in three parts. Ananda Ashram Sanskrit Series, Ananda Ashram, Poona, 1934

Chāndōgya — Text with Eng. trans. and copious notes by Swami Swahananda. Sri Ramakrishna Math, Mylapore, Madras, 1956

Eight Upaniṣads (excluding *Bṛhadāraṇyaka* & *Chāndōgya*) in two vols. — Sanskrit text with Eng. trans. of Śaṅkara's commentary by Swami Gambhirananda. Advaita Ashrama, Calcutta

Māṇḍūkya

(1) with Gauḍapāda's *Kārikā,* Śaṅkara's commentary and Ānandagiri's gloss. Ananda Ashram Sanskrit Series, Ananda Ashram, Poona, 1928

(2) with Gauḍapāda's *Kārikā* and Eng. trans. of Śaṅkara's commentary with notes by Swami Nikhilananda. Sri Ramakrishna Math, Mylapore, Madras, 1956

Muktika included in *Twenty-eight Upaniṣads,* text only. Nirnaya Sagar Press, Bombay

Nṛsiṁha-pūrva-tāpanīya — with Śaṅkara's commentary. *The Works of Śaṅkara,* vol. IV. Sri Vanivilas Press, Srirangam, 1910

Nṛsiṁha-uttara-tāpanīya included in *108 Upaniṣads,* text only. Nirnaya Sagar Press, Bombay, 1932

Śvetāśvatara

(1) (Beng. edn.) Text and commentary (attributed to Śaṅkara) with explanation by Pandit Durgacharana Samkhya-Vedanta-tirtha. Calcutta, 1931

(2) with Sanskrit text, Eng. trans. and comments by Swami Tyagisananda. Sri Ramakrishna Math, Mylapore, Madras, 1937

(3) included in *The Upanishads,* vol. II — Eng. trans. of text with notes and explanations based on Śaṅkara's commentary by Swami Nikhilananda. Harper & Bros. Publishers, New York, 1952

Vaiśeṣika Sūtras (Sūtras of Kaṇāda)

(1) with Śaṅkara Miśra's commentary "Upaskāra" and Praśastapāda's exposition "Padārthadharma-saṁgraha." Chowkhamba Sanskrit Series, Chowkhamba, Varanasi, 1924-31

(2) with Udayanācārya's gloss "Kiraṇāvalī" on Praśastapāda's and other commentaries. Sanskrit Book Depot, Calcutta

Vākya-padīya (Brahma-kāṇḍa) by Bhartṛhari — Edited with commentary and notes by Pandit Suryanarayana Sukla. The Kashi Sanskrit Series, no. 124, Chowkhamba, Varanasi, 1937

Vākya-vṛtti (Exposition of Mahāvākya "Thou art That") by Śaṅkarācārya.

(1) with commentary. Ananda Ashram Sanskrit Series, no. 80, Ananda Ashram, Poona

(2) Text with Eng. trans. and notes by Swami Jagadananda. Sri Ramakrishna Math, Mylapore, Madras

Vedānta-paribhāṣā by Dharmarājā Adhvarīndra

(1) Edited by M. Anantakṛṣṇa Śāstrī with introduction and commentary "Paribhāṣā-prakāśikā." University of Calcutta

(2) with Rāmakṛṣṇa Adhvarīndra's commentary "Śikhāmaṇi" and Amaladās's gloss "Maṇiprabhā." Sri Venkatesvara Press, Bombay, 1911

(3) (Beng. edn.) Text with explanation and notes by Saratchandra Ghosal, and with a preface by Hirendranath Datta. White Lotus Publ. Co., Calcutta

Vedāntasāra of Sadānanda

(1) with text and the commentaries of Nṛsiṁha Sarasvatī and Rāmatīrtha. Edited with notes and indices by Col. G.A. Jacob. Nirnaya Sagar Press, Bombay, 1925

(2) Text with Eng. Trans., intro., and comments by Swami Nikhilananda. Advaita Ashrama, Mayavati, Himalayas, 1931

Viveka-cūḍāmaṇi by Śrī Śaṅkarācārya

(1) *The Works of Śaṅkara,* vol. X. Sri Vanivilas Press, Srirangam

(2) Sanskrit text with Eng. trans., notes and index by Swami Madhavananda. Advaita Ashrama, Mayavati, Himalayas, 1944

(3) (Eng. edn.) *The Crest-Jewel of Discrimination* — trans. with an introduction to Śaṅkara's philosophy by Swami Prabhavananda and Christopher Isherwood. Vedanta Press, Hollywood, 1947

The Works of Śaṅkara, vols. III-VI, VIII-XI. Sri Vanivilas Press, Srirangam

Yōga Sūtras of Patañjali
(1) (Sanskrit edn.) Patañjali's Aphorisms with the commentary of Vyāsa and the sub-commentary of Vācaspati Miśra. Appendix contains "Rāja-mārtaṇḍa" of Bhōjadeva. Ananda Ashram Sanskrit Series, Ananda Ashram, Poona, 3rd edn., 1932
(2) (Beng. edn.) entitled *Pātañjala-darśanam*. Patañjali's Aphorisms with the commentary of Vyāsa and the sub-commentary of Vācaspati Miśra attended with explanatory notes and exposition in Bengali. Appendix dwells on the Yōga system in general. Compiled by Kalibara Vedanta-vagisha and edited by Durgacharana Samkhya-Vedanta-tirtha. Calcutta

Yōga-vāśiṣṭha Rāmāyaṇa of Vālmīki (in Beng. characters) — consisting of six main divisions — Sanskrit verses with the commentary "Vāśiṣṭha-mahārāmāyaṇa-tātparya-prakāśa" of Ānandabōdhendu Bhikṣu. Appended with Bengali translation of the Sanskrit verses. Compiled and edited by Pandit Kalibara Vedanta-vagisha. Published from "Vasumati Sahitya Mandira," Calcutta

INDEX

Acts, the, 215n
Adhyāsa, defined and types of, 104-5
Advaita, Vedanta: theory of causal relation, 113; theory of creation, 110-11
Ahaṁkāra (function of ego-consciousness), 122
Aitareya Upaniṣad (Ai.U.), 46, 72n, 88n, 114, 259
Ajātaśatru, 210-12
Ajñāna (ignorance): causes ego-idea, 95-96; causes inapprehension and misapprehension, 93, 154-55; eradicated by knowledge of Brahman, 34, 93n, 179, 188, 216, 252; meaning of term, 156n; product of māyā, 88, 217
Ākāśa (ether), 119, 120, 121, 122
Antaḥkaraṇa, 122, 260
Ap (water), 119, 120, 121, 122
Apāna, 122-23, 123n
Aparā-vidyā (subsidiary knowledge), 179
Appearance: differences in realm of, 174-75; no integral part of Reality, 162, 163
Appearance and Reality (Bradley), 163n
Āraṇyakas (forest treatises), section of Vedas, 34
Aristotle, 73, 126
Asatkārya-vāda (theory of non-preexistent effect), 113
Ātman: attaining, 186; unity of, 86
Avatāra, 148
Avidyā, 94, 95, 99; reality appears through, 93-94; two functions of, 93
Avyākṛta (undifferentiated), 94, 111
Avyakta (the indefinable), 94, 95, 130

Being: —Consciousness-Bliss, 218, 243, 254, 255; and nonbeing, 165-66; pure, all reality in, 168
—, Supreme: aspects of, 42; both immanent and transcendent, 157; self of man is, 23, 24, 25, 28, 258-59; realization of, 23, 155, 159, 286
Bergson, Henri, 169
Berkeley, George, on reality of perceptions, 84
Bhagavad-gītā (BG), 64, 263; quoted, 50, 54n, 69-70, 77n, 90, 91n, 99n, 102n, 116n, 117n, 130, 130n, 131n, 144n, 148n, 158n, 159n, 164n, 165n, 167n, 182n, 186-87, 193n, 205n, 206n, 209n, 215n, 219n, 225n, 226, 227, 228, 232n, 233n, 237n, 238n, 240n, 244, 245, 248, 250n, 252n, 253n, 257, 265
Bhagavān, 244, 244n
Bhāgavatam. See *Śrīmad-bhāgavatam*
Bhakti-sūtras, 249n, 250n
Bhakti-yōga, 43, 49, 50, 229, 265, 266, 267; leads to complete Freedom, 237; preparation for, 244, 266
Bigg, Charles, 146n
Bliss, of Brahman, 41, 192-93, 198
Body: causal, produces subtle, gross bodies, 112, 119; gross, death of, 287; gross, subtle, composition of, 119; human, privilege of, 248, 272-73; subtle, development of, 119, 123; subtle, develops gross, 125
Bradley, F.H., 163
Brahma, N.K., 178
Brahmā, 110n, 143; length of day and night of, 130. *See also* Hiraṇyagarbha
Brahmalōka, 88, 290-91; gradations of, 129
Brahman: apara (subordinate), immanent, 75-77, 200, 204-5, 215; attempting to describe, 42, 195-97, 200-202, 203-4; cause of universe, 72, 73, 75, 77, 110-11, 144, 145; comprehending, 87-88, 202-3, 208; knower of, 186-87, 209-10; mahāvākyas on, 46-47, 87-88, 258-59; manifests all else, 41, 131, 138, 156, 205, 209; one only without a second, 100, 194-95, 207-8; para (supreme), transcendent, 200, 201, 206-7; realization of, 181-82, 260-61; relative, manifestations of, 81, 82; śabda-, 139, 144; six nondualistic categories of, 106; three aspects of, 131; world real as, 80, 105
—, Saguṇa (Personal God), 42, 43, 54, 215-16, 219, 231, 291; goal of Bhakti-yōga, 43, 48, 243, 266; as Īśvara, Supreme Ruler, 76-77; three aspects of, 216
—, Nirguṇa (Impersonal God), 42, 43, 54, 219, 231, 291; goal of Jñāna-yōga, 42, 48, 50, 243, 254, 266

Brāhmaṇa, section of Vedas, 33, 34, 142; list of, 38-39
Brahma-sūtras (BS), 76n, 88n, 203, 205n, 218n; part of triple basis of Vedanta, 36
Bṛhadāraṇyaka Upaniṣad (Br.U.), 41, 46, 47n, 50n, 51n, 88n, 91n, 102n, 111n, 118n, 128n, 138n, 142n, 151, 153n, 160n, 161n, 164n, 173n, 174n, 180n, 186n, 190n, 192n, 195n, 196, 199n, 201n, 204n, 205n, 207n, 210-12, 216n, 254n, 255-56, 259
Buddhi (determinative function), 122
Buddhism: Idealist view of waking and dream states, 84-85; on karma as means of Nirvāṇa, 239-40; Mahāyāna, three forms of Buddha, 213; schools of, 83n

Cause: and effect, 113-14; material and instrumental, 144; Ultimate, 183
Chāndōgya Upaniṣad (Ch.U.), 41, 46, 72n, 74n, 80n, 88n, 102, 115, 121n, 135n, 170-72, 183-85, 192n, 193n, 194, 199n, 202n, 203n, 205n, 215n, 216n, 254n, 259
Change, philosophy of, 168-69
Christian: doctrine of Omnipresence, 215; and Vedantic view of Divine Incarnation, 147-48
Christian Platonists of Alexandria (Bigg), 146n
Citta (function of recollection), 122
Civilization on Trial (Toynbee), 152n
Cognition, primary function of mind, 122
Cognizer, of all external objects, 44-45
Concentration, of mind, 251
Consciousness, everything arises from, 41, 190-91, 264
Cosmic: cycle, 128-29, 130; ideation, 135, 136, 138, 139, 140; soul. *See* Hiraṇyagarbha
Creation, of universe (sṛṣti), 73-74, 89; Advaita theory of, 110-11; beginning of, 111-12; cosmic ideation of, 135, 136, 138, 139, 140; order of eternal process, 128-29; why, 107-8; from the Word, 132-33
Creative Evolution (Bergson), 169n
Critique of Pure Reason (Kant), 79n

Dakṣiṇāmūrti stōtram (Śaṅkara), 90n
Darwin, Charles, 125
Death, four main courses after, 287-91
Desire: freedom from, 29, 185, 224-25, 229; sense, 51, 285
Detachment, through Karma-yōga, 221
Diversity, and unity, problem of, 103
Divinity, within man, 66
Dream, and waking states, distinguished, 84-85
Dṛgdṛśya-viveka (Tīrtha), 173n
Dualities, inescapable, must be disillusioned of, 55, 158, 223, 264
Duty: for duty's sake, 225-26; as form of worship, 240, 267; universal, worship is, 250-51

Earthly life, limits of, 284, 285, 287
Eastern Religions and Western Thought (Radhakrishnan), 134n, 147n
Eckhart, Meister, 213
Eddington, A.S., 163
Education, limits of, 27
Ego: origin of, 45-46, 97-98, 154; renouncing as doer of work, 225, 228; in samādhi, 189; surrendering, 99, 251-52
Einstein, Albert, 168n
Elements, gross and subtle: compose body of jīva, 119; composition of, 119-22; origin of, 121-22; properties of gross, 121
Emotion, scope for in Jñāna-yōga, 266
Equanimity, mark of Karma-yōga, 228
Essentials of Biology, The (Johnston), 124
Essentials of Indian Philosophy, The (Hiriyanna), 157n
Evil, and good, 81-82; going beyond, 222, 228, 264
Evolution: of jīva, 125; preceded by involution, 126
Evolution (Geddes, Thomson), 125
Existence: of man self-evident, 43, 173; the one fundamental fact, 166-67; three orders of, 81, 174-75
—, relative: Brahman beyond, 81, 202; reality of, 86; three main categories of, 87
Experience: intuitive, and reason, 178; three daily states of, 191; world of, as aspect of Brahman, 216 (*See also* Jagat)

Fact: basis of reason and religion, 177; Brahman the only, 188

Fear, freedom from, 198-99
Forces, vital, 122-23
Fourth, the (turīya), 191

Gārgya, and Ajātaśatru, 210-12
Gauḍapāda: on Brahman and māyā, 75, 106, 107; on creation, 108, 119
General Biology and Philosophy of Organisms (Lillie), 125 n
Genesis, 133 n
Goal: of human life, 23, 50, 54, 59; Supreme, through good, 82, 264
God: cause of universe, 77; devotional relationships with, 49, 247-48; ignored by modern man, 26; Impersonal, difficult to attain, 29 (*See also* Brahman, Nirguṇa); logical proof impossible, 79; proof of through experiences, 176; realization of, 60, 264, 265; realization of, through different religions, 60; seeing in all, 32, 68-70, 240-41, 242, 252-53, 273-74; sole Reality, 137, 264; son of, Jesus Christ as, 145-46; son of, the Word as, 147; worship of, 240-41, 250-51, 252-53
Good: highest, beyond duality, 29, 264; and evil, 81-82; and evil, going beyond, 222, 228, 264
Gospel of Sri Ramakrishna (GSR), 49 n, 60 n, 100 n, 104 n, 155 n, 161 n, 174 n, 189 n, 190 n, 193 n, 196 n, 197 n, 209 n, 274 n
Grace, through self-surrender, 251-52
Guide to Modern Thought (Joad), 125 n
Guṇas, 42, 78, 227, 227 n; in creation, 112; explained, 42 n. *See also* Rajas; Sattva; Tamas

Heart, purification of, 184, 185
Hegal, Absolute of, 195
Heraclitus, 168
Hinduism: derivation of word, 33 n; names of, 33
Hiraṇyagarbha (cosmic soul), 110, 110 n; abode of, 129; birth, lifetime of, 118, 130; created from words, 142; role in cosmic process, 128
Hiriyanna, M., 157
History of Philosophy (Weber), 146 n
Holy persons, association with, 249, 271
Human life, privilege of, 248, 272-73, 290

Ideal, actual never approximates, 150
Idealism, subjective and absolute, 83
Ideation, cosmic, 135, 136, 138, 139, 140
Ignorance, 161; of real self, 45. *See also* Ajñāna; Avidyā
Īkṣaṇa (reflection on creation), 114, 115
Illumined ones, ways of, 186-87
Impressions, mental, and perception, 85
Incarnation, Divine, Christian and Vedantic view of, 147-48
India: derivation of word, 33 n; influence on other cultures, 57-58
Indian Philosophy (Radhakrishnan), 63 n, 83 n, 157 n
Indian Realism (Sinha), 84 n
Individual, experience of ascertains reality, 87
Indriyas (organs), 123
Infinite, the, 102, 184
Intellect, limits of, 279
Intuition, mystical, 63
Īśa Upaniṣad (Is.U.), 59, 70, 77 n, 192, 206 n, 215 n
Involution, precedes evolution, 126
Īśvara: as conscious self in all, 91; highest manifestation of Absolute, 101-2, 217; īkṣaṇa (reflection of) — how he starts creation, 114-15, 135; originator of Hiraṇyagarbha, 118-19; position as Creator, 116, 135-36; relation to jīva and jagat, 87, 88, 89, 90, 100, 218; ruler of māyā, 76-77, 92-93, 99-100; as third aspect of Brahman, 216-17; three aspects of, 90; unborn, 89; "unmoved mover" of prakṛti, 116-17; why He creates world, 107-8
Jagat (world of experience): relation to Īśvara, 87, 89, 90; unborn, 89
Jeans, James, 163
Jeremiah, 215 n
Jesus Christ, 185; St. John identifies Word with, 133 n, 145-46
Jīva (individual experiencer), 87, 87 n; evolution of, 125, 126; four kinds of, 124; gaining freedom from māyā, 99, 117; karma of, part in creation, 114, 115, 119, 135; psychophysical constitutions of, 122-24; purpose of world for, 108; really Brahman, 100; relation to Īśvara, 87, 88, 89, 90; unborn, 89; veiled by avidyā, 93
Jīvanmukta, 291
Jīvātmā (individual self), 54; related to body-mind through ajñāna, 99
Jñāna-yōga, 43, 48, 49, 50, 229, 266, 267; four prerequisites of, 232, 257:

Śaṅkara's view of, 233-36; threefold path of, 232, 235
John, St., 132, 133, 133n, 136, 281n; conception of Word compared to Vedanta, Philo, 145-47
Johnston, James, 124
Joy, 192-93, 250

Kalpa (cycle), 89
Kant, Immanuel, 79
Kapila (Sāṁkhya founder), 79, 217
Karma: Buddhist view of, 239; effects of at death, 288; of jīva, part in creation, 114, 115, 116, 119, 135; as used by Śaṅkara, 234; as used by Swami Vivekananda, 236, 238
Karma-yōga, 229, 265-66, 267, 268; equanimity common feature of, 228; not mere unselfish work, 222; preparation for, 223-25; as preparatory to other yōgas, 53-54, 55, 65, 226, 228-29, 266; Śaṅkara's view of, 233-36, 238; spiritualizes common duties, 221, 267; Swami Vivekananda's view of, 236, 238, 239-40
Kaṭha Upaniṣad (Ka.U.), 41, 47n, 75n, 116n, 153-54, 155, 156n, 157n, 164n, 180n, 185, 186n, 201n, 205n, 206n, 215n, 258
Kena Upaniṣad (Ken.U.), 47n, 50n, 74n, 182n, 195n, 196n
Knower, real self of man is, 154, 172
Knowledge: direct, immediate, 179; end of, through intuition, 102-3, 180, 188; gained through reason, limits of, 61-62, 78-79, 102, 178; goal of, 160, 161; mediate, indirect, 178-79; path of. *See* Jñāna-yōga; -section of Vedas (jñāna-kāṇḍa), 35; supreme, subsidiary, 179
Kṛṣṇa, Śrī: on devotion, 65, 270, 271-72; on Divine Incarnation, 148; first and last messages of, 263-64, 268, 275; instructs Arjuna, 263, 268-69; instructs Uddhava, 263, 268, 269-70, 272, 273; on seeing God in all, 67, 273

Lao Tzu, 212
Leviticus, 60n
Liberation, way of, 290
Life: earthly, 284, 285, 287; goal of, 181-82, 255; human, physical and psychical aspects of, 276-77; human, privilege of, 248, 272-73, 290; sense-, 279, 282; spiritual, 280, 282
Līlā (sport of God), 108
Limitations, time and object, 194
Logos: meaning of, 133, 133n, 134, 136, 136n; Philo's conception of, 147
Love: is expansion, 280; universal, way to, 30, 59
Luke, 60n

Mahābhārata (Mbh.), 52, 142, 143n, 263
Mahāvākyas (great sayings), 46-47, 87-88, 258-59
Maitreyī, 173, 174, 189-90, 255-56
Man: difference from animals, 276; ever seeking the Divine, 59, 151; identification with body, 97-98, 285; real self of, 54, 59, 154, 170, 255, 287
Manas (deliberative function), 122
Māṇḍūkya-kārikā (MK), 75n, 81n, 106n, 107n, 108n, 114n, 118n, 119n
Māṇḍūkya Upaniṣad (Ma.U.), 46, 88n, 191, 259
Mantras, types in the Vedas, 34n
Manu, 111, 132n, 142
Manu-smṛti (MS), 37, 111n, 132n
Mark, 60n
Material values, insecurity of, 24, 25, 26-27, 286
Matthew, 60n, 185n, 281n
Māyā: as ajñāna, avidyā, 93; as appearance of Brahman, 75-77, 92-93, 217; beginningless, 106-7; causes ego-idea, 97-98; cosmic and individual aspects of, 98-99, 131; defined by Śaṅkara, 95; different names of, 94-95; explained, 76-78; evident as contraries — couples Real and unreal, 95-97; going beyond bondage of, 99, 117; guṇas constituents of, 42n, 78; non-dualistic conceptions of, 91-93; as prakṛti, 78, 92; resolves unity-diversity problem, 103-4; Śaṅkara's Five Stanzas on, 109; veils Reality for the jīva, 88, 105
Māyā-śakti (creative energy), 136, 137, 138, 142, 147
Meditation: Its Process, Practice, and Culmination (Satprakashananda), 41n
Methods of Knowledge (Satprakashananda), 259
Milinda, King, 169, 169n
Mind: concentrating, 251; distinctive character of, 44, 123; four functions of, 260; purification of, 181, 185, 249-50, 271-72; purification of, through

Karma-yōga, 228-29, 232, 233, 267
Mithyā, 95
Momentariness, doctrine of, 85-86, 169
Monistic (nondualistic) school of Vedanta, 41, 42, 43, 88, 91; on prakṛti, 92; on creation, 116
Monotheism: schools of Vedanta, 41, 42, 43, 88, 91 n (listed); Vaiṣṇava, 231
Müller, Max, on Word and Logos, 134-35, 146
Multiplicity, must be apparent, unreal, 162, 164
Muṇḍaka Upaniṣad (Mu.U.), 35, 47 n, 50 n, 73 n, 102 n, 110, 121, 122 n, 156 n, 161, 179, 180 n, 181, 186 n, 199 n, 205 n, 207 n, 254-55, 257, 261, 291
Mysticism (Underhill), 214 n
Mysticism and Catholicism (Stutfield), 57
Mysticism East and West (Otto), 213 n

Naciketā, 185
Nāgasena, 168
Naimittika pralaya (intermediary dissolution), 130
Naiṣkarmya-siddhi (NS), 104 n, 232-33
Nāma-rūpa (names and forms), 116, 131, 137-38
Names, source of, 138
Nārada, 183-85, 249
Nature of the Physical World, The (Eddington), 163
Needham, Joseph, 163
Neo-Platonists, view of Ultimate Reality, 197-98, 214
Neti, neti (not this, not this), 196
Nicholson, Reynold, 215 n
Nirguṇa Brahman (Impersonal God), 42, 43, 54, 219, 231, 291; goal of Jñāna-yōga, 42, 48, 50, 243, 254, 266; Saguṇa is, apart from māyā, 77
Nirvāṇa, karma means of, 239-40
Nirvāṇa-ṣatkam (Six Stanzas on Nirvāṇa), 259-60
Nirvikalpa samādhi, 48, 50
Nonbeing, and being, 165-66
Nondualism. *See* Vedanta, nondualistic
Nonresistance, of evil, 269
Nous, 214
Nṛsiṁha-pūrvatāpanīya Upaniṣad (NPT.U.), 192 n, 243 n, 254 n
Nṛsiṁha-uttaratāpanīya Upaniṣad (NUT.U.), 192 n

Nyāya school: theory of causation, 113; view of elements, 121

Object, distinct from subject, 97, 172, 173
Ōm, as symbol of Vāk, 139-41, 144
One only without a second, meaning of, 194-95
Opposites: inevitability of, 96, 158, 264; not mere negations, 81-82
Organs, of perception, action, subtle and physical aspects of, 123, 124
Otto, Rudolph, 213 n

Pañcadaśī (Pd.), 120 n, 167 n, 170 n, 194 n
Pañcīkaraṇa (quintuplication), 120
Paramātmā (all-pervading self), 54
Parā-vidyā (supreme knowledge), 179, 180
Pariṇāma (actual modification), 111, 116
Patañjali, 127, 230, 268; accepts two reals, 230, 231
Perception: of external objects, 83, 85; Vedantic view of, 82-83
Philo: conception of Word compared to Vedanta, St. John, 145-47; doctrine of Logos, 133, 133 n, 134, 147
Philosophy, function of, 178
Philosophy of Hindu Sadana (Brahma), 178
Physical life, 276-77; vs. inner life, 278
Physics (Aristotle), 73 n
Physics and Philosophy (Jeans), 163 n
Pippalāda, on cognition, 154
Plants, consciousness in, 124
Plotinus, 197-98, 214
Plotinus: The Ethical Treatises, 197, 198, 214
Politics (Aristotle), 126 n
Porphyry, 197 n
Positive Sciences of the Ancient Hindus (Seal), 121 n
Prajāpati, 128
Prākṛta pralaya (basic dissolution of universe), 113, 129, 129 n
Prakṛti (primary cause): guṇas of, 227, 227 n; is māyā (appearance), 78, 92; Īśvara "unmoved mover" of, 115-16; undifferentiated (avyākṛta), 111, 112, 129, 135
Prāṇa, 122-23, 123 n, 184; Gārgya saw Brahman as, 210-11
Praśna Upaniṣad (Pr.U.), 154 n, 182 n
Principles of Human Knowledge (Berkeley), 84 n

Pṛthivī (earth), 119, 120, 121, 122
Problems, of life, 21, 28, 29, 30; root cause of, 22; solution attempted externally, 22; solution internally through religion, 21, 28-30
Psalms, 133n
Purification: through devotion, 249-50, 271-72; of mind through Karma-yōga, 228-29, 232, 233, 267; necessary for direct knowledge, 185

Questions of King Milinda, The, 169n
Quintuplication (pañcīkaraṇa), 120

Radhakrishnan, S.: on mystic intuition, 63; on Pantheism, 157; on Philo and Logos, 134, 147; on subject-object, 83
Rajas, 42n, 78, 227, 227n; in forming organs, 123, 124
Rāja-yōga, 230, 267-68; based on Sāṁkhya system, 231
Rāmacandra, Śrī, nine course for devotion, 245-46
Ramakrishna, Sri, 67, 104, 152; on Īśvara, 100; message of, 51; on the One Self, 281-82; on samādhi, 49-50, 189
Ramakrishna Math and Mission, 274-75
Rāmānuja, on Differentiated Brahman, 208n
Rāmāyaṇa, 245
Reality: appears through avidyā, 93-94; conforming mind to, 260-61; defined, 165; only One exists, 40, 41-42, 54, 74, 75; Supreme, man's conception of, 150-51
—, Ultimate: beyond conditions, 103; goal of all, 153, 198; Neo-Platonic view of, 197-98
Realization, 264, 265, 280-81; goal of life, 181-82; person of, 186-87; requisites for, 60, 63, 260-61
Reason: aid to knowing God, 79-80; facts necessary for, 177; and intuitive experience, 178; uses and limitations of, 61-62, 78-79
Reincarnation, way of, 289
Religion: common background of, 23, 60, 151; facts in, 177; message of complete freedom, 24; modern attitude towards, 26; solution to man's problems, 21, 22, 28
Renunciation, in and of work, 239
Representative Men (Emerson), 58
Revelation, book of, 146
Ṛg-Veda, 90n, 107n, 111, 112n, 118, 132n, 188, 207n
Ṛg-Veda Saṁhitā, 40
Rūmī Poet and Mystic (Nicholson), 215n
Rūpa, and nāma (form and name), 116, 131, 137-38

Śabda (sound or word), 134, 136, 137, 143; -Brahman, 139, 144
Sages, association with, 249, 271
Saguṇa Brahman, 42, 43, 54; apart from māyā is Nirguṇa, 77; Bhakti-yōga approach to, 43, 48, 243, 266; as Īśvara, Supreme Ruler, 76-77
Śakti (Īśvara's power), 92
Samādhi, 189, 190; nirvikalpa, 48, 50; savikalpa, 49, 50
Samāna, 123, 123n
Saṁhitā, section of Vedas, 33-34, 34n; list of, 38-39
Sāṁkhya, school, 231; theory of causation, 113, 116
Sāṁkhya-darśanam (SD), 79n
Saṁskāra (impression), 222
Sanatkumāra, 183-85
Śaṅkara: on bliss of Brahman, 193; on creation from Word, 144; defines māyā, 95; denies coordination of jñāna and karma, 233-36, 238; on describing Brahman, 196; on Īśvara as Creator, 116; on Īśvara and jīva, 100; *Māyā-pañcakam* (Five Stanzas on Māyā) of, 109; Nirvāṇa-ṣatkam (Six Stanzas on Nirvāṇa) of, 259-60; on perception, 83, 85; on real and unreal, 167; on twofold world view, 82; on waking-dream states, 85; on why world is created, 108
—, commentaries on: *Bhagavad-gītā* (BG), 119n, 167n, 195n, 234n, 235n, 237n; *Bṛhadāraṇyaka Upaniṣad* (Br.U.), 34, 82n, 113n, 118n, 142n, 173n, 196n, 211n; *Brahma-sūtras* (BS), 79n, 80n, 83n, 85n, 89n, 92n, 94n, 100n, 101n, 104n, 108n, 112n, 114n, 116n, 126n, 131n, 132n, 139n, 144n, 160n, 162n, 165n, 169n, 196n, 203n, 206n, 207n; *Chāndōgya Upaniṣad* (Ch.U.), 85n; *Māṇḍūkya Upaniṣad* (Ma.U.), 75n; *Māṇḍūkya-kārikā* (MK), 170n; *Muṇḍaka Upaniṣad* (Mu.U.), 180; *Praśna Upaniṣad* (Pr.U.), 72n; *Taittirīya Upaniṣad* (Tai.U.), 81n, 115n, 135n, 174n, 195n

Saradananda, Swami, 68
Sat-cit-ānanda (Being-Consciousness-Bliss), 201-2, 218, 243
Śatapatha Brāhmaṇa (Sat.Br.), 132 n
Satkārya-vāda (theory of preexistent effect), 113
Sattva, 42 n, 78, 227, 227 n; in forming organs, 123, 124; predominant in cosmic māyā, 98
Satyalōka, 129
Sceptical Biologist, The (Needham), 163 n
Science, seeks unity, 160, 161
Science and the Modern World (Whitehead), 151 n
Seal, Brajendranath, on elements, 121
Self: awareness, only in man, 126; -control, 29, 185-86; the dearest of all, 173-74, 256; at death, 288; finite, as aspect of Brahman, 216; interest, limits of, 25, 27-28, 285; knowing, constant, 172-73; -lessness, 28, 285, 286; -realization, urge for, 127; realization of, 191-92; -surrender, grace of, 251-52
—, Supreme: cause of universe, 72; oneness with, 47, 101, 153; separation from, 46-47
Selfishness, root of all vices, 25
Sense: desires, 51, 285; life, 279, 282
Sidgwick, Henry, 161 n
Sinha, Jadunath, on perception, 84
Smṛti, defined, 37-38, 132
Sphōta, 139-41
Spirit, real self is, 280, 281
Spiritual: life, 280, 282; outlook on life, 23, 25, 27, 242
Sri Ramakrishna, the Great Master (Saradananda), 50 n, 68 n
Śrīmad-bhāgavatam (SB), 263; quoted, 65, 67, 99 n, 102 n, 182 n, 219 n, 226, 229, 231, 242, 244, 248, 250, 251 n, 253 n, 265 n, 266, 269 n, 270 n, 272 n, 273 n, 274 n
Sṛṣti, 89. *See also* Creation
Śruti, defined, 35, 37, 132; testimony on God, 80
Sthūla bhūtas (gross elements), 119-22
Subject-object: distinct, yet related, 97, 172, 173; going beyond, 188; intellect cannot go beyond, 102
Sūfism, view of Absolute Reality, 214-15
Sūkṣma bhūtas (subtle elements), 119-22
Sūkṣma śarīra. *See* Body, subtle
Sureśvarācāryya, 104
Svargalōka (heaven-world), 289-90
Śvetaketu, 171-72
Śvetāśvatara Upaniṣad (Sv.U.), 40 n, 43, 50 n, 59 n, 72 n, 77 n, 78 n, 88 n, 89 n, 91 n, 92 n, 98 n, 113 n, 118 n, 128 n, 131 n, 142 n, 152 n, 156 n, 157 n, 159 n, 180 n, 186 n, 205 n, 206 n, 216 n, 220 n, 246, 261, 290 n

Taittirīya Āraṇyaka (Tai.Ar.), 107 n, 117 n, 196 n
Taittirīya Brāhmaṇa (Tai.Br.), 141 n, 142 n
Taittirīya Upaniṣad (Tai.U.), 41, 72 n, 73 n, 115, 122 n, 135 n, 182 n, 193, 194 n, 198, 202 n, 204 n, 241 n
Tamas, 42 n, 78, 123, 227, 227 n; preponderant in individual māyā, 98-99, 120, 122
Tantra, Śākta, on power of God, 92
Tao, the, 212-13, 212 n
Tao Te Ching (Lao Tzu), 212, 213 n
Teacher: need for, 257-58; spiritual, qualities of, 176
Tejas (fire), 119, 120, 121, 122
This-worldly attitude, limits of, 26, 285, 286, 287
Toynbee, Arnold J., 152 n
Truths, suprasensuous, beyond reason, 61-62; discipline for realizing, 63

Udāna, 122-23, 123 n
Uddhava, 263, 268, 269-70
Uddālaka, 170-72
Underhill, Evelyn, 214 n
United Nations, and world harmony, 31
Unity, world, basis of, 31
Universe: beginning of, 73-74, 90; cause of, 72, 73, 75, 77, 78; cause determined through intuition, 78-79; dissolution of, 112; states of existence, 89, 90
Unselfishness, 25, 224, 280
Upaniṣads: individual, 36-37, 38-39; part of triple basis of Vedanta, 36; section of Vedas, 34-35; term explained, 34

Vaināśikas (Buddhist Nihilists), 165
Vaiśeṣika school: theory of causation, 113; view of elements, 121
Vaiśeṣika Sūtras, 52 n
Vaiṣṇavism, 43, 231, 263

Vāk (the Word): creation from, 132-33, 137-38, 145; mother of Vedas, 141; para-, 139, 140; Ōm as symbol of, 139-41, 144; significance of, 134-46; as son of God, 147
Vākya-vṛtti, (VV), 88n
Values, material, insecurity of, 24, 25, 26-27, 286
Vāyu (air), 119, 120, 121, 122
Vedanta: as absolute idealism, 83; and Christian view of Divine Incarnation, 147-48; conception of Word compared to Philo, St. John, 145-47; defined, 33, 35-36; definition of reality, 165; denial of world, 86; fundamental teachings of, 46, 54; idea of evolution, 124, 125-26; not pantheism, 157; practicality of, 64; purpose in delineating creation, 117-18; triple basis of, 36; two specialities of, 55-56; view of the manifold, 156; view of perception, 82
—, monotheistic, 41, 42, 43, 88, 91, 91n; on prakṛti, 92; schools of, 91n
—, nondualistic (monistic), 41, 42, 43, 88, 91; on prakṛti, 92, on creation, 116
Vedānta-paribhāṣā (VP), 81n, 113n, 114n, 115, 117n, 118n, 130, 193
Vedanta Philosophy (Müller), 135n, 146n
Vedānta-sāra, 35-36
Vedas: extant texts listed, 38-39, 292-94; mahāvākyas in, 46-47, 87-88, 258-59; manifested by Supreme Being, 141-42; mantras in, 34n, 142; prescriptions of, 51-52; sections of, 33-34, 35
Vice, proceeds from selfishness, 25
Vidyā, leads to immortality, 99
Virāt, Hiraṇyagarbha as, 118
Virtue: necessity of, 25, 27, 52, 185; provides harmony, security, 52-53; universal duty, 52
Vital forces, 122-23
Vivarta (apparent modification), 111
Vivarta-vāda (Advaita theory of creation), 111
Viveka-cūḍāmaṇi (VC), 95n, 159, 189n, 193, 235, 258, 290n
Vivekananda, Swami, 32; applications of Karma-yōga, 66-67; on attaining Personal God, 218-19; on cause of māyā, 107; on creation from Word, 145; on differing capabilities of spiritual aspirants, 64; on evolution, 126, 127-28; on facts in reason and religion, 177; on Karma-yōga, 236, 238, 239-40; on knowledge, 160; on limits of reason, 62; on māyā, 96; on Ōm, 139-41; on reality of Īśvara, 217; on service as worship, seeing God in all, 67, 240-41, 274; on unity of Ātman, 86
—, *Complete Works of* (CW), 59n, 62n, 64n, 66n, 67n, 74n, 77n, 86n, 96n, 107n, 126n, 127n, 128n, 140n, 157n, 160n, 166n, 167n, 177n, 217n, 219n, 236n, 237n, 238n, 239n, 241n, 274n, 280n
Vyāna, 122-23, 123n

Waking, and dream states, distinguished, 84-85
Weber, Alfred, 146n
Whitehead, Alfred North, 151n
Word, the: creation from, 132-33, 137-38, 144; St. John identifies with Jesus Christ, 133n, 145-46; significance of, 134-36; Vedantic conception compared to Philo, St. John, 145-47
Words: and ideas, 134, 137, 142, 143; and meanings, 140; Vedic, source of names and forms, 141-43
Work: with desire, 225; good, 224; necessity of, 159; as offering to God, 226; without attachment, 221-23, 227
Work-section of Vedas (karma-kāṇḍa), 35, 51
World: appearance due to māyā, 93-94, 95, 105; cannot be ideal existence, 23; cause of, 79; real as Brahman, 80; -system, composition of, 129; Vedanta's denial of, 86
Worship: of God in all beings, 252-53, 273; through service, 240-41, 267; universal duty, 250-51

Yājñavalkya, 160; on Internal Ruler, 204-5; on nondual experience, 189-90; on self being dear, 173-74, 256; on self-knowledge, 255-56
Yōga, 265. *See also* Bhakti-; Jñāna-; Karma-; Rāja-
Yōgācāra (school of Buddhism), 83n; doctrine of momentariness, 85-86; on perception, 84, 85; on waking and dream states, 84-85
Yōga-sūtras (YS), 62n, 127n, 141n
Yugas, explained, 130n